Studies in Celtic History XVIII

THE IRISH IDENTITY OF THE KINGDOM OF THE SCOTS IN THE TWELFTH AND THIRTEENTH CENTURIES

The close ties between Gaels of Ireland and Scotland are well known, but in the twelfth and thirteenth centuries the elite in the core areas of the kingdom of the Scots apparently turned their backs on Gaelic culture. This book takes a new look at the issue, investigating the extent to which Scottish men of letters of the period identified the Scottish kingdom and its inhabitants with Ireland, and exploring the function of the kingdom's Irish identity. Dr Broun argues that a perceived historical link with Ireland was a fundamental feature of the kingdom's identity throughout the period, particularly as there is no evidence that Scotland, rather than Ireland, was portrayed earlier than the 1290s as the Scottish homeland. He concludes with a discussion of the beginnings of a Scottish national identity in the 1290s and early 1300s.

The study is based on a thorough examination of accounts of Scottish origins, the royal genealogy, and regnal lists, which articulate the ways in which Scottish men of letters expressed perceptions of the kingdom's identity; although few texts written in the period are extant, there are some dating from the fourteenth and fifteenth centuries which can be shown to derive from lost sources, enabling earlier texts to be partially recovered. The book includes a new edition of the origin-legend material in Book I of Fordun's *Chronica Gentis Scottorum*, editions of hitherto unknown witnesses of Scottish king-lists, and a new edition of texts of the royal genealogy.

Dr DAUVIT BROUN teaches in the Department of History at the University of Glasgow.

STUDIES IN CELTIC HISTORY

ISSN 0261–9865

General editors
Dauvit Broun
Máire Ní Mhaonaigh
Huw Pryce

'Studies in Celtic History' aims to provide a forum for new research into all aspects of the history of Celtic-speaking peoples throughout the whole of the medieval period. The term 'history' is understood broadly: any study, regardless of discipline, which advances our knowledge and understanding of the history of Celtic-speaking peoples will be considered. Studies of primary sources, and of new methods of exploiting such sources, are encouraged.

Founded by Professor David Dumville in 1979, the series is now relaunched under new editorship. Proposals or queries may be sent directly to the editors at the addresses given below; all submissions will receive prompt and informed consideration before being sent to expert readers.

Dr Dauvit Broun, Department of History (Scottish), University of Glasgow, 9 University Gardens, Glasgow G12 8QH

Dr Máire Ní Mhaonaigh, St John's College, Cambridge CB2 1TP

Dr Huw Pryce, School of History and Welsh History, University of Wales, Bangor, Bangor, Gwynedd LL57 2DG

For titles already published in this series
see the end of this volume

THE IRISH IDENTITY OF THE KINGDOM OF THE SCOTS IN THE TWELFTH AND THIRTEENTH CENTURIES

DAUVIT BROUN

THE BOYDELL PRESS

First published 1999
The Boydell Press, Woodbridge

ISBN 0 85115 375 5

The Boydell Press is an imprint of Boydell and Brewer Ltd
PO Box 9, Woodbridge, Suffolk IP12 3DF, UK
and of Boydell and Brewer Inc.
PO Box 41026, Rochester, NY 14604–4126, USA
website: http://www.boydell.co.uk

A catalogue record for this book is available
from the British Library

Library of Congress Cataloging-in-Publication Data

Broun, Dauvit.
The Irish identity of the kingdom of the Scots in the twelfth and thirteenth centuries / Dauvit Broun.
p. cm. – (Studies in Celtic history, ISSN 0261–9865 ; 18)
Includes bibliographical references and index.
ISBN 0–85115–375–5 (hc. : alk. paper)
1. Scotland – History – 1057–1603. 2. Scotland – Civilization – Irish influences. 3. Nationalism – Scotland – History – To 1500. 4. Scotland – Relations – Ireland. 5. Ireland – Relations – Scotland. 6. Civilization, Celtic. I. Title. II. Series.
DA780.B76 1999
941.1–dc21 98–50019

This publication is printed on acid-free paper

Printed in Great Britain by
St Edmundsbury Press Ltd, Bury St Edmunds, Suffolk

CONTENTS

PREFACE AND ACKNOWLEDGEMENTS

This book is the result of more than a decade studying accounts of Scottish origins, king-lists and texts of the royal genealogy. Parts of chapters IV and V started life in my Ph.D. dissertation, 'The Scottish origin-legend before Fordun', and I began working seriously on Scottish king-lists while I was a British Academy post-doctoral research fellow 1989–90. My original intention was to work towards a wider study of Scottish identity spanning the period from *c.*900 to *c.*1300, and to this end I turned my attention in the following years to origin-legend, king-list and genealogical material relating to the tenth and eleventh centuries, and particularly to the Picts. At the same time, however, I became increasingly concerned that fundamental aspects of my Ph.D. thesis were flawed, particularly the reliance on Skene's edition of Fordun's chronicle and my rather superficial analysis of Scottish identity. I am sorry to say that the first deadline for delivering the script to Boydell & Brewer was back in September 1993, and that it was only after this had passed that I gradually realised that I must abandon my intention of simply producing a revised and expanded version of my Ph.D. dissertation. I decided that the only way forward was to start again from scratch, re-doing the research according to sounder methodological principles. The most conspicuous result of this was to attempt a new edition of the origin-legend material in Book I of Fordun's chronicle. It later became apparent that the project needed a tighter focus, which meant jettisoning almost all my labours on material earlier than the twelfth century. Finally, study leave in the session 1996–7 gave me the opportunity to finish the research and write it up.

I have acquired many debts over the years that I have worked with this material, and I am very grateful for the help, support and encouragement which so many people have offered so willingly. I owe much initially to the supervisors of my Ph.D. dissertation, Professor Geoffrey Barrow and Dr John Bannerman, who guided me through my first faulty steps in the subject, and to the external examiner, Professor Alfred Smyth, for his enthusiastic reception of the finished product and his subsequent support. I was very fortunate to belong to a thriving community of postgraduate students in the Department of Scottish History at Edinburgh University, and benefited much from the stimulation of their company. I would not have survived my days as a postgraduate student, however, without the support of Mrs Jean MacGregor and her family, for which I am eternally grateful, and the ready assistance of my parents.

I am also very grateful to Richard Barber and Caroline Palmer of Boydell & Brewer, and to Professor David Dumville as general editor of the Studies in Celtic History series, for their patience and understanding in keeping faith with a book which was many years overdue before they saw any evidence of its existence. I am sorry that David Dumville had ceased to be general editor before I was ready to submit any of the book, for I know it would have benefited greatly from the immense care and scrupulous scholarship which he has brought to other work of mine which he has edited. As it is, the encouragement he gave me while work was in progress, and the inspiration of his example, were a great help to me in my determination to start the project again from scratch. I am also very grateful to Dr Thomas Owen Clancy, Dr Stephen Driscoll, Dr Katherine Forsyth, Dr Simon Taylor and Mr Alex Woolf of the PictFest working party at Rosemarkie in August 1995 whose constructive discussion of a draft of the pre-twelfth-century section of the original book helped me reach my decision to jettison it. Much of my labour on the book has been undertaken during 'vacations' staying with my parents-in-law, Mr Eddie and Mrs Bethan Jones, and I am very grateful for their unstinting support and patience.

I am happy to acknowledge the help and assistance I have received from staff at the British Library, Corpus Christi College, Cambridge, the National Library of Scotland, Edinburgh, the National Library of Wales, Aberystwyth, Scottish Catholic Archives, Edinburgh, Trinity College, Cambridge, Trinity College, Dublin, the Bodleian Library, Oxford, and the Libraries of the Universities of Edinburgh, Glasgow, St Andrews, and University College, Aberystwyth. I am particularly grateful to the Keepers of Manuscripts and the Librarians at the Bibliothèque nationale, Paris, the British Library, Corpus Christi College, Cambridge, Herzog August Bibliothek, Wolfenbüttel, the National Library of Scotland, Scottish Catholic Archives, and Trinity College, Cambridge, for their cooperation and the help of their staff in allowing me to use manuscripts in their care for the editions of texts in the book. My work on manuscripts of Fordun's chronicle has been greatly facilitated by the ready access I have been given to microfilms obtained by St John's House, University of St Andrews, and in particular by the help I have received from Professor Donald Watt in whose care the microfilms have been kept. I am also very grateful to Dr Marjorie Anderson for allowing me to use her microfilm of the 'Poppleton manuscript'. It is my pleasant duty, also, to acknowledge my debt to the British Academy for awarding me a post-doctoral fellowship, and especially to the School of History and Archaeology and the Faculty of Arts, University of Glasgow, for granting me study leave in the session 1996–7, which was vital in giving me the opportunity to finish the research and write the book.

I have been fortunate to get much helpful advice and feedback from Professor Richard Sharpe, Dr Simon Taylor and Professor Donald Watt, who read a draft of chapters II to IV, and Richard Barber, Dr Máire Ní Mhaonaigh, and Dr Huw Pryce, who read the whole script. I am especially grateful to Dr Ní Mhaonaigh and Professor Sharpe for the considerable improvements they suggested to my edition of passages from Fordun's chronicle. I have also been greatly assisted on specific points by discussions I have had with Dr Thomas Owen Clancy, Professor A. A. M. Duncan, Dr Tom O'Loughlin, and Dr Roibeart Ó Maolalaigh.

I owe profound thanks to all these people, and ask forgiveness from the many others who have contributed in various ways to my efforts who I have not mentioned. I accept full responsibility for all errors and defects which remain, for there is genuinely no excuse for them.

The most profound debt which I owe is to my wife, Dr Nerys Ann Jones, who has throughout been a vital source of support and encouragement and has willingly and selflessly given much of her time and energy to make sure that work on the book could progress. It is with enormous gratitude and everlasting love and affection that I dedicate this book to her.

Dauvit Broun — St Thenew's Day, 1998

ABBREVIATIONS

AClon	Annals of Clonmacnoise (ed. Murphy)
AFM	Annals of the Four Masters (ed. O'Donovan)
AI	Annals of Inisfallen (ed. MacAirt)
ALC	Annals of Loch Cé (ed. Hennessy)
AT	'Annals of Tigernach' (ed. Stokes)
AU	Annals of Ulster (edd. MacAirt and MacNiocaill)
BB	Book of Ballymote (ed. Atkinson)
BBCS	*Bulletin of the Board of Celtic Studies*
CGH	O'Brien, *Corpus Genealogiarum Hiberniae*
CMCS	*Cambridge Medieval Celtic Studies*
CS	*Chronicum Scotorum* (ed. Hennessy)
DIL	Quin, *Dictionary of the Irish Language*
DOST	*Dictionary of the Older Scottish Tongue*
EHR	*English Historical Review*
IHS	*Irish Historical Studies*
IR	*Innes Review*
Lec.	Book of Lecan (ed. Mulchrone)
LG	Macalister, *Lebor Gabála Érenn*
LL	Book of Leinster (edd. Best and O'Brien; ed. O'Sullivan)
PSAS	*Proceedings of the Society of Antiquaries of Scotland*
RRS, V	Duncan, *Regesta Regum Scottorum*, V
RSCHS	*Records of the Scottish Church History Society*
SHR	*Scottish Historical Review*
TRHS	*Transactions of the Royal Historical Society*
ZCP	*Zeitschrift für celtische Philologie*

I

INTRODUCTION

Within months of being inaugurated as king of Scots in March 1306, Robert I's hopes of leading Scotland to independence lay in ruins, and he himself was forced to flee his kingdom with a small band of dedicated supporters. In this his darkest hour, taking refuge probably on the island of Rathlin off the north coast of Ireland, he turned to the Irish for support in his bid to make a comeback. A letter he sent at this time to Irish kings, clerics and residents fortunately survives.[1] In it he appealed to the 'common language and custom' shared by 'our people and yours, free since ancient times, sprung from one seed of a nation',[2] and talked of his enthusiasm for 'permanently strengthening and maintaining inviolate the special friendship between us and you so that with God's will our nation may be able to recover her ancient liberty'.[3]

Robert's idea of Irish and Scots as a single people, and his expectation that the Irish might be willing to involve themselves in Scottish affairs, was not, however, the self-delusion of a desperate man, but was grounded on long established cultural and political reality. From Munster in the south to Moray in the north, people had for centuries been united by the same Gaelic language, high culture and major saints' cults, identifying themselves in their own language as *Gaídil*. In 1165, for example, a chronicler in Armagh could write of Mael Coluim IV, king of Scots, that he was 'the best Christian of the *Gaídil* to the east of the sea'.[4] Exactly one hundred years earlier another Armagh chronicler referred to a leading cleric, who died in Armagh, as 'chief confessor of Ireland and Scotland':[5] the cleric in question had the epithet *Albanach*, denoting either that he was from Scotland or

1 *RRS*, V. 695; Nicholson, 'A sequel to Edward Bruce's invasion'; translated in Barrow, *Robert Bruce*, 3rd edn, 314 (see also 379 n. 9 for comment). For the dating of this letter, see Duffy, 'The Bruce brothers', 64–5. For discussion see also Duffy, *Ireland in the Middle Ages*, 135–6; Duncan, 'The Scots' invasion', 110; Lydon, 'The impact', 283.

2 *. . . populus noster et uester ab olim liberi ab uno processimus germine nacionis quos tam lingua communis quam ritus . . .* An alternative translation of *germine nacionis* is given in Duffy, *Ireland in the Middle Ages*, 135: 'from one seed of birth'. On the terms *populus* and *nacio* see below, n. 43.

3 *. . . amicicie specialis inter nos et uos perpetue conuectende et inuiolabiliter obseruande per quam Deo disponente nostra nacio in antiquam reduci ualeat libertatem*; translation from Barrow, *Robert Bruce*, 3rd edn, 314.

4 Hennessy and MacCarthy, *Annála Uladh*, II. 148–9: *Mael Coluim Cennmór mac Éanric ardrí Alban in Cristiadhe as ferr do bai do Gaidhelaibh re muir anair. . .* For the most recent discussion of the Armagh provenance of this part of the Annals of Ulster, see Bannerman, '*Comarba Coluim Chille*', 36–40.

5 AU 1065.1: *Dubthach Albanach primhanmcara Érenn 7 Alban i nArd Macha quieuit.*

had some particular association with Scotland.[6] A bishop of Cennrígmonaid (St Andrews) was described at his death in 1055 as 'the splendour of *Gaídil*' in a chronicle kept at Clonmacnoise.[7] The reality of a single people stretching across Ireland and Scotland was also evident in the political sphere too. Seán Duffy has observed that 'men from one part of this Gaelic region involved themselves in the affairs of another part',[8] an involvement which is strikingly illustrated by the first recorded *mormaer* of Mar in the far north-east of the Gaelic world, whose single appearance in history is as a casualty fighting for Brian Bóruma at the battle of Clontarf (1014).[9] When Brian Bóruma came to Armagh in 1005 the title he assumed was *imperator Scottorum*,[10] which may have signalled a claim to superiority over all *Gaídil*.[11] And when a scholar, writing in or soon after 1119, attempted to synchronise the reigns of provincial Irish kings with those of kings of Ireland in the Christian era, he included Scottish kings alongside kings of Ulster, Leinster, Ossory, Munster and Connacht.[12]

Whatever justification there may have been for such a view of the Scottish kingdom as part of the Irish polity, there can be little doubt that practitioners of Gaelic high culture in Scotland looked to Ireland (and perhaps Armagh in particular) for leadership and learning. In 1169 Ruaidrí Ua Conchobair, king of Ireland, made an endowment to assist the *fer léginn* (lector) of Armagh in the instruction of students from Scotland as well as Ireland.[13] In the early tenth century St Catroe was sent from eastern Scotland to Armagh to complete his studies; indeed, according to Catroe's biographer, writing in 982x3,[14] 'the Scots have

6 See Duffy, 'Ireland and the Irish Sea Region', 25.

7 AT 1055.5: *Maeldúin mac Gilla Odran, espoc Alban 7 ordan Gaedel o cléircib, in Christo quieuit* (Stokes, 'The Annals of Tigernach. The fourth fragment', 397); the same wording is found in CS 1053.2, except that Mael Dúin's father is given as Gilla Andrias, and *o cléircib, in Christo* is omitted (Hennessy, *Chronicum Scotorum*, 282). For the identification of a Clonmacnoise chronicle, see Dumville 'The peculiarity of the Annals of Tigernach', 'Where did the "Clonmacnoise Chronicle" originate?', and 'When was the "Clonmacnoise Chronicle" created?'.

8 Duffy, 'The Bruce brothers', 59.

9 AU 1014.2; he is named as Domnall mac Éimín meic Cainnig, *mormhaer Marr i nAlbain*, and comes last in AU's long list of notables who fell along with Brian.

10 Gwynn, *Book of Armagh*, facsimile edn, fo. 16vb; Gwynn, *Liber Ardmachanus*, 32, col. 2; Stokes, *The Tripartite Life*, II. 336. See also Gwynn, 'Brian in Armagh'.

11 See Duffy, 'Ireland and the Irish Sea Region', 27, where it is suggested that the title used by kings of Scots, *rex Scottorum*, may have denoted a claim to being the leading king in the Gaelic world.

12 Thurneysen, 'Synchronismen'; Boyle, 'The Edinburgh synchronisms'. On the dating of this text, see below, 171 and n. 23.

13 Hennessy and MacCarthy, *Annála Uladh*, II. 160–3. The *fer léginn* at the time was highly qualified, having spent twenty-one years training in France and England (Hennessy, *The Annals of Loch Cé*, I. 150–1; O' Donovan *Annála Ríoghachta Éireann*, III. 12–13; Anderson, *Early Sources*, II. 267 n. 6).

14 The most recent discussion of the Life of Catroe is Macquarrie, *The Saints of Scotland*, 199–210; see 200 for date and authorship. The Life was written just over a decade after Catroe's death by a monk of the monastery where Catroe had been abbot. At 207 Macquarrie observed that 'it is clear that the writer had access to material probably

many thousand teachers, but they have not many fathers . . . because from the time of his [Catroe's] arrival none of the sages had crossed the sea, but they continued to dwell in Ireland'.[15] And according to Gerald of Barri, writing in the late 1180s,[16] Scotland looked to Ireland *quasi fons artis*;[17] Gerald maintained that the Welsh also sought to imitate the Irish in music due to their proximity to Ireland, but the Scots sought to imitate the Irish because of their ancestry (*propagacio*)[18] which (he explained in another passage) was shown to be from Ireland because of affinity of language, dress, arms and customs.[19] *Gaídil* in Scotland would appear, therefore, to have been culturally an Irish offshoot between the tenth and twelfth centuries at the very time when Gaelic was the dominant culture in the Scottish kingdom.[20]

This raises a key issue for Scottish identity in this period. As Seán Duffy has put it, 'we regard *Alba* and *Éire* as separate countries, and the *Gaídil* as one people, but were the *Gaídil Alban* and the *Gaídil Érenn* one nation or two?'[21] This book aims to address this question by investigating how Scottish men of letters located the kingdom of *Alba* in relation to the *Gaídil*, and to explore what role this played in defining the kingdom's identity. Did Scots see themselves as merely an Irish offshoot, or did they see the Scots and Irish as separate peoples sharing equally a common ancestry and culture?[22] And would this have mattered much either way?

Scottish men of letters in this period could typically have expressed their identity as a people and a kingdom in one of three ways. The more elaborate of the

---

related by Catroe himself referring to his parentage and early life in Scotland'. The primary witness of the Life is Colgan, *Acta Sanctorum*, facsimile repr., 494–507 (which was partially reproduced in Skene, *Chronicles*, 106–16).

15 . . . *Scoti multa millia pædagogorum habeant, sed non multum patres . . . nam a tempore aduentus sui, nullus sapientum mare transierat; sed adhuc Hiberniam incolebant*; translation from Anderson, *Early Sources*, I. 437. Again, the education on offer at Armagh would appear to have been of a very high standard: see Boyle, 'St Cadroe', 4–5, and Macquarrie, *The Saints of Scotland*, 202.

16 Bartlett, *Gerald of Wales*, 213.

17 Brewer, Dimock and Warner, *Giraldi Cambrensis Opera*, V. 154–5 (*Topographia Hibernica* III. 11)

18 Ibid.; see Bartlett, *Gerald of Wales*, 205–6.

19 Brewer, Dimock and Warner, *Giraldi Cambrensis Opera*, V. 147 (*Topographia Hibernica* III. 7): *Scotia quoque pars insule Britannice dicitur aquilonaris, quia gens originaliter ab his propagata terram illam habitare dignoscitur. Quod tam lingue quam cultus, tam armorum etiam quam morum, usque in hodiernum probat affinitas*. On Gerald's use of *lingua*, *cultus*, *arma*, and *mores*, see Bartlett, *Gerald of Wales*, 188–92.

20 Note Jackson's observation (Jackson, *The Gaelic Notes*, 126) that idiosyncracies evident in the orthography of the Deer property records (written *c.*1130 x *c.*1150) were 'not at all unnatural, considering that Deer is on the remotest edge of the Common Gaelic civilisation-area; its writing-masters must have been out of touch and poorly qualified'.

21 Duffy, 'The Bruce brothers', 59.

22 As, for instance, it was possible for the English to say of their brotherly relationship with Saxons as late as the mid-twelfth century; see Foot, 'The making of *Angelcynn*', 44 and n. 83. This kind of relationship would appear to have been what was intended in Robert I's letter to the Irish, where Scots and Irish were referred to as different peoples sprung (ultimately) from one seed of a nation (see above, 1).

three was in an origin-legend, stating where the Scots came from, and how their kingdom came into being. The other two focussed on the kingship in particular, either by listing the predecessors of the currently reigning king or by charting the reigning king's pedigree (typically, in a Gaelic context, through the male line only). A crucial aspect of every king-list was the first king, founding father of the kingdom; it was also important if the list showed that the kingdom was an ancient institution. The royal genealogy was also concerned with founding figures and the kingship's claim to antiquity, although it potentially added a new dimension to a king-list's information by showing the descent of the first founding king in the king-list. It can thus serve as an important link between king-list and origin-legend. If origin-legend, king-list and genealogy are taken together, therefore, it is possible to assemble the key elements in the kingdom's past as this was understood by Scottish men of letters, and therein view the essential contours of the kingdom's identity.[23] This can reveal, for instance, to what extent the kingdom was regarded as a community of common descent in its own right; how intimately it was associated with a particular territory; and what its relationship with other kingdoms was (ideally) considered to be. This is not to say that there were not other ways of expressing or promoting a kingdom's identity apart from origin-legend, king-list and genealogy,[24] or that every kingdom in this period was furnished by its historians with texts of this sort.[25] The absence of one or other of these genres from a kingdom's historiographical profile, however, may point to an important facet of its identity which made an origin-legend, king-list or genealogy seem unnecessary or inappropriate.[26] It was hardly because scholars lacked the means to devise such texts when they felt the need; the raw material for a king-list, for instance, could be

23 Such texts can often contain much more ideologically important information than will be discussed here: see esp. Dumville, 'Kingship, genealogies and regnal lists'; Ó Corráin, 'Irish origin-legends and genealogy'; Sims-Williams, 'Some functions of origin stories'; Reynolds, 'Medieval *origines gentium*'.

24 For example, the way English identity was constructed by King Alfred, discussed in Foot, 'The making of *Angelcynn*', 27–38.

25 Reynolds, *Kingdoms and Communities*, 272–3, has observed the lack of a specifically English origin-legend in the thirteenth century; Dumville, 'Kingship, genealogies and regnal lists', has commented (at 96–7) that in Wales 'regnal lists were not cultivated'.

26 The lack of Welsh king-lists could readily be explained as a result of the tendency for kingdoms occasionally to be divided among the deceased king's sons or segments (Davies, *Wales in the Early Middle Ages*, 123–5). Reynolds, *Kingdoms and Communities*, 272–3, wondered whether 'the claims which [English] kings made to overlordship of Wales, Scotland, and Ireland, as well as to inherited fiefs in France, inhibited them from writing in such terms' as a specifically English origin-legend. The English, however, probably already looked to Brutus for their origins, which would suggest that they had an origin-legend, but one which made plain their identification with Britain, and not just England, as their homeland. This would be apparent in the *Brut*, a history of the rulers of Britain and subsequently England, which survives in numerous versions, chiefly in English or French. It is sometimes said that the prose *Brut* originated shortly after 1333, although it is conceded that an earlier version ending in 1272 may have existed in the late thirteenth century (see Gransden, *Historical Writing*, II. 72, and Taylor, *The Universal Chronicle of Ranulf Higden*, 15). There are, however, no fewer than eleven manuscripts of the French prose *Brut* listed in Tyson, 'Handlist', 333–44, which run from Brutus to 1272 (as well as others which run from Brutus to 1154, 1199

found in a genealogy,[27] and there was by this time a number of standard ways of extending a genealogy to become an origin-legend.[28] It may be expected, therefore, that origin-legends, king-lists, and genealogies contain a rich seam of encoded information about what was regarded as important to contemporaries about the collectivities, kingdoms and kingships these texts were written to explain. When the evidence of all three genres is combined, therefore, a picture of the most important (and sometimes contradictory) elements in a kingdom's identity should emerge.

An inquiry such as this into the identity of the Scottish kingdom in this period must tackle two basic problems. The first is that there is a critical shortage of material. There are no readily identifiable accounts of Scottish origins before the end of the thirteenth century[29] and there is only one surviving text of a Scottish

---

and 1216). It would be premature at this stage to pronounce confidently on when these versions were written, but it seems likely that at least a version (or versions) ending in 1272 was produced during the reign of Edward I (1272–1307), and that the text existed earlier (even in the twelfth century). There were also poetic treatments of the *Brut* which predate the reign of Edward I, for instance by Wace and an anonymous author writing in the first third of the thirteenth century; see for instance Bell, *An Anglo-Norman Brut*. Royal genealogies seem to have become less prominent where a king-list was devised which connected with an origin-legend (as in the *Brut*). In those kingships where the succession made it difficult to present a simple linear genealogy in the male line it would not be surprising if the genealogy became less prominent. It is all the more significant, therefore, when a linear pedigree continued to be important despite such difficulty; for instance the Scottish royal genealogy which included the descent of Donnchad ua Maíl Choluim (d.1040) through his mother: see below, 173–4.

27 The extension of the list of kings of Ireland back to the first *Gaídil* to settle in Ireland was achieved by taking names from the existing genealogical scheme; see, for instance, Dumville, 'Kingship, genealogies and regnal lists', 102. A later example is the concoction from the royal genealogy of a succession back to the first king in Scotland in Boece, *Scotorum Historiae*, which was exposed by Innes, *A Critical Essay*. A cogent case has been made in Royan, 'The *Scotorum Historiae*', that Boece himself was not the author of this material. It is conceivable that this king-list existed already in 1301; see Broun, 'The birth', 21–2. It was also possible to construct a genealogy from a king-list, although this seems to have been much rarer: a Welsh scholar, for instance, converted a list of Roman emperors into a patrilinear pedigree; see Dumville, 'Kingship, genealogies and regnal lists', 96–7, where it is suggested that this was because the Welsh scholar regarded the list as a pedigree because he was unfamiliar generally with regnal lists; Dumville noted (at 96 n. 132) that confusion of regnal list and genealogy persists into modern times.

28 Reynolds, 'Medieval *origines gentium*', 375–8.

29 There is a reference to Scota daughter of Pharoah and to Scythian origins in a curious mixture of extracts from Isidore's *Etymologiae* entitled *Cronica de origine antiquorum Pictorum* (edited in Anderson, *Kings and Kingship*, 243–5); the title is problematic, not least because the text is concerned as much with the origins of *Scoti* as *Picti* (see ibid., 243, n. 233). The passage on Scythia and Scota can be dated 1202x14 (Miller, 'Matriliny by treaty', 138). Cowan, 'Myth and identity', 122, stated that the tract (including this passage) 'cannot be dated much later than 877', but this is based on a misunderstanding of Anderson, *Kings and Kingship*, 101–2, where the 'substantial section of pseudo-history' attached to the beginning of king-list 'P' 'not much later than 877' refers to the

king-list written in Scotland which can definitely be dated to before 1198.[30] There is one extant text of the genealogy, datable to 995x7, attached to the late-tenth-century *Senchus Fer nAlban*, and only a few thereafter.[31] As far as the tally of surviving manuscripts of these texts is concerned in the twelfth and thirteenth centuries, the picture is (not surprisingly) even more bleak: none of the origin-legend; two relatively brief king-lists, both in the same thirteenth-century codex (the Chronicle of Melrose: one is written on a folio inserted into the chronicle, the other is written piecemeal into the margins);[32] and four twelfth-century manuscripts of the genealogy (in Rawlinson B.502 and the Book of Leinster, and in two early copies of *Imagines Historiarum* by Ralph of Diss).[33] To rectify this shortage of material it is necessary to analyse surviving texts not only from this period but also from the fourteenth and fifteenth centuries to see if lost archetypes can be identified – and (if so) to what extent these can be recovered, and how accurately they may be dated and provenanced. This is particularly fruitful in revealing texts of the origin-legend datable to the thirteenth century and texts of the king-list datable to the period 1093x4–1214.

Such a thorough-going campaign of textual archaeology is necessarily painstaking and technical, especially given the shortage of material surviving in manuscripts of the period. It is important to show how each step in the process has been achieved and to make it as transparent as practicable. Because this study is focussed on origin-legends, king-lists and genealogies, and is based so heavily on a critical analysis of the surviving texts of these genres, I have incorporated into the discussion, at the appropriate places, such new editions of origin-legend, king-list and genealogy as have been required, rather than dispatching these to the relative oblivion of appendices. Thus the keystone of the book – a discussion of the account of Scottish origins in John of Fordun's *Chronica Gentis Scottorum* – includes a chapter devoted entirely to a new edition of the material under consideration, which is intended to provide a sound and transparent basis for the analysis thereafter. To some extent this approach, and the predominance of textual archaeology generally in the book, is a response both to the shortage of material available for study, and to the lack of attention which most of these texts have received this century (with the notable exception of the outstanding work of Marjorie Anderson, without which this book would have been impossible).[34] It is true, however, that a thorough-going investigation of the type attempted here should, in any case, be regarded as essential if the potential of texts such as these as a source for a kingdom's identity is to be properly realised. Peeling back the layers of copying, editing or rewriting behind an extant text can reveal how radical or conservative an author has been with his materials. When this procedure is replicated for a number

---

material preceding Gilgidi/Gud in the longer Pictish king-list, not to *Cronica de origine antiquorum Pictorum*.

30 The Chronicle of the Kings of Alba: see below, 167.

31 See below, 151, 174–5, 180–2.

32 The former commences only with Mael Coluim Cenn Mór (1058–93) (see below, 138–9); the latter, known as the Verse Chronicle, begins with Cinaed mac Alpín (see below, 136–7).

33 See below, 151 n. 98, 174, 180.

34 Especially her discussion of king-lists in *Kings and Kingship*.

of texts it becomes possible to identify elements which were new – and which may therefore have been particularly relevant at the time of writing – as well as other elements which were entrenched either because they retained their validity over a long period or because they were accepted as unobjectionable. In this way a critical understanding of the kingdom's identity in this period can emerge.

The second fundamental problem which must be confronted by this inquiry is a question of semantics which lies at the heart of the issue of the relationship of the Scottish kingdom to *Gaídil*. When writing about this subject in English it is impossible to use 'Gaels', 'Irish' and 'Scots' as translations of contemporary terminology without appearing to have decided matters in advance. 'Gaels' would imply a people of whom Scots and Irish could have been equally a part; to say the Scots thought of themselves as 'Irish' would be to deny this, and imply that they were regarded as an Irish offshoot. It is therefore unsatisfactory to adopt at the outset either the usual translation of *Gaídil* as 'Irish', or the alternative translation as 'Gaels'. A frequent Latin term for *Gaídil* was *Scoti*, which raises similar difficulties, especially in a Scottish context. If *Scoti* is rendered as 'Scots', then this would most naturally be used of a people separate from the Irish.[35] If *Scoti* is translated as 'Gaels' or 'Irish', however, then the same problem is encountered as in translating *Gaídil*. The straightforward (if slightly cumbersome) solution to all this which I will adopt is to leave *Gaídil* and *Scoti* untranslated, and to use these terms instead of 'Gaels', 'Irish' and 'Scots' where appropriate in order to emphasise that we are dealing with questions of identity which we cannot at the outset interpret with any certainty, even in the special context of origin-legends written by Scottish men of letters. Moreover, this problem is not simply a semantic minefield, but continues to touch sensitive chords in Scottish and Irish identity which pull in opposite directions. Thus in Ireland the use of 'Gaelic' rather than 'Irish' can seem like an attempt to deny national status, while in Scotland the use of 'Gaelic' rather than 'Irish' (Scots *Erse*) serves to affirm a native affinity with Scotland. It is a challenge, therefore, for us in the twentieth century, when trying to understand the identity of our forbears seven centuries or more ago, to take our minds out of our own times and discard the often painful memories and powerful emotions which are stirred by the choice between using or not using national and cultural names. Yet this is what we must do if we wish to understand how Scottish men of letters identified their kingdom in relation to the *Gaídil*. The outcome should be a keener, more informed awareness of the history of Scottish identity and of the importance of the *Gaídil*, not only as a dimension of Scottish and Irish history, but as a prominent feature in the social and political configuration of the islands of Britain and Ireland in the period under consideration.

The question of how Scots located themselves in relation to the *Gaídil* is also a key issue in Scotland's emergence as a nation within these islands. The background to this is a fundamental change in the way men of letters across western Europe thought about peoples and kingdoms. Susan Reynolds has observed that 'in the sixth century peoples were probably thought of as communities of common descent, law and language; then, as government developed, taking over more jurisdiction and law enforcement, units of descent and law came to be accepted as

35 As in the Declaration of Arbroath (see below, 119–20).

communities of government too, and quintessentially kingdoms'.[36] As a result, 'kingdoms and peoples came to seem identical – not invariably, but sufficiently often for the coincidence of the two to seem the norm to contemporaries',[37] so that 'stories invented by learned writers of the very early middle ages were unconsciously adapted . . . in quite different circumstances centuries later'.[38] The significance of Reynolds' observation may be more keenly appreciated if the definition of 'peoples' in this context is sharpened. Europe (and indeed the world) was consistently viewed in the Middle Ages as divided into peoples who were frequently accorded primordial beginnings in one (or more) of three ways: either through an origin in biblical times, or by an eponym in the Trojan era, or through descent from a son of Mannus/Alan(e)us.[39] These 'primordial peoples' were often defined in terms of observed cultural characteristics;[40] they were not, of course, primordial in fact, and the ethnic identity which was constructed in these terms was rooted in contemporary circumstances and was open to change.[41] The key development in the way men of letters thought about kingdoms between the tenth and thirteenth centuries, then, was that they began to see it as normal for kingdoms to coincide with one of these 'primordial peoples'. It may be inferred therefore that in the imagination of the politically active classes in this period it was increasingly likely that a kingdom's inhabitants would be regarded as constituting an ancient people.

This corresponds with the idea of a nation in modern times as essentially a community of common descent of great antiquity which forms a natural unit of government.[42] We should perhaps not be too squeamish about recognising this

36 Reynolds, 'Medieval *origines gentium*', 389. On this process see more fully Reynolds, *Kingdoms and Communities*, 256–302.

37 Ibid., 260.

38 Reynolds, 'Medieval *origines gentium*', 382.

39 Ibid., 375–8. They could also be regarded a sharing the same law or custom, which before the growth of government in the twelfth and thirteenth centuries was as much an idea rather than a reality as the notion of common descent. See Davis, 'The Peoples of Britain and Ireland 1100–1400. III. Laws and Customs'.

40 As in Bede's account of the four peoples of Britain: *HE*, I.1

41 Note, for instance, the striking comment in Wolfram, 'Gothic history', 313, that '*gentes* are always mixed; their origin is not a matter of blood but of constitution'. Most work done on ethnic identity in the medieval period has focussed on the fifth and sixth centuries in areas historically within the Roman empire. The most recent studies in English are Amory, *People and Identity*, esp. 13–39; Geary, 'Ethnicity as a situational construct'; Wolfram, '*Origo et religio*'.

42 Note, for instance, Gellner's view that nationalism is 'primarily a principle which holds that the political and national unit should be congruent' (*Nations and Nationalism*, 1), or Benedict Anderson's definition of a nation as an imagined community (*Imagined Communities*, 5–7) whose most distinctive characteristic (in his checklist at 6–7) is the aspiration to self-government, or Anthony Smith's comment that 'nation signifies a cultural and political bond, uniting in a single political community all who share an historic culture and homeland' (*National Identity*, 14–15). The emphasis placed by some recent commentators on mass communication (Anderson, *Imagined Communities*) or on common legal rights and duties (Smith, *National Identity*, e.g. 10–14) as important elements in the modern idea of a nation may thus be seen as developments from this

new way of thinking about peoples and kingdoms as the beginnings of the modern idea of a nation.[43] This is not to say that modern and medieval ideas of nationhood did not differ. Neither does this necessarily suppose that a kingdom's inhabitants all shared such ideas about their society, merely that these ideas were meaningful for men of letters and, therefore, potentially for the upper echelons of society in general of which men of letters were a part, and whose opinions they unconsciously reflected or actively sought to inform.

The key question this book will aim to answer, then, is whether Scottish men of letters portrayed the inhabitants of *regnum Scottorum* in similar terms as a nation between the twelfth and thirteenth centuries.[44] It will be argued that they did not, and that there is good evidence that, up to and including the thirteenth century, they identified the kingdom of the Scots and its inhabitants with Ireland. Moreover, this Irish identity was not simply a reflex of the cultural importance of Ireland which Scottish men of letters unthinkingly perpetuated after the retreat of Gaelic as a language of literacy and status in the kingdom's heartlands. However important the cultural ties with Ireland of Scottish men of letters may have been when Gaelic was predominant before the mid-twelfth century, something more than this would seem to be needed to explain the kingdom's Irish identity. A key objective will be to discern what function the kingdom's Irish identity may have served which could have allowed it to retain its vitality among the kingdom's non-Gaelic men of letters in this period.

Tracing the evidence for the kingdom's Irish identity and exploring its function will not add up to a complete history of Scottish identity itself in this period; that

---

medieval idea of a nation as a kingdom corresponding to a perceived 'primordial' people. It should be acknowledged, however, that none of these writers would be comfortable with the theory of pre-modern national identity I have articulated here. See most recently Smith, 'The problem'.

43 Reynolds, *Kingdoms and Communities*, 251–6, argues cogently that words like 'nation' and 'national' should be avoided (preferring the more neutral 'people' and 'regnal'). The advantages of using the term 'nation', however, outway the disadvantages, especially if it makes clearer the change in perception which (as I understand her) Reynolds was arguing occurred in this period, as well as highlighting the significance of this change for European history generally. Some medieval writers seem in their use of *nacio* or *gens* and *populus* to have applied a similar distinction between peoples which were 'primordial' and those which were not – although it would be rash to assert that these terms were generally employed systematically (see for instance Davies, 'The Peoples of Britain and Ireland 1100–1400. I: Identities', 5). Reynolds, *Kingdoms and Communities*, 256 n. 12, identified one writer (Anselm of Laon) who distinguished between *populus* and *nacio*. Another was apparently whoever drafted Robert I's letter to the Irish in the winter of 1306–7 (a fair guess would be his brother, Alexander, dean of Glasgow and graduate of Cambridge University, who was himself one of the bearers of the letter; Duffy, 'The Bruce brothers', 64–5). In the letter *populus noster et uester* referred to the inhabitants of Ireland and Scotland as separate communities, but *nacio* referred to both as a single community sharing the same language and customs, while *nostra nacio* meant, in effect, *Gaídil*.

44 The first appearance in contemporary record of what may be recognised as Scottish identity was two centuries earlier, in 900. See most recently Broun, 'Dunkeld', and Dumville, 'Ireland and Britain', 181–3.

would require a more wideranging discussion of the various ways Scots constructed their identity and how that may be explained by the social and political realities which they experienced. The book's focus on the kingdom's Irish identity should not obscure the possibility that the kingdom had other identities which served other functions.[45] Also, it should be emphasised that the historiographical texts with which this study is concerned can only safely be regarded as a direct witness to currents of opinion among men of letters. The extent to which such currents of opinion were shared by the elite in general in the kingdom's heartlands (never mind the population at large) depends on the nature of the relationship which men of letters had with their social peers and with other sectors of society. It is possible to envisage men of letters as not only reflecting some of the aspirations and assumptions of their age but also, to an unquantifiable degree, as opinion-formers as well. The issues which are addressed in this book and the aspects of Scottish identity with which it is concerned should, however, shed important light on the identity of the Scottish kingdom in the twelfth and thirteenth centuries, and ultimately contribute to our understanding of Scotland's origins as a nation.

45 For instance the kingship's English identity in the twelfth and thirteenth centuries enunciated through St Margaret's ancestry: see below, 196.

II

THE SCOTTISH ORIGIN-LEGEND IN JOHN OF FORDUN'S *CHRONICA GENTIS SCOTTORUM*: PROSPECTS AND PROBLEMS

John of Fordun's *Chronica Gentis Scottorum*, 'Chronicle of the Scottish People', completed in the 1370s, is the earliest extant text that contains a lengthy treatment of Scottish origins.[1] In outline, this tells how Gaedel (*Gaythelos*) son of Nél (*Neolus*) went from Greece to Egypt, married Scota daughter of Pharaoh, and left Egypt after Pharoah perished in the Red Sea while pursuing the Children of Israel; he then arrived in Spain and settled at *Brigancia* where he built a high tower; from Spain his sons Éber (*Hiber*) and *Hymec* set sail for Ireland and conquered it; some *Scoti* remained in Spain, and sometime later Éber, Éremón, and Partholón (*Hibertus*, *Hermonius*, and *Partholomus*), sons of Míl Espáine (*Micelius Espayn*), king of *Scoti* in Spain, set off for Ireland and conquered it; later still, Simón Brecc (*Smonbrec*), a son of the king of *Scoti* who yet remained in Spain, also made the journey to Ireland and conquered it, taking with him the Stone of Scone which he placed at Tara; sometime later Eochaid *Rothay*, a descendant of Simón Brecc, became the first to settle in the Hebrides, giving his name to Rothesay; eventually a descendant of Eochaid named Fergus, son of Ferchar or Feredach, arrived in mainland Scotland with the Stone of Scone and became the first king of *Scoti* in Scotland. There are no readily identifiable Scottish accounts of Scottish origins earlier than the first war of independence (1296–1328), and those which survive from the war, as in the Declaration of Arbroath (1320) or the material prepared by the Scottish procurators in Rome in 1301, consisted of little more than a couple of sentences.[2] It is little wonder, therefore, that John of Fordun has been credited as the first to formulate fully the Scottish origin-legend.[3]

Fordun's role, however, was much more limited. It will be argued from the textual archaeology of Fordun's account that it was based chiefly on a thirteenth-century synthesis of at least four versions of the origin-legend. It will also be

1 Skene's presentation of Fordun's work as consisting of an account of Scottish history from its origins to the death of David I in 1153 in five books followed by material (which Skene entitled *Gesta Annalia*) covering the period 1153–1385 is unsupported by the manuscript evidence. Only the *Chronica* in five books (up to David I's death) and 15 chapters of an incomplete sixth book (on St Margaret's English royal ancestors) may be safely attributed to Fordun. See Broun, 'A new look'. The misleading nature of Skene's arrangement was first brought to light by Professor Watt in MacQueen, MacQueen and Watt, *Scotichronicon*, III. xvi–xvii.

2 Discussed below, 119–21.

3 Mason, 'Scotching the Brut', esp. 63.

shown that some of this material was related to sources behind accounts of Scottish origins in Grey's *Scalacronica* and Wyntoun's *Original Chronicle*. Following on from this a picture of the relationship between accounts of Scottish origins before *c.*1300 can be assembled which will make it possible to distinguish some of their most important elements. One of these key features, it will be argued, is that Ireland rather than Scotland was portrayed as the homeland of *Scoti*, and that the Scottish kingship and its people were represented by its men of letters as an offshoot of the Irish.

The quest for the sources of Fordun's account of Scottish origins

It may be acknowledged at the outset that the legend given by Fordun can readily be recognised, in its essential details, as much older than Fordun himself. His telling of the legend conformed in outline with Irish accounts of Irish origins in *Lebor Gabála*, in which Gaedel son of Nél, Scota daughter of Pharaoh, and Míl Espáine and sons were also mentioned, and in which Egypt and *Brigancia* in Spain were also included on the itinerary from Greece to Ireland.[4] This similarity between Fordun and *Lebor Gabála* has usually been explained by referring to Fordun's alleged quest for sources in Ireland, as described in the prologue to the 'Book of Coupar Angus', a version of Bower's *Scotichronicon* which Bower himself prepared in the 1440s.[5] If, indeed, Fordun's account was based on Irish sources, then he could be regarded as the first to have employed this material extensively as an explanation of Scottish origins.

It has to be said, however, that disagreement between Fordun and *Lebor Gabála* is more apparent than agreement. For instance, Fordun in the Egyptian episode has Gaedel son of Nél in the leading role, but this was given in *Lebor Gabála* to Nél or Míl, and Gaedel was made Scota's son, not her husband;[6] Fordun has Gaedel lead

4 *LG*, II. 8–125; V. 11–135.

5 See e.g. MacQueen and MacQueen, 'Latin prose literature', 233: see also MacQueen and MacQueen, *Scotichronicon*, II. xvii. The passage reads: *idcirco et ipse pedester tamquam apis argumentosa, in prato Britannie et in oraculis Hibernie, per ciuitates et oppida, per uniuersitates et collegia, per ecclesias et cenobia, inter historicos conuersans et inter cronographos perhendinans* . . ., 'therefore [he went] on foot like a busy bee, in the plain of Britain and the oratories of Ireland, through cities and towns, universities and colleges, churches and monasteries, talking among historians and visiting chroniclers . . .' (see Watt, *Scotichronicon*, IX. 12–15). It has been suggested that Fordun's description of Edward the Confessor's chapel at Westminster (V. 29) may be an eye-witness account (Anderson, *Kings and Kingship*, 214). For the Book of Coupar Angus (Edinburgh, National Library of Scotland, MS Adv. 35.1.7), the only complete copy of this version of Bower's work, see Watt, *Scotichronicon*, IX. 193–6: at 193 the manuscript is dated by watermark evidence to *c.*1450 x *c.*1480. The prologue is printed in Skene, *Johannis de Fordun Chronica*, xlix–l, and more recently (with translation) in Watt, *Scotichronicon*, IX. 12–19. For the date of composition, see D. E. R. Watt's comments in Shead, Stevenson and Watt, *Scotichronicon*, VI. xv, and Watt, *Scotichronicon*, IX. 18. The prologue to Bower's *Scotichronicon* itself (see ibid., 2–5) has no mention of Fordun's travels.

6 *LG*, II. 10–11, 32–5, 38–41, 48–9, 52–3, 58–63, 68–9.

his people from Egypt, but in *Lebor Gabála* this role was played by one of Gaedel's descendants;[7] in *Lebor Gabála* the only *Scoti* who conquered Ireland were the eight sons of Míl, only two of whom were known to Fordun.[8] The most striking differences between Fordun and *Lebor Gabála*, however, were in their treatment of Partholón and Simón Brecc. In *Lebor Gabála* Partholón led the first settlement of Ireland after the Flood, a role attested for him in *Historia Brittonum* (829/30).[9] It would have been extraordinary, therefore, to have regarded him as a son of Míl and thus one of the first *Gaídil* to colonise Ireland. As for Simón Brecc, in *Lebor Gabála* he appeared as no more than a space-filling king of Ireland descended from Míl.[10] According to *Lebor Gabála*, the sequence of colonisations of Ireland culminated in the triumphant conquest by *Gaídil* led by the sons of Míl. It would have been highly unorthodox, therefore, for descendants of Míl still to have been in Spain, and for one of them, Simón Brecc, to have led yet another conquest of Ireland. Not only, therefore, were there few details which Fordun shared with *Lebor Gabála*, but key elements in Fordun's account drove a coach and horses through the long-established pseudo-historical scheme elaborated by Irish scholars for centuries before Fordun.[11] This means either that Fordun chose to refashion radically what he learnt from Irish historians, or that he himself was ignorant of *Lebor Gabála*, and acquired this material from an independent source. In the absence of a plausible explanation for the former proposition, it is hard to accept that Fordun based his account on material acquired in Ireland. The whole notion of Fordun's research-trip to Ireland, therefore, must be called into question. A context for inventing the trip is found in the prologue to the 'Book of Coupar Angus' itself. It was claimed there that Edward I had denuded Scotland of her chronicles;[12] it would have been consistent with this, therefore, to have stated that Fordun (on whom the credibility of much of the 'Book of Coupar Angus' itself depended) must have found his sources outside Scotland.

Some (at least) of the sources that lay directly behind Fordun's account have, in fact, remained visible in Fordun's text itself. The text in book I is presented as an assemblage of passages drawn from a number of different accounts which are attributed either to a 'legend of St Brendan', a 'legend of St Congal', an author called *Grossum Caput*,[13] or more often than not simply to 'a chronicle' or 'another chronicle'. None of these sources can be identified with an extant text, so that

7 *LG*, II. 14–17, 36–7, 62–5.

8 *LG*, V. 20ff, 70ff, 98ff.

9 LG, II. 268–73. Dumville, *Historia Brittonum*, III. 67–8 (see concordance at 56 for where this appears in other recensions); see also text quoted extensively in Carey, *The Irish National Origin-Legend*, 5–6, which is taken from a text supplied by David Dumville as part of his ongoing edition of the work. For the date of *Historia Brittonum*, see Dumville, 'Some aspects'. On Partholón, see Carey, *The Irish National Origin-Legend*, 8–9, and references cited there.

10 *LG*, V. 252, 507.

11 On the history of this scheme, see most recently Carey, *The Irish National Origin-Legend*, and Scowcroft, '*Leabhar Gabhála* Part II'.

12 Skene, *Johannis de Fordun Chronica*, xlix. On this claim see esp. Hughes, *Celtic Britain in the Early Middle Ages*, 3–7.

13 The name suggests Robert Grosseteste (d.1253), bishop of Lincoln, although none of the passages cited to *Grossum Caput* correspond to anything he is known to have written.

Fordun would appear on the face of it to have preserved uniquely a notable amount of material which would otherwise have been lost. It is little wonder that, as a result of reproducing material from different sources, Fordun's account is characterised by repetition and contradiction. For example, it opens in book I, chapter 8, with four passages which each related how Gaedel left Greece for Egypt and married Scota, daughter of Pharaoh. In the first and third it was claimed that Gaedel was wayward and insolent and was therefore driven out of Greece into exile in Egypt where his royal blood and courage earned him the hand of Scota; in the second passage it was said that Gaedel went to Egypt to assist an ally and married Scota, Pharaoh's only daughter, as a way of cementing the treaty between his father and Pharaoh; in the fourth passage, however, we are told how Gaedel was expelled from Greece because of his attempt to usurp and tyrannise his father's kingdom, and that he fled to Egypt where he assisted Pharaoh in persecuting the children of Israel and married Pharaoh's only daughter, Scota, in the hope of succeeding to Pharaoh's kingdom.[14] The reader is thus left in confusion, wondering whether Gaedel was a friendly ally, a ruthless self-enhancer, or something in between. It is striking that such ambivalence has been permitted concerning the founding-father of *Scoti*, and that some thoroughly unflattering material has been relayed without comment.

In theory it should be possible, therefore, to attempt to piece together passages such as these and reassemble Fordun's sources (at least partially) from those pieces which he has preserved. A serious difficulty, however, is that Fordun has evidently used more than one source identified simply as 'a chronicle' or 'another chronicle': of the four passages which described how Gaedel left Greece for Egypt and married Scota, for example, three have been attributed to nameless sources. A major problem, therefore, is how to disentangle these nameless sources and attempt to reconstruct the accounts from which these passages have been derived.

John and Winifred MacQueen have proposed one way in which this task might be accomplished. After deducing that three nameless sources may have been used throughout book I, they proposed that the passages reproduced first in a chapter all belonged to the same source, which Fordun regarded as primary; that all the passages attributed to 'another chronicle' which were given second in a chapter belonged to another source; and that a third source was used on the rare occasions when yet another passage attributed to 'another chronicle' was given. Finally, the MacQueens argued that all three sources were in agreement in the two instances in book I in which 'chronicles' in the plural were referred to.[15] The MacQueens would be the first to admit, I suspect, that their method was rather rough-and-ready: indeed, they candidly described it as based on 'possibly over-bold assumptions',[16] and even abandoned it in one instance when they assigned to their primary source both the first and third extracts attributed to a nameless source within the one chapter.[17] Moreover, the texts which they reconstructed contain contradictions which the MacQueens did not discuss. Their primary nameless source, for

14 See below, 34–6, for text.

15 MacQueen and MacQueen, *Scotichronicon*, I. xxiii–xxvii, esp. xxiii.

16 Ibid., xxiii.

17 Ibid., xxiii: 33–5 (ch. 12, lines 1–18, 26–34). Note that the chapters in *Scotichronicon* are numbered one more than the equivalent chapter in Fordun's *Chronica*.

instance, has Gaedel making a vow on leaving Egypt to seek uninhabited lands to settle, but later it describes Gaedel sending armed men to Ireland, their long-awaited homeland, who kill the inhabitants they find there.[18] Another example concerns their second source, which is either incomplete or provided only a partial account of the legend. It is the only one which does not have Gaedel leaving Egypt by boat, so that it might be expected that the only passage in which Gaedel was described journeying from Egypt across land rather than traversing the seas would also have come from this source.[19] Because the passage in question appears first in a chapter, however, the MacQueens assigned it to their primary rather than their second putative source.[20]

Another problem which confronts any attempt to reconstruct these lost sources is that it may be unsafe to assume uncritically that Fordun's account is no more than a scissors-and-paste composition in which sources have been mechanically repeated verbatim. James Goldstein, indeed, has argued that 'most of the details in Fordun's version are his own invention'. Goldstein has proposed that Fordun drew on 'several conflicting traditions', including different portrayals of Gaedel – characterised by Goldstein as the 'strong' Gaedel who is 'aggressive and rebellious' and the 'good' Gaedel who is 'a passive victim who would prefer not to fight at all' – and that Fordun has reworked these to reflect political attitudes current in fourteenth-century Scotland.[21] Although Goldstein looked for antecedents of these 'traditions', notably in *Lebor Gabála*, he did not attempt to isolate any text or texts which Fordun used. Unfortunately Goldstein's dependence on the account of Scottish origins in Grey's *Scalacronica* as a base version 'not produced in the climate of a war of independence' which he contrasted with Fordun in order to unravel the 'various skeins of Fordun's narrative'[22] will be shown to be misguided. It will become apparent that Grey has preserved an innovative version of the legend datable to the reign of King John (1292–1304) when the kingdom's sovereignty was challenged successfully by Edward I.[23]

The most acceptable basis for reconstructing the sources which lie behind Fordun's account from internal evidence alone, therefore, is to use contradictions between passages as a way of distinguishing one source from another, and match passages together which share specific details (such as Gaedel travelling from Egypt on land rather than by sea). It is not possible in this way to assign all such passages with equal conviction to a reconstructed source, but it is possible to recreate in outline at least two accounts of Scottish origins. The strength of this method is that it depends on details which are inherently unlikely to have been introduced by Fordun (or any intermediary): the contradictions are not individually advertised in a self-conscious manner (for instance with the formula 'others say') which would immediately suggest editorial activity by Fordun (or someone

18 Ibid., xxiii: 33 (ch. 12, lines 1–18), 41 (ch. 17).

19 Ibid., xxiv: 33 (ch. 12, lines 20–4), 35 (ch. 13, lines 1–12).

20 Ibid., xxiii.

21 Goldstein, *The Matter of Scotland*, 109–32; quotations from 114.

22 Ibid., 121, 110.

23 Edward I's challenge to Scottish sovereignty began in May 1291 at the outset of the process which led ultimately to the establishing of John Balliol as king; see most recently Duncan, 'The process of Norham'.

else). A careful examination of the text cannot be expected to show how far these sources have been reproduced verbatim, but it should be possible to recover at least those details which are the subject of contradiction between passages. As an aid to analysing Fordun's account I will refer to each passage attributed to a lost source according to its chapter-number and the order in which it appears within each chapter: the first such passage in chapter 8 will therefore be referred to as VIII.1, and the fourth as VIII.4. (Some chapters have ostensibly been taken from only one source, for instance chapter 15, or have not been subdivided into passages attributed to different sources; these chapters will be referred to simply by a roman numeral.) Because the analysis will perforce be rather detailed, each passage will be further subdivided, if necessary, with each subdivision (typically a sentence) indicated by a lowercase letter: the first subdivision of VIII.1 will thus be referred to as VIII.1.a, and the first two subdivisions as VIII.1.ab. (The first subdivision of XV will simply be referred to as XV.a.) All these divisions and subdivisions are indicated in an edition of the text which follows in the next chapter.

The need for a new edition of Fordun's Chronica

The first problem which an enquiry into the origin-legend material in Fordun's *Chronica Gentis Scottorum* faces is that there is no edition which meets modern scholarly standards. The most recent was published by W. F. Skene in 1871 (the translation by his nephew Felix Skene was published a year later).[24] W. F. Skene made a crucial contribution by publishing Fordun's text for the first time; previous editions had not made such a clear distinction between Fordun's work and Walter Bower's *Scotichronicon*, written in the 1440s, which expanded and continued Fordun's *Chronica* at great length.[25] The way Skene went about preparing his edition does not, however, allow the modern student to have much confidence in the status of Skene's text. Skene stated that his edition 'presents the text exactly as he finds it' in his base text **A**,[26] reporting any emendations in the notes appended to the translation, and noting variants in the other manuscripts in the usual way in the apparatus.[27] On inspection, however, it appears that he not only corrected **A**

24 Skene, *Johannis de Fordun Chronica*; Skene, *John of Fordun's Chronicle*.

25 Skene, *Johannis de Fordun Chronica*, x–xxxiii. The text of *Scotichronicon* has recently been edited in eight volumes: Watt, *Scotichronicon*. (A ninth volume is devoted to editing texts associated in the manuscripts with *Scotichronicon* and to studies of particular aspects of the work as a whole.) Previously the most recent edition was Goodall, *Joannis de Fordun Scotichronicon*. One of the manuscripts of Fordun's text (**C** below) had been published in 1722 by Thomas Hearne along with a continuation consisting of parts of books VI to XIV of Bower's *Scotichronicon* and all of books XV and XVI: Hearne, *Johannis de Fordun Scotichronicon Genuinum*. For Skene's rather misleading presentation of Fordun's work, see Broun, 'A new look'.

26 For an explanation of sigla and a description of the manuscripts, see below, 20–7.

27 Skene, *Johannis de Fordun Chronica*, xlvi. Skene's instinct (xlvi n. 1) was evidently to reproduce **A**'s orthography too, but he was persuaded to modernise it out of 'respect to the opinion of others'.

silently on a number of occasions[28] but that, more seriously, he frequently and inexplicably preferred **C** ahead of **A** (and all other manuscripts). For instance, in VIII.1.b he has *dum*, which is the unique reading of **C**, instead of *inde*; in XV.a he has **C**'s unique reading *omnium* (for *omnino*); likewise in XV.g he has **C**'s *enunciantes* (for *nunciantes*); in XVI.l **C**'s *successione* (for *successiue*); in XVII.3 **C**'s *incitatas* (for *incitatus*); in XXI.a **C**'s *antecessoris* (for *antecessorum*); and in XXIX.1 **C**'s *reuoluto* (for *euoluto*). Skene did not explain why he privileged **C** in these instances. Furthermore, there is no example in the extracts edited below where a variant unique to **C** represents a superior reading; indeed, some which Skene preferred are ungrammatical (as in *incitatas* for *incitatus* in XVII.3).[29] It would appear that the reason for Skene's occasional and silent use of **C** rather than **A** in arriving at his text is that, despite his declared intention to take **A** as his base, at some stage in his work he took **C** as his standard. The situation is even more serious than this, however. There are clear signs that Skene made little or no use of **C** itself, but took his text of **C** from the transcription published by Thomas Hearne in 1722.[30] Thus, Skene reported that **C** uniquely rendered the year-totals in X.1.a in roman numerals;[31] in fact, **C** used arabic numerals.[32] Hearne, however, changed **C**'s arabic numerals to roman numerals; it is this, then, that has been diligently reported by Skene. Other instances would appear to be in XVI.b, where Skene, like Hearne, has *notum* for *uotum*; XXI (title) where Skene followed Hearne in correcting *Hispeniensium* to *Hispanensium*; and XXXI.d where Skene shares Hearne's misreading of *continua* as *contraria*.[33] None of these readings in Hearne are supported by **C** (or any other witness). Finally, in XXVI.d, Skene has *adoptione* rather than the clearly preferable *adepcione*; all the witnesses except for **C**, in fact, read *adepcione*. Skene did not get *adoptione* direct from **C**, however; **C**'s reading is the meaningless *adopocione*, which was corrected silently by Hearne to *adopcione*. It might be supposed that had Skene seen **C**'s nonsense for himself he would have been alerted to **C**'s lack of authority here; if, however, he was dependent on Hearne for his knowledge of **C**, and indeed used Hearne's work in establishing the text of the chronicle, then it would not be so surprising that Hearne's unique reading slipped through the net.[34] It must be suspected, therefore,

28 The following are unique to **A**, but were not reported by Skene: in XI.1.d **A** reads *terra* (for *terras*); in XIV.1.e *Brigancia* (for *Briganciam*); in XVI.a *seruo* (or *serno*) (for *sereno*); in XVI.k *accipite uobis* (for *accipite et uobis*); in XVII.1.a *quidem* (for *quidam*); in XXI.2.a *docebatur* (for *dicebatur*); in XXVII.f *desum* (for *decisum*); in XXXIV.c *deiebat* rather than *degebat*. In every instance Skene's amendments were justified, but he did not include these among the amendments in his 'notes and illustrations' which he published along with his nephew's translation: Skene, *John of Fordun's Chronicle*, 375–438.

29 Skene corrected this reading in his notes (Skene, *John of Fordun's Chronicle*, 382) without showing any awareness that he was restoring the reading in all other witnesses apart from **C**.

30 Hearne, *Johannis de Fordun Scotichronicon Genuinum.*

31 Skene, *Johannis de Fordun Chronica*, 8, nn. 4–8.

32 In common with all but **S**.

33 Note also XIV.1.a where Hearne's *gracia victus* is shared by Skene but by no manuscript witness.

34 For another example of Skene relying on Hearne for his knowledge of **C**, see the edition

that in each case where Skene has silently preferred a unique reading in **C**, this represents the influence of Hearne's text, rather than **C** itself, on his edition. Skene's text may thus be characterised as **A** with a sprinkling of Hearne. The problem for the modern student wishing to take Skene's edition as a guide is that there is no way of knowing what has been taken from **A**, what is **C** via Hearne, and what may be a silent emendation (or even a mistake) in Hearne's rendering of **C**.

Another serious problem is that Skene's record of variant readings was very patchy. Skene did not explain his policy on this, and it must be suspected that he did not have one (which may to some extent be because he himself worked only on **A**, Hearne's transcription of **C**, and **F**).[35] On the one hand he took care in X.1.a, as we have seen, to note the use of roman rather than arabic numerals in one witness; on the other hand, however, although he reported that XVI was attributed in **C** (in the margin) and in **F** to a legend of St Brendan,[36] he failed to note that this attribution also appeared in **E** and in **B**[37] – an omission which misled John and Winifred MacQueen into thinking they could disregard it and assign XV to the legend of St Brendan and XVI to their 'chronicle-source A'.[38] A more striking example of the inadequacy of Skene's apparatus is his treatment of four lines of verse in X.1.c. It is impossible to guess from the information supplied by Skene that the verse does not appear in **B** and **E** in the same position as in **A**, but has been added later in different places;[39] moreover, although Skene divulged that the verse is absent from **C**,[40] he did not record that it is also absent from **F**. It is apparent from this that the

---

of the genealogy of Alexander III, below, 00. Some of Skene's misreadings inherited from Hearne almost certainly have a longer pedigree. The earliest edition of Fordun's *Chronica* is Gale, *Historiae*, II. 562–699, published in 1691, based on **C**; it is incomplete, stopping at book V, chap. 11. Gale also has *notum* for *uotum* at XVI.b, and *contraria* for *continua* at XXXI.d (Gale, *Historiae*, II. 574, 582).

35 Skene, *Johannis de Fordun Chronica*, xlviii, thanked Mr Andrew Gilman of London for making the collations with **B** and **E**, and Mr Thomas French of Trinity College Library, Dublin, for making collations with **D**. Skene was allowed three months to work on **A**, and would have had ready access, presumably, to **F**, then in the Catholic Archives in Edinburgh. The shortcomings in recording variant readings are, however, apparent in the manuscripts (and Hearne's text of **C**) which Skene consulted personally, as well as in those he did not.

36 Ibid., 14 n. 1.

37 It is also found in **G**: in all these instances (bar **C**) it appears in the rubric for XVI, so that its absence from **A** is due simply to the common absence of rubrics in that manuscript.

38 MacQueen and MacQueen, *Scotichronicon*, I. xxii, where they maintained that the ascription of XVI (= Bower's I.17) 'occurs in no other Fordun MS' apart from **C** and **F**, and argued that XV rather than XVI may have been derived from the 'legend of St Brendan' because it 'follows very naturally' on XIV.2, while XVI 'appears to derive from another source' because it recapitulates the beginning of XV. Any overlap between XV and XVI is not a problem, however, if (as the manuscripts indicate clearly) XIV.2 and XVI were derived from the same account (the 'legend of St Brendan'). For their 'chronicle-source A' see ibid., xxiii–xxiv.

39 Skene, *Johannis de Fordun Chronica*, 11. In **B** the stanza has been added, in a later hand, in the bottom margin of fo. 9r (which runs from X.2.b to XII.1.a); in **E** it has been added, in a later hand, in the bottom margin of fo. 6v (which includes X.1.c).

40 Skene, *Johannis de Fordun Chronica*, 11 n. 4.

verse was not originally in Fordun's text; in Skene's edition, however, it is presented as if it was. Finally as far as this verse is concerned, Skene reported inaccurately that **B** and **E** read *Josephum* instead of *populum* in the third line of the verse:[41] in fact, they both read *populum*.

A final problem for the modern student is that Skene was unaware of **G** when he produced his edition, and evidently did not appreciate the value of **S**, which he ignored.[42] It has been shown that **A** was derived from **G**, and that **S** and **G** represent the earliest extant copies of Fordun's text.[43] Not only is Skene's text laced with readings from Hearne, therefore, but it is based on a manuscript, **A**, which (it transpires) has no independent authority;[44] and not only is Skene's treatment of variant readings haphazard, but no account has been taken of the two earliest witnesses.

A new edition of Fordun's chronicle is plainly needed. This would be a considerable undertaking;[45] there is no one currently engaged in this task.[46] It would hardly be practical, therefore, to delay an analysis of the account of Scottish origins in Fordun's chronicle until such time as a new edition of the chronicle as a whole were to be completed. Neither, however, would it be sustainable to use Skene's edition for the detailed investigation of the text which is intended. The remaining course of action is to produce a new edition of only those parts of the chronicle with which our quest for lost accounts of Scottish origins is chiefly concerned; that is, those passages of origin-legend material which are or may be attributed to one or more lost anonymous or nameless sources. This amounts to six extracts from book I: (i) chapter 8; (ii) chapters 10–17;[47] (iii) chapters 20–1; (iv) chapters 26–9;[48] (v) chapter 31; and (vi) chapter 34; plus book II, chapter 12 (which completes the account of Fergus the first king of *Scoti* in Scotland begun in book I, chapter 34). This does not mean that the rest of the chronicle will be ignored; merely that these are the parts for which there is an immediate need for a

41 Ibid., 11 n. 6.

42 He devoted only a brief paragraph to it (ibid., xvi) in which he averred that 'there is nothing to indicate by whom the MS. was transcribed'. It must be doubted whether he ever saw it. It may be noted that the material from Cambridge, Corpus Christi College MS 139, published in Skene, *Johannis de Fordun Chronica*, 449–52, was apparently obtained by Skene from Henry Bradshaw of Cambridge University Library (see ibid., xlviii).

43 See below, 26 and n. 97.

44 Skene, 'Notice of an early MS.', attempted to argue otherwise; but see below, 28. In 1868, shortly after inspecting **A** for himself, Skene was prepared to regard it very highly; he declared that 'if not his [Fordun's] autograph, [it] has certainly been transcribed in his lifetime'; Skene, 'Notice of the existing MSS.', 247; see also 239 and 246.

45 A few of the problems are discussed in Broun, review of *Scotichronicon*, V and VI.

46 The recent edition of **S** (*Scotichronicon*, I–VIII), moreover, may well prove sufficient for most purposes (especially if my tentative conclusion, below, 30–1, about **S**'s place in the stemma of Fordun's witnesses was to be confirmed), which makes it unlikely that the hard-stretched resources available for research in medieval Scottish history generally will be devoted to a new edition of Fordun's chronicle for some time.

47 Omitting the material in 13 and 17 quoting Geoffrey of Monmouth and Peter Comestor.

48 Omitting the material in 26 which does not relate to Scottish origins.

new edition to support the detailed investigation into lost accounts of Scottish origins which follows.[49]

Manuscripts of Fordun's Chronica

I will begin with a fresh account of the witnesses. Because only a small part of the whole work is being edited, and (as will become clear) there is significant uncertainty about the relationships of the manuscripts to each other and to Fordun's original, I have retained the sigla used by Skene (except for **B** where, I will argue, three witnesses rather than one may be identified).[50]

A. Wolfenbüttel, Herzog August Bibliothek, Cod. Guelf. Helmstadiensis 538. Parchment. 219 folios. Written in two neat hands which Lyall has dated to '1450 or a little later'.[51] It consists of Fordun's Chronicle (books I to V) (fos 1r–132r); a blank page (fo. 132v); and fifteen chapters (fos 133v–139r), apparently for a sixth book; another blank page (fo. 139v); a collection of documents beginning with the Declaration of Arbroath, found also in **C**, **D** and **G** (fos 140r–164r); another blank page (fo. 164v); and finally an account of events up to 1385, beginning with St Margaret's English royal ancestors (fos 165r–219r), which corresponds to Skene's *Capitula ad "Gesta Annalia" Præfixa* and *Gesta Annalia* (without any differentiation between the two). Chapter-headings and other rubrics have frequently not been supplied in the gaps left for them. There is an *ex libris* of the Augustinian priory at St Andrews on fo. 1r.[52] This was adopted by Skene as his base manuscript. I have only examined it on microfilm.[53]

49 The account in I. 19 of Gaedel giving laws to his people, attributed to 'another chronicle', has been omitted from the edition because there is no scope for identifying telling details which could enable it to be linked to one or other of the nameless sources, although it has doubtless been derived from one of them. This passage has been assigned by the MacQueens to their 'chronicle-source B' (ibid., xxiv): for their methodology, see above, 14–15. Passing references to chronicles as sources (e.g. XXVI.a *ut docent cronice*, 'as chronicles teach') are somewhat looser than the attribution of a specific passage to one or more chronicles: the MacQueens were inclined to take seriously such a reference to chronicles as the source for XXVI, and assigned it 'probably' to their chronicle-sources A and B and 'possibly' also chronicle-source C (MacQueen and MacQueen, *Scotichronicon*, I. 139: see also xxiii) – but were careful not to include it in their listing of passages drawn from these sources (ibid., xxiv).

50 Skene's sigla (including **B**) were retained in the discussion of these manuscripts in the new edition of *Scotichronicon*, except that 'F' was prefixed to each (e.g. Skene's **A** was referred to as 'FA', **B** as 'FB', and so on). The dating of these manuscripts, unless otherwise stated, is based on Lyall, 'Fifteenth century Scottish manuscripts'. (I am grateful to Professor Donald Watt for bringing Lyall's paper to my attention.)

51 Lyall, 'Books and book owners', 254 (n. 13).

52 Skene, *Johannis de Fordun Chronica*, xxvi.

53 Courtesy of Professor D. E. R. Watt at St John's House, University of St Andrews. I am very grateful to Professor Watt for allowing me frequent access to the collection of microfilms in his care, which include all the manuscripts of Fordun's text.

B. London, British Library, MS Cotton Vitellius E xi. Paper. 279 folios. It has been described as 'a scrappy manuscript'.[54] It is a compilation of four different elements, of which three are copies of Fordun's *Chronica*, a fragment of the same, and part of *Gesta Annalia* (with which Fordun's chronicle is sometimes associated); the fourth contains documents relating to Anglo-Scottish relations up to 1401.[55] The volume has had each folio mounted in modern times, but unfortunately fire-damaged folios have been bound out of position, which has disturbed the coherence of the first element.[56] These damaged folios were overlooked in Skene's edition. The folios of the first element in the volume's make-up are, in their original sequence:[57] 3–23 (chasm made good by **H**), 28–33,[58] 35–37, 169, 38–51, 176, 173, 52–65, 170–171, 66–83, 175, 174, 84–95, 172, 96–115. This represents books I to V of Fordun's chronicle with a lacuna between fos 23 and 28 (breaking off during II.3 and resuming during II.11); fo. 115 is blank.[59] The second element (**H** below) is fos 24–27, and makes good the lacuna in the first element. The third element, fos 84–166, contains only the account of events 1153–1363 published by Skene under the title *Gesta Annalia*. This has probably been produced as a continuation of the first element, and begins a new gathering. The second and third elements are written in a pre-secretary hand, in contrast to the neat cursive hand of the first element, and are quite different from the first in quality and layout;[60] the second and third elements may be dated on palaeographical grounds to as late as the end of the fifteenth or early sixteenth century. Although these are now three elements of the same book, and the third element was apparently produced as a continuation of the first, it would be useful to distinguish between them as witnesses; the second would appear to be a fragment of a manuscript which has been cannibalised to fill a gap in the first, and the third has evidently been copied from an exemplar which was significantly different from the first, as is shown by a comparison between them and other witnesses (the first element is intimately affiliated with **E**,[61] while the third is closely related to **D**).[62] The siglum **B** will therefore denote only the first element; **H** will denote the

54 Watt, *Scotichronicon*, IX. 201.

55 See Watt, *Scotichronicon*, IX. 201–2.

56 They now follow the third element, and probably became detached after the third element had been added to the first.

57 Fo. 1 is a modern cover; fo. 2 is the medieval cover and may have been part of **B**, although there is no positive indication that it is earlier than whenever **B** and **I** were bound together.

58 Fo. 34 is a scrap mounted on a separate folio.

59 Except for a comment in a modern hand: *Desunt multa. Sequitur pars Lib. VII.*

60 The same post-medieval hand which added chapter-numbers to it has given it a separate foliation up to 51.

61 See below, 28–9. For examples where the first element agrees with **E** against all other witnesses (including **D**) see Skene, *Johannis de Fordun Chronica*, 217 n. 8, 227 n. 13, 236 n. 8. There are no idiosyncratic readings which it shares uniquely with **D** or with both **D** and **E**.

62 For instance it shares with **D** the inclusion of a passage (published in Skene, *Johannis de Fordun Chronica*, 377 n. 3) in which Archibald Douglas was referred to as earl of Douglas and lord of Galloway, titles which he did not secure until April 1389 (see Boardman, *The Early Stewart Kings*, 147–53, 159–68).

second; and **I** will denote the third. (**I** has no role in the edition of origin-legend material from Fordun's chronicle, but it will be referred to in the edition of Alexander III's genealogy in chapter VIII, below.)

B has been dated to the late fifteenth century both on palaeographical grounds and because it once belonged to William Schevez, archbishop of St Andrews (ob.1497),[63] for whom it may have been made.[64] The text is written in two hands. The first is a skilled cursive hand which is neat, tidy, compact and rounded;[65] the second, which is expansive and more cursive and gives an untidy impression, begins on fo. 174v and is also found in chapter rubrics from fo. 70r (the beginning of book IV). There are numerous additions and corrections in medieval hands throughout **B**. The most prominent of these (referred to hereafter as B^1) is small and neat, usually in a darker ink than the text hands, and was responsible for supplying most chapter rubrics up to fo. 70 as well as collations with *Scotichronicon* (or a version thereof). In the edited extracts below there are a number of instances where B^1 has altered the text to agree with readings unique to *Scotichronicon* (which is referred to as **S** in the edition below); for instance at XXI.2.d *certas* has been scored out and *terras* added above; at XXVI.c *Hibert* has been corrected to *Hiberti*; at XXVII.d *postere* has been altered to *posteri*; at XXVII.f *ferunt* has been added after *Hibernicum*; at XXVII.k *probari* has been changed to *probatur*, and at XXXIV.e *immanes* has been added after *reperiuntur*.[66] Skene has caused some confusion by reporting in his edition that in XXVII.a *Milo nomine* has been interlined in **B** as the name of Simón Brecc's father, without explaining that this was not written in the text hand.[67] *Milo nomine* is, in fact, simply another collation from *Scotichronicon* by B^1. Unfortunately, however, the MacQueens

63 Skene, *Johannis de Fordun Chronica*, xxvii. His name appears on fos 3r, 3v, 70r, 91r and 114r. His name is not found elsewhere in the volume apart from in **B**.

64 Schevez had a keen interest in Scottish history, and was responsible for the production of a copy of *Scotichronicon* (London, British Library, Harley 712) and a copy of the revision of *Scotichronicon* (known as the 'Book of Pluscarden') (Glasgow, Glasgow University MS Gen. 333 [*olim* F.6.14]); see Skene, *Johannis de Fordun Chronica*, xvii–xviii, xxi; Lyall, 'Books and book owners', 245–8. It is possible to recognise the same occasional glossing hand in black ink in both **B** and Glasgow University MS Gen. 333, which may therefore be the hand of Schevez himself.

65 According to Skene (ibid., xxvii) it resembled the text hand of **C**; the poor state of the text in **B**, however, would suggest that if the same scribe produced both manuscripts then he may have written **B** when he was not in full command of his powers.

66 Other instances of collations with *Scotichronicon* include the addition of phrases and sentences: e.g. fo. 19r (I.32) in the margin has *Priapus* [text cut away] *ortorum* which corresponds with MacQueen and MacQueen *Scotichronicon*, I. 76 (I.33, line 40); further down the margin on fo. 19r there is another insertion relating to *Priapus* in the next chapter, *Priapum ob m*[text cut away]*tudinem uir*[cut away] *uirilis habit*[cut away] *pro deo a fe*[cut away], which corresponds to MacQueen and MacQueen, *Scotichronicon*, I. 76 (I.34, line 9); on the next folio (fo. 20r, I.35) the exact duration of the earliest Scottish kingdom has been inserted interlineally, adding *lxu et trium mensium* following *ducentorum*, which corresponds with MacQueen and MacQueen, *Scotichronicon*, I. 86 (I.37, lines 6–7).

67 Skene, *Johannis de Fordun Chronica*, 23 n. 3.

took *Milo nomine* to be not only an original feature of Fordun's text, but also of the source to which XXVII is attributed.[68]

C. Cambridge, Trinity College, MS O.9.9. Paper. 227 folios (foliated in two series: the second begins with fo. 169). One skilled cursive hand, described by James as 'rather current'.[69] It is similar to the first hand in **B**,[70] which has been dated to the late fifteenth century (probably 1480x97).[71] It consists of books I–V of Fordun's chronicle (fos 1r–121r); a list of rubrics for a book VI corresponding to Bower's *Scotichronicon*, book VI (fos 121v–122v), followed by a chapter from *Scotichronicon*, book V, on Alexander I and the foundation of Scone as an Augustinian priory[72] (fo. 122v) and Henry I's manumission of the English (fos 122v–123v), presumably also derived from *Scotichronicon*, book V;[73] 23 chapters (fos 123v–134v), of which the first eight correspond to the first eight in book VI of Bower's *Scotichronicon*, and the remaining fifteen correspond with the fifteen chapters which follow book V in **A** and **G**; and material on Margaret's English royal ancestors and on events up to 1285 (fos 135r–168v) corresponding to Skene's *Capitula ad "Gesta Annalia" Præfixa* and *Gesta Annalia* chapters 1–66 (without any differentiation between the two).[74] The next item is the collection of documents (corresponding with that in **A**, **D** and **G**), which marks the beginning of a new foliation (fos 1–34v; this is not contemporary with the script, however); an account of events from 1285 to 1385 follows (fos 35r–60v) corresponding to Skene's *Gesta Annalia* chapters 67 to 190. The manuscript was presented to King's College, Aberdeen, by Hector Boece, the college's first Principal.[75] The

68 MacQueen and MacQueen, *Scotichronicon*, I. 144. In fact it is clear from their edition that *Milo nomine* is an addition to their base-text, Bower's extant working-copy of *Scotichronicon* (**S** below): ibid., 64 (for their editorial conventions see Watt, *Scotichronicon*, VIII. xx–xxi). It appears that 'Milo' was introduced by Bower from *Liber Extrauagans* in a section datable to 1296x1306 (see below, 123–5).

69 James, *The Western Manuscripts*, III. 447.

70 Skene, *Johannis de Fordun Chronica*, xxvii.

71 Watt, *Scotichronicon*, IX. 202 (suggestion of Prof. Lyall). (Presumably '1496' is a slip for 1497.)

72 MacQueen, MacQueen and Watt, *Scotichronicon*, III. 108 (= **S** fo. 110r): the chapter was inserted into **S** by Bower, and is numbered 36a in the edition by the MacQueens and Watt.

73 Ibid., 118–22; this is numbered as chapter 39a in the edition, and was inserted into **S** by Bower at fo. 110r immediately following the chapter on Alexander and Scone's foundation (printed as chapter 36a in the edition).

74 A colophon in a contemporary hand (not the text hand) at this point informs us that the text fails here and that book seven is contained in the remaining writing; for the rest of the narrative we are directed to the opening line of the chapter printed by Skene as *Gesta Annalia* ch.67: *Hic deficit. Residuo scripto finiatur liber uii[us]. Uide residuum, uidelicet Dominus Alexander 3[us] rex Scocie diem. Et hoc post duos quaternos integros, et rel.* (from *Dominus* to *diem* [read *die*] is the opening of *Gesta Annalia* ch.67). There are, in fact, 34 folios between this point and *Gesta Annalia* ch.67, and there is no correspondence with any gatherings in the MS (if that was what was intended by *post duos quaternos integros*).

75 Skene, *Johannis de Fordun Chronica*, xxv.

curious inclusion of a stray chapter from *Scotichronicon* on the foundation of Scone (fo. 122v) may indicate that the scribe or his patron may have had a particular association with Scone. It is apparent from the items on fos 121v–122v and the first eight chapters of book VI that the scribe of **C** had a copy of Bower's *Scotichronicon* before him. In the extracts edited below, however, there is no indication that his text of Fordun's chronicle has been contaminated in any way by Bower's *Scotichronicon*.[76]

D. Dublin, Trinity College, MS 498 (*olim* E.2.28).[77] This volume consists of two manuscripts, which are paginated rather than foliated; there are 398 pages in all. The first manuscript (pp. 1–222)[78] contains the 'Book of Coupar Angus' version of Bower's *Scotichronicon*, breaking off abruptly towards the end of the fourth book; it is written in one hand across the page. The second (pp. 223–398; a folio has been lost at the end)[79] is earlier,[80] and may be dated to *c.*1450 x *c.*1465.[81] It is a paper manuscript written in two columns by one hand throughout. It consists first (pp. 223–355) of book V of Fordun's chronicle followed immediately by the account of events from 1153–1363 printed by Skene as *Gesta Annalia*; there is then a blank page (p. 356), followed (pp. 357–396) by the collection of documents (corresponding with that in **A**, **C** and **G**, but additionally including King John of England's submission to the papacy and the absolution of Robert I);[82] finally (pp. 397–8) there is an incomplete copy of *Vita Sancti Servani*.[83] It does not contain a copy of books I and II of Fordun's chronicle, and will not therefore play any role in the edition which follows.

E. London, British Library, MS Harley 4764. This volume has two parts produced

76 A convincing explanation of the inclusion of chapters from Bower *Scotichronicon*, book VI, has been advanced by Donald Watt; [Watt], 'Fordun: appendices'. Bower concluded his VI.23 (MacQueen, MacQueen and Watt, *Scotichronicon*, III. 342; see 461 for comment) with a verse in which he stated that Fordun was the author up to this point and that, from now on, Bower himself was the author. This could have misled the scribe of **C** into regarding Bower's VI.1–8 as Fordun's work as well as VI.9–23 (which correspond to the fifteen chapters following book V in **A** and **G**). It would appear that the scribe of **C** has made a scrupulous attempt to reproduce Fordun's work alone, although he may have flirted with the idea of copying *Scotichronicon* book VI when he drew up the chapter-headings on fos 121v–122v.

77 The volume is fully described in Colker, *Trinity College Library Dublin: Descriptive Catalogue*, II. 916–18. I follow the pagination adopted there. The earlier part of the codex (1–220, with a stub remaining for 221–2) is an incomplete copy of the Coupar Angus version of Bower's *Scotichronicon*.

78 The final folio (221–2) is a stub.

79 The final gathering lacks a folio: see ibid., II. 918.

80 It is possible that 1–222 was not originally independent, but was produced to be added to 223–398; the stub at 221–2, however, could be the result of cutting away a folio when 1–222 was detached from the remainder of a manuscript.

81 Watt, *Scotichronicon*, IX. 200 (referring to advice from Prof. R. J. Lyall).

82 Published in Lawlor, 'The absolution of Robert Bruce'.

83 The Life of St Serf may provide a clue to its provenance, suggesting possibly Glasgow; see Broun, 'A third manuscript of *Vita Sancti Servani*'.

at different times. The original part (fos 1–113) consists of books I to V of Fordun's chronicle; the second (fos 114–188), which is later, continues the first with books VI–X of the abbreviation of *Scotichronicon* written at the Carthusian house at Perth;[84] this second part was probably produced as a continuation of fos 1–113.[85] It is with the original manuscript (fos 1–113) alone, however, that we are concerned. This is vellum, and is of very high quality. It may be dated on palaeographical grounds to the third quarter of the fifteenth century. There is one hand throughout, with corrections and additions which are chiefly by two medieval hands: one, small and neat in black ink, is confined to fos 1–113, while the other is very cursive and is found throughout the volume. The later section beginning on fo. 114 was transcribed sometime between 1497 and 1515 by a Richard Striveling (Stirling) for George Broun, bishop of Dunkeld:[86] if fos 114–188 were produced as a continuation of fos 1–113, then this would suggest that the manuscript was at Dunkeld by that time.

F. Edinburgh, National Library of Scotland, MS Acc. 10301/6 (*olim* Edinburgh, Scottish Catholic Archives, MS MM2/1). There are i + 210 folios which are numbered in roman numerals.[87] This volume also has two parts. The first and older part consists of books I to V of Fordun's chronicle and is written in one hand which may be dated to the last quarter of the fifteenth century.[88] The second part is a later continuation, dated 1509 (fo. CLXXXXIXv), and consists of chapters drawn from the 'Book of Coupar Angus' version of Bower's *Scotichronicon*, beginning at book IX. There can be no doubt that the second part was written as a continuation of the first. The earlier hand, responsible for Fordun books I to V, ceased at fo. LXXVIIr before reaching the end of a gathering at fo. LXXX. The principal hand of the continuation begins at fo. LXXVIIr with a contents-list for book IX of the 'Coupar Angus' version, with book IX following from fos LXXVIIv–LXXX. Only the first part, therefore, is a witness of Fordun's chronicle.

G. London, British Library, MS Add. 37223.[89] 216 folios.[90] Parchment; high quality, bound in wooden covers. The manuscript has been dated on palaeographical

84 Skene, *Johannis de Fordun Chronica*, xix–xx; Watt, *Scotichronicon*, IX. 196–7. Skene suggested that the exemplar may date to 1451 or before.

85 Not only does fo. 114 represent the beginning of a new gathering and a later hand, but the style of quire-signatures is quite different before and after fo. 114. Letters are used for signatures at beginning of gatherings at fos 9r (B), 19r (C), 29r (d), 39r (E), 49r (F), 59r (g), 67r (h), 75r (J), 83r (K), 91r (L), 107r (N); most of the gatherings are also numbered. After fo. 114 the order of the quires has been indicated by writing the first words of the new quire at the bottom margin of the previous quire (see fos 121v, 129v, 137v, 151v, 159v, 167v, 173v, 179v, 185v; most have suffered from being cut away partially, or in the case of fo. 143v entirely).

86 Skene, *Johannis de Fordun Chronica*, xxix; Watt, *Scotichronicon*, IX. 198.

87 Ker, *Medieval Manuscripts*, II. 523, pointed out that two successive folios are numbered 'lxxi'.

88 Ker described it as 'a skilled cursiva of a French type'; ibid., 524.

89 It was previously known as the 'Whytbank MS' (Skene, 'Notice of an early MS') and the 'Largs MS' (Lawlor, 'Notes on the library of the Sinclairs', 100).

90 The second is numbered 1 and there are unnumbered folios between fos 116–117 and

grounds by Lyall to '1450 or a little later'.[91] It was probably the exemplar of **A**.[92] The principal scribe (up to fo. 91r) has been identified as A. de Haliday.[93] It consists of books I to V of Fordun's chronicle (fos 1r–116r); fo. 116v has a couple of notes including a colophon in a medieval hand which identified John of Fordun as the author of books I to V;[94] this is followed by a blank folio (unnumbered) which forms a bifolium with fo. 116; fos 117r–123v contain the fifteen chapters corresponding to those following book V in **A**; fo. 124 is blank; fos 125r–151v contain the collection of documents corresponding to that found in **A**, **C** and **D**; there is then another blank unnumbered folio; fos 152r–212r contain the account of Margaret's royal ancestors and of events to 1385 corresponding to Skene's *Capitula ad "Gesta Annalia" Præfixa* and *Gesta Annalia* (without any differentiation between the two). There are notes of ownership on fo. 212r–v (Henry Sinclair, bishop of Ross; William Sinclair of Roslin, AD 1565; Master Robert Elphinstone),[95] as well as the royal genealogy from Noah to Gaedel, and a note of the inscription on the tomb of George Dunbar earl of March (d.1416).

H. London, British Library, MS Cotton Vitellius E xi, fos 24–27 (treated by Skene as if an integral part of **B**). Paper. This is the fragment which has been used at some stage (it is impossible to say when) to make good the lacuna in **B** between the course of II.3 and II.11. There is some overlap with **B**; the fragment begins during II.2 and ends during II.12.[96] It is written in a very cursive pre-secretary hand, varying in colour between brown and black, and it is crudely decorated with red initial capitals for each chapter and lines around chapter-headings. It may perhaps be assigned palaeographically to the end of the fifteenth century. There are marginal additions by two further medieval hands. It presumably once belonged to a manuscript of Fordun's chronicle which has been cannibalised. It is used only in the edition of II.12 below, and will not therefore be considered in the discussion of relationships between witnesses as revealed in the edited extracts as a whole.

S. Cambridge, Corpus Christi College, MS 171. Paper. 391 folios. Walter Bower's working copy of his *Scotichronicon* produced at Inchcolm during the 1440s.[97] A

151–152; these were presumably not included in the figure of 213 given in Watt, *Scotichronicon*, IX. 199.

91 Lyall, 'Books and book owners', 254 (n. 13).

92 *A Catalogue of Additions*, 376, where it is noted that many of Haliday's exclamations have been repeated in **A**. Skene attempted to argue otherwise, unconvincingly: see below, 28.

93 The most recent discussion of this manuscript is Watt, *Scotichronicon*, IX. 199.

94 The colophon is also found in the 'Donibristle' MS of *Scotichronicon* (D in the new edition); it was printed in Skene, *Johannis de Fordun Chronica*, xv from that MS. Patrick Russell, a Carthusian at Perth, is identified in the colophon as Fordun's continuator, which would only have been appropriate in the case of Russell's adaptation of Bower's *Scotichronicon*, of which neither of these manuscripts is, of course, a copy.

95 Rector of Kincardine, cousin and tutor of Alexander, 2nd Lord Elphinstone, *c.*1518–26; see *A Catalogue of Additions*, 376. For a full account of its owners see Lawlor, 'Notes on the library of the Sinclairs', 100–1.

96 Skene made no reference to these areas of overlap.

97 Watt, *Scotichronicon*, VIII. x. See also Watt, 'Editing Walter Bower', esp. 165,

full account of this manuscript is given by James.[98] Bower copied Fordun's books I to V as the first five books of *Scotichronicon* (fos 1–109);[99] he also included the fifteen chapters following book V in **A** and **G** (fos 113r–117v).[100] He was careful to distinguish his own contributions (indicated by *scriptor* in the margin) from Fordun's text (indicated by *autor* in the margin). Because Bower occasionally added whole chapters to Fordun's text, or made errors in numerations, the chapter numbers in **S** for the edited extracts do not coincide with those in Fordun's chronicle itself. The concordance of chapter numbers in book I is as follows:

First extract: Fordun 8 = **S** 9
Second extract: Fordun 10–17 = **S** 11–18
Third extract: Fordun 20–21 = **S** 22–23 (see MacQueen and MacQueen, *Scotichronicon*, I.52n.*a*)
Fourth extract: Fordun 26–29 = **S** 28–31
Fifth extract: Fordun 31 = **S** 33
Sixth extract: Fordun 34 = **S** 37

Editorial problems and principles

There are obvious difficulties in editing approximately only a tenth of Fordun's chronicle. In particular, there may not be enough data to enable a stemma to be

169–70, 172–3. At 173 he commented that 'we have therefore to bear in mind the possibility that the version of Fordun which we find incorporated into Bower [in CCCC 171] is not only certainly one of the earliest existing manuscripts, but it may also provide a purer, indeed the best, guide to Fordun's original text'. In the recent edition of *Scotichronicon* it is referred to as C.

98 James, *A Descriptive Catalogue*, I. 390–5. See also Watt, *Scotichronicon*, IX. 148–9.

99 This is the foliation used in the recent edition. These books are edited and translated in MacQueen and MacQueen, *Scotichronicon*, I and II; and MacQueen, MacQueen and Watt, *Scotichronicon*, III. 2–287.

100 Edited and translated in MacQueen, MacQueen and Watt, *Scotichronicon*, III. 306–43 (notes at 446–61). The exemplar of **S** also included the material on St Margaret's ancestors and events up to the fourteenth century (found in **A**, **C** and **G**, and in a reduced form in **D** and **I**), but Bower did not treat this with the same discretion as he did Fordun's chrionicle. As far as the material for the 1360s, 70s and 80s is concerned Professor Watt has observed that after XIV. 34 (Scott and Watt, *Scotichronicon*, VII. 358–60), Bower's account of David II's marriage in 1363 (the latest event recorded in **D** and **I**), 'Fordun [i.e. *Gesta Annalia*] is now becoming unavailable for the core of Bower's story' (ibid., 502). There is some verbal similarity, however, between XIV. 46, lines 6–10 (ibid., 402) and the account of Walter Wardlaw's promotion to cardinal in 1384 in the so-called *Gesta Annalia* (Skene, *Johannis de Fordun Chronica*, 383), and almost identical wording between XIV. 47, lines 7–13 (Scott and Watt, *Scotichronicon*, VII. 406) and the account of Richard II of England's invasion of 1385 in *Gesta Annalia*. There is a formal possibility therefore that Bower acquired these two passages independently of *Gesta Annalia* from a common source, which would mean that Bower's copy of *Gesta Annalia* may, like **D** and **I**, have terminated with events of 1363. The most economical explanation of the material in *Gesta Annalia* relating to the 1370s and 1380s is that it is fresh prose added as a continuation of the earlier text of *Gesta Annalia* which terminated in 1363.

constructed with any confidence. There is also the general problem of distinguishing mistakes which may be regarded as typical of the performance of the scribe of a witness from errors which may have been inherited from the scribe's exemplar.[101] Admittedly, if the text-history was likely to be a simple linear progression with discrete branches, then there might be grounds for more optimism. It is apparent from the above account of the witnesses, however, that there was significant interaction within the textual tradition initiated by Fordun and continued with Bower's *Scotichronicon* (1440s) and its subsequent revisions and abridgements.[102] Only **A** and **G**, it appears, have not come into contact with *Scotichronicon* or a version of it,[103] while in the cases of **B** and **C** material from *Scotichronicon* has been copied into the text either by the scribe himself (in **C**) or a later hand (B^1).[104] It would not be surprising, therefore, if there was also interaction between copies of Fordun's chronicle itself. This could have occurred in the seventy years which approximately separated Fordun's original from the earliest witnesses (**A**, **G**, and **S**), as well as later. This would certainly help to explain the rather confusing evidence of interrelationships which emerges from an examination of variant readings in the edited extracts (below). A couple of simple relationships can be demonstrated with confidence, but the discussion of this evidence will generally be kept brief and should be regarded as provisional. I will discuss **S** in detail in due course; it is more than just a copy of Fordun's chronicle, and therefore raises problems of its own.

Turning to **ABCEFG**, it is notable that there are no clear-cut instances where one of these has a unique reading which is grammatically or syntactically correct. None of these, therefore, would appear on its own to be closer to Fordun's original than the others. I will begin with **A**. **A** shares almost all the variants found in **G**.[105] Given that **A** has many more unique errors than **G**, this raises the possibility that **A** could be derived from **G**. This is effectively proved by a mistake in **G** in the arrangement of fos 152v–155r and fos 158v–161r so that the text is seriously disturbed. Donald Watt has pointed out that this disturbed text is precisely replicated in **A**.[106] Given that **A** can not be much younger than **G**, it seems probable that **A** is a copy of **G**.

Moving on to **B**, it is evidently very closely related to **E**, sharing numerous variants.[107] Most impressive of all is the lengthy passage in VIII.1.a which is found

101 A method for distinguishing between fresh and inherited errors is explained in Engels, 'Bower's Latin', 284–6, where he also gives a preliminary impression of the results of applying this method to the performance of the scribe of **S**.

102 On these see Drexler, 'The extant abridgements'.

103 Except the colophon added to **G** at fo. 116v, which originated in Patrick Russell's revision of *Scotichronicon*; see n. 94, above.

104 A full investigation of medieval scribal activity in all these witnesses may reveal other instances where collations have been made with these (and later) versions of Fordun's text.

105 A rare example of **A** having a better reading than **G** is in book II, chapter XII, where **A** reads *quidem* rather than *quidiem* in **G**; for another, see n. 111.

106 [Watt], 'Fordun: appendices'. I am grateful to Professor Watt for giving me a copy of this important unpublished paper.

107 Examples include X.1.b *obigebant* for *abigebant*; XI.1.b *tumis* for *turmis*; XI.3.a *iuge* for *coniuge*; XIV.1.a *fagitacione* for *fatigacione*; XVI.g *qua* for *quia*; XXI.1.a *caute* for

in these two witnesses only.[108] There can be no doubt, however, that **B** and **E** are independent of eachother: **B** has about fifty unique readings, while **E** alone has miscopied the numeral in XXVI.b. Both **B** and **E**, therefore, have an ancestor in common which is shared by no other witness. **E** overall has only a few unique readings – notably fewer than any other witness; **B**, in contrast, represents the poorest copy of the text (at least before being corrected), with a remarkable number of nonsensical readings. There can be little doubt, therefore, that **E** is closest to the ancestor shared with **B**, and that this shared ancestor is likely to have been **E**'s exemplar. The beginnings of a stemma can thus be discerned:

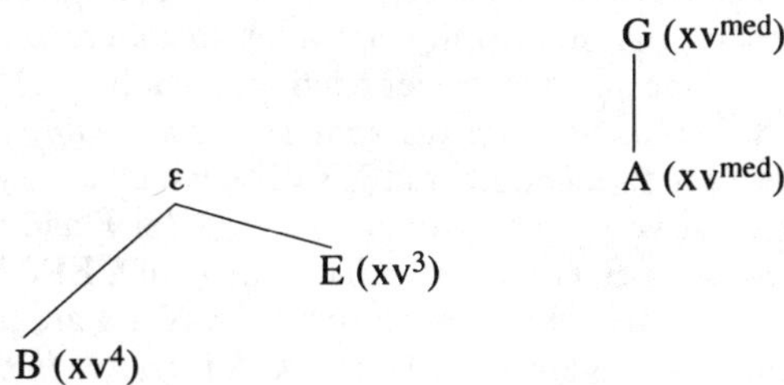

Relationships between **C E F** or **G** can not be so clearly discerned, however. (In what follows it may be assumed, unless otherwise informed, that **B** agrees with **E** and **A** agrees with **G**.) Taking **C** first, there are a few instances where it shares readings with **E** alone, such as VIII.1.a *nullum* for *nullam*; VIII.4 *alia cronica* rather than *item alia cronica*; VIII.4.a *tiranniidi* for *tirannidi*; XXI.2.c *iter* for *inter*; and XXVII.i *prophant* (**C**) and *prophantur* (**E**) as against *prophetatur* (**F**), *prophatur* (**G**) or *profatur* (**S**). There are also instances, however, where **C** and **F** alone share a correct reading (XVI.c *lustrata*; XXVIII.b *fides*; and possibly also XVII.4 *fuerat*). **C** and **F** also share an extra letter in the first word of XXIX.1 (*Reuoluto* **C**, *Eeuoluto* **F**, for *Euoluto*), which could be explained if at some stage the first letter (usually left unwritten and supplied later as an enlarged colour capital) had been written mistakenly (hence *Eeuoluto*, as in **F**), and that this may have been rationalised as *Reuoluto* by the scribe of **C** (or an ancestor of **C**). It may also be noted that **C** and **F** share X.1.b *de* instead of *e*, and that in one instance in II.12 a Latin genitive ending has been attached to *Fer(e)chard* in these witnesses alone. Looking outside the edited extracts, the most striking feature is that **C** and **F** share a peculiar version of III.25 which includes much additional information (notably a brief account of St Constantine). There are very few noteworthy readings shared by **C** and **S**; a rare example is XXVII.j *invenient* rather than *inveniant*. There are no significant readings in the sample which are peculiar to **C** and **G**.

tante; XXI.2.c *tenuerat* for *tenuerant*; XXVII.a *nota* for *nomen* and *cum* for *tamen*; XXVII.b *uetussima* for *uetustissima*, XXVII.m *que* for *quo*, and XXXIV.c *probilitatis* for *probitatis*; there are also omissions, such as XI.1.d *possidendas*, or XV.a *a* (in *a populis*), and additions, such as XII.1.a *et* (before *licet*), XIV.1.c *et* (before *victi*), XVII.7 *tradunt*, and the omission of *sexto Darium* in book II chapter 12.

108 Although, as is noted in the apparatus, some of this passage is found elsewhere in **S**.

Turning to **G**, therefore, there are a few noteworthy variants shared with **E**: XXI.1.d *Hispanis* (for locative *Hispanias*); XX.1 *quecumque* (for *quemcumque*).[109] **G** also shares a striking error with **F**, however: XXVI.c *Frachach* (for *Fiachach*); less striking is XXI.2.d *produceret* (for *perduceret*). It is noticeable that **G** has no significant variants shared alone with **S**.[110]

Finally, we come to **S**. In the small sample edited below, **S** shares no significant clear-cut errors with another witness; the most noteworthy involves only an extra minim: it and **F** read *Pirrimiis* (for *Pirriniis*) at XX.2.b. There are, however, significant variants shared only with **E** or **F**. Thus only **E** and **S** read *nacioni* (rather than *nacionem*) in XXIX.2.a, and omit *ergo* in XI.1.e. And only **F** and **S** give *Partholom/Bartholom* a genitive ending in XXVI.c, and read *Papireus* rather than *Papirius* in II.12. It is especially noteworthy, however, that there are a number of instances where **F** and **S** alone share a correct reading, notably XI.2.b *ueteres* (as against *ueteras*), and XV.e *Hispanicum* (as against *Hispanicam*). But pride of place must go to the position of *et hoc sicut* in XXVII.j, which appears illogically in the middle of two lines of verse in all witnesses except for **F** and **S**.[111]

The most striking feature of **S**, however, is that it alone of **CEFGS** has significant instances of unique readings which are correct:[112] XIV.1.a *gracia* (as against *gracias*); XVI.c *redeunt* (as against *rediunt*); XVI.i *compediri* (as against *compediti*); XVII.7 *quodque* (as against *quique*); XXI (title) *Hispaniensium* (as against *Hispaniensis*); XXVI.d *quod* (as against *quiddam*[113]); XXIX.2.c *Albionem* (as against *Albioniam*); and XXXI.b *Albionice* (as against *Albionici*) and *tenderunt* (as against *tenderant*);[114] note also XI.1.d where **S** alone has added *ab*, and II.12 (beginning) *Albionis* (as against *Albion*). **S** does not, however, represent a particularly clean copy. There are a number of instances where its unique readings are clearly erroneous: VIII.1.b *insulas* (for *incolas*); VIII.3.b *repulsus* (for *repulsa*); and *successit* (for *seccessit*); X.1.a *cccix*[115] (for *cccxxx/ 330*: one must also suspect *i^mdl* v. *1510*); XIV.1.c *ingente* (for *ingenti*); XXVII.d *cui* (for *qui*); XXVII.d *posteri* (for *postere*); XXVII.g *regis* (for *regni*); and II.12 *orientali* (for *orientalis*). A number of these may be explained as errors which the scribe of **S** was prone to make: Professor Engels in a preliminary study of the scribe's performance has remarked on 'a tendency . . . to mistake letters, especially *a/e*, *a/o*, *e/i* and *n/u* or *m/iu/ni* and the like, to omit or add letters syllables and words, and to misread or ignore abbreviations'.[116] There are other instances where **S** has unique readings

109 Note also XXXIV.c *silicet* (for *scilicet*) which is spelt out in **E** and **G**, but this may have been obscured in the abbreviated forms found in **C**, **F** and **S**.

110 With the possible exception of X.1.b *uolentes* rather than *nolentes*, but the misreading of minims may too readily be replicated independently.

111 There is one instance (in XXXI.b) in which **A** alone shares a correct reading with **S** (*tenderunt* as opposed to *tenderant*); probably the scribe of **A** here corrected what had been inherited from **G**.

112 Note XVII.8 where **G** alone (with **A**) has *relinquerat* as against *reliquerat*; but this should probably not be regarded as more significant than an orthographical variant.

113 **C** has *queddam*.

114 This is shared also by **A**; see n. 111, above.

115 Corrected from *ccc.lx.iii*.

116 Engels, 'Bower's Latin', 285–6.

which may be regarded as inferior, although not outrightly erroneous: XIV.1.e *adhoc* (as against *adhuc*); XXI.2.d *terras* (as against *certas*, the *lectio difficilior*); XXXIV (title) *regnancium* (as against *regnante*); XXXIV.c, omission of *et inmodice probitatis iuuenis*.

What conclusions may be reached from all this? Only **S** would appear to have a claim to be regarded as an independent witness of Fordun's own copy. Although **S** is not simply a copy of Fordun's chronicle, Bower's approach to Fordun's text (certainly up to book V) was evidently that of a copyist.[117] It is encouraging that there are instances where correct readings are shared only with one other witness: **F**. The formal possibility remains, however, that Fordun's text may have been altered by Bower, if only very occasionally.[118] In the circumstances it would be premature to regard as definitive any conclusion on the status of **S** based on only a small sample of Fordun's text. The evidence for relationships between **CEFGS** is also insufficiently conclusive, and possibly suggests a significant level of interaction between archetypes.[119]

This uncertainty about the status of **S** and the relationship between **CEFGS** makes a choice of witness as the base for the edition rather problematic. This is felt most acutely, of course, in those instances where there is significant disagreement. There are three areas in which this is important for our purposes: (i) when the difference could alter the sense of a word (ii) when the acceptance or rejection of a word or words is at stake, and (iii) when there is a difference in the spelling of a proper noun (unless the different spellings are phonetically equivalent). No final judgement can be pronounced in the edited extracts on what would have been the reading in Fordun's own text in these instances; attention will be drawn to these by using braces, { }, which will serve to emphasise that the readings offered within these brackets may be regarded as provisional. Each case will be discussed in the notes (as far as is necessary). The tendency will be to prefer whatever variant is correct (if this is obvious); the possibility remains, however, that readings which seem unorthodox or erroneous may have originated with Fordun himself (or may, indeed, have been copied by him from his sources). For this reason braces will still be used in cases where the correct reading is obvious. It is hoped that the edition will as a result be sufficiently transparent to enable these small areas of boggy ground to be distinguished readily from *terra firma*. A final issue which should also be made transparent is the possibility that superior readings found uniquely in **S** may preserve what was originally in Fordun's text. When **S** is the only witness to a reading which is grammatically correct, therefore, I will adopt its reading in the edited text, but mark this clearly by using angled brackets, < >, to indicate if this involves amending or adding to the testimony of the other witnesses, and rounded

117 Watt, *Scotichronicon*, IX. 210.

118 Suspicion falls, for instance, on the omission of *et inmodice probitatis iuuenis* (XXXIV.c), and the precise reckoning in I. 37 (= I. 35 of Fordun's *Chronica*) of the duration of the early Scottish kingdom before the Picts had kings: *ducentorum quinquaginta et quindecim annorum et trium mensium* as opposed to *ducentorum uidelicet ad minus annorum* (MacQueen and MacQueen, *Scotichronicon*, I. 86; Skene, *Johannis de Fordun Chronica*, 30). For figures similar to Bower's see below, 125–6.

119 For instance, it might be argued that **C** and **E** share an ancestor, and **C** (or an ancestor of **C**) acquired at least III.25 from an ancestor of **F**.

brackets ( ), to indicate if this involves deleting any letter(s) found in the other witnesses.[120] Finally, minor orthographical details will be standardised: *i*, *y* and *j* will be rendered *i*;[121] *v*, *u* will be rendered *u*, and *w* as *uu*. There is also standardisation of *c* and *t* (preferring *c* to *t* before *i* plus vowel in medial position), and of words which are prone to ambiguous contractions or compendia that make the recording of variants a fruitless task; thus *sed* is preferred to *set*, *quemdam* to *quendam*, and *compulsus* to *conpulsus*.

A translation of the edited text has not been provided, although a fresh translation will be offered on each occasion that part of the text is quoted in the discussion which follows.[122]

120 As a precaution this procedure will still be applied even when **S** and **F** alone have a correct reading.

121 *y* will be retained in some proper nouns; only in the case of *Gaythelos* will variation in the use of *y* and *i* be noted systemmatically.

122 Anyone wishing to gain a quick general impression of Fordun's account can do so from the translation by Felix Skene (*John of Fordun's Chronicle*) or (in a more modern style of English) from the translation of **S** by John and Winifred MacQueen in MacQueen and MacQueen, *Scotichronicon*, I (taking care, of course, to observe where Bower has indicated his own additions to Fordun's text).

III

THE SCOTTISH ORIGIN-LEGEND IN FORDUN'S *CHRONICA GENTIS SCOTTORUM*: EDITED EXTRACTS

Key: braces { } — indicate provisional readings where there is disagreement over a matter of substance among more than one of **CEFGS**.

angled brackets < > — show where unique readings in **S** have been preferred against all other witnesses.

rounded brackets ( ) — show where unique readings in **S** have been preferred, deleting a letter or letters found in the other witnesses.

Contractions have been expanded silently. The use of *v/u*, *uu/w* and *i/y/j* has been standardised respectively to *u*, *uu* and *i* (although *y* has been retained in some proper nouns).[1] The use of *c* and *t* has also been standardised, preferring *c* to *t* before *i* plus vowel in medial position. Punctuation is editorial. For an explanation of editorial procedure, see 31–2 above.[2]

As an aid to analysing Fordun's account I will refer to each passage attributed to a source according to its chapter-number and the order in which it appears within each chapter. (Where there is no subdivision into passages attributed to different sources a roman numeral alone will be used.) Each passage will be further subdivided, if necessary, with each subdivision (typically a sentence) indicated by a lowercase letter. For further explanation, see 16, above.

1 Only in the case of *Gaythelos*, however, has variation in the use of *y* and *i* been noted systemmatically.

2 In the apparatus, if notice is given of variants involving more than one word (e.g. n. 6, *rex quidam*), the words from the text and its witnesses will be given before the variant readings are noted (e.g. *rex quidam* AG; *rex quidem* C; *rex quidj* (final syllable ambiguous) FS; om. BE). The same procedure will be adopted in the case of a single word if there is a risk of ambiguity (which may result, for instance, from the use of braces).

First extract: I. 8

A 4v–5r; B 7v–8r; C 4r–v; E 5v–6r; F IIIv–IVr; G 3v–4r; S 5r–v[3]

De motu primo Scotorum originis.[4] Capitulum 8m[5]
[VIII.1]
[a] In etate uero tercia temporibus Moysi, rex quidam[6] unius regnorum Grecie[7] nomine[8] Neolus[9] uel Heolaus[10] filium habens uultu[11] elegantem[12] animo tamen instabilem nomine Gaythelos[13] quem null{a}m[14] in regno potestatem habere permiserat,
[b] unde[15] concitatus in iram et manu multorum munitus iuuenum horrenda crudelitate[16] paternum regnum multis affecit[17] cladibus et insolenciis, patrem et incolas[18] offendens uehementer.

[3] The foliation of S is that adopted in MacQueen and MacQueen, *Scotichronicon*, I.

[4] *De motu primo Scotorum originis* ACFG; om. B (*De motu primo Scotorum originis* B^1); *De primo motu Scotorum originis* E; *De primo motu originis Scotorum et eorum rege primo Gaythelos* S.

[5] The chapter numbers are different throughout in S.

[6] *rex quidam* AG; *rex quidem* C; *rex quidj* (final syllable ambiguous) FS; om. BE. The sense demands *rex quidam*, 'a certain king'.

[7] BE add (text from E): *regno dicta Elladia* [corrected in B from *Alladia*] *a rege Ellana Deucalionis et Pirre filio nunc dicta, ipsa quoque est Attica terra ab Atis fil<i>a inter Macedoniam et Achaiam iacet media a septentrione* [*septemtrione* B] *iungitur Archadie; ipsa est uera Grecie cuius due sunt partes Boecia et Peloponensis, quarum metropolis est Athena ubi quondam uigebat studium literarum nacionumque* [*nacionum quoque* B] *cunctarum ad discendum confluebat. De qua inuiunt autores quod Grecia cum suis prouinciis regnorum sit domina, milicie nutrix prophecie mater omnium bonarum arcium inuentrix et magistra, cuius gens bellicosissima dono sapiencie et sciencie predita sermone desertissima legibus subdita pia circa extraneos benigna circa incolas et domesticos quieta contra hostium iniurias minium intollerabilis et infesta, cuius ideonia omnium clarius et sonancius a quodam nomine Greco ibidem regnante Grecia dicta est. De quo quidam regno rex quidam* [*quidem* B]
The passage from *inuiunt autores* to *intollerabilis et infesta* is also found in S fos 206v–207r (book X chapter 2), with *est* for *sit*, *scienciarum* for *arcium*, *ministra* for *magistra* and *pacifica* for *benigna*; Taylor and Watt, *Scotichronicon*, V. 294, 296.

[8] ABCEFG; om. S

[9] *originis* add C

[10] ABCEFG; *Eolaus* S

[11] ACFGS; om. BE: *milicie* added superscript by B^1, and in later hand in E.

[12] ABEFGS; *eligantem* C

[13] ABEG; *Gaithelos* S; *Geythelos* CF

[14] *nullam* AFGS; *nullum* BCE: *nullam* agrees with *potestatem*, 'no power'.

[15] ABEFGS; *dum* C. Skene has *dum*.

[16] ABCEGS; *crudilitate* F

[17] ABCEGS; *effecit* F

[18] ABCEFG; *insulas* S

[c] Quapropter a patria uiolenter[19] expulsus nauigio diuertit in Egiptum et ibidem quia fortitudine simul et audacia prepollens atque regali propagine natus extiterat filia Pharaonis[20] Scota coniugio sibi fuerat copulata.

[VIII.2]
Alia cronica
[a] Infestabant omnem Egiptum Ethiopes illis diebus more solito uastantes a montibus usque ciuitatem Memphym[21] et mare magnum, ideo Neoli[22] regis filius Gaythelos[23] Pharaonis[24] confederati[25] in adiutorium sibi cum exercitu[26] magno missus est.
[b] Cui confederacionis[27] gracia pacti, rex unicam filiam tradidit in uxorem.

[VIII.3]
Legenda Brandani[28]
[a] Legitur inibi[29] quemdam militem cui principales generis sui dignitatem attribuunt Athenis in Grecia regnasse, cuius filium nomine Gaythelos[30] filiam Pharoanis[31] regis Egipti Scotam a qua Scoti nomen eciam traxere coniugio perhibent habuisse.
[b] Qui scilicet Gaythelos[32] uiribus prestans et audacia dum patrem uel ceteros insolencia perurgeret, causa repulsa[33] pocius quam uoto discedens animosa fretus manu iuuenum in Egiptum secessit.[34]

[VIII.4]
{Item} alia cronica[35]
[a] Gaythelos[36] autem quidam nepos ut fertur Nembro{t}ht[37] per generis succes-

19 Corrected in S from *uehementer* (*uiolenter* omitted in MacQueen and MacQueen, *Scotichronicon*, I. 26).
20 BCEFGS; *Pharonis* A
21 ABCEGS; *Nemphim* F
22 corrected in A from *Neolo*
23 ABCEGS; *Gathelos* F
24 BCEFS; *Pharonis* AG
25 BEFGS; *confiderati* AC
26 ABCEFS; *excercitu* A; *exerceritu* G
27 AFGS; *confideracionis* BCE
28 *Legenda Brandani* BCEFG; gap in A; *In Legenda Sancti Brandani* S
29 ABCEGS; *ibi* F
30 ABCEFG; *Gaitelos* S
31 BCEFS; *Pharonis* AG
32 BCES; *Ga^os^* AFG
33 ABCEFG; *repulsus* S
34 ACEFG; corrected from *secesset* in B; *successit* S
35 *item alia cronica* FGS; *alia cronica* CE; gap in AB (*alia cronica* supplied by B[1]).
36 ABCEG; *Gaithelos* S; *Gathelos* F
37 *Nembricht* A; *Nembrotht* B; *Nembroht* CE; *Nembroutht* (with suspension-stroke over *o*) F; *Nembritht* G; *Nemproth* S. Skene has *Nembricht*.

sionem regnare {u}olens[38] per indigenas ipsius tirannidi[39] nolentes[40] subesse auxiliantibus finitimis ex patria cessit, quem secutus est populus multus iuuenum cum exercitu.
[b] Denique[41] multis[42] per loca uaria bellis, lacescitus[43] et inopia uictualium compulsus uenit in Egiptum, et cum rege Pharaone iunctus filios Israel unacum Egiptiis nisus[44] est in seruitutem perpetuam tenere.
[c] Unde filiam Pharaonis unicam nomine Scotam uxorem duxit animo tendens ut regnum Egipti socero succederet.[45]

Second extract: I. 10–17

A 5v–8v; B 8v–12r; C 5r–8r; E 6v–9v; F IIIIr–VIv; G 4v–7r; S 6r–8r.

[46]De tempore quo Scoti primam[47] habuerunt originem et a quibus {et eorum}.[48] Capitulum 10m
[X.1]
[a] A mundi quoque principio transactis 3689[49] annis in tercie uidelicet[50] etatis anno 505o[51] qui fuit ante captiuitatem Troie 330[52] ante condicionem urbis 760[53] et

38 *uolens* G; *uolens* more likely than *nolens* AE; *volens* BS; *nolens* CF. *Uolens* would contrast with *nolentes*. It is possible, however, that the description of Gaythelos' rule as *tirannis* could suggest that he was not ruling *per generis successionem*, 'by the [lawful] succession of the country', which would point to *nolens* as the original reading. Skene has *nolens*.
39 *tirannidi*, AFGS; extra minim in BCE.
40 ACEFGS; *volentes* B
41 ABCEGS; *deinde* F
42 ABEFGS; *multus* C
43 AFGS; *lacescitus* BCE
44 ACEFGS; *visus* B
45 *socero succederet* originally omitted in BE; added later in both (by B1, and possibly by text hand in E)
46 Title originally left blank in B (filled in by B1).
47 CEFGS; *prima* A
48 *et eorum* ACG; *etc* ES; om. F. Something is missing after *et eorum*; as it stands this makes no sense, hence the resort to *etc* in ES and omission in F.
49 ABCEG; *iiim dc.lxxxix* S; *389* F
50 ABCEFG (B corrected to *uero* by B1); *uero* S
51 ABCEG; *505* F; *d.u* S
52 ABCEG; *3309* F; *ccc.lx.iii* scored out and replaced by *cccix* S. Note that both A and G read *330'* which could point to the origin of *3309* in F.
53 ABCEFG; *dcclx* S

ante Domini Nostri Ihesu Christi natiuitatem[54] 1510,[55] [56]supradicto Pharaone cum suis exercitibus[57] submerso sexcentis scilicet curribus quinquaginta milibus equitum et ducentis[58] milibus peditum armatorum.
[b] Hii uero repente qui superfuerant domi superstites a seruitute frugum olim illata per Ioseph tempore famis sperantes[59] absolui[60] generum regis Gaythelos Glas, insontes Hebreos {n}olentem[61] persequi ne super eos dominium inuaderet cum suis {e}[62] regno penitus abigebant.[63]
[c] Cunctos[64] itaque Grecorum pariter et Egipciorum[65] nobiles quos nequaquam uorax absorbuit pelagus[66] allecti pagenses seruili tumultu[67] crudeliter a se propulerunt.

[X.2]
Alia cronica[68]
[a] Gaythelos[69] autem ex[70] industria inter ipsum et regem Pharaonem condicta[71]

54 ABCFGS; *natiuitantem* E (with horizontal suspension-stroke over penultimate syllable)
55 ABCEFG; *i^m dl* S. AG add here the following which is also found in B (added at the foot of the following page, probably by B[1]) and in E (added at foot of the current page in a later hand). The text is from G, with variants in A, B and E noted:

Alii dicunt sic

Quingentis mille cum sexaginta monosque[a]
Annis ut reperi[b] *precessit tempora Christi*
Rex Pharao[c] *populum fugientem per Mare Rubrum*
Cuius rex Pharao[d] *mergitur in medeo*[e]

[a]AG; *nouesque* BE
[b]BEG; *repi* A
[c]AG; *Pharo* BE
[d]G; *Farao* A; *Pharo* BE
[e]ABG (second *e* uncertain in B); *medio* E

Skene included this verse in his edition. Its appearance in the body of the text only in A and G suggests that it is unlikely to have been originally part of the text.
56 add *et* F
57 BCEFS; *excercitibus* AG
58 Corrected from *ducentes* in B and E.
59 Corrected from *superantes* in B (by B[1]).
60 ACFGS; *obsolui* BE
61 *nolentem* BCF (in B corrected to *volentem*); *uolentem* AG; *volentem* S; ambiguous in E. *Nolentem* would mean that Gaythelos did not wish to pursue the Hebrews, which would make sense as an explanation of why Gaythelos was not with his father-in-law when Pharaoh was submerged with his army in the Red Sea.
62 *e* ABEGS; *de* CF. Skene has *de*.
63 CFS; *abiegebant* AG; *obigebant* BE (altered in B to *abigebant*)
64 ABEFGS; *Cunctis* C
65 ABCEFS; *Egipcorum* G
66 ACFGS; *pellagus* BE
67 BCEGS; *tumulti* A; *timultu* F
68 BCEFGS; *cornica* A (note that G has *c^onica*)
69 ABCEGS; *Gathelos* F
70 BCEFGS; om. A
71 Erasure in C of *est* after *condicta*.

post exercitum[72] ciuitate remansit Heliopoleos, suo quasi regno forsan[73] successurus.

[b] At populus Egipcius qui residuus adhuc fuerat quid de suo rege contigit aduertens simulque precauens ne iugo tirannidis aliene semel submissus, excutere denuo non ualeret. Collectis igitur uiribus Gaythelo[74] mandat quod si ocius[75] e regno non maturaret exitum inexterminabile sibi suisque[76] proueniret excicium[77] absque mora.

De eleccione Gaythelos[78] in regem et eius profeccione[79] {uersus occidentem}[80] Capitulum 11^{m}

[XI.1]

[a] [81]Preterea[82] Gaythelos[83] quoniam gener regis omniumque nobilissimus ab expulsis utriusque gentis nobilibus in regem erigitur.

[b] Sed nichilominus[84] exercitu quamquam numeroso[85] stipatus caute perpendit se tante multitudinis hostium turmis[86] seuiencium non posse resistere.[87]

[c] Sed et iterum in Greciam sciens obstructam redditus[88] orbitam[89] ob perpetrata prius ibidem[90] scelera,

[d] suorum consilio maiorum pro rato[91] quippe[92] decreuit ut aut regnum et terras[93]

72 ABCFGS; *exerccitum* E
73 ABEFGS; *forsitan* C
74 ABCEGS; *Gathelo* F
75 ABCEGS; *cicius* F
76 ABEFGS; *fuisset* C
77 ACGS (*exitum* erased in C); *excisium* BEF (glossed *excicium* by B^{1}). Skene corrected silently to *exitium*, 'destruction'.
78 *Gaithelos* E; *Gaythelos* S; *Ga*^{os} F; *Geythelos* ACG; title blank originally in B, and supplied later by B^{1}.
79 ABEFGS; *profeccioe* C
80 *uersus occidentem* EF; *uersus* C; om. AG; *etc.* S (for B see n.78). Possibly the incomplete reading in C was shared by an ancestor of S and perhaps G, and has been resolved by resorting to *etc* or by omission.
81 *item alia cronica* add F
82 ABCEGS (the second last letter has been corrected/clarified in B); *Preteria* F
83 BECS; *Ga*^{os} AG; *Gathelos* F
84 Scored out in B, and *nichillominus* inserted in margin.
85 ABEFGS; *numerosa* C
86 *turmis* C; *t*^{r}*mis* AG; *t*^{2}*mis* S; *t*^{a}*mis* BE (i.e. *tramis*; corrected in B to *t*^{2}*mis* in later hand); *tramis*, F
87 Corrected in B from *recistere*.
88 Corrected in S from *reditus*.
89 ABEFGS; *orbatam* C. The subject of the sentence is Gaythelos; *redditus* is genitive singular, therefore *redditus orbitam* 'return route'.
90 *prius ibidem* ABEFGS; *ibidem prius* C
91 ABEFGS; *rata* C
92 ABCEFG; om. S
93 BCEFGS; *terra* A

<ab>[94] aliis abriperet[95] gentibus[96] armis perpetuo colendas[97] seu diis sibi fauentibus desertas saltem mansiones conquereret[98] possidendas,[99] quodque pro uiribus omnes execucione debita prosequi communi proposito coniurantur.
[e] Sublimato quidem Gaythelo {ergo} duce[100] nobiles expulsi[101] ut in extremis[102] mundi finibus uelud opinantur adhuc uacuis[103] nouas terras sibi[104] colendas acquererent.[105] Iuuenilibus[106] ducti quodammodo lasciuiis classem non modicam immissis[107] uictualibus cum ceteris nauigio necessariis oneratam citissime[108] prepararunt.

[XI.2]
Alia chronica
[a] Collectis igitur Gaythelos[109] suis omnibus[110] cum uxore Scota ab Egipto recessit,
[b] et quia propter ueter{e}s[111] inimicicias timuit in partibus e quibus in Egiptum uenerat repedare,[112] uersus occidentem[113] iter uertit ubi nouerat et pauciores et minus bellicosos habitare populos cum quibus congredi necesse fuerit hominibus armis minus doctis.

94 *ab* S; om. ABCEFG.
95 ABCEGS; *abripere* F
96 ABEFGS; *gentilibus* C
97 ABCEGS; om. F
98 ABCEFG; *conquireret* S
99 ACGS; *possedendas* F; om. BE, with *possedendas* added in B by B[1] as interlinear gloss, and in E superscript in later hand.
100 *Gaythelo ergo duce* C; *Gaythel- ergo duce* AG; *Gaythelos ergo duce* F; *Gaythelo duce* BE (in E there is a larger than usual gap between these words); *duce Gaythelo* S. For other examples where *Gaythelos* is treated in some witnesses as declinable, see XIV.1.d and XVII.3.
101 Corrected from *compulsi* in B by B[1].
102 ABEFGS; *extremi* C
103 ABEFGS; *uacans* C
104 ABEFGS; *igitur* C
105 BCE; *acquirerent* FS; *acqreret* AG (with suspension-stroke above *qr*)
106 ABCEGS; *iuuenibus* F
107 Corrected in B from *missis*, possibly by text hand.
108 ABCEGS; *certissime* F
109 *Gaythelos* BCE; *G*^{os} AG; *Ga*^{os} F; *Gae*^{dy}*los* S (the suprascript letters are faint and have been added by a contemporary hand; they were not noted in MacQueen and MacQueen, *Scotichronicon*, I. 32 and n.*c*).
110 BCEFS; *hominibus* AG. Skene has *hominibus*.
111 *ueteres* FS; *ueteras* ABCEG: *ueteres* is grammatically orthodox.
112 BCEFS; *ropedare* AG
113 BCEFGS; *occedentem* A

[XI.3]

Item[114] alia cronica

[a] Denique paratis omnibus Gaythelos[115] cum coniuge[116] totaque familia ceterique duces deorum suorum regimine fidentes scaphis aduecti naues conscendunt paratas et anchoris funditus subductis nautarumque funibus[117] diligenti cura solutis uela lacius uentorum afflatibus expanduntur.

[b] Mediterraneum deinde[118] fretum petentes inter australes Europe fines et Affricam proris pelagi secantibus undas uersus occidentales mundi plagas tetendere.

De tempore quo Gaythelos stacionem fecit in Affrica {et causa qua primo uenit in Hispaniam}.[119] Capitulum 12ᵐ

[XII.1]

[a] Gaythelos[120] itaque prouinciis pluribus peruagatis et uariis per loca stacionibus que repperit[121] oportuniora[122] factis, quia populum quem duxit mulieribus ac paruulis multisque sarcinis oneratum ultra modum uexari nouerat, per Ansaga flumen Affricam[123] intrans per aliquod temporis spacium Numidie prouincia[124] quieuit, [125]licet illius patrie cultores nullam requiei certam habent sedem.[126]

[b] Igitur per annos xl. quibus habitauerunt filii Israel in deserto sub Moyse et ipse Gaythelos[127] cum suis nunc hac nunc illac per plures uagabatur terras,

[c] sed Affrica[128] tandem relicta nauibus quas habere tunc[129] poterat ascensis[130] iuxta Gades insulas aduehitur in Hispania.[131]

114 BCEFGS; om. A

115 *Gaythelos* BCE; *G^os^* AG; *Ga^os^* F; *Gaytelos* S

116 Corrected in B (possibly by text hand) and E from *iuge*.

117 Corrected in B from *finibus*.

118 ABEFGS; *inde* C

119 *Gaythelos stacionem fecit in Affrica et causa qua primo uenit in Hispaniam* C; *G^os^ stacionem fecit in Affrica* AG; om. B, but *Gaythelos stacionem fecit in Affrica et causa qua primo* squeezed into gap by B[1]; *stacionem in Affrica fecit Gaithelos et eam qua primo peciit Hispaniam* E; *Ga^os^ stacionem fecit in Affrica et causa qua primo etc.* F; *G'* *stacionem fecit in Africa* S.

120 ABCG; *Gaithelos* ES; *Gathelos* F

121 BC; *reperit* AEFGS

122 ABEFGS; *optuniora* C

123 ABCEFG; *Africam* S

124 Altered in B to *prouincie*.

125 *et* add BE

126 ABCEGS; *fidem* F

127 BC; *Gaithelos* E; *G^os^* AG; *Ga^os^* F; *G'* S

128 ABCEFG; *Africa* S

129 *habere tunc* ABCEG; *haberi tunc* F; *tunc habere* S

130 BCEFS; *abscensis* A; *a scensis* G

131 BCEFS (altered in B to *Hispaniam*); *Hispaniam* AG. Skene has *Hispaniam*.

[XII.2]
Alia[132] cronica
[a] Sic quidem diu per maris incogniti[133] loca huc illucque uagi plura pertransiunt[134] et prout contrario uentorum agebantur impetu pericula multa discriminaque[135] uaria perpessi,
[b] cogente tandem alimentorum penuria quasdam[136] insperatas Hispaniarum ad horas[137] incolumes aduentant ubi naues eiectis anchoris affixe tenacibus quieuerunt.

[138]De causa sui recessus ex Egipto secundum quosdam.[139] Capitulum 13[m]
[XIII.1]
[a] Perhibetur[140] tamen alibi multos Egipcios et aduenas simul Grecos non solum humano metu sicut superius expremitur[141] sed pocius timore diuino perteritos[142] ab Egipto procul et patria natiua fugisse.
[b] Uidentes autem terribiles plagas et signa quibus per Moysen afflicti fuerant timuerunt ualde, nec ausi sunt ibidem amplius prestolari.
[c] Nam sicut Gomorreorum[143] regiones cum populis et Sodomorum olim in cineres propter peccata redacte fuerant sic totam sperabant Egiptum cum incolis subito[144] subuertendam.

[Two further passages follow, one from Peter Comestor *Historia Scholastica*, the other attributed to *Grossum Caput*][145]

Qualiter Gaythelos primam optinuit sedem in Hispania.[146] Capitulum 14[m]
[XIV.1]
[a] Illis interim diutina maris fatigacione[147] uexatis et acquirendi <uictus gracia>[148] ac quietis ad terram Hispanie properantibus

132 BCEFGS; om. A
133 BCEFG (in B altered to *incognita*); *incognita* AS
134 ABCEGS; *transiunt* F
135 *discriminaque* BFS; *discreminaque* ACG; second syllable in E ambiguous
136 BCES; *quasdem* AG; final syllable ambiguous in F
137 ABCEFG; *oras* S
138 B om. title, which was supplied later (as given here) by B[1].
139 *secundum quosdam* ACG; *secundum quosdam etc.* E; om. FS; for B, see n. 138, above.
140 ABCEGS; *Prohibetur* F
141 ABCEFG; *exprimitur* S
142 Corrected in G from *perteritas*.
143 ACEFGS; *Gemorreorum* B
144 ABCEGS; *cito* F
145 See MacQueen and MacQueen, *Scotichronicon*, I. 120, for comment.
146 *Qualiter Gaythelos primam optinuit sedem in Hispania* CFGS (except for *Gaythelos* F reads *Ga[os]*, and G reads *Gey[os]*, and S reads *Gaithelos*); *Qualiter primam optinuit sedem in Hispania Gaithelos* E; AB om. title and leave gap: B[1] has squeezed in *Qualiter Gaythelos primam optinuit sedem in Yspania.*
147 ACFGS; *fagitacione* BE
148 *uictus gracia* S; *gracias uictus* ABCEFG. S makes better sense: the whole phrase can be translated ‘for the sake of obtaining food and rest’. Skene has *gratia victus*; Hearne, *Johannis de Fordun*, I. 24, likewise has *gracia victus*.

[b] ex omni parte concurrunt ciues eorum indigne ferentes aduentum, bello proponunt et armis obsistere,
[c] sed et pugna mox ingenti[149] contencione commissa [150]uicti sunt indigene[151] pariter et fugati.
[d] Patrata deinde uictoria Gaythel{os}[152] ciues insequitur et aliquantis agrorum predatis ad[153] litora reuersus in quodam[154] alcioris loci monticulo tentoria uallo circumdata confixit ubi tucius hostium insultantibus cuneis poterat obuiare.
[e] Quo postmodum subactis aliquantisper incolis opidum interpolate[155] fortissimum nomine Briganciam[156] edificans cuius in medio maxime celsitudinis[157] turrim[158] constituit profundis adhuc[159] patentibus fossis circumceptam.
[f] Omnibus igitur diebus uite sue continuis affectus[160] bellorum incursibus ibidem deguit uariisque fortune casibus iugiter obuolutus.

[XIV.2]
Legenda Sancti Brandani[161]
[a] Gaythelos[162] autem ex Egipto pulsus et sic per Mediterraneum mare uectus nauibus ad Hispaniam applicat,
[b] atque[163] super Hiberim flumen turrim condens nomine Briganciam locum et sedem uiolenter ab[164] incolis usurpauit.

[165]De continua cede[166] suorum ibidem[167] propter quod[168] exploratores pro terris [169]occeano[170] scrutandis direxit. Capitulum 15[m]

149 ABCEFG; *ingente* S
150 *et* add BE
151 ACEFGS; *indigine* B
152 *Gaythelos* C; *Gaithelos* S; *Gaythel-* AG; *Gaithel-* BE; *Ga[os]* F. For other examples where *Gaythelos* is treated in some witnesses as declinable, see XI.1.e and XVII.3.
153 ABEFGS; *at* C
154 BCES; *quodem* AG; final syllable ambiguous in F
155 BCEFS; *interpollate* AG. From *interpello*, 'to interupt'; it is translated 'by degrees' in Skene, *John of Fordun's Chronicle*, 12, and 'gradually' in MacQueen and MacQueen, *Scotichronicon*, I. 39.
156 BCEFGS; *Brigancia* A. This place has been derived from Orosius; see discussion in MacQueen and MacQueen, *Scotichronicon*, I. 121.
157 BCEFGS; *celcitudinis* A
158 CFS; *turrem* ABE; in G the final syllable is blotched.
159 ABCEFG; *adhoc* S (*ad hoc* in MacQueen and MacQueen, *Scotichronicon*, I. 38)
160 BCEFS; *affectis* AG
161 *Legenda Sancti Brandani* BCEFG; *Legenda Sancti Brendani* S; om. A
162 C; *Gaithelos* BEFS; *Gaythe[os]* AG
163 Added superscript in A.
164 ACEFGS; *ad* B
165 Title om. AB; B[1] has squeezed in *De continua sede suorum ibidem propter quod exploratorum pro terris occeano scrutandis direxit.*
166 CEFS; *sede* G (for AB see n. 165)
167 CEGS; om. F (for AB see n. 165)
168 CFGS; om. E (for AB see n. 165)
169 *in* add E
170 CEFG; om. S (for AB see n. 165)

[XV]

[a] Multimodis interim afflictus ibidem incommodis[171] Gaythelos[172] cuius circa gentis sue[173] tuicionem sicut utilem[174] decuit et curiosum principem tota uersabatur intencio cum aliud illac euentum sibi nullatenus aduenire prospexerat[175] quam aut a[176] populis Hispanorum fortissimis ipsum cum gente de superficie terrarum omnino[177] deleri[178] uel iugo perpetue subici seruitutis.

[b] Et licet aduersariis sepius strages plurimas ipsum inferre contigerat nuncquam tamen aut una potitus est uictoria absque sue gentis exigue detrimento quam cotidiano[179] iugique dispendio minui pocius prospicit quam augeri.

[c] De tali uero continua cede[180] necnon imminent{i}[181] discidio[182] seu deinceps de dicto quid agendum negòcio dum cura peruigili precauens mente diuolueret, secum tandem deceptans[183] animaduertit quod quas paciebatur merito tulisset angustias ut cumque suum primitiue deliberacionis propositum terras scilicet uacuas nulli molestiam inferens acquirere[184] dimiserat sed et solum insultans aliis diuinitus adhibitum[185] populis[186] quod in hoc suos multipliciter deos offendisse sperauit.

[d] Ad preconceptum igitur in Egipto propositum intendens regredi suorum consensu maiorum nautas conuocat et eos armis instructos cum nauiculis uictualibus refectis terras quesitum desertas ad infinitum confestim dirigit occeanum p{er}scrutandum.[187]

[e] Illi nimirum abeuntes naues petunt et explicatis uelis[188] litus linquentes Hispanic{u}m[189] ad incognita maris loca relictis cognitis[190] adueniunt.

[f] Quique cursu uelocissimo fauore conducti deorum procul eminentem uiderunt insulam undique salo[191] circumfusam, ad quam in portu cum applicarent proximo locatis nauibus eam explorantes circuiunt,[192]

171 ABCEFG; *incomodis* S

172 *Gaythelos* ABCGS; *Gaithelos* EF

173 ACEFGS; *sui* B

174 ACEGS; *ultime* B corrected by B[1] to *utilem*; *utile* F

175 ACEFGS; *prospexirat* B

176 ACFGS; om. BE originally, and supplied by B[1] and by a later hand in E.

177 ABEFGS; *omnium* C. Skene has *omnium.*

178 ACEFGS; *delere* B

179 *cotidiano* BEFS; *cothidiano* AG; *quotidiano* C

180 Corrected from *sede* in B.

181 *imminenti* ES; *iminenti* F; *imminente* ABCG (in B altered to *imminenti*, possibly by B[1]). Skene has *imminente.*

182 ABEFGS; *discidie* C. Skene has the phonetically identical *dissidio.*

183 I.e. *disceptans*, 'debating', 'discussing'.

184 CFS; *acquerere* ABEG

185 BCEFGS; *adibitum* A

186 ABCEGS; om. F

187 *perscrutandum* CS; *proscrutandum* ABEFG (which is nonsense).

188 ABEFGS; *uel* C (note that BES have *uel-*)

189 *Hispanicum* FS; *Hispanicam* ABCEG (an unorthodox treatment of *litus* as feminine).

190 ACEFGS; *cognotis* B

191 BCEFS; *solo* AG (corrected in G to *salo*)

192 ABCEFG; *circumiunt* S

[g] atque uisa quoad poterant insula celeri remige Briganciam repetunt de quadam plaga terre pulcherima occeano reperta suo regi Gaythelo[193] nunciantes.[194]

{De eodem, Legenda Brandani}.[195] Capitulum 16^{m}

[XVI]

[a] Gaythelos[196] namque cum esset incolis ingratus die quodam sereno[197] cum[198] de Brigancia spectans eminusque terram contemplatus esset in mari agiles et bellicosos iuuenes armat et cum tribus nauiculis exploratum dirigens alto se committunt freto.

[b] At illi spirantibus[199] auris ad uotum[200] tandem ad insulam conueniunt et eam contemplando circuiuntes[201] et remis incolas repertos inuadentes[202] perimerunt,[203]

[c] sicque tellure lustrat{a}[204] mirantes eius decorem ad Briganciam red<e>unt.[205]

[d] Sed Ga{y}thelos[206] morte repentina preuentus filios hortando commonuit ut predictam certamine terram inuaderent, eorum[207] pariter segniciem arguens[208] et ignauiam si tante nobilitatis regnum desererent[209] quod sine bello uel quouis discrimine penetrare ualerent.[210]

[e] Uobis, inquid,[211] hanc insulam quicquid de mea salute contigerit facere {poteritis habitabilem ut asseritur}.[212]

193 CFS (in C a final *s* has been erased; in S a final *s* has been crossed out); *G^{o}* ABEG

194 ABEFGS; *enunciantes* C. Skene has *enunciantes.*

195 *De eodem et exortacione filiorum* (with *Legenda Brandani* in margin in text hand) C; *Legenda Beati Brandani de eodem* E; *De eodem, Legenda Sancti Brandani* F; *De eodem, capitulum .16., Legenda Brandani* G; *De eodem et exortacione filiorum ut dictam adirent insulam* S; om. AB; in B a later hand has squeezed in *Legenda Beati Brandani de eodem*. There can be little doubt that the archetype included at least *De eodem, Legenda Brandani.*

196 *Gaythelos* ABCFGS; *Gaithelos* E

197 BCEFGS; *seruo* A

198 ACEFGS; *est* B

199 CFS; *sperantibus* ABEG

200 Hearne, *Johannis de Fordun*, I. 27, has *notum*; Skene also has *notum.*

201 ABCEFG; *circumiuntes* S

202 ABCEGS; om. F

203 Skene has *peremerunt*

204 *lustrata* CF; *lustrato* ABEGS. It would be more orthodox to treat *tellus* as feminine; see, however, XXXI.b, where *tellus* is treated as masculine in all but S.

205 *redeunt* S (which is correct); *rediunt* ABCEFG

206 *Sed Gaythelos* C; *Sed G^{os}* AG; *Sed Gathelos* F; *Sed Gaethelos* S (the suprascript letters are very faint and have been added by a contemporaneous hand); *Sed Go$^{e'}$* B (*Go$^{e'}$* expanded by B^{1} to *Gaythelos*); om. E (*Sed Gathelos* squeezed in).

207 ACFGS; *eorumque* BE (*que* originally absent in E, and has been squeezed in later)

208 ABCEGS; *arguans* F

209 ACEFGS; *deserrerent* B

210 This sentence is on the face of it illogical: Gaythelos is urging his sons to invade *certamine*, 'with armed force', but then expects them to enter *sine bello uel quouis discrimine*, 'without war or any danger'. See below, 64–5 for an explanation of this.

211 ABCEG; *inquit* FS

212 *poteritis habitabilem ut asseritur* BEF; *poteritis ut habitabilem asseritur* AG; *poteritis ut asseritur habitabilem* C; *ut asseritur poteritis habitabilem* S

[f] Applicantibus in hac regione nobis[213] urgente uictus inopia dii[214] nostri de obstantibus incolis iustam dedere uictoriam si[215] quamcicius ut refectis alimentorum copia nauibus recedentes, hanc quam dii nobis iam offerunt insulam uel consimilem cultoribus uacuam adiremus.
[g] Hec[216] igitur nobis aduersancia merito patimur quia[217] iustis deorum uotis nullatenus obedire[218] curauimus.[219]
[h] In hiis estimo partibus dominii possessio difficilis[220] acquiritur[221] nisi caro nimis precio seruili uidelicet subieccione seu nostrum[222] omnium morte quod absit [223]redimatur.
[i] Sed et[224] nobis iocundius est laudabiliusque mortem compati bello strenue[225] quam ignobiliter quasi uiuentes moriendo[226] cotidie[227] sub execrabilis onere subieccionis iugiter compedi<r>i.[228]
[j] Hominis enim nullatenus dignus est nomine cuius continuum uelud[229] azini collo iugum imponitur seruitutis.[230]
[k] Nunc igitur, o filii, munera deorum oblata gratanter accipite et[231] uobis paratam adite nec tardetis insulam qua uelud[232] nobiles et liberi degere poteritis,
[l] cum sit hominum summa nobilitas et cordis cuiusque generosi desideratissima rerum iocunditas immo gemma cunctis mundi merito preferenda iocalibus nullius alienigene[233] dominantis imperium pati,[234] sed successiue[235] solummodo proprie nacionis uti spontaliter potestate.

213 BCEFS; *uobis* AG
214 ABEFGS; *dum* C
215 ABCEGS; *sed* F
216 ABCEFG; *Hic* S
217 ACFGS; *qua* BE (corrected in B by later hand to *quia*)
218 ABCFGS; *obdire* E
219 Corrected in B from *curauius*: note that in F *curauimus* is rendered *curauius* with curled suspension-stroke above the *a*.
220 BCEFS; *defficilis* A, and probably originally in G, where the second letter is blotched, probably in an attempt to alter *e* to *i*.
221 CS; *acqueritur* BE; *acqritur* (with suspension-stroke above *qr*) AFG
222 ACFGS; *urm* (with suspension-stroke above *m*) E; *uerium* B (later scored out and *nostrum* added in margin by B^{1})
223 add *mortibus* C
224 ABCEGS; *eciam* F
225 ABEFGS; *strenuo* C
226 BCEFGS; *moriendi* A
227 *cotidie* BFS; *totidie* AG; *quotidie* CE
228 *compediri* S (which is correct); *compediti* ABCEFG
229 ABEFG; *uelut* CS
230 ABCEGS; om. F
231 BCEFGS; om. A
232 ABCEG; *uelut* FS
233 ABCEGS; *alienegine* F
234 ABCEGS; om. F
235 ABEFGS; *successione* C. Skene has *successione*.

[236]Qualiter Hiber[237] filius Gaythelos[238] dictam{}[239] aggrediens insulam optinuit.[240] Capitulum 17m

[XVII.1]

[a] Auditis igitur Iber[241] patris sermonibus cum Hymec fratre nauigio predictam aggressus[242] est insulam et eam non ui sed uacuam ut quidam[243] uolunt omni cultore carentem obtinuit,

[b] et obtentam[244] fratri sueque familie committens ad Hispaniam reuersus est.

[XVII.2]

[*Passage from Geoffrey of Monmouth*]

[XVII.3]

Legenda Brandani[245]

Ex filiis Gaythel{}[246] unus quidem Hiber[247] nomine iuuenis sed de etate ualens incitatus[248] ad bellum animo cepit arma paratoque pro posse nauigio predictam aggressus insulam partem paucorum incolarum quos reperit[249] necat sibique partem subegit. Sed et totam sibi possidendam et fratribus terram uendicat[250] eam ex nomine matris [251]Scociam nuncupando.

[XVII.4]

Grossum Capud[252]

Et quia ipsa[253] ducissa[254] eorum inter omnes qui aderant nobilissima {fuerat}[255]

236 Title om. A
237 BCEGS; *Iber* F
238 BC; *Gaithelos* E; *Ga^os* F; *G^os* G; *Gaelos* S
239 *dictam* EFS; *dictamque* BCG
240 *insulam optinuit* BEGS; *insulam* C; *etc.* F
241 ACEFG; *Hyber* B; *Hiber* S
242 ACEFGS; *egressus* B
243 BCEGS; *quidem* A; final syllable ambiguous in F
244 ABCEFG (altered to *obtentem* in E); *optentam* S
245 *Legenda Brandani* BCEFG; *Legenda Brendani* S; om. A
246 *Gaythelis* BE; *Gaythel-* ACG; *Gaithel-* S; *Gathel-* F. For other instances where *Gaythelos* is treated (by some witnesses) as declinable, see XI.1.e and XIV.1.d. Elsewhere (for instance, the title to this chapter) *Gaythelos* is treated as indeclinable. The coyness about the final syllable here makes it impossible to be sure what was intended. Skene has *Gaythelos*; MacQueen and MacQueen, *Scotichronicon*, I.44 (based on S) has *Gaithelis*.
247 CBEF; *Iber* AG; *Hib-* S
248 ABEFGS; *incitatas* C. Skene has *incitatas*, which he amended to *incitatus* in his notes (Skene, *John of Fordun's Chronicle*, 382).
249 ABCFGS; *repperit* E
250 *terram uendicat* ACEFGS; *uendicat terram* B. Skene silently corrected this to *terram uindicat*.
251 *sue* add F
252 BCEFS; *Grossum Caput* G; om. (with gap) A
253 BCEFS; om. AG
254 *ditussa* in B crossed out in red and *ducissa* added by B[1] in margin.
255 *fuerat* CF; om. ABEGS

Scota dicebatur ipsam partem terre cui prius applicuerant[256] scilicet Oylister[257] Scociam uocauerunt.[258]

[XVII.5]
Legenda[259]
Postmodum autem ab eodem Hibero[260] rege uel mari pocius Hiberico Hiberniam uocauerunt.

[XVII.6]
Ex Cronicis[261]
Hiber igitur sua postmodum tam crebra nauigacione uersus insulam proficiscens indeque tociens iterum per mare rediens eidem mari sicut et insule de suo nomine uocabulum reliquit[262] eternum, ita uidelicet quod Hibericum mare de cetero[263] sicquidem[264] et[265] insula uel ab eodem rege uel pelago[266] Hibernia uocentur interim et usque tempus presens.

[XVII.7]
Quidam quoque tradunt[267] scriptores Hiberum ampnem toti Hispanie Hiberia[268] nomen dedisse qu<od>que[269] no{men}[270] ab ipso rege sicut legitur accepit.

[XVII.8]
Citeriorem autem Hispaniam, Ianuensis[271] scripsit, primo uocari Hiberiam[272] sed ulteriorem Hesperiam[273] uel ab Hespero[274] stella que in ipsa parte celi lucet uel ab

256 BCEGS (in B *applicauerant* scored out and followed by *applicuerant* in text hand); *applicauerant* A; *applicuerunt* F.

257 EFS; *Olyster* B; *Olister* AG; om. C

258 *Oylister* add C

259 BCEFGS; om. A

260 BCEFS; *Ybero* AG

261 BCEFGS; om. A (with gap)

262 CF; *reliquid* ABEG; *dereliquit* S

263 *de cetero* has originally been written *deceto* in BE, and altered to *de cetero* by B^1 (probably) and by a later hand in E

264 BCEFGS (in C the first syllable is squashed as if originally written *si* and altered to *sic*); *siquidem* A. *Sicquidem* here is an unorthodox form of *siquidem* (see also XXXIV.b); Skene has *sicquidem* which he corrected to *sic quidem* in his notes (Skene, *John of Fordun's Chronicle*, 382).

265 BCEFGS; om. A

266 ACEFGS; *palago* B

267 ACFGS; om. BE, and inserted later above line by B^1 and a later hand in E.

268 ACG; *Hiberiam* S; *Hyberiam* BEF.

269 *quodque* S (which is better grammatically); *quique* ABCEFG

270 *nomen* AFGS; *nota* BCE

271 I.e. Giovanni Balbi; the passage has been derived from his *Catholicon* (see MacQueen and MacQueen, *Scotichronicon*, I. 126).

272 *Citeriorem . . . Hiberniam* om. B, and probably supplied by B^1 in margin in a gloss (now faded and cut away) beginning *citeriorem autem*.

273 ACEFG; *Hisperiam* BS

274 BCEFS; *Espero* AG

Hespero rege Athlantis fratre qui pulsus a germano Italiam tenuit[275] eamque de suo nomine, uel nomine prestine[276] regionis quam reliquerat,[277] Hesperiam[278] nominauit.

Third extract: I. 20–21

A 9v–10v; B 13r–14r; C 9r–v; E 10v–11r; F VIv–VIIr; G 7v–8r; S 9r–v

[279]De successione filii Gaythelos[280] Hiber.[281] Capitulum 20m

[XX.1]

Ad regimen uero Scotorum in Hispanis permanencium post mortem patris successit Hiber cui filius eius[282] Nonael[283] deinde quidem que{m}cumque[284] regimen[285] iure successionis attigerat hunc gens prefecerat[286] suum regem.

[XX.2]

Alia cronica

[a] Per ccos circiter et xl[287] annos inter Hispanos qui eos iugiter infestabant egro uictu et uili habitu moram fecerunt.

[b] Deserta quippe loca montibus Pirriniis[288] et saltuosa sibi sunt ab Hispanis contradita ut uix uiuere poterant solummodo lacte caprino[289] et melle siluestri uitam sustentantes.

[c] Hiis igitur erumpnis uel peioribus multo tempore uixit populus iste siluis[290] degens et abditis preter quod ex rapinis habere ualuit et predis propter quod a circumsitis[291] undique populis maxime detestatus nichil habens nudipes gradiens male pastus habitu uilissimus[292] nam pene nudus exceptis saltem pelliciis uel pilosis[293] uestibus quibus fuerat informiter coopertus.

275 AEFGS; *tenet* BC

276 CF; *pristine* S; first syllable ambiguous in ABEG

277 BCEFS; *relinquerat* AG

278 ACEFGS; *Hisperiam* B

279 Title om. A.

280 BCES; *Gathelos* F; *Geyos* G

281 *in regnum Scotorum* add S

282 BCEFGS; om. A

283 CEFS; probably *Uonael* ABG (corrected in B to *Nonael*, possibly by B1)

284 CFS; *quecumque* ABEG (altered in B to *quicumque*, possibly by B1)

285 BCEFS; om. AG

286 *prefecerat* AEFGS; *preficerat* B; *prefecerat* C

287 *Alia cronica. Per ccos circiter et xl* BEG; *Alia cronica. Per ccos circiter xl* C; *circiter et xl* F; *Alia cronica. Per ducentos circiter et xl* S; om. A

288 ABCEG; *Pirrimiis* FS. Skene has *Pirreniis*.

289 ABCEGS; *cano* F

290 ABCEGS; *filius* F

291 Corrected in B from *circumsitus* by erasure of a minim.

292 Corrected in B from *uilissius*, possibly by B1.

293 BCEFGS; *piolosis* A

[d] Et in omnibus hiis malis et angustiis nuncquam ut regi subderetur[294] alieno[295] uel ad obediendum flecti poterat quin pocius humilis semper et deuotus sub rege proprio cum libertate tantum hanc uitam eligeret[296] ducere bestialem.

[XX.3]
Grossum Caput[297]
Scoti quoque[298] quasi a principio regnum ab aliis distinctum et regem semper proprium habuerunt.

De Micelio rege Scotorum Hispaniens<ium>.[299] Capitulum 21^{m} [300]
[XXI.1]
[a] Peruenit tandem [301]regiminis culmen ad uirum eque strenuum et industrium regem uidelicet Micelium Espayn[302] cuius antecessorum[303] quidam sibi suisque gentibus cum libertate sedem mansionis acquesiuit[304] liberam sed tante[305] numerositatis gentibus nimis modicam.
[b] Desiderate uero pacis tranquillitate pro qua diu certasset optenta[306] per circuitum ab omnibus hoc tempore populus fruebatur.
[c] Erant enim[307] Micelio tres filii quorum nomina sunt [308]Hermonius,[309] P{a}rtholo{m}us,[310] et Hibertus, ipsos interim ad Hiberniam parata classe[311] copioso transmisit exercitu[312] sciens ibidem eos ad colendam spaciosam[313] reperire terram sed pene uacuam[314] licet paucis et ex eodem genere gentibus fuerat antiquitus incolata.
[d] Quo post breue spacium cum aduenissent et eam uel bello uel ab incolis sponte

294 Corrected in B from *suderetur*.
295 BCEFS; *alieono* AG
296 ACEGS; *elegeret* BF
297 ACFGS; *Capud* BE
298 BCEFS; om. AG
299 *Hispaniensium* S; *Hispaniensis* ABCEFG. Only S has a grammatical reading. Hearne, *Johannis de Fordun*, I. 36, corrected silently to *Hispanensium*, as did Skene.
300 ACEFG; *22* B (altered to *21*, possibly by text hand). For S see 27, above.
301 *et* add B (subsequently scored out).
302 ACGS (in A *Hyspan* deleted before *Espayn*); *Espaen* BE; *Ospayn* (with superscript stroke above *n*) F
303 *antecessorum* ABEFGS (B altered to *antecessoris*, possibly by B^1); *antecessoris* C. Skene has *antecessoris*.
304 ACEFG; *acquisiuit* B; *acqsiuit* (with suspension-stroke above *qs*) S
305 ACFGS; *caute* BE (changed in B to *tante*)
306 ABCEGS; *obtenta* F
307 ABCEGS; *autem* F
308 *hec* add B.
309 ACEFGS; *Hermoneus* B
310 *Partholomus* CEGS; *Partholonius* AB; *Pertholonius* F (only in F is the first syllable spelt out).
311 *classe* added above line in text hand in C.
312 CFS; *excercitu* ABEG
313 ABCFG; *spasiosam* E; *spaci*[(lacuna) S
314 *uacuam* altered in B from *uacciam* (by B^1).

recepti faciliter occupassent,[315] Hermonius ad patrem Hispani{a}s[316] rediit, fratres uero sui P{a}rtholo{m}us[317] et Hibertus cum gentibus in insula commanserunt.

[XXI.2]
Alia cronica
[a] Post mortem Gaythelos[318] et Scote suorumque filiorum in illo successerunt ducatu quique[319] proximi singillatim[320] sicut casus se casibus optulit usque quemdam qui proprio nomine P{a}rtholo{m}us[321] dicebatur.[322]
[b] Is animo sagax et eque sensu industris dolere cepit se populumque[323] suum in illis partibus crescere[324] uel multiplicare non posse propter acerimas[325] et crebras infestancium molestias Hispanorum.
[c] Igitur a tam arido solo quod eciam erumpnose[326] tenuerant[327] inter[328] quos itaque qui eos tamquam hominum uilissimos reputabant sese proponunt[329] eripere et ad mansiones pro posse laciores transducere.
[d] Consilio proni demum inito cum senioribus ad Mare Gallicum cum sportellis et sarcinis accedunt et comparatis uel undecumque poterant quesitis nauibus marino discrimini sese committunt certas[330] quesituri[331] quo se fortuna p{er}duceret[332] et perpetuas cum libertate mansiones.
[e] Igitur ad Hiberniam P{a}rtholo{m}us[333] cum sua familia nauigio profectus est et eam subactis indigenis in perpetuam sibi possessionem optinuit.[334]

315 BCEFS; *ocupassent* AG
316 CFS; *Hispanis* ABEG
317 *Partholomus* BCEGS; *Partholonius* A; *Pertholonius* F (only in F is the first syllable spelt out).
318 BCEF; *Gaithelos* S; *Gay^os^* AG
319 Corrected from *quinque* in B
320 ABCEGS; *singilatim* F
321 BCS; *Partholonius* E; *Protholonius* F; *Partholous* AG (in G squeezed in over an erasure). In all cases apart from F a contraction is used for the first syllable which normally represents *per*, but can also be used for *par*.
322 BCEFGS (in G written over an erasure); *docebatur* A
323 ABEFGS; *populum* C
324 ACEFGS; *cressere* B
325 BCEFGS; *acerrimas* A
326 ABEFGS; *erumpnoso* C
327 ACFGS; *tenuerat* BE (in B altered to *tenuerant*)
328 ABFGS; *iter* CE
329 BCEFGS; *proponuntur* A. Skene followed A here; there is no need for the passive, however.
330 ABCEFG (scored out in B and *terras* added above by B[1]); *terras* S
331 ABCEGS; *quesitari* F
332 BCES; *produceret* AFG
333 *Partholomus* ABCEGS; *Pertholonius* F (only in F is the first syllable spelt out). In view of the variation between *m* and *ni* elsewhere in this section, it is best to regard the *m* here as uncertain.
334 ABCEGS; *obtinuit* F

Fourth extract: I. 26–29

A 12r–13v; B 15v–17r; C 11r–12v; E 12v–14r; F VIIIr–IXr;
G 9v–10v; S 10v–11v

[335]De profeccione tercia Scotorum ad Hiberniam facta { }[336] Capitulum 26^{m} [XXVI]

[a] Ad insulam preterea supradictam processu temporis ab Hispanensium[337] finibus ut docent cronice, eciam tercius adueniens accola Scotici generis cui nomen Scotice S{m}onbricht[338] Latine uero Simon uarius uel lentiginosus ibique regni fastigium arripiens indigenis habunde nouis insule populos ampliauit.[339]

[b] Eo tempore regnauit ut asserunt in Iudea Manasses filius Ezechie qui cepit anno quarte[340] etatis ccco lxiiii^{o}.[341]

. . .

[c] Erat enim idem Simon filius regis Fonduf,[342] qui tunc temporis super Scotorum reliquias Hispania degentes regnauit, qui fuit filius[343] Etheon, filii[344] Glach{^{s}},[345] filii Noethath Fail,[346] filii Elchata Ol{c}haim,[347] filii Sirue,[348] filii De{in},[349] filii Demail,[350] filii Ro{t}ho{t}ha,[351] filii Ogmain,[352]

335 Title om. A.

336 *facta* om. G; F continues *per Simonbritht*; S continues *per Simon brek et eius genealogia.*

337 BCEFS; *Hispanencium* AG

338 CG; *Smonbrich* A; *S^{i}monbritht* BE; *Simonbritht* F; *Simon brek* S. On this name, see below, n. 378.

339 ACEFGS; *amplicauit* B

340 Altered subsequently in G to *quarto*.

341 ABCFGS; *ccc^{o} luiiii^{o}* E

342 I.e. Eoin Duib (genitive: in discussion below the genitive forms will be given). Ralph of Diss, *Imagines Historiarum*: London, Lambeth Palace MS 8 (the royal genealogy is at fo.107va32–b28) has *Eon Duf.* On Diss's and related copies of the genealogy, see 180–2, below.

343 ACEFGS; om. B

344 In F corrected from *filius*

345 *Glach^{s}* BE; *Glachus* AG; *Glash^{s}* F; *Glachez* S; *Glach^{o}* C. It is difficult to know exactly what was intended by the raised *s*, which was presumably also the reading in an archetype of G. *Etheon filii Glach^{s}* is Aedáin Glais; Diss has *Etheon filii Glachs.* Skene has *Glachus.*

346 *Fail* om. B (added probably by B^{1}); i.e. Nuadat Fáil; Diss has *Noethath Fail.*

347 *Elchata Olchaim* GS; *Elthata Olchaim* A; *Elchata Olthaim* BEF; *Elchata Oltbaim* C. This is a telescoped rendering of Giallchada meic Ailella Ólchain; Diss has *Elchatha Olchaim*. Skene has *Elchata Olchaim*.

348 ACEFGS; *Sirne* possibly in B; i.e. Sírnai; Diss has *Sirne.*

349 BCS; *Dem* EF; *Deiu* AG; i.e. Déin (Diss has *Dein*).

350 ACEFGS; *Demael* B; i.e. Demáil (Diss has *Demail*).

351 *Rothotha* CF; *Rothocha* BE; *Rochotha* AG; *Rochocha* S; i.e. Rothechtada/Rechtada; Diss has *Rothotha.*

352 BCG; *Ochmam* S; *Ogmam* AEF; i.e. Ogmain. Diss has *Ogmain.* Skene has *Ogmam.*

filii Eugus Ol{um}c{a}tha,[353] filii F{i}achach[354] Labrain,[355] filii Emirnai,[356] filii S{m}recha,[357] filii Emba{t}ha,[358] filii[359] Thiernay,[360] filii Faleg,[361] filii Etheor,[362] filii[363] Iair Olfacha,[364] filii Hermonii,[365] fratris Partholo{m}[366] et Hibert.[367] [d] Et hii[368] tres[369] fuerunt filii regis[370] Micelii Espain[371] cuius supra mencionem fecimus,[372] de quo quidem[373] S{m}onbricht[374] et eiusdem[375] adepcione[376] regni <id quod> sequitur[377] in legenda sancti Congalli reperitur inscriptum.

353 *Olumcatha* ABEG; *olim Cotha* C; *Olmucetha* F; *Olumchatha* S; i.e. Oengusa Ólmugaeda; Diss has *Enegus Olmucatha.* (It is doubtful whether much significance should be attached to the correct rendering of the minims in F.)

354 *Fiachach* CES; *Fiathach* B; *Frachach* AFG; i.e. Fiachach (Diss has *Fiachach*). Skene has *Frachach.*

355 BCEFS; *Labram* A; *Labraiu* G; i.e. Labrainn (Diss has *Labrain*).

356 I.e. Smirgnaith; Diss has *Smirnai.*

357 *Smretha* B; *Sinrecha* CS; *Smrecha* EG; *Smertha* A; *Surrecha* F; i.e. Smretha; Diss has *Sinrecha.* Skene has *Smertha.*

358 *Embatha* ABCES (first attempt scored out, C); *Embacha* FG; i.e. Enbotha/Senbotha; Diss has *Embatha.*

359 ACEFGS; *filius* B, and also in following two *filii*, each corrected to *filii* (probably by B^1)

360 *Th^{r}ernay* B (superscript *r* added with caret mark); *Chiernay* C; *Thrernay* E; *Thiernai* FS; *Thiernay* G; *Thernay* A; i.e. Tigernaig; Diss has *Thiernai.* Skene has *Thernay.*

361 All manuscripts have an indeterminate line (a hook in ABCEG) continuing from the final *g*, which may in original have been no more than a flourish. The name-form is Fallaig; Diss has *Faleg.* Skene has *Falegis.*

362 I.e. Ether/Ethriel (Diss has *Etheor*).

363 *Etheor filii* om. B (added later by B^1).

364 I.e. Íaréoil Fátha; Diss has *Iair Olfatha* (it would seem that the division between name and epithet has been incorrectly analysed at some stage). Skene has *lair Olfatha.*

365 I.e. Éremóin; Diss has *Ermon.*

366 *Partholom* CE; corrected to *Partholonii* in B; *Pertholonii* F; *Pertholomi* S; *Bartholom* AG. The name is Partholón (gen. Partholóin). Skene has *Bartholomi.*

367 ACEFG; corrected to *Hiberti* B (probably by B^1); *Hiberti* S. The name is Éber.

368 Corrected in B from *hiis* (possibly by text hand).

369 *ut supradictur* add S

370 ABCEGS; om. F

371 *regis* add F. *Micelii Espain* represents Míled Espáin; Diss has *Micel Espaine* showing the metathesis of *c* (presumably originally *t*) and *l* which explains the form *Micelius.* The explanation of *Micelius* in MacQueen and MacQueen, *Scotichronicon*, I. 134, is fanciful: it is argued there that *Micelius* has been derived from the phrase *Tánic asin Micil Gréc*, 'He came from *Micil* [Sicily?] of Greeks', used of Partholón in one place in *Lebor Gabála* (see *LG*, III. 4).

372 *cuius supra mencionem fecimus* ABCEFG; om. S

373 AEFGS; final syllable ambiguous in C; *quidam* B

374 CEG; *Smonbritht* AB (B corrected to *Simonebricht* by B^1); *Simonbritht* F; *Simone Brek* S. On this name, see below, n. 378.

375 ABCEGS; *eius* F

376 ABEFGS; *adopocione* C. Hearne, *Johannis de Fordun*, I. 44, has *adopcione*; Skene has *adoptione.*

377 *id quod sequitur* S; *quiddam ut sequitur* BEFG; *quidam ut sequitur* A; *queddam ut sequitur* C. Only S makes sense; *quiddam* is interrogative, and is inappropriate here.

De eodem S{m}o{}nbrek[378] et cathedra regali lapidea[379] et eiusdem uaticinio.[380] Capitulum 27m

[XXVII]

[a] Erat autem quidam Scotorum Hispanie rex[381] plures habens filios unum tamen cui[382] nomen[383] S{m}onbrec[384] quamuis natu non maior fuerat uel heres pre ceteris tamen[385] diligebat.[386]

[b] Misit igitur ipsum pater ad Hiberniam cum exercitu[387] donauitque sibi marmoream cathedram[388] arte uetustissima[389] diligenti[390] sculptam opifice qua Scotice[391] nacionis Hispanie reges sedere solebant unde diligenter[392] in sua regione quasi pro anchora tuebatur.

[c] Pergebat[393] autem idem S{m}o{}nbrec[394] magna comitatus[395] hominum

---

The discrepancy between S and the rest is striking, however; perhaps S here represents Bower's intervention in making sense of what may have been inherited from Fordun.

378 *Simonbrec* (with suspension-stroke above *o*) C; *Simonbritht* F; *Simone Brek* S; *Smo*a*nbrek* AEG; *Smonbrek* B. Skene has *Smonnbrek*. There is considerable variation elsewhere between the witnesses in how this name is rendered. The reading in AEG with a raised *a* (which is open and therefore looks like a *u*) would normally (although not exclusively) be interpreted as signifying either *ra* or *ar*; in a vernacular context, however, it would simply signify *u*. The *lectio difficilior* would certainly be a literal reading of AEG as *Smoranbrek*, which may have been rationalised to Smon/Simon Brek (especially if, as I argue below, 65, this individual has been identified with Simón Brecc [Diss *Sinonbricht*] in the royal genealogy, maybe only on the grounds that the names are similar). If 'Smoranbrek' was the original name, perhaps the first element represented *smir* (Old Irish *smiur*), 'marrow', found in the pseudo-historical names Smirdub and Smirgoll (see *DIL s.v. smir*). It would need to be explained, however, how the vowel came to be spelt *o*. It would seem safest to regard the original identity of this person as uncertain.

379 ACFGS; *lapide* BE (altered in B to *lapidea* by B1)

380 *et eiusdem uaticinio* BCES; om. AFG

381 *Milo nomine* added in later in B (by B1) and S

382 ABCEGS; om. F

383 ABCFGS; *nota* BE (corrected in B to *nomen* by B1)

384 *Smonbrek* AG; *Smonbrec* B (altered to *Symonbrec* by B1); *Smonbret* (with suspension-stroke above *o*) C; *Smo*a*nbrec* E; *Simonbritht* F; *Simon brek* S. Skene has *Smonbret*. See above, n. 378.

385 ACGS; *cum* BE (altered in B to *eum* by B1); om. F. Skene has *tum*.

386 BCEFS; *deligebat* AG

387 ACEFGS; *excercitu* B

388 BCEFGS; *cathederam* A

389 ACFGS; *uetussima* BE (attempt at clarification aborted in B, and *uetustissima* added in margin by B1)

390 ABCEG; *deligenti* F; *diligentique* S

391 BCEFS; *Scocie* AG

392 ABCEGS; *deligenter* F

393 ACEFGS; *Pargebat* B

394 *Smo*a*nbrec* C; *Smo*a*nbrek* EG; *Smonbrek* A; *Smonbrecht* B (altered to *Symonbrecht* by B1); *Simonbritht* F; *Simon brek* S. Skene has *Smonbrek*. See above, n. 378.

395 BCEFGS; *comittatus* A

caterua predictam[396] ad insulam et in ea suo subiecta dominio regnauit annis multis.

[d] Lapidem uero prefatum scilicet cathedram in eminenciori loco regni Themor nomine posuit qui[397] regia sedes locusque regni superior de cetero dictus est[398] quo sue propaginis postere[399] reges multis temporibus sedere solebant regiis honoribus insigniti.

[e] Attulit secum hanc cathedram Gaythelos[400] cum aliis ornamentis regalibus ad Hispaniam ut aiunt quidam ex Egipto.

[f] Alii quoque quod S{m}onbrec[401] in mari prope litus Hibernicum[402] emissas e naui confixit anchoras et eas iterum urgente uentorum aduersitate dum ex undosis omni conatu retrahere fluctibus ualide sategerat in formam cathedre decisum[403] ex marmore lapidem de pelagi[404] profundo sublatum[405] in naui cum anchoris introduxit.

[g] Hunc igitur lapidem quasi preciosum munus a diis oblatum certum eciam futuri regni[406] presagium accipiens et nimio fluctuans in gaudio suos in tantum ueneratus est deos[407] ac si regnum sibi tradiderant penitus cum corona.

[h] Accepit[408] ibidem et inde uaticinium a diis suis huiusmodi sicut scriptis asseritur quod ubicumque locorum regno seu dominio per aduersariorum de cetero potenciam ab eis inuitis delatum reperiant[409] lapidem pro firmo tenere iusserunt aruscipes ibidem se suosque[410] postea regnaturos.

[i] Unde quidam ex eorum diuinacione uaticinando metrice sic propha{tur}[411]

[j] Ni fallat fatum Scoti quocumque locatum
Inueni{a}nt[412] lapidem regnare tenentur ibidem.

[k] {Et hoc sicut}[413] uulgaris asserit hactenus opinio uerum in sua sepius primitiua

396 ABCEGS; *predictamque* F
397 ABCEG; *que* F; *cui* S
398 ABEFGS; om. C
399 ABCEGS, altered to *posteri* in B; *posteri* S
400 ABCEGS; *Gathelos* F
401 ABCEG (altered in B to *Symonbrec* by B[1]); *Simonbritht* F; *Simon brek* S
402 *ferunt* add S (and added in B by B[1])
403 BEFGS; *decisam* C; *desum* A
404 ACFGS; *pellagi* BE
405 ACFGS; *sullatum* BE (altered in B to *sublatum*)
406 ABCEFG; *regis* S
407 ACEFGS; probably *deo* originally in B, altered to *deos*
408 ACFGS; *Accipit* BE
409 ABCEGS; *repereant* F
410 ABCEGS; *suos* F
411 *prophatur* AG (in G altered to *prophantur*); *profatur* S; *prophetatur* F; *prophantur* BE; *prophant* C (no doubt an ancestor read *prophantur*); *uersus* add BE (*uersus* in margin in C); *scilicet* add C
412 *Inueniant* ABEFG; *inuenient* CS (also Wyntoun: see below, 103
413 *Et hoc sicut* FS; ABCEG have the phrase misplaced after *locatum* (end of first line of verse). Either FS alone preserve the original reading, or (less likely) the verse and its introductory sentence (XXVII.ij) have been added to the archetype in such a way that *et hoc sicut* could be copied out of position. Skene followed in placing *et hoc sicut* after *locatum.*

peregrinacione probari.[414] Nam ereptum per hostes lapidem non solum Hispanienses regulos uerum eciam et Hibernienses patriotas[415] hunc unacum eorum regionibus secundum assignatum superius uaticinium et ipsi[416] potenter ab hostibus receperunt.[417]

[l] [418]Uerum quia de Grecis et Egiptiis populus iste commixtus duxerat originem ne priorum memoria suorum principum[419] prolixi transcursu temporis ex hominibus forte periret eorum nomina suis coaptabant nominibus.

[m] Greci uidelicet ex sui principis nomine Gaythelos[420] se Gaythelenses[421] similiter et Egiptii de Scota se Scotos protinus uocabant quo[422] solo nomine postmodum hodieque communiter utraque gens perfrui[423] gratulatur.

[n] Unde quidam:

Scoti de Scota de Scotis Scocia tota
Nomen habent uetito Gaythelos[424] ducis adaucto.[425]

[426]De primo rege[427] Scotorum inhabitancium insulas {Albionis}.[428] Capitulum 28m

[XXVIII]

[a] Creuit autem in terra populus et ualde multiplicatus est, extendit enim a mari usque ad mare palmites suos et Albionis insulas ut traditur nullo cultore prehabitatas propagines eius.

[b] Primus autem eorum dux eas inhabitancium Echa{t}hius[429] Rothay pronepos supradicti Simonis Brec[430] interpretacione[431] sui nominis insule Rothisay[432] nomen dedit, quo quidem non parui[433] temporis spacio fruebatur nomine quousque Saluatoris Nostri fide{s}[434] per uniuersos orbis terre fines et insulas que procul

414 ABCEFG (altered in B to *probatur*); *comprobatur* S
415 ABCEGS; *patroatas* F
416 ABCEGS; *ipso* F. Refers to *Scoti.*
417 CGS; *reciperunt* AB; *recipererunt* E; *ceperunt* F
418 *postmodum* add AG (and Skene)
419 *suorum principum* BCEFS; *principum suorum* AG
420 BC; *Gaithelos* ES; *Geythelos* AFG
421 ACEG; *Geithelenses* F; *Gaythelenses* B; *Gathelenses* S
422 ACGS; *que* BE (altered in B to *quo*, possibly by B[1]); *eo* F. There is no need to doubt that the grammatically correct *quo* was the original reading.
423 ABCEGS; *persrui* F
424 *Gaythelos* BS; *Gaithelos* EF; *Geythelos* AG; *Gathelos* C
425 ACEFGS; *abaucto* B, corrected to *adaucto.*
426 Title om. (with gap) A.
427 *rege* scored out and *duce* written above in S
428 *Albionis* CS; om. BEFG (added by B[1])
429 *Echathius* B; *Echachius* ACEG; *Ecathius* S; *Ethachius* F; i.e. a Latin form of Eochaid, so *Echathius* was probably originally intended; the amendment may be justified by the instability of *c* and *t* here, rather than the reading in B which can have little authority on its own. Skene has *Ethachius.*
430 C; *Brek* ABEGS; *Britht* F
431 ABCEFS; *interpretacionem* G
432 ACEGS; *Roythysay* B; *Rothissay* F
433 CS; *perui* F; vowel in first syllable is ambiguous in ABEG.
434 *fide* ABEGS; *fides* CF (which is better)

sunt diffusa, sanctus Brandanus in ea botham idiomate nostro .bothe. i.[435] cellam construxit.

[c] Unde et deinceps et usque tempus nostrum habetur binomia quod aliquando Rothisay[436] .i.[437] insula Rothay[438] sic et aliquando insula[439] de Bothe ab indigenis[440] nuncupatur.

[441]De Pictis aduentantibus Hiberniam[442] pro sedibus.[443] Capitulum 29m

[XXIX.1]

[a] Euoluto[444] quidem[445] non pauco tempore dummodo prospera quiete degebant et pace populus quidam[446] ignotus ab Aquitannie[447] finibus emergens qui Pictus postea dicebatur suo litori[448] ratibus applicuit et quod uel per se loco deserto uel secum in insula passim cohabitare posset humiliter a maioribus postulauit.

[b] Ex propria namque patria se dicebat aduersancium ualida[449] manu licet immerito nuper expulsum ac eatenus[450] in mari periculis uexatum fuisse maximis et horrendis procellarum.

[c] Nec tamen[451] ut inter eos eadem maneret[452] insula{ }[453] fateri uolebant, immo sub amicicia sue pacis et proteccione susceptum ad finem Albionis aquilonalem desertum hactenus[454] cum quibusdam traditis secum comitibus transmiserunt.

[d] Illis igitur incipientibus ibidem terras incolere nec secum sue nacionis mulieres habentibus dederunt uxores Scoti filias suas sub pacto sempiterni federis[455] et dotis condicto speciali.

[e] Pictorum autem accessus ad hanc insulam per uarios uarie discribitur[456] auctores, quorum quidam tradunt quod a gentibus quas[457] secum ex Sithia[458] rex

435 BCES; *idest* F; *id est* AG rendered *ide* with suspension-stroke above *e* (altered in text hand in G from *i*)

436 ABCEGS; *Rothissai* F

437 ABCEGS; *idest* F

438 ABCEGS; *Rothissay* F

439 ABCEGS; *insulam* F

440 ABCEGS; *indegenis* F

441 Title om. (with gap) A.

442 *Hiberniam* BEFGS; *Yberniam* C.

443 *ibidem habendis etcetera* add S

444 *Euoluto* ABEGS; *Reuoluto* C; *Eeuoluto* F. Skene has *Reuoluto.*

445 BCE; *quidam* AG; ambiguous FS

446 ABCEGS; *quidem* F

447 ABCEG; *Aquitanie* FS

448 ACEFGS; *litori* B, corrected (possibly by B1) to *litore*

449 ABCEGS; *ualidi* F

450 BCEFS; *eatinus* AG

451 ACFGS; *tum* BE (corrected by B1 to *tamen*)

452 *eadem maneret* ABCEFG; *maneret eadem* S

453 *insula* BEFS; *insulam* ACG (which is ungrammatical)

454 ABCEF (*h* added later superscript in C); *actenus* S

455 ACEGS; *fediris* B; *fedis* (with superscript *r* added later) F

456 ABCEFG; *describitur* S

457 ACEFGS; *qua* B corrected (perhaps by B1) to *quas.*

458 BCFS; *Sichia* AEG

Humber ad Britanniam conduxerat cum a Locrino[459] filio Bruti propter occisionem sui fratris Albanacti submersus est fluuio Picti sumpserunt originem.
[f] Nam sublato gentes rege suo non recesserunt ab insula sed in extremis eiusdem finibus multo tempore causas iudicibus terminabant.

[XXIX.2]
Alia Cronica.
[a] Picti[460] quidem exorti de Sithia[461] fugam Agenoris comitati sunt et ipso duce insederunt Aquitanorum nacion{em}.[462]
[b] Huic assercioni nostre urbis testatur Agenorensis ab Agenore constructa et Pictauorum patria[463] in qua Picti de proprio nomine Pictauem condiderunt ciuitatem.
[c] Hii uero classe postmodum composita petentes[464] Albion<e>m[465] cum[466] Scotis hactenus[467] commanere dicuntur.

Fifth extract: I. 31

A 14r–v; B 17v–18r; C 13r–v; E 14v–15r; F Xr–v; G 11r; S 11v–12r

[468]De causa prima Scotorum aditus ad Albionem insulam.[469] Capitulum 31^{m}
[XXXI]
[a] Scotorum uero filias quas nuptum Picti sumpserunt et cognatas[470] dum secum ad propria paulatim mariti conducerent earum innumeri parentes secuti sunt, patres scilicet et matres fratres eciam[471] et sorores neptes similiter et nepotes.
[b] Sequuntur[472] autem et ceteri plures, quos non solum affeccio filialis urgebat uel sororia sed pocius quos telluris Albionic<e>[473] quo tender<u>nt,[474] herbosa fertilitas[475] atque suorum amplissima pecorum pascua penitus prouocabant.

459 ACGS; *Alecrino* B, corrected (probably by B^1) to *Alocrino* (one word); *Alacrino* E, corrected to *a Locrino*; *Alocrino* F.
460 ACEFGS; *Pica* B, corrected by B^1 to *Picti*.
461 BCF; *Sichia* AEG; *Scithia* S
462 *nacionem* ABCFG; *nacioni* ES
463 ACEFGS; *patriam* B
464 ABCEFS; *petentee* G, corrected to *petentes*.
465 *Albionem* S (the most orthodox reading); *Albioniam* BCEFG; *Albionam* A
466 ACEFGS; *a* B, corrected to *cum* (unclear by whom).
467 ABCEFG; *actenus* S
468 Title om. A (with gap).
469 *insulam* BCEFS; om. G
470 ACEFGS; *cognas* B, altered to *cognotas* by B^1.
471 ABCEFG; om. S
472 *sequuntur* CF; *secuntur* ABEGS
473 *Albionice* S (which is correct); *Albionici* ABCEFG. Compare with XVI.c, where *tellus* is treated as masculine in all except C and F.
474 *tenderunt* AS; *tenderant* BCEFG. The perfect *tenderunt* seems preferable to the pluperfect. Note that on this occasion there is no reduplication, as in XI.3.b (*tetendere*) and XXXIV.d (*tetenderat*). S is not alone in giving a correct reading, but the reading in A may represent an independent correction (see 28, above).
475 ACFGS; *farcilitas* B, altered to *fartilitas*; *farcilitas* E (vowel in first syllable ambiguous).

[c] Utriusque uero sexus tanta sequacis uulgi copia secum armenta deducens[476] cum Pictis mansura per exigui temporis exiit interuallum quanta non legitur propriam[477] linquisse patriam absque duce.
[d] Sed et[478] eorum itaque numerum augebat proscriptorum continua[479] progressio malificorum[480] quia legis disciplinam quisquis[481] subire timescens cohabitare Pictis securus adiit ubi deinceps accersitis paruulis et[482] uxore[483] pacifice remanens nullatenus de cetero reuersus est.
[e] Aduentum uero tante multitudinis interim Picti moleste ferentes nam timor eorum eos peruaserat ne quis aduena sedem de cetero mansionis usquequaque finibus suis optineat[484] ex preconio proclamari iubebant, sed et hiis qui secum prius ad uotum[485] manere contenderant occasionem dedere multiplicem recedendi.
[f] Nam primo cum intrabant ad insulam, per suorum responsa deorum sed pocius demonum quibus antequam operis cuiusque quicquam facerent immolantes intellexerunt futurum esse quod si non Scotos expugnare satagerent ab eis penitus delerentur.
[g] Ideoque[486] uidentes eorum inter eos augeri numerum magis ac magis timere ceperunt et eos acrius a sua regione propulerunt.
[h] Quod autem uerum non statim postea[487] sed post mille annos expertum est quoniam genus eorum eo tempore cum lingua per eos penitus deletum est.

Sixth extract: I. 34

A 16r; B 19v; C 14r–v; E 16v; F Xr–v; G 12r–v; S 13v

[488]De primo rege Scotorum regnant{e}[489] in Albione. Capitulum 34[m] [XXXIV]

[a] Preterea[490] dum Picti Scotos aduenas huiusmodi dampnis affligerent et angustiis nunciatum est clamculo gentis sue maioribus quali quantaque per eos degebant erumpna.

476 ACEFGS; *ducens* B, altered by B[1] to *deducens*.
477 ABCEGS; *pro patria* F
478 ACEGS; om. BF (added by B[1])
479 *continua* ABCEFGS; Hearne, *Johannis de Fordun*, I. 51, has *contraria*, as does Skene (although Felix Skene translated this as *continua*: Skene, *John of Fordun's Chronicle*, 27).
480 ABCEFG; *maleficorum* S
481 ABCEFG; *quisque* S
482 ABCEFG; *cum* S
483 BCEFS; *utere* A; in G the second letter has been erased and *uxore* written in margin in later hand.
484 ABCEGS; *obtineat* F
485 *ad uotum* CEFGS; *aduotum* (or *adnotum*) AB.
486 ABEF; *idioque* CG; *idoque* (with suspension-stroke above *o*) S
487 ABCEFG; om. S
488 Title om. (with gap) in A.
489 *regnante* BCG; *regnancium* S; ambiguous after *t* in EF. The better reading is *regnante*, agreeing with *rege*.
490 ACEFGS (in C first attempt erased); *preteria* B

[b] Sed et interim accedentes quidam qui tam ample tanteque fecunditatis amenitatem regionis eciam sibi prodiderant, in qua uolatilia tantum et fere siluestres inerant et bestie redigenda si(c)quidem[491] faciliter in culturam.[492]

[c] Hec igitur ut audiuit nobilis quidam et inmodice[493] probitatis[494] iuuenis[495] Fergus[496] filius Fer{ec}had[497] siue Ferchardi[498] ex antiquorum prosapia regum[499] progenitus[500] quod scilicet[501] acephila[502] gens sue nacionis absque rectore per Albionis uastas uagando solitudines a Pictis eiecta degebat[503] cordis ob iram candescere cepit.

[d] Insuper et illius commendacione regionis qua forsan regnare tetenderat multum allectus est quam qui uidissent uberimam[504] predicabant, preter quod[505] operiebatur eo tempore condensis ualde nemoribus omnis humus.

[e] Unde certum nobis[506] et hactenus[507] huiusmodi patet indicium cum in[508] locis contigerit et sepe planissimis quibus terra fortassis effossa fuerit seu cauata subterranee radices[509] arborum ingentes et trunci reperiuntur[510] immo quo[511] nusquam antea siluas creuisse diceres ullo signo.

[f] Hiis igitur exhortacionibus et ambicione regnandi stimulatus magnam sibi iuuenum copiam accumulans[512] ad Albionem continuo progressus est, ubi segre-

491 *siquidem* S; *sicquidem* ABCEFG, which (although it is phonetically identical) is a rather unorthodox form: cf. n. 00, where all witnesses have *sicquidem* for *siquidem*; perhaps, therefore, this is a case where Bower has corrected Fordun.

492 *in culturam* CEFS; *inculturam* ABG

493 *imodice* with horizontal suspension-stroke above *im* in ACG; *inmodice* F; *immodice* BE; om. S

494 ACFG; *probilitatis* BE (corrected in B to *probitatis*, probably by B[1]); om. S

495 *et inmodice probitatis iuuenis* om. S

496 ABCFG (reading *Fergus* with tail on final *s* in ABG as *Fergus*); *Fergusius* ES

497 *Ferechad* AG; *Feraghad* S; *Ferehad* C; *Ferchad* F; *Ferchard* BE. In the genealogy of Alexander III (edited below, 183–7), which shows knowledge of the account of Scottish origins preserved in Fordun's Chronicle, we are told *Fergusius fuit filius Feredach quamuis a quibusdam dicitur filius Ferchere*; Diss also has *Feredach* for Fergus's father. It would appear, therefore, that the reading here was *Ferechad*, a metathesised miscopying of *Feredach*. Skene has *Ferechad*.

498 *Ferchardi* BF; *Farchardi* AEG; *Ferehardi* C; *Ferardi* S. Skene has *Farchardi*.

499 *prosapia regum* ABCEFG; *regum prosapia* S

500 ABCEFG; *genitus* S

501 *sc* followed by compendium for *et* in C; *s* FS; *silicet* ABEG

502 ABCEFG; *acephala* S

503 BCEFGS; *deiebat* A

504 ABEFGS; *uberrimam* C

505 *quod* add S

506 ACEFGS; *uobis* B (correction obscured by blotch).

507 ABCEFG; *actenus* S

508 ACFGS; om. BE

509 Skene has *radicis* (which he amended in his notes to *radices*: Skene, *John of Fordun's Chronicle*, 384).

510 *immanes* add S and B[1] interlineally.

511 BCEFS; om. AG

512 AEFGS; *accumulas* corrected to *accumulans* B; *accumilans* C

gatos e medio Pictorum Scotos accolas una cum hiis quos secum attuler{a}t[513] in occidentis[514] [515]insule locando finibus ibidem super eos regem primum se constituit.

Appendix: II. 12

A 25r–v; B 28r–v; C 21r–v; E 25v–26r; F XVr–v; G 18v–19r; H 27v; S 18v–19r

[516]De tempore quo Fergus[517] {filius}[518] Fer{e}chardi.[519] Capitulum 12^{m}

Ad hanc insulam Albion<is>[520] memoratus, adueniens Fergusius Scotorum primus rex in ea creatus est, quibus et ipse datis legibus et statutis ab occidentali quidem occeano[521] regnum et ab insulis usque dorsum Albanie[522] dilatans limites ibidem inter regna constituit nam orientalis[523] occeani regnum Picti coluerunt. De regni quoque[524] principio dicti regis et armis bellicis sic habetur:

Albion in terris rex primus germine Scotis,
Ipsorum turmis rubri tulit[525] arma leonis.
Fergusius fuluo Ferchard[526] rugientis in aruo[527]
Christum tricentis ter denis prefuit annis.

Hoc uero tempore uidelicet anno etatis quinte 255° magnus Alexander[528] patri Philippo[529] succedens anno regni sui postea[530] sexto Darium[531] regem Persarum

513 *attulerat* EF; *attulerit* ACGS; word crossed out in B and word ending *]lerat* added in margin by B^1. The pluperfect *attulerat* is clearly preferable to the future perfect *attulerit*. Skene has *attulerit*, but it is translated as a pluperfect by Felix Skene.

514 ACFGS; *occidentes* BE

515 add *in* BE

516 Title om. in B and added by B^1 (with *Fergusius* for *Fergus* and *Farchar* for *Ferechardi*).

517 *De tempore quo Fergus* ACEGH; *De tempore quo Fergusius* E; *De Fergusio* F; *Quando Fergus* S

518 CHS; om. AEFG

519 *Ferechardi* CES; *Ferchardi* AG; *Farchard* H; om. F, and has instead *primo Scotorum rege*.
E continues *regnare cepit*; H continues *electus est in regem Scotorum*; S continues *rex Scotorum primus in Scocia regnare cepit et armis eius bellicis*.

520 ABCEFGH; *Albionis* S. Only S is grammatically orthodox; perhaps, however, Albion was treated here by Fordun as undeclinable.

521 ABEFGHS; *oceano* C

522 ABCEFGS; *Albionis* H

523 ABCEFGH; *orientali* S

524 ABCEGHS; *quaque* F

525 ABCEGHS; *tenet* F

526 BCEFHS; *Ferchad* AG

527 Bower has added a paragraph here in S.

528 ABCFGHS; *Alaxander* E

529 ACEFGHS; *Phillippo* B; *regi Macedorum* add S

530 ABCEFGH; om. S

531 In both B and E a gap has originally been left where *sexto Darium* would have been; and in both cases a later hand (B^1 in B) has supplied the missing words.

interfecit atque Babiloniam optinuit[532] per idem itaque tempus apud[533] Romanos[534] Lucius Papir{i}us[535] dictator effectus adeo tunc ut ait Eutropius inter bellicosissimos urbis milites[536] habebatur ut cum[537] diceretur Alexandrum in Italiam[538] transgredi Romani inter ceteros[539] duces hunc eligerent precipue qui bellis sustineret impetum[540] Alexandri.[541]

Historia Beati Congalli.[542] Deinde post multum tempus uenit quidam[543] rex ex Hibernia nomine Fergus[544] filius Ferchard[545] regalem in Scocia secum deferens[546] cathedram [547]marmoreo[548] lapide decisam in qua[549] primus ibidem rex a Scotis coronatus est. Cuius exemplo succedentes postmodum in regno ceteri reges eadem cathedra rite coronam [550]susceperunt. Hanc quoque cathedram S{m}o{ }nbrec[551] ut supradictum est primus[552] attulit ad Hiberniam.[553]

Post cuius uero regumque quorundam aliorum decessum abnepos[554] eius Rether quem Beda Reudam uocat ad regimen regni Scotorum Albionencium[555] succedens sui regiminis temporibus indefesso[556] labore regionis[557] limites proten-

532 ABCEGHS; *obtinuit* F
533 ACGHS; om. BEF; added above line by B[1], and in E also added above line by later hand.
534 ABCEGHS; om. F
535 ABCEGH; *Papireus* FS
536 ABCEGHS (written in C over crossed-out word); *limites* F
537 ACEFGHS; om. B
538 *Italiam*, ACEFGHS; *Italeam* B
539 ABCEFGH; *eos* S
540 *sustineret impetum* ABCEFGH; *impetum sustineret* S
541 ABCEFGH; om. S
542 *Historia Beati Congalli* CFGHS; *Legenda Beati Congalli* E; om. AB (supplied by B[1])
543 BCEHS; *quidem* A; *quideim* G; final syllable ambiguous in F
544 *Fergus* ACFGS; *Fergusius* BEH. Skene has *Fergusius*.
545 *Ferchard* BEHS; *Ferchad* AG; *Ferechardi* C; *Ferchaddi* F. Skene has *Ferchad*.
546 *secum deferens* ABCEFGH; *postea ferens* S
547 *ma* add A (as separate word).
548 ACEFGHS; *marmorio* B
549 Originally *aqua* in E, altered to *qua*.
550 *acceperunt siue* add H
551 *Smo*[a]*nbrec* AEG; *Smo*[a]*nbr*[c] B; *Simo*[a]*nbrek* F; *Symonbrec* C; *Symonbrek* H; *Simon brek* S. Skene has *Smonbrec*. For discussion, see n. 378.
552 BCEFHS; om. AG
553 H terminates here.
554 BCFS; *ab nepos* AEG (in G the word-division coincides with a line-division)
555 ABCEFG; *Albionensium* S
556 ACFGS; *in defesso* BE
557 BCEFGS; *regiones* A

dere studuit nam et aliquas[558] Pictorum regni[559] partes adauxit[560] sollicitus[561] suo regno. Insuper nec arridentis ei tam felicis fortune[562] dono contentus, immo prorogandi regni fines auiditate nimia deditus apposuit eciam et ex terris Britonum quasdam[563] extremi limitis prouincias uersus boream sibi[564] dominio subiugare.

558 *regni* add F
559 ABCEG; om. FS
560 BCEFGS; *aduxit* A
561 BCEFHS; *solicitus* AG
562 BCEFHS; *fortunio* AG
563 BCEFHS; *quosdam* A; probably *quosdam* G, but the *os* has been disturbed.
564 ABCEFG; *suo* S

IV

THE SCOTTISH ORIGIN-LEGEND IN JOHN OF FORDUN'S *CHRONICA GENTIS SCOTTORUM*: ANALYSIS

Armed with a detailed account of the text as it is found in the manuscripts, it is now possible to embark on a study of the textual archaeology of the origin-legend material in Fordun's chronicle, focussing in the first instance on material derived from nameless sources. This will lead in the first instance to the identification of two lost accounts. In this chapter it will be shown that in one of these accounts Ireland was emphatically portrayed as the current homeland of *Scoti*. The other account will be discussed more fully after further lost accounts of Scottish origins have come to light following an analysis of passages attributed to *legenda Sancti Brandani* and *legenda* or *historia Sancti Congalli* in the next chapter.

The Scottish origin-legend in Fordun's Chronica *as far as the taking of Ireland*

As noted already,[1] there are three passages attributed to nameless sources (VIII.1, VIII.2, and VIII.4) which relate, in different ways, how Gaedel left Greece for Egypt and married Scota daughter of Pharaoh. Other key episodes have also been given three different treatments derived apparently from unnamed sources, such as Gaedel's departure from Egypt which is told in X.1, X.2 and also XIII.1; his journey from Egypt in XI.1, XI.2 and XI.3; and his arrival in Spain in XII.1, XII.2 and XIV.1. On the face of it, then, no fewer than three nameless accounts have been used. Some of these accounts would, of course, have been more elaborate and contained elements which were not present in others, as in the discovery of Ireland described in XV.

We will begin our attempt to disentangle this material by examining a key idea expressed in XV.c–f. In XV.c Gaedel is described reflecting on the relentless and unsustainable pressure his people were suffering, and he realises that these troubles were deserved because he had abandoned his original plan 'to obtain empty tracts, bringing trouble to no-one'.[2] He recognised that, by taking lands in Spain which were already inhabited, he was 'treating arrogantly what was divinely offered for other peoples'.[3] He decided (XV.d) 'to return, therefore, to the plan he

1 14, above. The fourth passage is attributed to *legenda Sancti Brandani*.

2 *uacuas nulli molestiam inferens acquirere*.

3 *insultans aliis diuinitus adhibitum populis*.

had previously drawn up in Egypt',[4] and directed sailors to search the ocean for some uninhabited land: in due course (XV.f), 'by favour of the Gods', they came upon an island (presumably Ireland: see below).[5] In XVII.1.a there is a clear echo of this concern to settle virgin territory. There we are told that Gaedel's sons Éber and 'Hymec' arrived on the island, and that 'Éber took it, not by force, but empty (as some people suppose), entirely without an inhabitant.'[6]

The original vow to look for uninhabited land takes us back to XI.1, which described how Gaedel and his followers left Egypt. Although there is possibly some ambiguity in XI.1.d about what they all swore to do,[7] their intention is made clear in XI.1.e where we are told that they prepared a fleet 'so that they might obtain for themselves new lands to settle in the outermost limits of the world, hitherto uninhabited (as they supposed)'.[8] This contrasts with XI.2.bc., where it is said that Gaedel headed west from Egypt because he knew the inhabitants there would be easy to overcome. The land anticipated as the ultimate goal in both XI.1 and XI.2 – whether empty or easily conquered – was evidently Ireland. Certainly it can not have been Spain: the stay of *Scoti* there – the only lengthy stopping-off point described before reaching Ireland – was never referred to as anything but a struggle (XIV.c.f, XV.ab, XX.2.a–c, XXI.1.b,[9] and XXI.2.bc).

The issue of whether Ireland was inhabited or not before the arrival of *Scoti* sheds particular light on the make-up of XVI, attributed in the chapter's rubric to *legenda Sancti Brandani*. In XVI.ab. Gaedel sees Ireland from *Brigancia* and directs some warlike youths to set off and explore it: they arrive, attack the inhabitants, and kill them.[10] In XVI.fg, however, Gaedel, addressing his sons on his death-bed, blames the unbearable adversity they have hitherto endured in Spain on the fact that they had not proceeded immediately to an uninhabited land after arriving in Spain and taken provisions on board, and had thus paid no heed to the just wishes of the gods (*iustis deorum uotis*); the gods, he goes on to declare (XVI.k), now offered them uninhabited Ireland as a settlement in freedom.

4 *ad preconceptum igitur in Egipto propositum intendens regredi.*

5 The only realistic alternative, presumably, would be Britain. Ireland appears as the island in question in all accounts of the legend, including the others which underlie Fordun's text. Moreover it is probable that XVII.6, where we are told how Éber (*Hiber*) gave his name to *Hibernia*, included material drawn from the same account as XVII.1: see below, 75.

6 *eam non ui sed uacuam ut quidam uolunt omni cultore carentem obtinuit.*

7 XI.1.d may be translated: 'by the advice of his elders he [Gaedel] on balance decreed indeed that either he would wrench from other peoples a kingdom or land – which would need to be inhabited perpetually by arms – or, with the gods favouring him, he would seek out at least uninhabited settlements which would be there for the taking; and this they all swore by common purpose to put duly into effect so far as they were able'.

8 *ut in extremis mundi finibus uelud opinantur adhuc uacuis nouas terras sibi colendas acquererent.*

9 Although this passage is generally more upbeat than the others, it is quite specific that the calm they enjoyed had been hard-won, saying that they enjoyed the 'tranquillity of peace for which he [one of Míl's ancestors] had contended for a long time' (*pacis tranquillitate pro qua diu certasset*).

10 As will be shown in the next chapter, this agrees with accounts elsewhere attributed to a St Brendan source or drawn from a source related to it.

Gaedel's speech, therefore, would appear to have been taken from a different source than *legenda Sancti Brandani*, and to have belonged originally to the same source as the other passages in which the ultimate goal of settling uninhabited land was a key feature (XI.1, XV, and XVII.1). Indeed, Gaedel's speech to his sons provides a natural bridge between XV, which finishes with Gaedel receiving news about the discovery of an uninhabited island, and XVII.1, in which Gaedel's sons set sail and occupy the empty island after hearing their father's words. The material in XVI drawn (ultimately) from *legenda Sancti Brandani* would seem, therefore, to have extended at most only as far as XVI.d: Gaedel's exhortation at that point that his sons 'should invade the aforesaid land by force'[11] would seem to imply that some resistance was expected.[12]

Another aspect of Fordun's account which repays close examination is the repeated migrations of *Scoti* from Spain to Ireland. In XV.ab and XVI.h–k the explanation given for why *Scoti* had to leave Spain is that they were faced with either annihilation or slavery at the hands of the Spaniards. Nevertheless, in XVII.1.b we are told that Éber returned to Spain, leaving the newly-conquered island to his brother 'Hymec'. In XXI.1 *Scoti* in Spain, this time led by three sons of Míl (a descendant of Gaedel),[13] are forced into another exodus, which concludes in XXI.2 with the immigrant *Scoti* subduing the natives (*indigeni*) they find in Ireland. Again, however, despite being told in XXI.2.bc that they left Spain because of their wretched circumstances, Éremón son of Míl is said to have returned to Spain (XXI.1.d), and *Scoti* are still to be found in Spain generations later when yet another expedition to Ireland is mounted, this time led by Simón Brecc, a descendant of Éremón (XXVI–XXVII). This pattern of returns to Spain – despite the explanation given each time for the necessity of leaving Spain – appears decidedly contrived. This could readily be explained, however, if each exodus originally represented a distinct account of how *Scoti* left Spain and settled Ireland, with a different person in each cast in the role of leading the expedition – Éber son of Gaedel, the sons of Míl, and Simón Brecc. The idea of arranging these into a chronological sequence could readily have been inspired by the appearance in the royal pedigree of Éber son of Gaedel, Míl and Simón Brecc – in the same order as Fordun's account of the colonisation of Ireland.[14] Moreover, the character described as returning from Ireland to Spain is in each case the ancestor in the genealogy of the leader(s) of the next expedition from Spain to Ireland.

John and Winifred MacQueen have argued, however, that there is no need to see these repeated invasions as being derived from different versions of the legend. They pointed out that in *Lebor Gabála* (and earlier in *Historia Brittonum*) Ireland is colonised in a series of invasions, and they suggested that 'Scottish tradition too, it might appear reasonable to assume, had preserved the idea of a series of

11 *ut predictam certamine terram inuaderent.*

12 In apparent contrast, XVI.d ends with Gaedel anticipating that his sons would enter the island 'without war or any risk whatever' (*quod sine bello uel quouis discrimine penetrare ualerent*). There is evidence, however, that a statement like this appeared in the exemplar of Fordun's *legenda Sancti Brandani*: see below, 110.

13 This is only stated explicitly in XXI.2 with reference to Partholón, who is identified in XXI.1 as a son of Míl: see below.

14 See below, 174–87, for texts of the royal genealogy.

invasions by kindred Gaelic-speaking peoples, whose immediate origin was Spanish.'[15] There is a crucial difference, however, between the repeated expeditions to Ireland described by Fordun and the series of invasions in *Lebor Gabála* cited by the MacQueens: Fordun's invaders are not linked by a remote common ancestor, as in the scheme in *Lebor Gabála*, but belong to the same line of descent. The scheme elaborated in *Lebor Gabála* did not, therefore, produce Fordun's awkward pattern of descendants of the eponymous Gaedel and Scota colonising Ireland by taking over a land already peopled by *Gaídil/Scoti*.[16] There was no requirement, therefore, in *Lebor Gabála* for conquering heroes to make an unconvincing return to Spain so that their descendant might lead a later expedition to Ireland. The closest parallel in Irish versions of the legend to what is found in Fordun's account is the second recension of *Lebor Gabála* in which two different accounts of the Egyptian episode were brought together – one with Nél father of Gaedel cast as leader and husband of Scota, the other with Míl in this role. This was achieved in the same way as I have suggested the different accounts in Fordun's text were stitched together: Nél appeared as Míl's ancestor in the pedigrees, so both Nél and, generations later, Míl, were made to go to Egypt and marry a daughter of Pharaoh called Scota.[17]

On closer examination, however, it would appear that Fordun's account has been composed by incorporating not just three versions of the exodus from Spain to Ireland – featuring Éber, the sons of Míl, and Símon Brecc – but a fourth as well, in which the expedition was led by yet another character: Partholón. As it stands, XXI contains two passages from different sources (XXI.1 and XXI.2) which both seem to describe the same exodus – that undertaken by three sons of Míl. A significant contradiction between the passages, however, serves to confirm that they originally belonged to different accounts. Among the reasons given in XXI.2 for the decision to migrate to Ireland was that they (*Scoti*) experienced 'fierce and frequent troubles from hostile Spaniards' (XXI.2.b):[18] in XXI.1 we are told, in contrast, that Míl's people 'at this time [the reign of Míl] enjoyed indeed the tranquillity of longed-for peace maintained by everyone round about' (XXI.1.b).[19] A more striking difference is in how the leadership of the migration is presented. In XXI.1 Éremón, Partholón and Éber, sons of Míl, take Ireland together; in XXI.2 Partholón alone is named and he holds Ireland 'as a perpetual possession for himself' (XXI.2.e).[20] No brothers of Partholón are alluded to in XXI.2, and his parentage is not actually stated: his association with Partholón son of Míl is only

15 MacQueen and MacQueen, *Scotichronicon*, I. xxv–xxvi (quotation at xxvi).

16 The only awareness of this difficulty in Fordun's account is shown in XXI.1.c, where Ireland prior to being colonised by Míl's sons is described as 'almost empty, although it was anciently settled by a few people also of the same lineage' (*pene uacuam licet paucis et ex eodem genere gentibus fuerat antiquitus incolata*). As will become apparent (77–8, below), XXI.1 can not convincingly be assigned to any particular nameless account which it might have shared with other passages.

17 As argued by Macalister in *LG*, II. 2–3.

18 *acerimas et crebras infestancium molestias Hispanorum.*

19 *desiderate uero pacis tranquillitate . . . per circuitum ab omnibus hoc tempore populus fruebatur.*

20 *in perpetuam sibi possessionem optinuit.*

implied because the passage follows XXI.1. The most fundamental difference between these passages, however, is that in XXI.1.a Míl is the ruler of *Scoti* in Spain and, as such, initiates the expedition to Ireland; in XXI.2.a Partholón is described unambiguously as Gaedel and Scota's successor in the leadership (*ducatus*).[21] It appears that XXI.2 has not, in fact, been taken from an account of the invasion by the sons of Míl, but from a version of the legend which gave the leading role to Partholón alone. Suspicion falls, therefore, on the only detail which links XXI.1 with XXI.2 – the notion that Míl had a son called Partholón. That this has been invented for a specific purpose seems all the more likely because although Míl's sons (in varying numbers) appear regularly in Irish accounts of the legend – and Éremón and Éber are always mentioned – not once is a Partholón named among them.[22] Partholón does regularly appear, however, as leader of the first post-diluvian colonisation of Ireland.[23] It would seem, therefore, that the contention in XXI.1 that Partholón was a son of Míl was simply a device designed to bind an independent account featuring Partholón into the chronological scheme adopted for the accounts featuring Éber son of Gaedel, the sons of Míl, and Simón Brecc. Unlike Éber, Míl and Simón Brecc, Partholón (or any name like it) did not appear in the royal genealogy, hence, no doubt, the need to resort to another way of fitting Partholón son of Míl into the scheme.

Of these four invasions of Ireland from Spain, three appear in passages which can be attributed to nameless accounts – namely those led by Éber son of Gaedel; Éremón and Éber sons of Míl; and Partholón. The account of the fourth invasion led by Simón Brecc (XXVII) is attributed in the text to *historia Sancti Congalli* (XXVI.d). Nevertheless, as the MacQueens have pointed out, not all of XXVII has been derived from that source.[24] XXVII.e–k is concerned with the stone throne which Simón Brecc brought with him from Spain, beginning with a brief statement of its origins according to what 'some people say' (XXVII.e), followed by an involved story told by 'others also' (XXVII.f–h) concerning Simón's discovery of the stone in the sea near the Irish coast.[25] There is then a prophecy in verse

21 It may also be noted that the clear statement of Gaedel and Scota as Partholón's ancestors in XXI.2.a contrasts with the rather vague explanation of Míl's antecedents in XXI.1.a where we are told how 'one of his [Míl's] ancestors had procured for himself and his peoples an unoccupied dwelling-place, in freedom' (*cuius antecessorum quidam sibi suisque gentibus cum libertate sedem mansionis acquesiuit liberam*).

22 See, for instance, Carey, *Irish National Origin-Legend*, 10 (and n.18 for references), and discussion in Kelleher, 'The pre-Norman Irish genealogies'.

23 *Partholón* is a Gaelic form of Latin *Bartholomeus*, which was apparently interpreted as 'the son of the one who holds up the waters', hence his role as first settler after the Flood: see Meyer, 'Partholón mac Sera'; Carey, 'The Irish vision of the Chinese'; and Carey, *Irish National Origin-Legend*, 5–8, esp. 8.

24 MacQueen and MacQueen, *Scotichronicon*, I. 145.

25 The MacQueens (ibid.) suggested that XXVII.e has been derived from their 'chronicle-source A', and they divided XXVII.f–h into two: XXVII.f–g from 'chronicle-source B' and XXVII.h 'less plausibly' from 'chronicle-source C', on the strength of the phrase 'as is upheld by writings' (*sicut scriptis asseritur*) in XXVII.h – although this phrase is notably less specific than the others, and reads more like a general appeal to written authority (hence, no doubt, the MacQueens' reservations about attributing XXVII.h to their chronicle-source C).

(XXVII.ij, possibly belonging to the same account as XXVII.f–h, which finishes with a reference to this prophecy), and a passage about the prophecy attributed to 'popular opinion' (*uulgaris . . . opinio*) (XXVII.k). This is followed, finally, by a tail-piece on the mixed Greek and Egyptian origins of *Scoti* (XXVII.l–n). At the very least, therefore, it would appear that a nameless source apart from *historia Sancti Congalli* has been used to supply an alternative account of how Simón acquired the stone throne.[26]

I mentioned earlier how passages from three different nameless sources are given for a number of key episodes in Fordun's account, such as how Gaedel left Greece for Egypt and married Scota daughter of Pharaoh, Gaedel's departure from Egypt, his journey from Egypt, and his arrival in Spain. As far as the migration of *Scoti* to Ireland was concerned, however, it appears that four nameless accounts have been used which each featured different leaders of the exodus – Éber son of Gaedel, Éber and Éremón sons of Míl, Partholón, and also Simón Brecc (in the material in XXVII following the passage attributed to *historia Sancti Congalli*). All we can note at this juncture are two possible explanations: either there was a fourth nameless account which may have begun with Simón Brecc, or Simón Brecc was featured in one of the other nameless accounts which therefore included not one but two expeditions from Spain to Ireland. Leaving aside for the moment the nameless source for Simón Brecc, I will refer for convenience to the other putative accounts respectively as the 'Éber', 'sons of Míl' and 'Partholón' accounts. I have also argued that these have been stitched together using the royal genealogy as a chronological framework, with the result that the exodus from Spain to Ireland was led by a figure in the royal genealogy who had to return to Spain to ensure that his lineal descendant could lead the next exodus. In the case of Partholón, who did not appear in the royal genealogy, he was made out to be a son of Míl. The account of Scottish origins in Fordun's *Chronica Gentis Scottorum* can thus be recognised as a deft attempt to bring together a number of conflicting versions of the legend.[27]

26 The MacQueens have suggested that the phrase *ut docent cronice*, 'as chronicles teach', in XXVI.a could indicate that XXVI as a whole (including therefore some material on Simón Brecc) may be assigned 'probably' to their chronicle-sources A and B and 'possibly' also chronicle-source C (MacQueen and MacQueen, *Scotichronicon*, I. 139: see also xxiii): they have carefully not included it, however, in their listing of passages drawn from these sources (ibid., xxiv). This chapter serves to introduce Simón Brecc and his invasion, synchronising Simón with kings of Rome and Judea (XXVI.b) and giving an account of Simón's pedigree (XXVI.c). The only respect with which XXVI could be said to duplicate XXVII or provide an alternative account is in the notice of Simón's invasion given in XXVI.a, which seems simply to help introduce Simón by anticipating what is told in detail subsequently. I would suggest, therefore, that XXVI is the work of the synthesist (on whom see further, below, 72–3): indeed, Simón's pedigree may represent a fragment of the text of the royal genealogy which provided the chronological framework for the synthesis of origin-legend accounts.

27 It follows from this that a description of a return to Spain by a conquering hero (XVII.1.b and XXI.1.d), or a sentence linking different invasions of Ireland (XX.1) or alluding to a previous settlement of *Scoti* in Ireland (XXI.1.c at end, from *licet paucis*) are unlikely to have been derived from a nameless account.

The settlement of Scoti *in Scotland*

It might be expected that the synthesis included some account of how *Scoti* reached Scotland itself. In Fordun's account this again took the form of a number of migrations. In XXVIII Eochaid *Rothay* was said to have been the first leader of *Scoti* who had spread into *insulas Albionis*, which were previously uninhabited. He was a great-grandson of Simón Brecc, and we are told that he gave his name to the island of Rothesay (which was also known as Bute from St Brendan's cell or *bothe* there). In XXIX there are three different accounts of Pictish origins, followed in XXX by Bede's account of womanless Picts arriving in Ireland and taking *Scoti* as their wives before moving to settle in Scotland. In XXXI we are told that *Scoti* first arrived in (mainland) Scotland because the wives of the Picts were followed from Ireland by their kin; the Picts eventually became fearful of the growing number of *Scoti* in their midst and banished them. After a couple of chapters on heathen gods, the account resumes in XXXIV in which the banished *Scoti*, 'wandering rulerless through the remote wastelands of Albion' (XXXIV.c),[28] came to the attention of Fergus son of *Ferechad* or Ferchar,[29] an ambitious youth of the ancient royal lineage, who was greatly angered to hear of their plight and resolved to become their first king, establishing a kingdom in the west of Albion. Book I closes with an inconclusive discussion of whether Picts or *Scoti* were the first to inhabit Scotland, and the history of the kingdom established by Fergus son of Ferchar is not resumed until book II, chapter XII. There we are told that Fergus arrived in 330 BC and (in an extract attributed to *historia beati Congalli*) that he brought with him the stone throne of Simón Brecc which was used thereafter in the coronation of Scottish kings; in due course Fergus was succeeded by his descendant *Rether*, equated with Bede's *Reuda*, who (according to Bede) brought *Scoti* from Ireland to Argyll. The next chapter continued by explaining that *Rether* aimed to expand his kingdom and recruited men from Ireland, described as a 'second coming of *Scoti* from Ireland to Alba'.[30] In book II chapter XLV, however, we are told that this first kingdom of *Scoti* in Scotland came to grief, overwhelmed in AD 360 by Britons and Picts led by the tyrant Maximus; *Eugenius* king of *Scoti* was killed and his brother and nephew, Eochaid and Erc, fled to Ireland with many *Scoti*. But in the opening chapters of book III we are informed that this reverse was righted by Fergus son of Erc (and grandson of Eochaid) who returned from Ireland in AD 403 and in three years restored the kingdom of *Scoti* in Scotland extending in the west from Stainmore to the Orkneys. We are also told that he reigned sixteen years, and for three years was the first king of *Scoti* to rule beyond Drumalban in the land of the Picts as far as the North Sea.

Unlike the exodus of *Scoti* to Ireland, there are few instances here in which different accounts of the same episode have been juxtaposed[31] or in which

28 *absque rectore per Albionis uastas uagando solitudines.*

29 For the variation in the patronymic of Fergus, see below, 104–5.

30 *secundus ex Hibernia Scotorum aduentus ad Albaniam.*

31 John and Winifred MacQueen tentatively assigned the three accounts of Pictish origins in XXIX to their chronicle-sources A, B, and C (MacQueen and MacQueen, *Scotichronicon*, I. 148).

significant contradictions in detail may be noted.[32] It is not so obvious, therefore, that this part of Fordun's chronicle represents a synthesis of a number of independent versions of the legend beginning with Gaedel and Scota; rather, it would appear to have been constructed from short accounts such as the story of *Reuda* in Bede's *Historia Ecclesiastica* and the legend of the Stone of Scone attributed to *historia* or *legenda Sancti Congalli* which featured Fergus son of Ferchar. The same method can be observed, however, of organising diverse material into a series of expeditions according to the chronology of the royal genealogy. Fergus son of Erc not only appeared in all texts of the royal genealogy but was also the first king of *Scoti* in king-lists current in Scotland in the twelfth and thirteenth centuries.[33] Eochaid *Rothay*, for his part, can be found in some copies of the Scottish royal pedigree.[34] The synthesist had to work much harder to place *Reuda* and Fergus son of Ferchar. *Reuda* in fact would seem to have been an earlier form of Eochaid Riata,[35] but the synthesist was evidently unaware of this and searched for a name which looked like *Reuda*. He settled for *Rether*, a rendering of Rothrir in some copies of the genealogy, twenty-nine generations earlier than Fergus son of Erc and twenty-one generations after Eochaid *Rothay*.[36] Fergus son of Ferchar must have posed a still greater challenge.[37] In the same copies of the genealogy a space-filling ancestor of Fergus son of Erc called Forgg mac Feredaig,[38] great-great-grandfather of Rothrir (*Rether*), was rendered (in the genitive) *Forgso filii Feredach*. The synthesist evidently seized on this[39] and equated the name with Fergus son of Ferchar, whom he introduced in XXXIV as *filius Ferechad siue Farchardi*: we may wonder if in the synthesist's copy of the royal genealogy *Feredach* had become *Ferechad* by metathesis. The net result was a sequence of four settlements led respectively by Eochaid *Rothay*, Fergus son of Ferchar, *Reuda*/*Rether*, and finally Fergus son of Erc. A more sophisticated approach has been adopted, however, than simply bringing each back to Ireland to become the ancestor of the next settlement. This was no doubt because of the crucial issue of how to reconcile two claimants to the role of first king of *Scoti* in Scotland – Fergus son of Ferchar by virtue of bringing the royal inaugural throne to Scotland, and Fergus son of Erc, first king of *Scoti* according to the king-list. The solution was to create the expulsion of *Scoti* from Scotland *c.*AD 360, thereby enabling Fergus son

32 Confusion about the extent of the kingdom ruled by Fergus son of Erc is one example: see below, 116–17.

33 See below, 146–57.

34 See below, 186 n. 197.

35 Also known as Coirpre Rígfota: see below, 182.

36 For text, see below, 186.

37 Could the name originally have been Fergus Fogae son of Froechar Fortrén, who was regarded in literary sources as the last king of Ulaid in Emain Macha, and who appears in genealogies of Dál nAraide (*CGH*, I. 324–5), the people to whom St Comgall of Bangor belonged? (This is not to say that Fergus Fogae was ever presented as an ancestor of Comgall himself; for Comgall's pedigree see Ó Riain, *Corpus*, 16.)

38 *CGH*, I. 329. Other forms of Forgg are Fuirgg and Forggo; cf. ibid., 657.

39 *Forgso* suggests Forgus rather than Forgg: perhaps the synthesist was aware of this. The text of the genealogy in the 'Poppleton collection', which preserves Gaelic orthography from a Scottish exemplar (see below, 178), has *Forgo* (Anderson, *Kings and Kingship*, 257). *Forgso*, therefore, would appear to be an error.

of Erc to re-establish the kingdom and thus justify his place as the first in the series of Scottish kings up to the present. Eochaid *Rothay* has a curious history: he was, it seems, created accidentally in a twelfth-century version of the royal genealogy[40] when *Echdach Buadaig* (genitive of Eochaid Buadach) was mistranscribed as *Echdach Rothai*.[41] It is possible that the synthesist himself noticed the coincidence between *Rothai* and Rothesay (which he plausibly interpreted as 'island of *Rothay*'),[42] and that this association with one of Scotland's west-coast islands, when combined with his genealogical position as supposed ancestor of Fergus son of Ferchar, was enough to inspire the synthesist to cast Eochaid in the role of leader of a colony of the western islands alone. Because Eochaid was kept off the mainland it would appear that he was deemed not to compromise the portrayal of Fergus son of Ferchar as first king of *Scoti* in Scotland itself.[43] As for *Rether/Reuda*, the claim that he brought a second wave of *Scoti* from Ireland as reinforcements would have served to satisfy Bede's description of him as leader of *Scoti* into territories won from the Picts.

The overall result is an even more impressive harmonisation of different accounts within a single narrative thread than was achieved when dealing with the colonisation of Ireland by *Scoti* from Spain. There can be little doubt that the synthesis also included other key texts relating to Scotland's early history. The role of the tyrant Maximus in the expulsion of *Scoti* in *c*.360, for instance, was taken from a pro-Scottish rewriting of material from Geoffrey of Monmouth's *Historia Regum Britannie* which John and Winifred MacQueen have convincingly identified as the principal source for book II.[44] The expulsion, moreover, is followed by an account of how Regulus brought St Andrew's relics to Scotland which has been derived from the longer version of the St Andrews foundation-legend.[45] Only the first part of the legend was included here, however; the latter part was placed in the ninth century.[46] This division of the foundation-legend solved a chronological contradiction which would have become apparent on acquaintance with Pictish and English king-lists: the legend dated the arrival of Regulus to the mid-fourth century, but at the same time featured kings who must have reigned centuries later. These kings were named as the Pictish 'Hungus *filius* Forguso' and his English foe Æthelstan. There were two Pictish kings with both this forename and patronymic (Onuist/Oengus son of Uurguist/Fergusso) who reigned (in real life) 729–61 and

40 The version's distinctive feature is that it departed significantly from Gaelic orthographical conventions; see below, 180–1.

41 See below, 179, 186 n. 197.

42 XXVIII.c: the final syllable is Old Norse *ey*, 'island'.

43 This suggests that the author did not regard the islands as part of Scotland. In the account in the Chronicle of Melrose of the negotiations of 1265–6 leading up to the cession of the western islands by Norway to Scotland, the islands were described as 'lying around the full kingdom (*ampla regio*) of the Scots': Anderson, Anderson and Dickinson, *The Chronicle of Melrose*, 128. See Broun, 'Defining Scotland and the Scots', 7 and n. 15 for discussion.

44 MacQueen and MacQueen, *Scotichronicon*, I. xxviii–xxix.

45 Skene, *Chronicles*, 183–93; Anderson, 'St Andrews', 7–9, 10–13 (where this version is designated 'Version B'). A new edition, with a translation, is being produced by Dr Simon Taylor of the St Andrews Scottish Studies Institute, University of St Andrews.

46 See Broun, 'The birth', 15–20, esp. 18 for discussion.

820–34 respectively. The nearest Æthelstan contemporary with either of these was the eldest son of Æthelwulf (king of Wessex 839–56) who predeceased his father but ruled parts of southern England under him. This Æthelstan was duly pressed into service as the opponent of 'Hungus' (perhaps without realising that Æthelstan actually outlived King Onuist who was supposed in the legend to have slain him).[47] This careful attempt to resolve contradictions may no doubt be recognised as the work of the synthesist, in particular the determination to achieve chronological coherence based on a given framework such as a genealogy or (in this case) a king-list.

It remains to explain, however, why the exile of *Scoti* from Scotland was dated to between *c.*360 and 403. These dates are found nowhere else and, indeed, appear to be rather eccentric: Fergus son of Erc would have flourished in the mid-sixth century (according to king-lists current in Scotland), while in the 'Annals of Tigernach' his advent and death appear *c.*500. Some effort, moreover, has been expended in extending the succession of kings in an attempt to make the early date of 403 carry conviction. In comparison with texts of the king-list current in Scotland in the twelfth and thirteenth centuries, Fordun's *Chronica Gentis Scottorum* has three additional kings (*Eugenius* son of Fergus Mór, 419–52, *Constantius*, another son of Fergus, 457–79, and *Eugenius/Eochodius* son of Comgall, 538–58), as well as an increase in the the duration of the reign of Fergus son of Erc from three years to sixteen (403–19). Where, then, has the all-important date of 403 come from? The answer can be found in *summae annorum* supplied in king-lists. It would appear that the archetype of Marjorie Anderson's X-group of lists gave 506 as the total number of years between the advent of Cinaed mac Alpín and the death of William I in 1214; the archetype of the principal list used in *Chronica Gentis Scottorum* apparently stated that the total number of years from Fergus son of Erc up to Cinaed's father Alpín was 305. This makes for a straightforward calculation: 506 + 305 = 811, so Fergus son of Erc would have begun to reign 811 years before AD 1214, which is AD 403. It has been suggested plausibly that the appeal of this date may have been because it placed the origins of the current unbroken succession of Scottish kings earlier than the arrival of the English in Britain.[48]

Fordun's source for his account of Scottish origins

It would appear, therefore, that the synthesis involved more than just differing accounts of Scottish origins, and amounted to a significant proportion of *Chronica Gentis Scottorum* as far as the part of the St Andrews foundation-legend placed in the ninth century and the Pictish king-list which precedes it (book IV, chapters 9 to 14). There are two considerations, however which suggest that John of Fordun himself was not the synthesist. First, there is a reference to the expulsion of *Scoti* in the mid-fourth century in one of the drafts prepared by Scottish procurators at the curia in 1301 (a version of the so-called 'Instructions' drawn up in response to English claims to sovereignty over Scotland presented to the pope earlier that

47 Anderson, 'St Andrews', 8.

48 MacQueen and MacQueen, *Scotichronicon*, I. 381.

year).[49] It can be shown that this reference betrays a knowledge of the synthesist's special treatment of Fergus son of Erc; it can also be inferred from this reference that much of the structure of *Chronica Gentis Scottorum*, from at least Eochaid *Rothay* to the ninth-century Pictish king who vanquished Æthelstan, was already in existence.[50] If the synthesis was written in or before 1301, then Fordun (who was certainly still alive in 1371) could not have been its author.[51]

Second, there is a striking piece of chronological nonsense in book V, chapter 50. This chapter consists of the genealogy of David I,[52] in which David's descent is traced back through his father to Noah, with sections omitted which it was claimed had been given earlier in the chronicle.[53] The genealogy is also interrupted by two notes: one about Gaedel Glas, the other about the first inhabitant of the Scottish islands. This last should, of course, have referred to Eochaid *Rothay*. Fordun, however, has selected an ancestor of Simón Brecc who appears in the genealogy in XXVI.c as *Rothotha*[54] twelve generations after Míl Espáine and nine before Simón Brecc. This makes a nonsense of the chronology established by the synthesist. Fordun's only concern would appear to have been the possibility of finding a more ancient eponym for Rothesay than Eochaid *Rothay*, and therefore an earlier date for the first *Scoti* within the bounds of the Scottish kingdom (as established in Fordun's lifetime).[55] Not all medieval authors were sensitive to chronological absurdities, but the synthesist certainly was. It is difficult on this evidence, therefore, to accept that Fordun and the synthesist could be one-and-the-same person. This would suggest that Fordun himself did little more than copy the origin-legend material under discussion, which had already been composed by the synthesist by 1301.

49 See Goldstein, 'The Scottish mission to Boniface VIII', and Shead, Stevenson and Watt, *Scotichronicon*, VI. 260–3.

50 Broun, 'The birth', 15–21.

51 For the dating of Fordun's *Chronica* to 1371x7 see Broun, 'A new look'.

52 See below, 180.

53 One of the omissions is between Fergus son of Ferchar and Simón Brecc which we are told appeared in book I chapter 26: book I chapter 26, however, has the section between Simón Brecc and Míl Espáine

54 The name is *Rothotha* in Diss's text of the royal genealogy, and as *Rodchada* in the text of the royal genealogy in the 'Poppleton' compilation. In Irish texts it appears as *Rothechtada* or *Rechtada*. See below, 179, 186 n. 197.

55 Skene argued (*Johannis de Fordun Chronica*, xxxiii) that V.50 was a later addition (partly because he thought that **D** represented an earlier version of the chronicle, which it is clear that it does not; see Broun, 'A new look'). A unique feature of **D** is the omission of chapters 50–52 (all of which are genealogical). Donald Watt has pointed out to me, however, that the list of chapters at the beginning of **D** includes chapters 50–52. It is apparent, moreover, that the scribe of **D** (or its archetype) was not interested in genealogy: he has omitted the copy of the royal genealogy which appears during the account of Alexander III's inauguration in all other manuscripts (including **I**, the close relative of **D**). There can be no doubt, therefore, that the genealogy of David I in V.50 was part of the archetype of Fordun's text.

Reconstructing the 'Éber' and 'Partholón' accounts as far as the settlement of Scoti *in Ireland*

Can any of the nameless sources for Scottish origins used in the synthesis be disentangled from the others, at least up to the taking of Ireland? The one which can most readily be pieced together is the 'Éber' account. A distinctive feature that unites some passages, which I have discussed already,[55a] is that Ireland was uninhabited before the arrival of *Scoti*, an idea denied in other passages (to whose number XXI.1.c and XXI.2.e can be added). This suggests that XI.1, XV, XVI.e–l and XVII.1.a (the taking of Ireland by Éber son of Gaedel) were drawn from the same source (which I have designated the 'Éber' account). Other passages can be added to this if we turn first to XI.1. The reference in XI.1.a to Gaedel's being set up as king 'by the banished nobles of both peoples' (*ab expulsis utriusque gentis nobilibus*) is evidently connected with X.1 which described (X.1.c) how the Egyptian peasants (*pagenses*) 'cruelly drove out from among them all the nobles of the Greeks as well as those of the Egyptians which the devouring sea had not swallowed up'[56] along with Pharoah in pursuit of the Israelites. In contrast to the peasant *versus* noble opposition in X.1, Gaedel's expulsion is presented in X.2 in terms of an Egyptian rising against Gaedel as a foreigner; in XIII.1 the departure from Egypt was explained in yet another way, in terms of a flight in terror by both Greeks and Egyptians from the biblical plagues.[57]

This leaves the 'Éber' account needing one of the nameless passages in VIII. The vital clue is the explanation in XI.1.c that Gaedel was unable to return to Greece 'on account of wicked deeds which he had done there earlier'.[58] This presumably referred either to VIII.1, which described how Gaedel was driven out of his father's kingdom because of his many cruel misdeeds (*horrenda crudelitate*) and insolence, or to VIII.4 in which the expulsion of Gaedel from Greece was attributed to his attempt to usurp the kingdom and tyrannise its inhabitants. In VIII.4.b, however, it is said that Gaedel 'strove together with King Pharaoh to keep the Children of Israel in perpetual bondage',[59] which does not tally with X.1.b in which we are told that Gaedel, 'not wishing to pursue the inoffensive Hebrews',[60]

[55a] Above, 63–5.

[56] *cunctos itaque Grecorum pariter et Egipciorum nobiles quos nequaquam uorax absorbuit pelagus . . . crudeliter a se propulerunt.*

[57] This passage is unusual, however, for acknowledging a difference in detail with previous passages (*non solum humano metu sicut superius expremitur sed pocius timore diuino*, 'not only through fear of men, as described above, but rather from divine terror').

[58] *ob perpetrata prius ibidem scelera.*

[59] *cum rege Pharaone iunctus filios Israel unacum Egiptiis nisus est in seruitutem perpetuam tenere.*

[60] *insontes Hebreos {n}olentem persequi*: see note on *nolentem* in the edition (above, 37 n. 61) where it is argued that *nolentem* is preferable to *uolentem* if (as is suggested by the context) this is meant to explain why Gaedel was still in Egypt when Pharaoh died and could thus be expelled by Egyptian peasants. MacQueen and MacQueen, *Scotichronicon*, I. 30–1, followed **S** in reading *uolentem* (without noting the alternative *nolentem*) and they translated the passage accordingly, commenting that Gaedel 'presumably intended to use a land-route in pursuit of the escaped Children of Israel'

stayed behind while Pharaoh and his army chased after the Israelites. VIII.1, rather than VIII.4, may thus be assigned to the 'Éber' account.

The 'Éber' account, therefore, can be identified as the source of VIII.1, X.1, XI.1, XV, XVI.e–l and XVII.1.a. It would seem also to have been the source of XIV.1, which is the only passage from a nameless source apart from XV to identify *Brigancia* as the home of *Scoti* in Spain.[61] In outline, then, the 'Éber' account would have told how Gaedel, allowed no authority in his father's kingdom, caused trouble and was driven out, landing in Egypt where he married Scota daughter of Pharaoh; following Pharoah's death in the Red Sea, Gaedel, along with Greek and Egyptian nobles, was driven out of Egypt 'by a servile insurrection' (*seruili tumultu*) of peasants; Gaedel was made king by the expelled nobles of both peoples, and they set sail, vowing to seek out uninhabited land to settle; they landed in Spain, fought off the natives, and Gaedel built a fortified town (*opidum*) called Brigancia with an exceedingly high tower in it; continual warfare against the powerful Spaniards, however, caused Gaedel to realise that his people faced only death or slavery, and he decided to resort to his original plan to seek out uninhabited land; he directed sailors to explore the ocean, who discovered 'a most beautiful tract of land';[62] Gaedel, at death's door, exhorted his sons to take this uninhabited land, and Éber duly colonised it.[63]

The possibility should be left open at this stage that material drawn from the 'Éber' account may in due course be identified relating to the settlement of *Scoti* in Scotland.[64] One passage which has probably been developed from the 'Éber' account (among others) is XVII.6 (introduced as *ex cronicis*, 'from chronicles'). It is told there how Éber left his name on *mare Hibericum* due to his travels between Spain and the island he had colonised, and how the island was called *Hibernia* either from him or the sea which bore his name. The prominence given to Éber suggests a relationship with the only nameless account which featured Éber as leading the exodus from Spain.[65]

(ibid., 117), but without explaining why Gaedel had not therefore set off at the same time as Pharaoh.

61 It also supplies a link in the narrative between XI.1 and XV. The MacQueens have suggested that XI.1 may have been followed immediately by XI.3, which is plausible simply in terms of how the passages read: it is not readily apparent, however, why, if both were derived from the same account, they have been divided rather than given *en bloc*.

62 XV.g: *quadam plaga terre pulcherima.*

63 Éber's brother *Hymec* – whose name is quite unlike anyone in Irish versions of the legend – has presumably been invented by the synthesist in order to enable Éber to return to Spain without seeming to give up the settlement his father had urged him to establish. The MacQueens suggested that it may have originated as *Hemir*, a possible spelling of Éber, and become *Hymec* as a result of misreading and misunderstanding (MacQueen and MacQueen, *Scotichronicon*, I. 124).

64 It will be argued below (115–16) that other passages include XXVII.fg (if not XXVII.h as well) and XXVII.l–n; and also material on Fergus son of Ferchar in XXXIV, and therefore the unattributed material on the arrival of the Picts and the first colony of *Scoti* in Scotland in XXIX and XXXI on which XXXIV depends.

65 Additional evidence to support this view will be identified in the next chapter (as will further confirmation that the island settled by Éber was, indeed, Ireland).

The next nameless source which may be pieced together is what I have designated the 'Partholón' account. The desperate plight of *Scoti* described in XXI.2 is closely paralleled by their miserable condition portrayed in XX.2. In particular, the detail in XXI.2.c that they wished to escape from the barren soil they possessed in misery 'among those who regarded them as the vilest of men'[66] matches XX.2.c in which *Scoti* are described 'living in forests and hidden places',[67] dependent on plundering their neighbours 'on account of which they were hated exceedingly by the peoples around them on all sides'.[68] This contrasts with the peace and freedom which they are said to have enjoyed in XXI.1.ab. It may also be noted that the departure from Spain via the Gallic Sea (XXI.2.d) makes sense following the siting of their settlement in the Pyrenees (XX.2.b).

Another pair of passages which appear to be linked are XII.1 and XI.2. In XII.1.a Gaedel is described as 'wandering through many provinces',[69] halting in various places 'because he knew that the people he led, burdened with wives and children and much baggage, were distressed beyond measure'.[70] Evidently an arduous trek across country was intended.[71] Only one of the passages relating to Gaedel's departure from Egypt, XI.2, does not specify that he left by sea.[72] Another detail in XI.2 appears to be a specific reference to an earlier passage: it is explained that Gaedel was reluctant to return to his native land 'on account of old emnities' (*propter ueteres inimicicias*). This presumably referred to VIII.4, which told how Gaedel arrived in Egypt after being expelled from his native land because its inhabitants feared his tyranny.[73] In contrast, Gaedel's departure from his homeland is presented in VIII.2 in positive terms as someone sent abroad to assist an ally. VIII.4, in turn, appears to be linked to X.2. Its thoroughly unflattering depiction of Gaedel as a power-hungry opportunist finishes with Gaedel's hoping that his marriage to Pharaoh's only daughter, Scota, would make him Pharoah's successor to the kingdom of Egypt. X.2 opens with the prospect of Gaedel's accession which, as in VIII.4, is only denied by his prospective subjects' rising against him because they feared tyranny.[74] Finally, if XI.2 and VIII.4 were derived from the same source, and VIII.4 and X.2 likewise, this would mean that X.2

66 *inter quos . . . qui eos tamquam hominum uilissimos reputabant.*

67 *siluis degens et abditis.*

68 *propter quod a circumsitis undique populis maxime detestatus.*

69 *prouinciis pluribus peruagatis.*

70 *quia populum quem duxit mulieribus ac paruulis multisque sarcinis oneratum ultra modum uexari nouerat.*

71 It may be noted, however, that the entry into Africa *per Ansaga flumen* could suggest travel by water. The River Amsiga (according to Isidore) represented a boundary of Numidia, one of the provinces of Africa; Lindsay, *Isidori*, XIV. 5 (see also MacQueen and MacQueen, *Scotichronicon*, I. 119).

72 Moreover, in XI.2.b it is explained that Gaedel sought to take his people *ubi nouerat et pauciores et minus bellicosos habitare populos cum quibus congredi necesse fuerit, hominibus armis minus doctis*, 'where he knew the inhabitants with whom he would have to contend were both fewer and less warlike – his men being not at all trained in arms', which matches the rather bedraggled followers described in XII.1.

73 VIII.1 is ruled out because it evidently belonged to the 'Éber' account: see above, 74–5.

74 In X.2.b they specifically feared the consequences of *iugo tirannidis aliene semel submissus*, 'submission once under the yoke of foreign tyranny'.

should be linked to XI.2: the beginning of XI.2 does, indeed, seem to follow naturally from the last sentence in X.2, and the description of Gaedel's departure in X.2 is consistent with his being accompanied by only a few men untrained in warfare in XI.2.

It is possible, therefore, to identify specific details that suggest that VIII.4, X.2, XI.2, and XII.1 were derived from the same account.[75] It is also apparent that XX.2 and XXI.2 shared a source. Unfortunately there are no points of narrative detail which specifically link XX.2 and XXI.2 with VIII.4, X.2, XI.2, and XII.1, but there are some distinctive elements which appear in both groups. There is a particular emphasis on the discomfort and/or vulnerability of *Scoti* in their travels in XI.2 and XII.1 as well as XX.2 and XXI.2; there is also a particular interest in geography (the nearest parallel elsewhere in this material is the mention of *Brigancia* in XIV.1 and XV) as well as on time spent – forty years traversing Africa, 240 years in Spain: these features may serve especially to link XII.1 with XX.2.

A number of detailed considerations can be assembled, therefore, which suggests that VIII.4, X.2, XI.2, XII.1, XX.2 and XXI.2 have been derived from what I have designated the 'Partholón' account. This account then would have told (in outline) how Gaedel grandson of Nimrod was expelled from his native land because of his tyrannous designs, and ended up eventually in Egypt where he assisted Pharaoh in keeping the Israelites enslaved and married Pharaoh's only daughter with a view to succeeding to the kingdom; following Pharaoh's death on the Red Sea, however, the Egyptians forced him out in case he became king; with his wife and retainers he set off westward where he knew the inhabitants were fewer and less warlike, and trekked wearily across Africa for forty years until, embarking on some ships they found, they landed in Spain near the islands of Cadiz; for 240 years they lived wretchedly in Spain, continually harrassed by the Spaniards who had left them only waste and forest in the Pyrenees to live in; they were finally led from their misery by Partholón across the Gallic Sea to Ireland which he obtained as a perpetual possession for himself after conquering the natives. Whether any more of Fordun's text can be attributed to the 'Partholón' account will be discussed later.

The remaining passages, unfortunately, do not furnish any details that would allow them to be identified positively as sharing a common source. As far as VIII.2, XIII.1, XI.3 and XII.2 are concerned they could only be deemed to derive from a single account by a process of elimination. If combined in that order, they would produce a narrative which told how Gaedel was sent by his father Nél to help his ally Pharaoh against the Ethiopians, after which Gaedel married Scota, Pharaoh's only daughter, to cement the alliance (VIII.2); the plagues visited on Egypt caused general flight and panic (XIII.1); Gaedel, his wife, *familia*, 'and the rest of the leaders', were brought to ships which had been made ready, and they departed westward on the Mediterranean Sea (XI.3); and after ranging hither and thither and suffering various dangers, they arrived unexpectedly in Spain just as they were running out of provisions (XII.2). There is a problem, however, about which taking of Ireland to attribute to such an account: either the passage in which

75 Note also the use of *suis* for 'his [Gaedel's] people' shared only by X.2.b, XI.2.a, and XII.1.b.

one of Míl's ancestors had found a place to live which was, however, too cramped, so that Míl sent his sons Éremón and Éber to take Ireland and settle there (XXI.1), or the story of Simón Brecc's discovery of a stone throne raised from the Irish Sea by the anchors of his ship, and how he took this to be a portent that he would gain a kingdom (XXVII.f–h).[76] Moreover, there must be some doubt about whether XIII.1 has been derived from such a putative account, not only because of its position in Fordun's text in relation to the other passages, but also because it may, in fact, be read as an authorial introduction to the material given in the rest of XIII which concerns the flight from the biblical plagues inflicted on Egypt. Furthermore, neither Gaedel or Scota are named in XIII.1. If XIII.1 were to be excluded, then it would no longer be possible to claim that a third account has been incorporated piecemeal even in outline, for there would be nothing to fill the gap between Gaedel's arrival in Egypt and marriage to Scota in VIII.2 and his departure with Scota in XI.3. Only circular arguments beckon if one has to make the choice between the proposition that all these passages (excluding one of the two takings of Ireland) have been derived from one account, or the alternative, that they have been derived from a range of possible sources, none of which would necessarily have given a complete telling of the origin-legend.

So far, therefore, two accounts of Scottish origins can be identified by analysing passages which may be attributed to nameless sources. It cannot be claimed that their contents have been reconstructed comprehensively, but it is possible to recognise at least the outline of these accounts and some of their distinctive detail. It emerges that the central idea in the narrative of each account is based on Ireland as the current homeland of *Scoti*. In the 'Éber' account the theme of seeking uninhabited lands to settle climaxed with Éber's colonisation of Ireland, while in the 'Partholón' account the wretched plight of *Scoti* in their travels was resolved by taking Ireland as a perpetual possession.

The vision of Ireland in the 'Partholón' account

To what extent did these portrayals of Ireland as homeland of *Scoti* reflect an aspect of Scottish identity which the authors of these accounts consciously accepted or promoted? Or was this view of Ireland simply repeated from their sources? The only one of these accounts whose sources can be identified at this stage is the 'Partholón' account. It can be shown that its author has substantially rewritten the materials at his disposal, and that in doing so he actively identified *Scoti* with Ireland. It appears that as far as he was concerned *Scoti* were Irish.

Much of the 'Partholón' account is reminiscent of the account of the origins of *Scoti* in *Historia Brittonum*.[77] There the (first) leader of *Scoti* (an unnamed Scythian in *Historia Brittonum*) is also an exile who established himself in Egypt (marrying Scota daughter of Pharaoh in one recension);[78] after Pharaoh and his

[76] For a solution, see below, 115.

[77] Dumville, *The Historia Brittonum*, III. 69–70 (for collation with other recensions, see 56).

[78] The 'Nennian' recension: for a detailed discussion of this passage as it appears in the manuscripts see David Dumville's comments *apud* Miller, 'Matriliny by treaty', 138.

army drowned in the Red Sea pursuing the Israelites, this first leader of *Scoti* too was expelled from Egypt by the remaining Egyptians who feared he might assume power over them.[79] There are some differences in detail between the 'Partholón' account and *Historia Brittonum* – notably the route across Africa – and the 'Partholón' account is somewhat more expansive than the rather skeletal version in *Historia Brittonum*, but none of this threatens the basic premise that they may be related in some way. It seems unlikely, however, that the 'Partholón' account has been drawn directly from a recension of *Historia Brittonum*. There is no indication in the 'Partholón' account of knowledge of other material relating to the taking of Ireland in *Historia Brittonum*.[80] In particular, although Partholón himself appeared in *Historia Brittonum*, there is no ostensible link (apart from the name itself) between Partholón in *Historia Brittonum* – who is described settling an empty Ireland and whose colony was wiped out by disease – and Partholón in the 'Partholón' account who subjugated Ireland's inhabitants and made it a perpetual settlement.[81] It is probable, therefore, that the 'Partholón' account derived material from *Historia Brittonum* only at second hand.

The immediate source for this *Historia Brittonum* material is likely to have been Henry of Huntingdon's *Historia Anglorum* (written in six different versions with endings at 1129, 1138, 1146, 1149, and 1154).[82] Book I, chapter 11 of *Historia Anglorum* is chiefly derived from the Vatican Recension of *Historia Brittonum* and Bede's *Historia Ecclesiastica*, and includes the account of the noble Scythian progenitor of *Scoti* and the exodus from Egypt to Spain and ultimately Ireland.[83] Among the few original contributions by Henry of Huntingdon himself in this chapter is the statement that the Egyptians banished the noble Scythian from their midst 'lest he should seize lordship over them',[84] and the curious 'observation' that the people of Navarre still spoke Irish.[85] The former could be the germ for X.2, while the latter may have inspired the author of the 'Partholón' account to place Partholón and his hard-pressed people in the Pyrenees.

The idea of placing Partholón in the Pyrenees could, however, have been taken from another twelfth-century history which may also have been the source from which Partholón himself was derived. In Geoffrey of Monmouth's *Historia Regum Britannie* a Partholón is described leading an expedition of 'Basques' from Spain (eventually) to Ireland;[86] the reference to Basques is comparable with Henry

79 In addition, he likewise wandered across Africa and settled with his people in Spain before eventually migrating to Ireland, but there is no compelling detail here which could corroborate a link with *Historia Brittonum*.

80 Dumville, *The Historia Brittonum*, III. 67–8 (for collation with other recensions, see 56).

81 *eam subactis indigenis in perpetuam sibi possessionem optinuit,*

82 Greenway, *Henry, Archdeacon of Huntingdon*, lxvi–lxxvii.

83 Ibid., 28–31; for Henry's use of *Historia Ecclesiastica* and *Historia Brittonum*, see lxxxvi–lxxxix, and xc–xci.

84 *ne dominium super eos inuaderet.*

85 *Nam et pars eorum* [i.e. *Scoti*] *que ibi* [Spain] *remansit adhuc eadem utitur lingua, et Nauarri uocatur.*

86 Wright, *The Historia*, I. 31 (§46); II. 40–1 (§46).

of Huntingdon's identification of *Navarri* as *Scoti*, and was presumably based on the same idea that the Basque and Irish languages were closely related. If Geoffrey of Monmouth was a source for the 'Partholón' account, however, then its author has taken care to refashion Geoffrey's portrayal of Partholón as subject to the king of Britain. Geoffrey of Monmouth recounted how Gargunt Babtruc, king of Britain, came upon Partholón and his people who were desparately roaming the seas looking for a place to settle after being expelled from Spain; Partholón did homage to Gargunt and Gargunt granted him Ireland which, according to Geoffrey, was then uninhabited; Partholón thus settled in Ireland, and his people remain there 'to this day'. The absence of Gargunt from the 'Partholón' account and the insistence that Partholón and his people, after taking Ireland by force, established 'perpetual settlements in freedom'[87] may be seen, therefore, as a deliberate attempt to deny Geoffrey's message that Ireland (and the Irish) were subject to the king of Britain.

This would not be the only instance in which a modified 'pro-Scottish' version of *Historia Regum* could be detected as a source behind Fordun's chronicle. John and Winifred MacQueen have argued that such a work, characterised by refashioning material in Geoffrey's *Historia Regum* in order to lessen, if not negate, Geoffrey's more stridently pro-British bias, is visible in much of Fordun's book II.[88] They have suggested, for example, that Fordun's account of the conversion of the Scots in AD 203 in a mission dispatched by Pope Victor I was concocted in this work in order to supply a Scottish equivalent for Geoffrey's account of the conversion of the Britons in the time of Eleutherius, Victor's predecessor.[89] Another example proposed by the MacQueens of a self-conscious attempt in this work to match Geoffrey of Monmouth is Julius Caesar's encounter with kings of *Scoti* and Picts related by Fordun in book II, chapters 14 and 15, which includes the text of these kings' forthright letter to Caesar defending their ancestral liberty. An account of Scottish origins which refashioned Geoffrey of Monmouth's description of Partholón's settlement of Ireland and emphasised the primeval freedom of *Scoti* would be consistent with this 'Scotticised' version of *Historia Regum*.

It appears, therefore, that the author of the 'Partholón' account identified *Scoti* with Ireland; not only was he keen to defend Ireland's independence, but he portrayed Ireland as the perpetual settlement of *Scoti*. The key themes which have been elaborated by him were the hardship endured by *Scoti* in the quest for a perpetual settlement in freedom, and the independence enjoyed by *Scoti* from the beginning of their history. These are so deeply embedded in the account's narrative framework that they can not plausibly be separated out and explained simply as later additions by Fordun or anyone else. These can be recognised as important concerns which motivated the account's author to expand and adapt his materials. They are, of course, interrelated, for the hardship endured by *Scoti* was for the sake of preserving their independence. It is possible, therefore, that it was the account's author who promoted the idea that 'in all these ills and difficulties [*Scoti*] could never be bowed into submitting or answering to a foreign king, but

87 *perpetuas cum libertate mansiones.*

88 MacQueen and MacQueen, *Scotichronicon*, I. xxviii.

89 Ibid., I. 381

chose rather to lead this bestial life, with freedom alone, always humble and loyal under their own king'.[90]

As far as the date and authorship of this account is concerned, all that can be said is that it was written in Scotland sometime after the publication of Geoffrey of Monmouth's *Historia Regum* in 1136 (or after one of the later versions of Henry of Huntingdon's *Historia Anglorum*) and sometime before 1301.[91] There is no indication that its author could read Gaelic; indeed, his apparent ignorance of Partholón in *Lebor Gabála* suggests that he is unlikely to have been literate in Gaelic.[92]

90 *Et in omnibus hiis malis et angustiis nuncquam ut regi subderetur alieno uel ad obediendum flecti poterat quin pocius humilis semper et deuotus sub rege proprio cum libertate tantum hanc uitam eligeret ducere bestialem.* This (and the similar passage XVI.i–l) have been interpreted differently as later statements by Fordun himself motivated by the experience of the wars of independence; see Goldstein, *The Matter of Scotland*, 124–7, and esp. Webster, 'John of Fordun' (I am grateful to Bruce Webster for sending me a copy of this prior to publication). It is possible within the date-limits suggested below, of course, that the 'Partholón' account was written sometime after Edward I began his challenge to Scottish independence in May 1291 (see esp. Duncan, 'The process'). Another context which could have inspired such appeals to freedom was the struggle by Scottish kings and churchmen to deny the claims of the archbishops of York and Canterbury to jurisdiction over bishops of St Andrews and Glasgow (and ultimately *ecclesia Scoticana* in general). This was particularly intense during the twelfth century (see esp. Barrell, 'The background'; Barrow, 'The idea of freedom', 18–19; Barrow, *Scotland and its Neighbours*, 3–4), but remained an issue in the thirteenth (Stones, *Anglo-Scottish Relations*, nos 6 and 9; note also no. 12, and comment in Barrow, 'The idea of freedom', 19–21; Barrow, *Scotland and its Neighbours*, 4–6).

91 1301 is the *terminus ante quem* for the synthesis (see above, 72–3). The MacQueens have suggested (*Scotichronicon*, I. 378) that *tribuni* (at ibid., I. 250) could suggest a date later than 1347 because the title was uniquely applied to Cola di Rienzo, tribune of the Roman people, 1347–54. The term can be found earlier, however, used for instance by Orderic Vitalis: he says of Edward, the victorious commander of David I's forces at the battle of Stracathro (1130), *sub Eduardo rege tribunus Merciorum fuit*; Chibnall, *The Ecclesiastical History,* IV. 276–7.

92 See below, 131.

V

ACCOUNTS OF SCOTTISH ORIGINS IN THOMAS GREY'S *SCALACRONICA* AND ANDREW WYNTOUN'S *ORIGINAL CHRONICLE*

The identification of Ireland as the perpetual (i.e. current) homeland of *Scoti* by the author of the 'Partholón' account raises the possibility that the kingdom's Irish identity was current after the mid-twelfth century when Gaelic was in retreat in the kingdom's heartlands as a language of status and literacy. Was the author of the 'Partholón' account unusual, however, compared with other Scottish writers on the subject of Scottish origins in the period 1136x1301, in displaying such an identification with Ireland?

It has to be admitted that the extreme difficulty in tracing versions of the Scottish origin-legend in this period means that a critical mass of material is unlikely to be achieved which could support any confident assertions about aspects which were or were not generally accepted. The most that can be hoped for is to show that the identification with Ireland in the 'Partholón' account was not restricted to one author. If an independent account with a similar identification of *Scoti* with Ireland could be found then this would at least make it a reasonable proposition that such an expression of Irish identity represented a genuine current of opinion, and was not just the predilection of a single author. The author of the 'Éber' account also portrayed Ireland as homeland of *Scoti*; but at this stage, without knowing his sources and how he has deployed them, it is impossible to determine how actively he promoted this feature.

In this chapter the investigation of pre-Fordun accounts of Scottish origins will be taken further by studying the accounts in Thomas Grey of Heton's *Scalacronica* and Andrew Wyntoun's *Original Chronicle*, and in particular how these relate to the material attributed in Fordun's *Chronica Gentis Scottorum* to *legenda Sancti Brandani* and *legenda Sancti Congalli*.[1] This will lead ultimately to a fuller disclosure of the likely contents of the 'Éber' account, and an identification of its principal source, which will, in turn, reveal its author's prime concerns and shed crucial light on his vision of Ireland. A more immediate result of analysing the accounts of Scottish origins in Grey's *Scalacronica* and Wyntoun's *Original Chronicle*, however, will be the recovery of four more lost accounts which may be dated *c.*1300 or earlier. These four accounts are (not surprisingly) closely related to each other. Only one of them may be regarded as a substantial reworking of its

1 This title is adopted for convenience; it is referred to variously as *historia* or *legenda Sancti* (or *Beati*) *Congalli*. It is possible, moreover, that *Congall* represents *Cougall* (i.e. Comgall).

exemplar; two of them, by contrast, are unlikely to be much more than copies of their sources.[2] These accounts have the capacity, therefore, to extend our knowledge of the kind of material which was in circulation, inherited from earlier writings; and they also have the potential, especially through the light they can cast on the preoccupations of the author of the 'Éber' account, to establish indirectly that the Irish identity visible in the 'Partholón' account represented a genuine current of opinion in the period 1136x1301.

The Scottish chronicle inserted into Grey's Scalacronica

Sir Thomas Grey of Heton began writing his *Scalacronica* while he was a prisoner in Edinburgh Castle following his capture in 1355. His declared intention was to translate the chronicles of Britain and deeds of the English into French. The majority of the text is a version of the *Brut* running from the Creation to the death of Henry III of England which Grey has continued from his own knowledge and from what he found while in Edinburgh Castle, concluding with David II's marriage to Margaret Logie in April 1363. *Scalacronica* survives in a single manuscript (Cambridge, Corpus Christi College, MS 133);[3] his text of the *Brut* has been described as certainly the least traditional of those in the Parker Library, Corpus Christi College.[4]

Following his account of the Scottish embassy to Edward I of England informing him of the death of Margaret the 'Maid of Norway' in 1290 (the last direct heir of Alexander III), Thomas Grey digressed to give an outline of Scottish history from origins to the accession of John Balliol in 1292. This brief history of the Scots has been described as an independent chronicle which he translated into French from Latin and inserted into his work.[5] It has the appearance of a compilation, and consists of (i) an account of Scottish origins; (ii) a list of kings of Dál Riata; (iii) an account of Pictish origins; (iv) a Pictish king-list; (v) an account of how the Picts were destroyed by *Scoti*; and (vi) an annotated list of kings from Cinaed mac Alpín. The whole of this inserted chronicle was published and translated by Skene;[6] the king-list material (sections ii, iv and vi above) was given the siglum **K** by A. O. Anderson,[7] and has been edited separately by Marjorie Anderson.[8] A. O. Anderson assigned the text of the king-list to the reign of King John Balliol[9] (whose inauguration is the latest event mentioned): the king-list

2 Nevertheless they have significant new features which make it useful to distinguish them separately.

3 The most modern edition is Stevenson, *Scalacronica*. Maxwell, *Scalacronica* is a translation of the latter part: at p. viii Maxwell explains that Grey began work on *Scalacronica* during his captivity in Edinburgh Castle, 1355–7.

4 Tyson, 'Les manuscrits du Brut en prose française', 111: 'certainement le moins traditionnel de nos cinque manuscrits'. (I am grateful to Professor David Dumville for drawing this article to my attention.)

5 Webster, *Scotland from the Eleventh Century*, 17.

6 Skene, *Chronicles*, 194–208.

7 Anderson, *Early Sources*, I. xlvii.

8 Anderson, *Kings and Kingship*, 286–9.

9 Anderson, *Early Sources*, I. xlvii.

material, therefore, may be dated to sometime after John Balliol's inauguration on 30 November 1292, and presumably before 9 February 1304 when those governing Scotland in King John's name finally surrendered to Edward I.[10] It is not immediately obvious, however, that this dating holds true for the rest of the 'inserted chronicle'.[11]

Two of the items in the chronicle – (iii) and (v) – may have been added by Thomas Grey himself from material at his disposal: one of his sources was evidently Higden's *Polychronicon*, and both these passages correspond closely with Higden's account of Pictish origins and the destruction of the Picts.[12] Grey can certainly be recognised in the first item interpolating cross-references to material earlier in his work.[13] The first item itself, an account of Scottish origins, is attributed in the text to a Life of St Brendan: it can not, however, be identified with a known extant source. The question, then, is whether Grey himself added it to the king-list material, or whether he found it already attached to the king-list in his exemplar of **K**.

Grey's account of Scottish origins and Fordun's passages attributed to legenda Sancti Brandani

We have already met passages in John of Fordun's *Chronica Gentis Scottorum* that were cited as derived from *legenda Sancti Brandani*. Once Grey's account is compared with Fordun's material attributed to *legenda Sancti Brandani*, it becomes apparent that they are, indeed, related. There is one immediate difference between them, however: Grey's account continues right up to the settlement of *Scoti* in Scotland, while Fordun's St Brendan material takes us only as far as the colonisation of Ireland. Before embarking on a discussion of how Fordun's *legenda Sancti Brandani* passages and Grey's account compare with each other, it will be useful to present the texts and highlight where there is clear agreement and disagreement between them.

10 King John himself surrendered abjectly to Edward I in 1296 and, after a spell as a prisoner in England, he was allowed to retire to his ancestral estates in Picardy. Although he never returned to Scotland, significant areas continued to be governed in his name in opposition to Edward I until the final Comyn surrender in February 1304. John may not have ruled after 1296, therefore, but as far as most Scots were concerned he certainly reigned beyond that. Although the cause of Balliol's kingship continued to attract support beyond 1304, no one governed in King John's name after 1304. (His son, Edward, regained the throne briefly in the last months of 1332, and also 1333–5, after which his support ebbed away decisively.) See esp. Watson, 'The enigmatic lion'. For Scottish government and resistance to English rule in the years after King John's surrender see Barrow, *Robert Bruce*, 3rd edn, 80–131.

11 Webster, *Scotland from the Eleventh Century*, 17, has suggested that the 'inserted chronicle' as a whole may have been written at the end of the thirteenth century.

12 Babington, *Polychronicon*, II. 70, 144 (on the origin of Picts; the idea that Rodric, king of Picts, was killed near Carlisle seems diagnostic of Grey's use of Higden); and 154–6 (on the destruction of Picts).

13 See below, 87, where there is a reference *com auaunt especifie*, 'as pointed out earlier', to an account of Pictish origins derived from Geoffrey of Monmouth.

Passages in Fordun's account of Scottish origins attributed to legenda Sancti Brandani

The text is divided according to divisions employed in the edition in chapter III (where a fuller record of the text and apparatus will be found).

Key: *italic*: notable similarity with account in Grey
underline: notable contradiction with account in Grey

/VIII.3/ Legitur inibi[14] *quemdam militem* cui principales generis sui dignitatem attribuunt *Athenis in Grecia* regnasse, *cuius filium nomine Gaythelos filiam Pharoanis regis Egipti Scotam* a qua Scoti nomen eciam traxere *coniugio perhibent habuisse*. Qui scilicet *Gaythelos uiribus prestans et audacia* dum patrem uel ceteros insolencia perurgeret, causa repulsa pocius quam uoto discedens *animosa fretus manu iuuenum* in Egiptum secessit.

/XIV.2/ Gaythelos autem ex Egipto pulsus et sic per Mediterraneum mare *uectus nauibus ad Hispaniam applicat*, atque super Hiberim flumen turrim *condens nomine Briganciam* locum et sedem *uiolenter ab incolis usurpauit*.

/XVI.a–d/ Gaythelos namque cum esset incolis ingratus die quodam sereno cum de Brigancia spectans eminusque terram contemplatus esset in mari agiles et bellicosos iuuenes armat et *cum tribus nauiculis* exploratum dirigens alto se committunt freto. At illi spirantibus auris ad uotum tandem ad insulam conueniunt et eam contemplando circuiuntes et remis incolas repertos inuadentes perimerunt, sicque tellure lustrata mirantes *eius decorem ad Briganciam redeunt. Sed Gaythelos morte repentina preuentus filios* hortando *commonuit ut predictam certamine terram inuaderent*, eorum pariter segniciem arguens et ignauiam si tante nobilitatis regnum desererent *quod sine bello uel quouis discrimine penetrare ualerent*.

/XVII.3/ *Ex filiis Gaythel unus quidem Hiber nomine* iuuenis sed de etate ualens incitatus ad bellum animo cepit arma paratoque pro posse nauigio *predictam aggressus insulam partem paucorum incolarum quos reperit necat sibique partem subegit*. Sed et totam sibi possidendam et fratribus terram uendicat eam ex nomine matris Scociam nuncupando.

/XVII.5/[15] Postmodum autem *ab eodem Hibero rege uel mari pocius Hiberico Hiberniam uocauerunt*.

[14] I.e. *legenda Sancti Brandani*.

[15] Attributed in text simply to *legenda*.

The first part of the account of Scottish origins in Grey's Scalacronica *(as far as the taking of Ireland).*[16]

Punctuation editorial (guided by MS punctuation);
contractions expanded silently.

Key: *italic*: notable similarity with account in Fordun
underline: notable contradiction with account in Fordun
[et com . . . especifie.]: sentence probably interpolated by Grey (see 85, above)

[17]En la vie saint Brandane est troue qen *le pays de Attenys en Grece, estoit vn noble cheualer, qi out vn fitz, qy auoit a noun Gaidel, qauoit en espouse la feile Pharao le Roy de Egypt, qe out a noune Scota*, de qei il auoit bele engendrure. *Gaidel estoit cheualerous, se purchasa lez iuuenceaux de soun pays* /fo. 191r/ *se mist en mere* en uese od sa femme Scota, et sez enfauntz se quist mansioun al auenture, en biaunce de le conquer, *arryua en Espayne*, ou sure vn haut mountain au couster de la mere Hiberynie, fist edifier vn fort chastel, *et le noma Brigans. Il viuoit od lez soens de rauyn sure lez paisens du pays.* Sez pescheours furount chacez vn iour par tempest parfound en la mere, qi ly reuindrent renouncier qils auoint aparsceu par voler dez flores dez chardouns et autres enseignes, qe il y out terre pres de outre mere. Gaidel od sez fitz, qui a surnoun auoient Scoti, apres lour mere Scota, se mist en mere *en trois naueaux*, seglerent aual la mere trouerent vn Isle grant mounterent a terre, trouerent *le pays* herbous et *plesaunt* de boys et reueres, mais noun pas bien poeple dez gentz; [et com est ymagine et suppose, procheignement deuaunt auoit Gurguyns le fitz Belin Roy de Bretaigne, assigne cel Ile as gentz extretiz Despayne queux il troua en Orkany com venoit de Denemarc com auaunt est especifie.] Gaidel *repaira* a soun chastel de *Brigauns*, ymaginaunt de realer al Ile troue, *mais ly surueint vn tresgref malady dount ly coueint murrir, si deuisoit a sez fitz qils alasent a cel Ile, et y demurasent com a vn pays saunz grant defens, leger a conquere.*[18] *Eberus le* eyne *fitz Gaidel* et de Scota la feile Pharao, *se adressa* od sez freirs *al auaunt dit Ile, qi le seisy, et tuerent et soutzmistrent a lour obeisaunce,*

16 The account of Scottish origins runs from fo.190vb to 191va, and is immediately preceded and followed by a blank line. The text here and in the following extract from Grey has been edited afresh from the manuscript. I am grateful to Professor Dumville for his assistance in the transcription of it. The text in Skene, *Chronicles*, 194–7, has a number of minor errors, the most serious being singular *auoit* for plural *auoint* in the account of the storm-driven fishermen finding evidence of land (although Skene [ibid., 195] translated *auoit* as plural). Also, Skene's folio numbers are misleading. (For an earlier edition, see Stevenson, *Scalacronica*, 112–14.)

17 The account attributed to a Life of Brendan is introduced with the following: *Et fait asauoir qe solonc lez cronicles Descoce, nestoit vnqes tiel difficoulte qi enserroit lour Roys de droit lingne, qe outriement estoit failly en le hour de troys Roys succiement, chescun fitz dautre; et pur ceo voet cest cronicle toucher la originaute dez Roys, et la processe de caux, qen Escoz ount regne.*

18 The rest of the line in the manuscript is filled with a wavy line, and the next line begins with *Eberus* (with a larger than normal initial capital).

ceaux qe ils y trouerent, et pius appellerent le Ile Iberniam, apres lour freir eyne *Eberus, ou apres la mere Eberiaco*, qe nomez estoit ensi dez Espaynolis, mais le surenoun Scoty demura od lez autres freirs, et od lour issu bon pece en cel Ile, qe entre nous est apelle Irrelande.

The story, in outline, is the same. Gaedel goes from Greece to Egypt and marries Scota daughter of Pharaoh; he leaves Egypt and sails to Spain where he founds *Brigancia*; Ireland is discovered and explored, and is then invaded and conquered by Gaedel's son, Éber. More significantly, both accounts share points of detail. In both, Gaedel is the son of an Athenian knight (*miles*, *cheualer*); the exploratory expedition to Ireland consists of three vessels; and on its return Gaedel is struck down with a mortal illnes and urges his sons to settle in Ireland, which he declares is easy to conquer. There are, moreover, also a few instances of significant verbal correspondence between the accounts, as in the description of Éber's arrival in Ireland:

. . . [Éber] predictam aggressus insulam partem paucorum incolarum quos reperit necat sibique partem subegit . . . Postmodum autem ab eodem Hibero rege uel mari pocius Hiberico Hiberniam uocauerunt.	. . . [Éber] se adressa od sez freirs al auaunt dit Ile, qi le seisy, et tuerent et soutzmistrent a lour obeisaunce, ceaux qe ils y trouerent, et pius appellerent le Ile Iberniam, apres lour freir eyne Eberus, ou apres la mere Eberiaco . . .

It is clear, therefore, that both accounts shared a common source. Given that both were attributed to a hagiographic text concerning a St Brendan, there can be little doubt that the common source was a *legenda* or Life of a St Brendan which included an account of the origins of *Scoti*, probably as a preliminary to its treatment of the saint's life. Unfortunately no extant Life (or *legenda*) of a St Brendan contains this material.

Grey's account of Scottish origins and Fordun's passages attributed to legenda Sancti Congalli

Although Fordun's passages attributed to a *legenda* of St Brendan took the account of Scottish origins only as far as Ireland, Grey's telling of the legend continued (without a break) with Simón Brecc, a son of a king of Spain. We are told that Simón was not in line to succeed his father as king, but that, because he was his father's best-loved son, Simón was given by his father the stone throne of the kings of Spain, which Simón took with him to Ireland. Later this stone throne was taken to Scotland by Simón's descendant, Fergus son of Ferchar, who was the first king of Scots to be inaugurated on it. All subsequent kings of Scots, we are informed, have been inaugurated on this stone (which is clearly the Stone of Scone). All this material can be found in Fordun's text, but in passages attributed to a *legenda* (or *historia*) of a St Congal rather than a *legenda* of St Brendan. Moreover, when Grey's account of Simón Brecc and Fergus son of Ferchar is compared with Fordun's passages attributed to *legenda Sancti Congalli*, it is apparent that they are related to each other. This can readily be appreciated if the texts are presented in a way which highlights where there is clear agreement between them; clear disagreement between them will also be noted.

Passages in Fordun's account of Scottish origins attributed to legenda Sancti Congalli

The text is divided according to divisions employed in the edition in chapter III (where a fuller record of the text and apparatus will be found).

Key: *italic*: notable similarity with account in Grey
<u>underline</u>: notable contradiction with account in Grey

/XXVII.a–d/ *Erat autem quidam* Scotorum *Hispanie rex plures habens filios unum tamen cui nomen Smonbrec*[19] *quamuis natu non maior fuerat uel heres pre ceteris tamen diligebat.* Misit igitur ipsum pater *ad Hiberniam* cum exercitu *donauitque sibi marmoream cathedram* arte uetustissima diligenti sculptam opifice *qua* Scotice *nacionis Hispanie reges sedere solebant* unde diligenter in sua regione quasi pro anchora tuebatur. *Pergebat autem idem Smonbrec* magna comitatus hominum caterua *predictam ad insulam* et <u>in ea suo subiecta dominio</u> *regnauit* annis multis. *Lapidem uero prefatum scilicet cathedram in eminenciori loco regni* Themor nomine *posuit qui regia sedes* locusque regni superior de cetero *dictus est* quo sue propaginis postere reges multis temporibus sedere solebant regiis honoribus insigniti. /II.12/ Deinde post multum tempus *uenit* quidam rex *ex Hibernia nomine Fergus filius Ferchard regalem in Scocia secum deferens cathedram* marmoreo lapide decisam in qua primus ibidem rex a Scotis coronatus est. Cuius exemplo *succedentes postmodum in regno ceteri reges eadem cathedra rite coronam susceperunt.* Hanc quoque cathedram Smonbrec ut supradictum est primus attulit ad Hiberniam.[20]

19 It is possible to argue that the confusion shown in rendering Simón Brecc (see below, 53) shows that he was not Simón Brecc at all (a name which should have caused no difficulty), and may have been *Smoranbrec* as suggested in some of the witnesses. *Smoranbrec* as a name is found nowhere else (see above, 53 n. 378, for discussion). Whoever he was he is shrouded in mystery. For the sake of convenience I will continue to refer to him as Simón Brecc.

20 MacQueen and MacQueen, *Scotichronicon*, I. 196 attributed the remaining section of this chapter to *legenda Sancti Congalli*, which consists of two sentences on a descendant of Fergus described as *Rether, quem Beda Reudam uocat*. The MacQueens (ibid., 353) remarked that 'the name Rether, derived from 'Riatai', Rigfhota', or most probably Bede's 'Reuda', is unique to the 'History of Blessed Congall.' It is, in fact, from the version of the royal genealogy witnessed in Diss and *Gesta Annalia*, where it represents (genitive) Rodchada (or variants of this name): see below, 186. Given the synthesist's use of this version of the royal genealogy for the chronological framework of his work (see above, 70), there can be little doubt that he was responsible for equating Bede's *Reuda* with *Rether*. The section following this extract should not, therefore, be regarded as derived from *legenda Sancti Congalli*.

The remaining part of the account of Scottish origins in Grey's Scalacronica *(following the taking of Ireland)*

Punctuation is editorial (guided by MS punctuation); contractions are expanded silently.

Key: *italic*: notable similarity with account in Fordun
underline: notable contradiction with account in Fordun
[Mais . . . recordez.]: sentence probably interpolated by Grey (see below)

[21]*En quel Ile apres arryua Symound Bret, le fitz* pusne *du Roy de Espayne, qi od ly aporta vn pere, sur quoi lez Roys Despayne soleient estre coronez, qi soun pier ly bailla* en signifiaunce qil en fust Roys, *com cely qil plus amast de sez enfauntz. Cesty Symound deuient Roy du pays de Ireland,* de par vn feile extreit de Scoty, *qi enmyst le auaunt dit pere en le plus souerain bele lieu du pays, qe au our de huy port le noune, li lieu real. Apres qoi, veint* vn dez fitz de vn dez Roys *de Ireland* extreit de Scota, *qy out a noun Fergous fitz* [22]*Ferthairy* en le plus lointisme pays outre Bretaine deuer septentrioun, et de cost lez Bretouns occupia la terre deuer Cateneys outre la laund Porry,[23] et y endemurrerent; et tout estoit il du nacioun de Ireland, et lez soens touz /fo. 191va/ vnqor lez firent nomer Scoty, et la terre Scocia apres Scota la feile Pharao roy de Egypt, de qei enuindrent lez Scotois. Mais lour pr<o>pre[24] pays est Ireland, lour coustom et patoys acordaunt, [qi puis furount mellez od Pices com apres serra recordez.][25] *I cesti Fergus aporta hors de Ireland la pere real auaunt nomez,* et la fist mettre ou ore est Labbai de Scone, *sure quoy furount faitez, assise et establis, les Roys Descoce touz puscedy,* tanqe Edward le primer Roy Dengleter apres la conquest len fist aporter a Loundres a Westmoustre[26] ou ore le sege du prestre a le haute auter.

Not only do these accounts betray coincidences of detail (such as Simón as the best-loved son of a king of Spain, though not the eldest, and Fergus son of Ferchar who took the stone throne to Scotland), but there are also occasional examples of verbal similarity, as in the description of where Simón placed the stone in Ireland:

21 Continues immediately from previous extract: see n. 16 above for details.
22 Preceded by *R*, erased.
23 *la laund Porry* is probably the north-west corner of the mainland with Cape Wrath at its point which is *Am Parph* in Gaelic. Taylor, 'Cape Wrath', showed that there were two forms of this name, of which one, /parau/, could be equated with *Porry*.
24 *prpre* in MS.
25 The passage on mixing with the Picts referred to here relates to the account of Pictish origins (item iii above, see 84–5) which was derived from Higden and therefore can be attributed to Grey himself.
26 *Westm* with curved suspension-stroke over the *m*.

Lapidem uero prefatum scilicet cathedram in eminenciori loco regni Themor nomine posuit qui regia sedes locusque regni superior de cetero dictus est . . .

. . . enmyst le auaunt dit pere en le plus souerain bele lieu du pays, qe au our de huy port le noune, li lieu real.

There can be little doubt, therefore, that Grey's account of Simón Brecc and the Stone of Scone and Fordun's passages attributed to *legenda Sancti Congalli* were related. The puzzle is that Grey evidently attributed this material, as well as his account of Gaedel and Éber, to a Life of St Brendan. Unfortunately this can not be solved by reference to a known hagiographical text: there is no surviving Life of a St Congal (or St Comgall, for that matter) that contains any of this material, just as there is no extant Life of a St Brendan that includes any of it either. The simplest explanation is that Grey has not preserved as specific a record as Fordun of where this material was ultimately derived from. The St Brendan source would, therefore, have given only an account of Gaedel and Éber, as represented in the passages attributed to *legenda Sancti Brandani* in Fordun, and the legend of Simón Brecc and the Stone of Scone would have appeared only in *legenda Sancti Congalli*, not a Life of Brendan as well; the two accounts would then have been brought together subsequently in a source shared (ultimately) by Grey and Fordun, but the attribution of the legend of Simón Brecc and the Stone of Scone has been lost in Grey's account either before it was copied by Grey, or by Grey himself.

An origin-legend plus king-list text written 1292x1304

Although there are obvious similarities between Grey's account and these passages attributed to St Brendan and St Congal sources in Fordun, there are also some serious contradictions which need to be investigated. The first cluster involves the discovery and conquest of Ireland by *Scoti*, which may be summarised:

1. In *legenda Sancti Brandani*, *Brigancia* was a tower built by Gaedel on the River Ebro; in Grey's account it was a castle built on the coast of the 'Hibernian Sea'.
2. In *legenda Sancti Brandani* Ireland was first discovered by *Scoti* when Gaedel spotted it from his tower in *Brigancia*; in Grey's account Gaedel was first made aware of Ireland when he was told by some fishermen that they had come across 'flowers, thistles and other signs that there was land nearby across the sea'[27] when they were driven off-course in a storm.
3. In *legenda Sancti Brandani* Gaedel armed some active and warlike young men and dispatched them to explore Ireland; in Grey's account Gaedel himself and his sons explored the island and then returned to *Brigancia*.

The notion in Fordun's *legenda Sancti Brandani* that Ireland was discovered by Gaedel when he saw it from his tower in *Brigancia* is corroborated by its appearance in all recensions of *Lebor Gabála*.[28] This suggests that Grey's version represents a recasting of this episode, presumably by someone who considered the idea

27 *flores . . . chardouns et autres enseignes qe il y out terre pres outre mere.*
28 E.g. *LG*, V. 10–13.

of sighting Ireland from Spain as insufficiently plausible, adopting in its place the motif of fishermen seeing signs of land on the sea as a more convincing explanation of how Gaedel came to know about Ireland.[29] The other differences can be interpreted as having followed on from this change. There was no need in Grey's account for *Brigancia* to be a tower, so it became a castle; the fishermen story may have made it seem more plausible to specify that *Brigancia* was on the coast of the 'Hibernian Sea'; and the notion that Gaedel himself went to explore Ireland may have been introduced to preserve the idea that Gaedel had set eyes on Ireland before his death – an idea which would otherwise have been lost when Gaedel's sighting of Ireland from the tower was abandoned. The narrative force of Gaedel's seeing Ireland before dying presumably hinged on the notion that Ireland was the homeland; whoever rewrote the account preserved by Grey may not, therefore, have wished to lose the original parallel with Moses sighting the Promised Land.[30]

It appears from this that Grey's account may represent a version of the legend which has been edited with a view to ironing out problematic features. Another difference between Grey's account and *legenda Sancti Brandani* which can be explained in this way is the omission in Grey's version of Gaedel's sojourn in Egypt: Gaedel and the band of young men (*fretus . . . iuuenum*; *lez iuuenceaux*) who accompanied him from Greece are described by Grey setting sail and arriving in Spain, rather than proceeding to Egypt first and then, after being expelled, setting sail for Spain. Again, corroboration of Fordun's version by Irish (and other) accounts of the legend confirms that it is Grey's account which is here at variance with what must originally have appeared in the St Brendan source both Grey and Fordun both ultimately shared. The Egyptian leg of Gaedel's exodus and his relationship with Pharaoh was an obvious cause of potential embarrassment, for it made the Scots vulnerable to accusations that their progenitor was on the side of the Israelites' persecutors – a charge which was met head-on in a later Scottish account of the legend (known as the *Scotis Originale*).[31] Bringing Gaedel directly to Spain from Greece would thus appear to have been another way of dealing with this awkward episode: it might also have seemed desireable to suppress the identity of Scota's father, but it was no doubt too well known that she was daughter of Pharaoh to make this feasible.

The only serious contradiction thrown up by a comparison of the remainder of

29 The notion of fishermen from Spain as the first people to see Ireland is also found (although without the same detail) in recensions of the story of Cessair in *Lebor Gabála*: *LG*, II. 178–9, 184–5, 198–9, and 214–17 (in poem XXII). Goldstein, *Matter of Scotland*, 123, assumed that the story of Cessair was the source of this account of fishermen discovering Ireland; there is no compelling detail to support this unlikely proposition, however.

30 On the parallel between *Gaedil* and Israelites see, e.g. Scowcroft, '*Leabhar Gabhála*: part II', 20–1.

31 *and gyf ony wald saye tyll us yat we ar cummyn of Egipt of ye ta syde quhilk oppressyt ye bairnes of Israell, argue us not wyt ye werst, for rycht sa comme Christ of ye Jowes. Versus: Sicut spina rosam genuit Judea Mariam. And alsua full worthye men ar cummyn of ye traytouris of Troye, and suppoise yat yai persuyte ye bairnis of Israell, yai resavyte Christ in to Egipt and nurest him nere sevin zere, quhen ye generatioun of ye sammyn bairnis persuyt him to ye ded, and at ye last yai crucifyte him*. Skene, *Chronicles*, 379–80.

this material in Fordun and Grey relates to how Simón Brecc became king of Ireland. In *legenda Sancti Congalli* in Fordun we are told not only that Simón's father gave him the stone throne on which kings of Spain were inaugurated, but also that Simón was sent to Ireland by his father with an army; Simón then conquered Ireland and reigned there many years, placing the stone throne at Tara. In Grey's account, however, we are told that Simón became king of Ireland peaceably by marriage to a daughter of *Scoti* descended from Éber. Presumably here, as before, Grey's version represents a modification of the original account: indeed, the notion of Simón as king by marriage seems rather to dissipate the narrative force of the gift of the stone throne by Simón's father 'signifying that he would be king',[32] which appears more credible backed up with an army.

What, however, could have made Simón's conquest of Ireland appear problematic? The *legenda Sancti Brandani* and *legenda Sancti Congalli* material in Fordun would each have given a different account of the conquest of Ireland, one by Éber, the other by Simón Brecc. There can be no doubt that Éber's conquest was understood as the settlement of Ireland by *Scoti*, for (apart from anything else) we are told that 'he called it *Scotia* from his mother's name'. If Simón's invasion was deemed to follow Éber's, therefore, then this would have meant *Scoti* in Ireland being conquered by an army from Spain. It is possible, moreover, that Simón was only specifically identified in Fordun as a *Scotus* as a result of the synthesis of differing versions of the Scottish origin-legend which underpinned Fordun's book I. It was argued in the last chapter that this synthesis was constructed by identifying key individuals in each account with figures in the royal genealogy, creating a series of invasions of Ireland by *Scoti* from Spain in which care was taken in each case to bring the ancestor of future invasions back to Spain. Simón may only have become explicitly a *Scotus*, therefore, when he was matched with the space-filling person of that name in the royal genealogy. Indeed, in Fordun's material attributed to *legenda Sancti Congalli*, Simón's affiliation as a *Scotus* is only apparent because we are told that the stone throne was used by kings of Spain *Scotice nacionis*. The same passage appears in Grey's account, but without anything corresponding to *Scotice nacionis*.[33] Moreover, nowhere in Grey's account is Simón said to be *Scotus*: in fact, it is maintained that *Scoti* was the name adopted by the colonists established after the conquest led by Éber, which would suggest that Simón was not regarded in Grey's account as *Scotus*.[34] The problem, then, which could have provoked the substitution of Simón's conquest with his marriage to a

32 *en signifiaunce qil en fust Roys.*

33 . . . *donauitque sibi marmoream cathedram* . . . *qua Scotice nacionis Hispanie reges sedere solebant*. . .;. . . *sur quoi lez Roys Despayne soleient estre coronez, qi soun pier ly bailla* . . .

34 *mais le surenoun Scoty demura od lez autres friers, et od lour issu bon pece en cel Ile, qe entre nous est apelle Irrlande*, and later Simón's wife is described as *extreit de Scoty* (meaning descended from Éber's brothers). As one of Gaedel's sons, Éber is clearly regarded as *Scotus* when we are told that Gaedel's sons *a surnoun auoient Scoti, apres lour mere Scota*. The implication of the sentence which claimed that *Scoti* remained as the 'surname' of Éber's brothers and their descendants would appear to be either that Éber had no offspring or that he and his successors adopted another name. There is no suggestion in Grey's account that Éber returned to Spain and was thus Simón's ancestor

descendant of the original colony of *Scoti* was that the source shared ultimately by Grey and Fordun could have been interpreted as presenting Simón as a foreigner who conquered *Scoti* – which would have made the Stone of Scone a potential symbol of victory over *Scoti*. Such reading was not, of course, originally intended if (as suggested above) the legend of Gaedel and Éber and the legend of Simón Brecc and the Stone of Scone were originally distinct, the former derived from *legenda Sancti Brandani*, the latter from *legenda Sancti Congalli*, each with their own account of a conquest of Ireland from Spain. The two legends would have appeared in the source shared ultimately by Grey and Fordun, but their separateness would still have been indicated by their attribution to different sources. Only in Grey's account can it be said that these two legends have been stitched together into a single narrative by finding a new explanation for how Simón became king. It is possible, also, that the deliberate attempt to recast all this material into a single narrative has further resulted in the loss or rejection of the attribution of the legend of Simón Brecc and the Stone of Scone to a source different from a Life of Brendan.

Each of these changes exhibited in Grey's account show a concern for the legend's credibility and a sensitivity to Scottish sensibilities which it would be difficult to attribute to Sir Thomas Grey himself. His viewpoint can be seen elsewhere, as in his account of Pictish origins (based on Geoffrey of Monmouth) in which 'Albany' was assigned to the Picts by the king of Britain for their homage, and the Picts defeated the 'Irish Scots' and held them in subjection; or when Grey explained that Ecgberht's successors as kings of a newly-united England were so busy with their own affairs that they allowed the Scots under Cinaed mac Alpín to establish their own kingdom.[35]

The key question to ask in considering when the account of Scottish origins preserved by Grey was edited is whether the origin-legend and king-list were combined by Grey himself or whether he already found them joined together in his exemplar. The answer lies in the beginning of the king-list. All extant texts of the king-list which are related to Grey's declare that the first king of *Scoti* in Scotland was Fergus son of Erc. Uniquely, however, Grey's list has replaced Fergus son of Erc with Fergus son of Ferchar. In the origin-legend which precedes this, the first king of *Scoti* in Scotland is, of course, explicitly identified as Fergus son of Ferchar. When origin-legend and king-list were brought together, therefore, the role of first king of *Scoti* in Scotland would have been performed by two kings called Fergus with different fathers. The alteration of the king-list's Fergus son of Erc to Fergus son of Ferchar solved this problem, displaying the same concern to produce a coherent and credible account of Scottish origins which evidently lay behind the other changes to the origin-legend material derived ultimately from *legenda Sancti Brandani* and *legenda Sancti Congalli*.[36] Again, it seems unlikely that this was Grey's work. This suggests, therefore, that origin-legend and king-list were already combined in Grey's exemplar.

– which would have made the implicit exclusion of Éber from those who were *Scoti* all the more extraordinary.

35 Skene, *Chronicles*, 199, 203 (the latter he took from Higden's *Polychronicon*).

36 Another unique feature of the king-list which may show the same concern to make origin-legend and king-list consistent with each other is its description of the realm of

It has been suggested above that the king-list, which concludes with the inauguration of King John, presumably took its present form during John's reign – that is to say probably sometime between 30 November, 1292, and 9 February, 1304.[37] This may now also be regarded as the dating-limits of the edition of the origin-legend preserved by Grey. It seems unlikely, given the editor's scrupulous concern for his text, that he would have finished with a grand-total for Pictish and Scottish kings 'to the coronation of John Balliol' if this had not been the latest royal inauguration. (If Grey has copied the figure accurately, the grand-total was calculated with impressive precision as 1,976 years, 9 months and 8 days.)[38] The edition was produced, therefore, sometime during a period which began with the inauguration of a king whose sovereignty was immediately challenged by Edward I, and which subsequently included English conquest, occupation and Scottish resistance. It is not difficult to envisage a connection between the editor's fastidious care for the credibility of his text and the threat which the Scottish kingdom was experiencing at the time in which he was working. The way he rearranged the origin-legend material he inherited may not, admittedly, amount to a strident defence of Scottish interests. Louder statements can be identified in the king-list, however, such as the claim (noted above) that the kingdom's history stretched back for nearly two thousand years, or the declaration attached to the conversion of Bruide *filius* Maelchon that 'it should be known that this nation was only converted once, so that they have carried on [the faith] from that time, and on account of this their priests do not use shoulder-straps on their vestments, while English priests have two, on account of being converted twice'.[39]

---

the first king of *Scoti* in Scotland as *outre Dunbretaine*, 'beyond Dumbarton'. Related texts of the king-list read *ultra Drumalban* (by which 'west of Drumalban' was intended). Dumbarton, which denoted 'fort of the Britons' in Gaelic, was the northern limit of British territory in historic times, so that 'beyond Dumbarton' could recall the legend's account (unfortunately uncorroborated by Fordun) of Fergus son of Ferchar settling *en le plus lointisme pays outre Bretaine deuer septentrioun, et de cost lez Britouns*, 'in the remotest country beyond Britain to the north beside the Britons': the idea may have been to emphasise that *Scoti* had nothing to do with Britain and thus subvert English claims based on a primeval division of Britain among the sons of Brutus.

37 See above, 84–5.

38 Anderson, *Kings and Kingship*, 289.

39 *Et fait a sauoir, qe cest nacioun nestoit vnqes conuerty fors vn foitz, qe tanque en sa ount perseure, et pur ceo ne vssent lours prestres point despaulers a lour aubes, ou lez prestres Engles ount dieus, pur ceo qe dieus foits ount este conuerty.* Skene, *Chronicles*, 200–1. (Note that Bruide *filius* Maelchon has been mistranscribed in Grey's text as *Drust fitz Methor*.) This passage is unique to this text of the king-list; its possible antecedents in an earlier king-list are discussed in Miller, 'The disputed historical horizon', 30–2.

Wyntoun's accounts of Scottish origins

Fordun and Grey were not the only late-medieval authors who used origin-legend material derived (ultimately) from *legenda Sancti Brandani* and *legenda Sancti Congalli*. Andrew Wyntoun wrote his *Original Chronicle* sometime between 1408 and 1424.[40] The most modern edition is that of F. J. Amours published by the Scottish Text Society in six volumes between 1903 and 1914.[41] Wyntoun produced three versions of his text; the earliest extant manuscripts are of the second and third versions.[42] London, British Library, MS Cotton Nero D xi (hereafter **C**), a copy of the third version of the chronicle, and British Library, MS Royal 17 D xx (hereafter **R**), a copy of the second version, have both been dated to the third quarter of the fifteenth century.[43] The earliest extant manuscript of the first version was, at the time of Amours' edition, the property of Randolph G. Erskine Wemyss, of Wemyss Castle, Fife, and has been dubbed the Wemyss MS (hereafter **W**).[44] Amours dated **W** to the early sixteenth century, and described it (and London, British Library, MS Harley 6909, hereafter **H**, a seventeenth-century manuscript containing an abridged copy derived from **W**) as the latest of the nine manuscripts known to him.[45] Not only is **W** a late witness, but Amours formed the

40 The dating of Wyntoun's second and third editions of his work (for which see below) is established by Wyntoun's eulogy of Robert, duke of Albany (died 3 September, 1420), and the lack of any allusion to James I's return from English captivity in 1424 (as argued by J. T. T. Brown and George Neilson *apud* Amours, *The Original Chronicle*, I. xxx). The *terminus post quem* for the first edition is established by the reference to Isabel, countess of Mar, as deceased (ibid., V. 252, 253 [bk. VIII, line 1327/line 1361]); she died in 1408. (The only event offered as a *terminus post quem* in Brown and Neilson's discussion at ibid., I. xxxi, was a cattle-plague in Ireland in 1407; they also suggested that Wyntoun began his work 'possibly before the death of Robert III in 1406'.)

41 Amours died on 9 September 1910; by then the text of his edition had been published, and the Notes, Glossary and Index intended for volume I were ready for press. Only the Introduction remained to be completed; this was achieved by J. T. T. Brown and George Neilson, who were able to utilise Amours' materials for all except the sketch of Wyntoun's life in I. xxx–xl. Earlier editions of Wyntoun's chronicle are Macpherson, *Ðe Orygynale Cronykil*, published in 1795, and Laing, *The Orygynale Cronykil*, published between 1872 and 1879; their shortcomings are discussed in Amours, *The Original Chronicle*, I. xliv–xlvii; II. vi–vii.

42 See Amours, *The Original Chronicle*, I. xlvii–liv, lxxxvii–xc; Craigie, 'The St Andrews MS'.

43 Amours, *The Original Chronicle*, II. vi; for descriptions and discussions of these, see ibid., I. lii–liv; lxii–lxiii. The sigla are those in Amours' edition (as listed in ibid., I. lxi; II. v–vi). **C** and **R** have been dated more precisely from their paper to *c.*1470 and *c.*1480 respectively (Lyall, 'Books and book owners', 254, n.13).

44 Ibid., I. xlvii–li; lxiii–lxiv.

45 Ibid., I. xlviii, lxxxvii; at I. xlviii n.1 it is suggested that **W** may be dated to sometime after 1527 (see further the note on bk. VIII, line 5652, at I. 120, although this is contradicted at I. lv). For **H** see ibid., I. liv–lv, where Amours declared that 'from testing inquiries, it appears that it is an abridged copy of the Wemyss [**W**] in its present state'.

opinion that its scribe 'undoubtedly took liberties with the text'.[46] Although **W** is clearly the most authoritative witness of the first version of Wyntoun's chronicle, it is regrettably much less certain than **R** is as a witness of the second version or **C** is of the third version. All three need to be taken into consideration when examining Wyntoun's text. Amours published **C** and **W**;[47] **R** had been published in two earlier editions, neither of which is satisfactory.[48]

In book II, chapters 8 and 9, Wyntoun gave no less than three different accounts of Scottish origins. The second of these was derived from Geoffrey of Monmouth on how *Scoti* reached Ireland;[49] the third was from Henry of Huntingdon's *Historia Anglorum* (book I, chapter 11).[50] The first and longest, taking up all of book II, chapter 8, was an account of the legend of Gaedel and Éber. When compared with the versions of this legend in Fordun's passages attributed to *legenda Sancti Brandani* and in Grey, it is apparent that it shared a common source with them. Not only is it similar in outline, but it contains detail which, I have argued, appeared in the source shared ultimately by Fordun and Grey. For example, it included Gaedel's building a tower called *Brigancia* on the River Ebro, and his subduing the local population; Gaedel's seeing Ireland from the tower, and his dispatching explorers in three ships who circumnavigate Ireland and kill some of the inhabitants; Gaedel's being struck down by a mortal illness which prevents him from settling Ireland himself, but his sons are advised that conquering Ireland presents no danger; Éber's mounting an armed expedition to Ireland, slaying some of the inhabitants and subduing the rest; and the naming of Ireland *Hibernia* after Éber.

What follows is Wyntoun's account of the legend of Gaedel and Éber highlighting where there are notable similarities with Grey's account and with Fordun's passages attributed to *legenda Sancti Brandani*. The intention is not to provide a new edition (which is hardly necessary given the high standard of Amours' work). The text below is taken from **C** as published by Amours, with variant readings from **R** itself and from Amours' text of **W**.[51] Only significant

46 Ibid., I. xlix. Amours was acutely aware of the difficulties posed by material unique to W (and its copy **H**): see ibid., xlix–l, and xlix n. 1 for further references.

47 See n. 51, below.

48 Macpherson, *Ðe Orygynale Cronykil*; Laing, *The Orygynale Cronykil*.

49 Amours, *The Original Chronicle*, II. 200–1. Wright, *The Historia*, I. 31 (§46); II. 40–1 (§46).

50 Amours, *The Original Chronicle*, II. 202–7. Greenway, *Henry, Archdeacon of Huntingdon*, 28–31.

51 The transcription of **C** was undertaken for Amours by a Miss Thompson and proofed against the manuscript before publication (see Amours, *The Original Chronicle*, II. xi). I have checked the published text against the manuscript and can vouch for its accuracy. **W** was transcribed for Amours by Henry Paton; it was not available when the text was being proofed (ibid.). Nevertheless, Amours (writing in 1902) described it as the manuscript he knew best (ibid., I. xlvii). Although I have not consulted it myself, it is most unlikely that any significant variants will have been missed or incorrectly reported by depending on the text in Amours' edition. As far as **R** is concerned, I have found Laing's edition to be not entirely reliable; because Amours says that he has taken his readings of **R** from Laing (ibid., II. x), I have, therefore, collated Amours' text of **C** against **R** myself.

variants will be noted (including all those that have a bearing on sense). There are only a few occasions in which **R** and **W** agree against **C**; attention will be drawn to these by amending **C** (using round brackets for material in **C** which may thus be deleted, and angled brackets to indicate additions or alterations to **C**).

The account of the legend of Gaedel and Éber in Wyntoun's Original Chronicle *(II, 8)*

Amours, *The Original Chronicle*, II.190–9 (C fos 15v–16r, W fos 37r–39r); R fos 24v–26r (pencil foliation)

The thorn and yogh have been rendered *th* and *z* respectively.

Key: *italic*: notable similarity with both Grey and *legenda Sancti Brandani* passages in Fordun
underline: notable similarity with *legenda Sancti Brandani* passages in Fordun alone
bold: notable similarity with Grey alone

Out of Sithi in that qwhile
In til Grece come Sir Newil,
That was of ded a worthi[52] man,
And in to Grece, gret worschep[53] wan.
He was nere into xx. gre
Be lyne discendande fra Noye
Off his[54] zongest son, but let,
That to nayme was callit[55] Iaphet.
Off Sem his brothir coyme presthade,
And of <this>[56] Iaphet coyme knichthade.
This Newel[57] was fra this Noye,
As I said are, the twenty degre,
And had a son callit Gedil-Glayis,
And, as the story of him sayis,[58]
To wif weddit Scota zynge,
Pharois douchtir of Egipte kynge.
This Gedilglayis was of gret pithe,
And warnyst weil of wit thar withe;
He gat on Scota barnys fayr,
And ane of tha suld haf beyn ayre
Til [59]Pharo that drownyt was
In to the Rede Se at that[60] chas
That the Egiptis made sa fel[61]
Apon the folk of Israel,

52 CR; *douchty* W
53 CR; *lordschip* W
54 CW; *this* R
55 CR; *hattyne* W
56 *this* RW; om. C
57 CR; om. W
58 CW; *mays* R
59 add *king* W
60 *at that* CR; *quhen he couth* W
61 line om. W

Qwhar al that folk[62] our past dry,
The Egiptis drownit hallely.
This Gedilglayis qwhen he saw
The lande of Egipte hie and law,
That in al thynge was profetabil,
And to his liffynge delitabille,
His dwellynge[63] thar he thoucht to ma,
And his awantagis of it ta,
Syn his barnnys apperit to be
Lordis of al that ryalte.
Bot the barnage of the lande
That ramanyt than liffande
Thoucht thai war agrewit sare
Throw[64] the wrakis thai tholit are
Be th<at>[65] exempil of[66] consaile
Al (the)[67] alyenys thai banyst haille.
Qwharfor thisilk Gedilglayis
His waye out of that lande[68] he tais,[69]
And throw the Mere Medyterrayne
He passit qwhil he coyme in Spayne
And on the wattyr of Hibery
He biggit the toure of *Brigancy*
Thar now is the towne of Galis,
Qwhar that thar sancte Iames lyis,[70]
And thai that duelt[71] than in that lande
He gert be til hym obeyssande.
Syne as he passit apon a day
Throw that lande[72] in til his play
Our fra hym be zonde the se
He kende[73] lyande a gret cuntre.
Than sperit he thraly of that lande
Qwha sulde be in it than duellande;[74]
Bot ansswer tharof gat he nane,
Na nakyn knawlage in certane.
In hy than gert he schippis thre
Withe armyt men son stuffit be,
And gert thaim passe be se thar way
To se that lande how that it lay,
And gif that it was ethe to wyn,
And qwha was duellande[75] it with in.
Withe wynde at wil thai folk than past,
And in the lande coyme at the last,

62 *that folk* CR; *the Israellis* W
63 CR; *wynnyng* W
64 *Throw* CR; *And thocht on* W
65 *the* C; *that* RW
66 CR; *throu* W
67 *the* C; om. RW
68 C; om. R (for W see next note)
69 In W this line reads: *Out of that cuntre tuke his waise*
70 In W this line reads: *Thare sanct Iames the appostill lyise*
71 CR; *duellis* W
72 *that lande* CR; *the cuntre* W
73 CR; *saw* W
74 In W this line reads: *Quhat thai wer therin wonnand*
75 CR; *wonnand* W

That ane ile was in the se,
Off gret space and of qwantite;
Bot thai that duelt in to that ile
Wnhonest was and wnwtyle;[76]
Tharfor thai at coyme to spy
That lande, thai dressit wnmodyrly;
For sum of thaim thai slew richt thar,
With aris, sum thai dange richt sare;[77]
Syne al the ile thai past about,[78]
And saw thai mycht *but dreid or dout*[79]
Wyn it hallely to thar wil,
Swa that thai wertu had thar til.[80]
Thai tuk wp sayl and past[81] in hy
Withe wynde at wil *to Brigancy*
Qwhar Gedilglayis was ourtane
Off casse, than ded richt subitane;[82]
Bot his body withe honoure
was put in[83] honest sepulture
With swylk oysse and solempnyte
As that tyme was in that cuntre.
Thir spyis taulde his barnys[84] sone
In to that ile as thai had done
And said that it was ethe to wyne
For thai that duelt that ile with in
war sottis sylde[85] of na walew
Na gouernyt thaim be na wertu;[86]
And at that lande was profitabil,
And till his[87] liffynge delitabil,
Tharfor thai said it was his[88] wil,
A ful consail thai gaf thar til,
For to passe that ile within
And it be conquest to thaim wyn
And with thar stuff[89] it occupy
For thaim and tharis heretabilly,
[90]Repruffand thaim as sottis wilk;[91]
Syn thai mycht doubtles but perille
Til thaim and [92]*thar lynnage*

76 *wnwtyle* CR; *rycht vile* W
77 Two lines added in W: *And thai that happinnit to get away / Held to thare schippis but delay*
78 In W this line reads: *And saillit all that ile about*
79 *but dreid or dout* CR; *with litill dout* W
80 In W this line reads: *Gif thai wald do thare mycht tharetill*
81 *tuk wp sayl and past* CR; *saillit out that way* W
82 This line in W reads: *With deid throu a chance on ane*
83 *put in* C; *put intyll* R; *had till* W
84 CR; *sonnys* W
85 *sottis sylde* CR; *bot vile* W
86 In W this line reads: *Nor of na gouernance na of vertew*
87 CR; *all* W
88 CR; *thar* W
89 CR; *avne* W
90 The six lines from *Repruffand* to *caytefly* om. W
91 *sottis wilk* C, *Scottis wyle* R.
92 add *all* R

That lordschipe wyn in heritage,
For to lieff it fayntly,
And lief [93]lowderaris caytefly,
A son of Gedil-Glayis than
Hiber, that was a drouchty man
Thought (at)[94] it was <tyll hym>[95] liffynge fayr,
Syn he was nocht his fadyr ayr;[96]
He son inclynyt to thar consail,
And chesit hym men and gat[97] wittaile
And laid[98] his schippis to the se
And enteryt in withe his menzhe,
And tuk up sayl and furthe he past
And in the ile coyme at the last.
Al the men[99] thar he slew [100]doune
That was nocht til his biddynge bowne;
Off (al)[101] the laif he tuk homage.
Thus al the lande in heritage
He wan al hail[102] and maid it fre
Til hym and his posteryte
Swa occupyit he furthe that lande
Withe al that euir[103] thar he fande,
And Scotland gert call that ile
For honoure of his modyr qwhile,
That Scota was withe al men calde,
As zhe (haf)[104] herde befor betaulde.
Hybernya thai call<it> it[105] syne
Off this Hiberius[106] in Latyne,
That Irlande we oysse to call
Now in til our langag<e>[107] [108]all.
Off Hiber thai coyme hallely
That we oysse to[109] call Irischery;
And this lady callit Scota
Al thir Scottis ar cummyn fra,
As zhe may in this process here
Qwhen we are cummyn to that mater.

Wyntoun took the account of Scottish origins in book II, chapter 8 only as far as Ireland, and delayed his description of *Scoti* reaching Scotland until book III, chapter 9, where he gave an account of the legend of Simón Brecc and the Stone of Scone. A detailed comparison with Grey's account and passages in Fordun

93 add *as* R
94 *at* C; om. RW
95 *tyll hym* RW; om. C
96 *ayr* CR; om. W (gap in MS)
97 *gat* CR; om. W
98 CR; *put* W
99 CR; *folkis* W
100 *haill* add W
101 *al* C; om. RW
102 *al hail* CR; *with forse* W
103 *al that euir* CR; *the gud* W
104 *haf* C; om. RW
105 *thai call it* C; *thai callyd it* R; *that callit is* W
106 CR; *Yber* W
107 *langage* RW; *langagis* C
108 add *Inglis* W
109 *oysse to* CR; om. W

attributed to *legenda Sancti Congalli* demonstrates that here, again, Wyntoun's origin-legend material was closely related to the source shared ultimately by Fordun and Grey.

The account of the legend of Simón Brecc and the Stone of Scone in Wyntoun's Original Chronicle *(III, 9)*[110]

Amours, *The Original Chronicle*, II. 344–7 (C fos 30v–31r, W fos 69r–70r); R fo 45r (pencil foliation)

The thorn and yogh have been rendered *th* and *z* respectively.

Key: *italic*: notable similarity with both Grey and *legenda Sancti Congalli* passages in Fordun
underline: notable similarity with *legenda Sancti Congalli* passages in Fordun alone
bold: notable similarity with Grey alone

In the meyne tyme that this fel
As zhe haf[111] herd of thir brethir tel
Thar was regnande a mychty *kynge*
That had al Spanzhe at gouernynge.
This kynge mony sonnys hade,
Off ane of tha zhit mast he made.
That Symon Brek was callit be nayme,
Ane honest man and of gude faym.
A gret stane the kynge than hade
That for th<is>[112] *kyngis set was made,*
And haldyn was a gret iowalle
Withe in the kynrik of Spanzhe hail.[113]
This kynge bad this Symon ta
That stane and in til Irlande ga,
And wyn[114] that lande and occupy,
And halde that stane perpetually,[115]
and mak *it his seigis thar,*
As thai of Spanzhe did of it are.
This Symon did than as the kynge
Fullely gaf hym in biddynge,

110 For explanation of text and variants, see above, 96–8.
111 *As zhe haf* C; *That* R; *That ze* W
112 *this* RW; *the* C
113 These two lines reflect Fordun's description of the stone as *diligenter in sua regione* [i.e., the kingdom of Spain] *quasi pro anchora tuebatur*; the idea of the stone as a 'jewel' conceivably suggests a link with Fordun's picture of it as *arte uetustissima diligenti sculptam opifice*.
114 *And wyn* CR; *Haue in* W
115 CR; *specially* W

And wan Irlande and chesit <his>[116] plasse
Qwhar honest and[117] mast likly was,[118]
Thar he made a gret cite,
And in it syne that stane gert he
Be haldyn and set for iowalle
And chartyr of that kynrik haile.[119]
Fergus Erchson fra hym syne
Down descendande ewyn[120] be lyne[121]
in to the v. and fifty gre,
As ewyn reknande[122] men may se,
Broucht this stane within Scotlande,
First quhen he come and wan th<at>[123] *lande*
and [124]it fyrst in Icolmkyll,
And Scone thar eftyr **it was broucht til**;
<And>[125] thar it was <syne>[126] mony (a)[127] day,
Qwhil Edward gert haff[128] **it away**
Kyng of Inglande, and syne he[129]
Gert it set in Lyndyn be.
Eftyr that Ihesu Criste was born
To sauff our lywis that was forlorn
A thousande and thre hundyr zher
And ten thar til or thar by nere.
Now[130] I wil the worde rahers
As I f<y>nde[131] of that stane in wersse:
Ni fallat fatum Scoti quocunque locatum
Inuenient[132] lapidem, regnare tenentur ibidem.
'Bot gif that werdis failzeande be,
Qwhar euir that stane ze segit se,
Thar sal the Scottis be regnande,
And lordis hail our all that lande.'

116 *his* RW; *that* C
117 *honest and* CR; *him thocht it* W
118 Compare Fordun's description of the site of the stone as *in eminenciori loco regni* and Grey's *le plus souerain bele lieu du pays*.
119 These three lines reflect Fordun's account of the stone's use in Ireland as an inaugural throne.
120 CR; *lyne* W
121 Compare Grey's account, where it was not specified that Fergus was a lineal descendant of Simón, but that Fergus was son of a king 'descended from Scota' (*extreit de Scota*).
122 *ewyn reknande* CR; *in the genology* W
123 *that* RW; *the* C
124 *set* add W
125 *And* RW; om. C
126 *syne* RW; *richt* C
127 *a* C; om. RW
128 *Edward gert haff* CR; *king Edward had* W
129 In W this line reads: *With the langschankis, and it he*
130 CR; *All* W
131 *fynde* RW; *fande* C
132 CW; *Inueniunt* R. For this Latin verse see also 54, above.

Wyntoun's account is closer to Fordun's material derived from *legenda Sancti Brandani* and *legenda Sancti Congalli* than to Grey's. This is brought out especially clearly in episodes where (as noted above) Grey's account represents improvements made by the author of his exemplar 1292x1304. Wyntoun agrees with Fordun's *legenda Sancti Brandani* material in including Gaedel's sojourn in Egypt, in its description of how Gaedel discovered Ireland, and in making Simón 'win that land [Ireland] and occupy it' as his father intended, rather than acquire it by marriage, as in Grey's account. Wyntoun wrote his chronicle independently of Fordun's,[133] so the similarity in detail shared by Wyntoun and Fordun against Grey can not be accounted for by supposing that Wyntoun acquired material from Fordun (directly or indirectly). There can be no doubt that Wyntoun's accounts of Gaedel, Éber, Simón and the Stone of Scone have been derived ultimately from the source shared by Fordun and Grey which brought together two originally distinct origin-legends from *legenda Sancti Brandani* and *legenda Sancti Congalli.* Details common to Wyntoun and Grey but absent from Fordun can therefore be accepted as features derived from the source shared by all three. This amounts to only three points – that Gaedel had 'fair offspring'[134] with Scota; Ireland was large and plentiful,[135] and that the Stone of Scone was taken to Scone. Both Grey and Wyntoun mention Edward I's removal of the Stone of Scone to London in 1296,[136] but this may have been so well known that it could have been added independently to each account.[136a]

Other witnesses of the origin-legend plus king-list text

There are some features of Wyntoun's account which differ from what is found in Grey or in Fordun's passages attributed to *legenda Sancti Brandani* and *legenda Sancti Congalli.* The most telling of these for our understanding of the source shared with Fordun and Grey is the alteration of Fergus son of Ferchar's patronymic to *Erchson*, 'son of Erc'. It will be recalled that in Grey the patronymic of Fergus – the first king in Grey's regnal-list which follows immediately after the origin-legend – had been altered from 'son of Erc' to 'son of Ferchar', and it was suggested that this was done in order to resolve a contradiction between the king-list (which would have originally represented the first king of *Scoti* in Scotland as Fergus 'son of Erc') and the account of Scottish origins (which gave the same role to a Fergus 'son of Ferchar'). It would appear, therefore, that the

133 There is a close relationship between Wyntoun and *Gesta Annalia* (attributed by Skene to Fordun) in their accounts of events between Alexander III's second marriage (1285) and *c.*1330. It can be shown that this has been derived independently from a common source; moreover, Fordun's authorship of *Gesta Annalia* is open to doubt. For all this see Broun, 'A new look'.

134 *bele engendrure*; *barnys fair.*

135 *vn Isle grant . . . herbous et plesaunt de boys et reueres*; *ane ile . . . off gret space and of qwantite.* Fordun's material from *legenda Sancti Brandani* has the same sentiment, if not the detail: indeed, Grey's *plesaunt* matches Fordun's description of Gaedel's explorers admiring *eius decorem.*

136 Misdated *c.*1310 by Wyntoun; book III, lines 1079–80 (see above).

136a The same may be true for the prophetic lines found in Wyntoun (above, 103) and XXVII.j.

same problem has arisen in Wyntoun's account, and that instead of changing the king-list to agree with the origin-legend, the origin-legend has been changed to conform with the king-list's Fergus 'son of Erc'.

Wyntoun did, indeed, use a king-list as a source. It was not he, however, who changed the origin-legend's Fergus 'son of Ferchar' into Fergus 'son of Erc'. It is plain, indeed, that Wyntoun had never heard of Fergus son of Ferchar, otherwise he should have been able to rescue himself from a chronological conundrum which caused him some embarrassment. In the first edition of his work Wyntoun had been content to repeat the claim made in his king-list source that the series of kings of Dál Riata preceded the series of Pictish kings lock, stock and barrel. He thus saw nothing amiss in describing Fergus son of Erc as a king in the mid-fifth century BC. By the time of the third edition of his work, however, Wyntoun had noticed that the period between Fergus son of Erc and Cinaed son of Alpín according to this scheme meant that, according to the royal genealogy (of which he had a copy), 1,200 years or more were covered by a mere ten generations. He admitted that this was unsatisfactory, and tentatively suggested that Fergus son of Erc and his successor kings of Dál Riata may not have reigned before the Picts but contemporaneously with them. He was not at all confident about this, however, and left the matter open to anyone else who might find a better solution. Had Wyntoun known about Fergus son of Ferchar it is difficult to see why he would not have (at least) mentioned him in this context; indeed, it might be expected that he would have suggested Fergus son of Ferchar in the role of first king of *Scoti* in Scotland in the mid-fifth century BC, which would have allowed him to put forward more forcibly his realisation that Fergus son of Erc must have been contemporary with Pictish kings, while at the same time retaining the early pre-Pictish date for the Scottish kingdom. Something like this is found in Fordun's chronicle, where (as noted at 70–1, above) the different kings called Fergus who appear as first king of *Scoti* in Scotland in the origin-legend and king-list have been reconciled by first placing Fergus son of Ferchar in 330 BC as king of the first colony of *Scoti* in Scotland, and then concocting an expulsion of *Scoti* from Scotland in AD 360 so that their victorious return under Fergus son of Erc (in AD 403) would present that king as the founder of a new kingdom, justifying his position as first king in the king-list.

In the case of both Grey and Wyntoun, therefore, the exemplar used by each for the origin-legend material they have in common must also have included a king-list. The question is, was the king-list and origin-legend in each exemplar brought together independently, or were they already combined in an earlier archetype shared by both? Marjorie Anderson has shown that Grey's and Wyntoun's king-lists were closely related, so there can be little doubt that their exemplars for origin-legend and king-list did, indeed, share an archetype which contained both origin-legend and king-list.[137]

This raises a further point: this archetype must have been at least closely related to (and may have been identical to) the source shared with Fordun's passages attributed to *legenda Sancti Brandani* and *legenda Sancti Congalli*. It is significant, therefore, that Marjorie Anderson has shown that the main king-list

137 Anderson, *Kings and Kingship*, 63–4.

underlying Fordun's chronicle was also closely related to Grey's and Wyntoun's.[138] This suggests that the archetype of the material on Scottish origins shared by Fordun, Grey and Wyntoun consisted of the king-list preceded by two origin-legends – one, the story of Gaedel and Éber, derived from *legenda Sancti Brandani*, the other, the tale of Simón, the Stone of Scone and Fergus son of Ferchar, derived from *legenda Sancti Congalli*.

It is apparent that no attempt had been made in the archetype shared ultimately by Fordun, Grey and Wyntoun to resolve contradictions between the two origin-legends or between the second legend and the king-list. This archetype, therefore, may be recognised as simply a collection of historical pieces.[139] This was the form in which it was incorporated into the origin-legend synthesis which underlies Fordun's account of Scottish origins. Some attempt had evidently been made in Wyntoun's exemplar to resolve at least the difference in patronymic between the two Ferguses cast in the role of 'first king'. Only in the 1292x1304 edition of this material preserved by Grey can it be shown (so far) that a concerted attempt was made to weld these different texts into a coherent and homogenous account of Scottish origins.

A final point to observe, however, is that although Fordun's main king-list source was closely related to Grey's and Wyntoun's, Marjorie Anderson has shown that it was not as close to Grey's and Wyntoun's king-lists as these were to each other.[140] It would appear, therefore, that Fordun's chronicle is a witness to an

138 Ibid., 63.

139 Conceivably, therefore, it may have included other texts. It is remotely possible, for example, that the compendium contained a king-list of Marjorie Anderson's Y-group (which would not have included Pictish kings) following the list of Marjorie Anderson's X-group (which would have included Pictish kings) attested in Fordun, Grey and Wyntoun. Fordun's chronicle shows knowledge of both X-and Y-type lists (Anderson, *Kings and Kingship*, 212–13), which on its own may not be remarkable, given its basis as a synthesis of various material; List **N** (closely related to List **D** which shares an exemplar with Wyntoun), however, consists of a Y-type Dalriadic list combined with an X-type list of Cinaed mac Alpín and his successors (see ibid., 63–4, 66–7 and 71, and 290–1 for edition of **N**).

140 Thus Grey and Wyntoun omit Nechtan son of Irb; and they have *Dergard* or *Dergert* for 'Derili', and *Frud* for 'Brude' father of Oengus (Fordun has, respectively, *Decili* and *Dereli*, and *Brude*; see Anderson, *Kings and Kingship*, 292, and also MacQueen and MacQueen, *Scotichronicon*, II. 302); they also omit the *l* from 'Melchon' (witnesses of Fordun read *Merlochon*, *Meilothonam* and *Meilochon*; see Miller, 'The disputed historical horizon', 20, and also MacQueen and MacQueen, *Scotichronicon*, II. 300); see Anderson, *Kings and Kingship*, 63–4. It may be noted that Miller saw the source of Fordun's Pictish king-list as different from the Pictish king-list in Marjorie Anderson's X-group (Miller, 'The disputed historical horizon', 21–5). Her view was based on the proposition that reign-lengths in Fordun's list and those of the X-group have been composed according to different chronographical schemes. It is unfortunate, therefore, that her analysis depended on an edition of Fordun's Pictish list based on **A** alone, disregarding two kings who have been omitted in **A** (ibid., 19). If these kings are included (as they should be), then her analysis of the chronographical scheme underpinning the list is compromised. It is difficult, moreover, to reject the evidence identified by Marjorie Anderson for regarding the source of Fordun's Pictish king-list as a member of her X-group, especially in the light of other evidence that an X-group list has been used in

earlier stage in the text history of the origin-legend-plus-king-list compilation. The difference between this earlier stage and the archetype shared ultimately by Grey and Wyntoun may not have been simply a matter of minor errors or amendments, but probably involved a fundamental change in how the king-list was understood. It is apparent that the main regnal-list ultimately behind Fordun's chronicle was a member of Marjorie Anderson's X-group whose archetype consisted of a list of kings of Dál Riata, a list of Pictish kings, and an annotated list of kings from Cinaed son of Alpín. Although the archetype of this group was arranged in a single sequence (beginning with Dál Riata, followed by Picts, and finally Cinaed and his successors), it was made clear that kings of Dál Riata were contemporary with kings of Picts. It is apparent, however, that the version of the origin-legend-plus-king-list compilation witnessed by Grey and Wyntoun included a textually tiny, but hugely significant amendment. Instead of regarding the lists of kings of Dál Riata and Picts as contemporary, followed by Cinaed son of Alpín and his successors, all three lists were presented as a continuous series so that the kings of Dál Riata were deemed to have reigned before the Pictish kings (which made for the chronological difficulties Wyntoun encountered when he compared this scheme with the royal genealogy). At a stroke, a reigning king of Scots in the thirteenth century was transformed from the most recent in a discrete succession of just under thirty kings into the latest in a series of about one-hundred-and-ten.[141]

Fordun noted the possibility that kings of Dál Riata reigned before the Picts,[142] and Marjorie Anderson has suggested that this may have been derived from the chronicle's principal king-list source.[143] The chronological scheme in Fordun's chronicle (almost certainly created by the synthesist writing sometime in or earlier than 1301) is a clear rejection of this idea, however, presenting the kings of Dál Riata in the regnal-list as contemporaries of the Picts, not their predecessors. The pre-Pictish kingdom of *Scoti* is mentioned only as an assertion made by others.[144]

---

the composition of Fordun's chronicle (see Anderson, *Kings and Kingship*, 63, 212–13).

141 See below, 170–3, 192–3.

142 Book I, chapter 35: 'Ancient histories tell us that Scotland had first of all been occupied by these two peoples of different nations and that their arrivals there were simultaneous or separated by only a short space of time, while on the contrary certain historians consider that the Scots reigned for many years before the Picts' (*Duabus autem hiis gentibus diuerse nacionis uetuste docent historie possessam primo fuisse Scociam, et earum inibi aggressus nullo uel pauco saltem interueniente temporis spacio, cum tamen ante Pictos quidam uolunt regnare Scotos multis annis*); MacQueen and MacQueen, *Scotichronicon*, I. 86–7 (their translation); the same is found in Skene, *Johannis de Fordun Chronica*, 30. Another mention of *Scoti* preceding Picts in Scotland is in book IV, chapter 9 (Skene, *Johannis de Fordun Chronica*, 152; MacQueen and MacQueen, *Scotichronicon*, II. 296–7), referring back to book I, chapter 35.

143 Anderson, *Kings and Kingship*, 64.

144 See n. 142 above. It may also be significant that no knowledge is shown of the specious date of 443 BC (or thereabout) which is found in Grey, Wyntoun (and List **D**, closely related to Wyntoun) as the date when this pre-Pictish kingdom was founded (see Anderson, *Kings and Kingship*, 221; on the relationship between Wyntoun and List **D** see ibid., 63–4). It is conceivable that the synthesist responsible for so much of the

The most economical explanation is that the principal king-list used by the synthesist conformed with the archetype of Marjorie Anderson's X-group and did not reconstrue the kings of Dál Riata as reigning before the Picts, but that he (or perhaps Fordun) knew of a list related to Grey, Wyntoun and List **D** which presented Fergus son of Erc and his Dalriadic successors as kings of a pre-Pictish kingdom of *Scoti*.

This chapter began with the recognition that there was a need to recover more accounts of Scottish origins than simply those yielded by an investigation of Fordun's chronicle. Only in this way could some sense of what was current be gained. Some progress has been achieved towards that end. The problems which remain to be tackled in the next chapter are the sources of the 'Éber' account and a fuller investigation of the dating and authorship of this material.

---

structure of Fordun's *Chronica Gentis Scottorum* realised the chronological absurdity of this pre-Pictish kingdom and restored the kings of Dál Riata to something approximating their proper position. If this were so, however, then it might be expected that he would have suppressed all mention of a kingdom of *Scoti* centuries earlier than the Picts; instead, however, he seems to have had a stab at reconciling this with the view that *Scoti* and Picts arrived in Scotland at about the same time: see book I, chapter 35, where it is claimed that the Picts were without kings for about two hundred years, while *Scoti* at the same time had kings continuously from their origin (Skene, *Johannis de Fordun Chronica*, 30; MacQueen and MacQueen, *Scotichronicon*, I. 86–7. The precise figure for the duration of the rule of these kings of *Scoti* is probably an addition by Bower; see above, 31 n. 118).

VI

ACCOUNTS OF SCOTTISH ORIGINS 1214–1306

It will be useful to summarise the progress made so far in identifying pre-Fordun accounts of Scottish origins and how they related to each other. The archetypes can from now on be denoted in the usual way by Greek letters. The following stemma can be constructed:

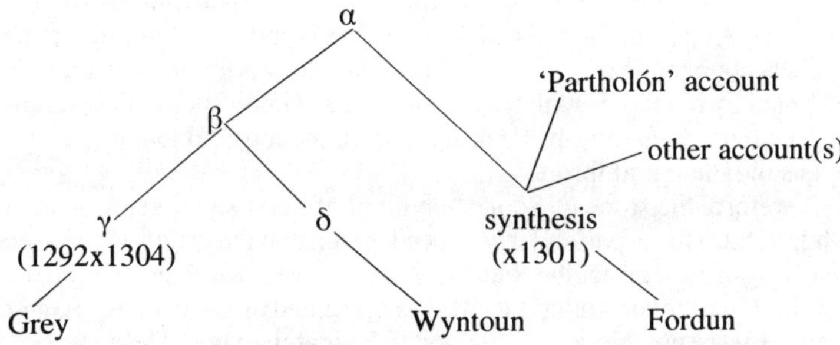

The chief characteristic of each archetype may be summarised:

α: a compendium of two origin-legends (the legend of Gaedel and Éber from *legenda Sancti Brandani* and the legend of Simón, the stone of Scone and Fergus son of Ferchar from *legenda Sancti Congalli*) followed by a Scottish king-list consisting of a list of kings of Dál Riata, a list of Pictish kings and an annotated list beginning with Cinaed mac Alpín running to the currently-reigning king of Scots.

β: a copy of α, but with a major change in how the king-list was understood; the Dalriadic and Pictish lists were no longer regarded as contemporary with each other, but were presented as a single series culminating in the list of Cinaed mac Alpín's successors.

γ: a reworking of β into a coherent history of the Scots and their kings in which material which posed problems for the credibility of the text, or which could otherwise prove awkward from a Scottish point of view, was ironed out or suppressed.

δ: a less drastic reworking of β than was the case with γ. The problem in β of different patronymics for Fergus the first king of *Scoti* in Scotland was resolved by adopting the king-list's Fergus son of Erc for this role; in γ the origin-legend's Fergus son of Ferchar had been preferred instead of Fergus son of Erc.

The role of Ireland in lost accounts of Scottish origins attested by Fordun, Grey and Wyntoun

It is possible at this stage to say something more about α and (in due course) δ. Detail in origin-legend material shared by Fordun and either Grey or Wyntoun can now be identified as inherited from α. Wyntoun's account in particular can thus serve to confirm that in the account of the legend of Gaedel and Éber in α *Brigancia* was described as a tower on the River Ebro from which Gaedel first caught sight of Ireland; Gaedel was said to have dispatched an armed expedition which attacked the inhabitants and explored the island; the expedition reported back that Ireland could readily be overcome without danger, and Gaedel's sons were reproved that they would be fools not to take possession of Ireland and instead choose to live meanly as cowards; this inspired Éber to mount an armed assault on Ireland and conquer it, and he named the island *Scocia* after his mother Scota – but it was afterwards called *Hibernia* from Éber himself, or from the 'Hiberic Sea'. As for the legend of Simón Brecc and the stone of Scone in α, Wyntoun's account confirms that it told how Simón was given the stone throne of kings of Spain by his father with the intention that Simón should take Ireland, and that Simón, after conquering Ireland, set it up in the most honourable place in the kingdom as the inaugural throne.

In α, therefore, the stone of Scone – symbol of Scottish kingship – was identified with Ireland. This is particularly striking given that the origin-legend preceded a Scottish king-list; in effect the Scottish kingship was portrayed as rooted in Irish kingship. In α, moreover, Ireland itself was presented as the original *Scocia*. Both these features were not, however, retained in later archetypes. The absence of Tara from Grey's and Wyntoun's accounts suggests that this detail may have been omitted in β. Furthermore, although the statement that Ireland was named *Scocia* was evidently preserved in β, it does not appear in Grey's account and may therefore have been dropped in γ. The author of γ may have made a point of reserving *Scocia* for Scotland; this would tally with his description of Fergus son of Ferchar and his followers readopting the name *Scoti*, which may have been intended to explain *Scoti* as 'Scots' in particular rather than Scots and Irish indiscriminately.[1] On the other hand, a strident assertion of the Irishness of the Scots may be attributed to γ. We are told in Grey's account that Fergus son of Ferchar was wholly Irish,[2] and that he and his followers' 'own country is Ireland, according to their custom and language'.[3] Such sentiments would not have been unprecedented around 1300; Robert I (it will be recalled) wrote to Irish kings in the winter of 1306–7 that common language and custom showed that 'we come from the seed of one nation'.[4] The Irishness of Fergus son of Ferchar may have been

1 Especially if *Scota . . . de qei enuindrent lez Scotois* was translated from γ.

2 *et tout estoit il du nacioun de Ireland.*

3 *lour propre pays est Ireland, lour coustom et patoys acordaunt.*

4 *ab uno processimus germine nacionis*: see above, 1. There may be a residual doubt, however, that the insistence that Fergus and his followers were Irish could be Grey's own comment, especially as it is followed immediately by a cross-reference to a later passage on the Picts which seems certainly to have been Grey's own addition. (After

deployed by the author of γ as part of an argument defending Scottish independence by portraying the Scots as thoroughly 'unBritish', thereby hoping to by-pass the argument based on an ancient British past which Edward I used to justify his conquest of Scotland.[5] A concern to present the Scots and Scotland as 'unBritish' may also be seen in the insistence that Fergus son of Ferchar settled 'the most distant country beyond Britain'.[6] A cultural identification with Ireland may therefore have been sufficiently current to be thought useful both by the author of γ and Robert I (in different contexts).

As far as δ is concerned, Wyntoun probably derived from it the idea that Ireland was named *Scocia* (Wyntoun's *Scotland*), an idea which the author of δ could have inherited from β. A number of innovatory features in Wyntoun's account may have been derived by him from δ (or conceivably from a descendant of δ); it seems unlikely that Wyntoun himself would have made any significant amendments – he appears to have done little more than translate or copy the various origin-legend accounts at his disposal.[7] Notable among these innovations is the notion that the Irish were named after Éber, while the Scots were named after Scota;[8] this would appear to have been designed to create a distinction between Scots and Irish while still apparently not denying that they formed a single people.

It is possible in these archetypes, therefore, to detect an association of Scottish

---

lour propre pays . . . acordaunt it continues *qi puis furount mellez od Pices com apres serra recordez*.) Nonetheless, it is difficult to see why Grey might have wished to reinforce the link between Scots and Ireland in this way. Moreover, in the passage on Pictish origins which Grey himself wrote, he retold how the Picts acquired wives from Ireland on condition that their children spoke Irish, and he went on to observe that Irish 'remains to this day in the Highlands among some who are called Scots' (*quel patois [Irrays] demurt a iour de huy hu haute pays entre lez vns qest dit Escotoys*: Skene's translation). As far as Grey was concerned, therefore, this rather than the colony led by Fergus son of Ferchar, was the event which he used to explain how Gaelic ('Irish') came to Scotland.

5 Particularly in 1301 when Edward I made a formal reply to papal condemnation of his action. See Stones, 'The appeal to history'.

6 *le plus lointisme pays outre Bretaine*. These elements in γ may be evidence that it was written sometime in or after 1301.

7 See further Drexler, 'Fluid prejudice', 66–8. These innovatory features could have included the notion that the inhabitants of Ireland conquered by Éber were *wnhonest* and *wnwtyle*; their moral degeneracy would thus have made it seem excusable to deprive them of their land, as well as explaining the idea (derived ultimately from α) that Ireland was easy to occupy. Another departure from α or β would have been the death of Gaedel before he could deliver the speech (derived ultimately from α) urging his sons to conquer Ireland; the speech is attributed instead to the returning explorers. No doubt this was deemed to be tidier than having Gaedel lingering on despite the claim that he suffered a sudden death (*morte repentina*; *ourtane off casse, than ded richt subitane*; cf. *ly surueint vn tresgref malady dount ly coueint murrir*, which is a little less dramatic).

8 *Off Hiber thai coyme hallely that we oysse to call Irishery; and this lady callit Scota al thir Scottis ar cummyn fra.* This is followed by a statement that Scota as eponym of the Scots would be mentioned later, but Scota does not get mentioned again in Wyntoun's chronicle. Has Wyntoun copied this from his exemplar, but omitted the relevant passage when he came to reproduce the legend of Simón and the Stone of Scone?

kingship with Ireland, but also a tendency (which may be discerned particularly in γ and δ) to emphasise a distinction between Ireland and Scotland or Irish and Scots.

The date and provenance of lost accounts of Scottish origins attested by Fordun, Grey and Wyntoun

What can be determined about the dating and authorship of these archetypes? The dating of γ to 1292x1304 establishes a *terminus ante quem* for α and β; the dating of the synthesis behind Fordun's chronicle to in or before 1301 offers only a slight refinement of this. As for δ, some indication of its *terminus ante quem* may be found by reference to the king-lists which Marjorie Anderson has identified as more closely related to Wyntoun than to Grey. These are lists **D** and **N**, which Anderson has argued shared a common ancestor.[9] **D** dates to the late fifteenth century; unfortunately it breaks off after Lulach mac Gille Comgáin, which deprives us of important evidence for the date of its exemplar.[10] **N** is more promising; it is part of a vigorously pro-English account of British history in a late-fourteenth-century manuscript.[11] **N** concludes with an account of the descent of King John Balliol and Robert I from three sisters (daughters of David earl of Huntingdon), finishing with 'Robert Bruce the third who had himself crowned king of Scotland at Scone and killed John Comyn'.[12] Robert I was the third Robert Bruce who was a claimant to the throne after the death of Alexander III's grand-daughter Margaret in 1290. This way of referring to Robert I and the detailed knowledge shown concerning King John and Robert suggests that the exemplar of **N** was probably written in or soon after Robert I's *coup* in 1306.[13] This, then, would be the *terminus ante quem* for the common ancestor with **D** which, if it was not identical with δ, was closely related to it.[14]

For a *terminus post quem* for these archetypes we must look to their king-list component. Marjorie Anderson has shown that this was derived from the archetype of her X-group, which she dated to the reign of Alexander II (1214–49). There can be little doubt, therefore, that α and β were produced sometime in the thirteenth century.

The provenance of these archetypes is difficult to pin down precisely. Marjorie

9 Anderson, *Kings and Kingship*, 63–4. This common ancestor may have also been shared (directly or indirectly) by Wyntoun: Wyntoun used the Verse Chronicle as a major source for his account of Cinaed mac Alpín's successors, which could account for the absence in his text of the errors shared by **D** and **N** (remembering that only the section from Cinaed in **N** belongs to Marjorie Anderson's X-group).

10 Anderson, *Kings and Kingship*, 64–6; edited 264–8.

11 Ibid., 66–7; edited 290–1.

12 *Robertus Bruys tercius qui seipsum fecit coronari in Regem Scocie apud Sconam et interfecit Johannem Comyn.*

13 Ibid., 67, where it is tentatively suggested that it may have acquired its sharply anti-Scottish tone as a response to Scottish propaganda circulating in the months before Edward I died in July 1307.

14 See below, 125–7, for further discussion.

Anderson has suggested that notes on St Serf and St Regulus in Grey's copy of the king-list could indicate an association with St Andrews.[15] Two derivatives of δ, Wyntoun and list **D**, have strong connexions with St Andrews, so δ may also have been a St Andrews text.[16] St Andrews is also the provenance of the fourteenth-century exemplar of list **F** which also belonged to Marjorie Anderson's X-group.[17] There are some indications that an important source for Fordun's chronicle which may have terminated with events of 1285 (possibly therefore the synthesis itself) had some association with Dunfermline.[18] The evidence for the provenance of all these archetypes, such as it is, takes us repeatedly back to Fife, therefore. Although it is difficult to pin down with confidence individual archetypes to particular churches, it is a reasonable presumption that all were produced in the east midlands of the Scottish kingdom.[19]

There are a couple of details unique to Fordun or Grey which probably originated in α, and which suggest that the author of α, or at least the author of his origin-legend sources, knew Gaelic. In Fordun's *legenda Sancti Congalli* material, the site where Simón placed the stone throne in Ireland is identified as *Themor*, i.e. Tara. Tara is Temair (or Temuir) in medieval Gaelic, which is obviously what was intended by *Themor*.[20] A knowledge of Gaelic in this passage from *legenda Sancti Congalli* preserved by Fordun may also be detected in the description of Tara as 'the loftiest site in the kingdom',[21] which may reflect Gaelic *temair*, 'a high place, eminence, hill'.[22] Another Gaelic form is attested uniquely in Grey's account, where Gaedel is rendered *Gaidel* rather than *Gaythelos* in Fordun and *Gedilglayis* in Wyntoun. The forms adopted in Fordun and Wyntoun would appear to have

15 Ibid., 66.

16 Ibid., 64–5.

17 Ibid., 54–9; see also below, 135.

18 See Broun, 'A new look'.

19 As far as the authors of the 'Éber' and 'Partholón' accounts and the synthesis are concerned, their lack of literacy in Gaelic (though not necessarily ignorance of Gaelic itself) is discussed below, 129–31.

20 The spelling *m* for /v/ is orthodox Gaelic; in Latin *u* would be expected (unless, of course, the Latin form *Temoria* were employed, which is not the case in this instance). The vowel in the final syllable, although unorthodox, would not be unprecedented in Gaelic writing (see Jackson, *The Gaelic Notes*, 132). *Th* for /t/, however, would be most unusual in a Gaelic context. If 'Themor' accurately reflected the spelling that would have appeared in α (and this is an important and unquantifiable 'if'), then it seems to be a cross between Gaelic and non-Gaelic orthography. This would not be unparalleled in eastern Scotland between the mid-twelfth and mid-thirteenth centuries; see Broun, 'Gaelic literacy'.

21 The stone throne is placed *in eminenciori loco regni* (reading *eminenciori* as a Medieval Latin instance of a comparative for superlative).

22 *DIL*, s.v. *temair* (a). Both Grey and Wyntoun's accounts at this point have an abstract rather than physical sense of 'loftiness'; the former has *le plus bele souerain lieu*, the latter has *that plasse qwhar honest* (i.e. honourable) *and mast likly was*: it is possible, therefore that this could reflect an interpretation of *eminencior* in β which may have arisen if β was the work of a scribe ignorant of Gaelic who failed to recognise the connexion with *temair*. He is likely, moreover, to be responsible for the absence of Tara in Grey and Wyntoun's accounts.

been taken from copies of the royal genealogy.[23] Grey's *Gaidel*, however, was doubtless copied from his exemplar; a particular feature is *d* for intervocalic /ð/ which would be orthodox in Gaelic orthography but much less usual than 'th' in a non-Gaelic context (whether Fordun's Latin or Grey's French). It is possible, therefore, that *Gaidel* was the form which appeared in α.[24] Given the loss of Gaelic among Scottish men of letters in the east midlands in this period,[25] it is likely that these Gaelic features were originally present in α, but were lost at different points in transmission.

These Gaelic forms probably present in α may, moreover, have been inherited from *legenda Sancti Brandani* and *legenda Sancti Congalli* (attributed in α as its sources respectively for the legend of Gaedel and Éber and the legend of Símón Brecc and the stone of Scone). The inclusion of so much origin-legend material is not at all common in a Life of a Gaelic saint, however. The closest parallel would appear to be the Life of Catroe – but it was written on the Continent and can not be taken, therefore, as a typical example of Gaelic or specifically Scottish hagiography.[26] Such an explanation of Catroe's ethnic background might have been thought desirable on the Continent as a way of locating the saint in the mental world-map of an audience for whom *Scoti* were foreign. It is possible, therefore, that *legenda Sancti Brandani* and *legenda Sancti Congalli* were produced in a part of Gaelic Scotland where the strength of Anglo-French acculturisation in the twelfth century could have encouraged the writing of hagiography designed to explain existing saints' cults in terms acceptable to the new culture and its personnel.[27] If so, the inclusion of an account of Scottish origins may have been intended to inform incoming Anglo-French men of letters that St Brendan belonged to an ancient people whose origins were located within the biblical scheme of early history and that St Congal[28] was closely associated with Scottish kingship. It has recently been argued that a body of hagiography from the twelfth century and earlier can be traced in the now lost sources of the Aberdeen Breviary, although it is impossible to determine whether any of these included an account of

23 Their texts of the genealogy are discussed below, 180–2.

24 A unique feature of Wyntoun's account which may with less conviction be attributed to α is its statement that the Stone of Scone was first brought to Iona (*first in Icolmkyll*) before eventually being taken to Scone. Wyntoun's *Icolmkyll* is clearly a Scots rendering of Gaelic *Í Choluim Chille*; this was, however, Wyntoun's preferred form for Iona – he evidently regarded *Icolmkyll* as Scots and *Iona* as Latin – so it is impossible to regard it necessarily as a feature of his exemplar. Nonetheless, it is still possible to argue that the idea of the Stone reaching Scone via Iona is more likely to have been inherited from α than interpolated in β.

25 See Broun, 'Gaelic literacy'.

26 Colgan, *Acta Sanctorum*, facsimile reprint, 494–507: partially reproduced in Skene, *Chronicles*, 106–16. The most recent discussion of the Life of Catroe is Macquarrie, *The Saints of Scotland*, 199–210; see also Boyle, 'St Cadroe in Scotland'. See also comments in MacQueen and MacQueen, *Scotichronicon*, I. xix–xx.

27 It has also been suggested in MacQueen and MacQueen, *Scotichronicon*, I. xx, that these texts may have been of Continental origin.

28 Possibly Comgall was intended, if *Congall* originally represented *Cougall*.

Scottish origins.[29] It is conceivable, therefore, that the origin-legend material preserved through α originated in Latin texts written by Gaelic churchmen in the twelfth or maybe the early thirteenth century.

The 'Éber' account and its source

The archetype α is particularly significant because it can be recognised as the ultimate source of the 'Éber' account. The 'Éber' account is not only the same in outline as the legend of Gaedel and Éber which would have appeared in α, but it also shares some significant detail. This is particularly evident in its description of Gaedel as 'elegant in appearance but unstable in spirit' who, 'fortified by a force of many young men', inflicted much damage in his father's kingdom because he had been denied any power, and was as a result of his arrogance 'driven by force from his native land' and set sail for Egypt.[30] The comparable passage attributed to *legenda Sancti Brandani* is notably similar. There we are told that Gaedel, 'conspicuous for his strength and boldness', left his father's domain for Egypt 'supported by a spirited force of young men . . . after oppressing his father and everyone else with his arrogance, . . . quitting because of the rejection of his position rather than on his own accord'.[31] Other details which would have been shared with α include Gaedel's building of a tower at *Brigancia* and the circumnavigation of Ireland by an armed expeditionary force who reported the discovery of a beautiful land. On this basis the first part of XVII.6 can be recognised as derived from the 'Éber' account, in which we are told that *Hibernia* was named after Éber or from the 'Hiberic' sea (which was itself named after Éber).[32] This would correspond closely with the very similar statement in XVII.5 derived from α. The 'Éber' account may be recognised, therefore, as a much more elaborate version of the legend of Gaedel and Éber found in α.

This raises the possibility that the 'Éber' account, like α, may have also included the legend of Simón Brecc and Fergus son of Ferchar as well as a version of the king-list beginning with Fergus son of Erc. It will be recalled that in XXVII the account of Simón Brecc attributed to *legenda Sancti Congalli* was followed by an alternative version (beginning at XXVII.f) which told how Simón brought up the stone of Scone from the sea when he lifted anchor beside the Irish coast. This introduced the prophecy that *Scoti* would rule wherever the stone was found (XXVII.ij), and the chapter concluded with a reference to the mixed Greek and

29 Macquarrie, 'Lives of Scottish saints in the Aberdeen Breviary'.

30 VIII.1: . . . *uultu elegantem animo tamen instabilem nomine Gaythelos quem nullam in regno potestatem habere permiserat, unde concitatus in iram et manu multorum munitus iuuenum horrenda crudelitate paternum regnum multis affecit cladibus et insolenciis, patrem et incolas offendens uehementer. Quapropter a patria uiolenter expulsus nauigio diuertit in Egiptum.*

31 VIII.3: *Qui scilicet Gaythelos uiribus prestans et audacia dum patrem uel ceteros insolencia perurgeret, causa repulsa pocius quam uoto discedens animosa fretus manu iuuenum in Egiptum secessit.*

32 XVII.6 is introduced as *ex cronicis*; the remaining part reports other opinions on how *Hibernia* acquired its name.

Egyptian origins of *Scoti* (XXVII.l–n). Mixed Greek and Egyptian origins are an important and distinctive part of the narrative in the 'Éber' account (notably in X.1 and XI.1), which reinforces the suggestion that XXVII.f–n may have been derived from the 'Éber' account. On this basis it is possible, further, to argue that the 'Éber' account may also have been the source of much of XXXIV, which contains the other account of Fergus son of Ferchar apart from the passage attributed to *legenda Sancti Congalli* in book II, chapter 12. If so, the 'Éber' account could also be the source of the material in XXX and XXXI in which it was explained who the banished *Scoti* were who in XXXIV Fergus came from Ireland to rule.

If the 'Éber' account told how Fergus son of Ferchar was first king of *Scoti* in Scotland, this raises the question of whether it also mentioned Fergus son of Erc and, if so, how the claims of Fergus son of Ferchar and Fergus son of Erc to be first king of *Scoti* in Scotland may have been resolved. A key passage which could point to an answer is the claim in book III, chapter 2, of Fordun's chronicle, that Fergus son of Erc in the last three years of his sixteen years as king 'reigned beyond Drumalban, that is beyond the ridge of Alba, the first of the kings from the nation of *Scoti* in the land of the Picts, from the mountains to the Firth of Forth'.[33] In Fordun's chronicle nothing more is made of this apparent conquest of the Picts by Fergus son of Erc; indeed, it cuts across the overall narrative in which *Scoti* and Picts are portrayed as in alliance during and after Fergus's reign.[34] It can plausibly be seen, however, as an attempt to reconcile the appearance of Fergus son of Erc as first in the king-list with the portrayal of Fergus son of Ferchar in the origin-legend as first king of *Scoti* in Scotland. Fergus son of Erc would thus have been presented as first king of Scotland,[35] thereby allowing Fergus son of Ferchar to remain as first king of *Scoti* in Scotland. As noted above, in Fordun's chronicle this problem was resolved differently (probably by the synthesist): Fergus son of Erc was portrayed as the first king of a re-established kingdom west of Drumalban following the expulsion of *Scoti* from Scotland forty-three years earlier, thereby

33 *ultra Drumalban hoc est ultra dorsum Albanie primus regum Scotici generis in terra Pictorum a montibus ad mare Scoticum regnauit.* It may be noted that Fergus son of Erc would have been accorded a three-year reign in α and its derivitives.

34 Note, however, the statement earlier in the chapter that Fergus took three years to re-establish the whole extent of the kingdom on both sides of *uadum Scoticum* which had been anciently possessed by his ancestors, that is from Stainmore and the Hebrides to the Orkneys (Skene, *Johannis de Fordun Chronica*, 88; MacQueen, MacQueen and Watt, *Scotichronicon*, III. 4: *Infra quoque spacium abinde trium annorum idem Fergusius uniuersas regni regiones cis citraque uadum Scoticum a patribus ab antiquo possesas, ad Mora Lapidea uidelicet et Inchegal ad insulas Orcades, sub sua composuit dicione*). If *uadum Scoticum* referred to the Firth of Forth (see MacQueen, MacQueen and Watt, *Scotichronicon*, III. 5, 190) then this would contradict the claim that Fergus only ruled in the east in the last three years of his reign. The rest of the passage suggests, however, that west of Drumalban was in fact intended; Drumalban was certainly regarded as the frontier between *Scoti* and Picts in the remainder of Fordun's *Chronica* until the Picts were conquered by Cinaed mac Alpín (see e.g. book IV chapter 4).

35 This would have been possible if the comment in all lists belonging to Marjorie Anderson's X-group (including α) that Fergus son of Erc ruled *ultra Drumalban* was misconstrued as east of Drumalban, rather than west (which was what was was originally intended): see Anderson, *Kings and Kingship*, 213, 212 n.2.

allowing Fergus son of Erc to be seen as first king of an unbroken succession which continued to the present day. The alternative solution, in which Fergus son of Erc was presented as first king of *Scoti* in the current heartland of the kingdom, may therefore have been adopted in the 'Éber' account which, when incorporated dutifully by the synthesist, would have made the claim that Fergus ruled for three years east of Drumalban appear extraneous. (The figure of three years was derived from Fergus's reign-length given in the king-list.)

Finally, this brings us to the question of whether the Éber' account used α or β as its source. The principal detectable difference between these archetypes is that the component parts of the king-list in α – Dalriadic king-list, Pictish king-list and list of successors of Cinaed mac Alpín – came in β to be regarded as a single succession. If the 'Éber' account included XXXIV, however, then *Scoti* could not have been portrayed in it as preceding the Picts; also, if Fergus son of Erc was presented as first king of Scotland by conquering the Picts beyond Drumalban, then this would obviously be incompatible with β in which Fergus son of Erc would have appeared as first king in a series of kings of *Scoti* who ruled before the Picts. It would appear, therefore, that the 'Éber' account was derived from α rather than β. If so, this would make it impossible in Fordun's chronicle for us to distinguish the 'Éber' account's king-list (if, indeed, there was one) from material derived from α by the synthesist.[36]

It is possible, therefore, to recognise the 'Éber' account as a reworking of material derived from α to create a coherent and more expansive narrative of Scottish origins. According to the above analysis of its probable contents it would appear to have been written with a readiness to confront problems in its source. One instance not discussed so far would have been how its author tackled the difficulty – which would arise from bringing the two origin-legends in α together – of the conquest of Ireland by Simón Brecc despite its prior occupation by *Scoti*. This has evidently been completely recast. The new version, in which Simón came across the stone of Scone by accident while sailing near the Irish coast, replaced the idea that Simón received the stone from his father as a token of his future taking of Ireland; there is no indication, moreover, that Simón was said in the 'Éber' account to have come from Spain (although this information may, for all we know, have been subsumed when the account was incorporated into the origin-legend synthesis).

The vision of Ireland in the 'Éber' account

The most significant departures from α traceable to the 'Éber' account were made to promote a central idea: that each people has a divinely ordained virgin territory. We are told that the attempt to settle in Spain was doomed because it infringed the God-given right of Spaniards; only once *Scoti* arrived in unoccupied Ireland did they find a land which they could possess in freedom and security. This stood in sharp contrast to how the colonisation of Ireland would have been described in

36 The synthesist (if he, rather than Fordun, included the references to a β-type list) would thus have gained his knowledge of β independently of the 'Éber' account.

either α or β: there the inhabitants whom *Scoti* found in Ireland were either killed or forcibly subjected. What is particularly striking about the 'Éber' account, however, is that its author has taken it for granted that Ireland, not Scotland, should be the virgin territory divinely ordained for *Scoti*. Indeed, if it is accepted that the 'Éber' account was the source for the narrative on Fergus son of Ferchar in XXXIV, along with the material in XXX and XXXI on which XXXIV depends, then its author would appear to have been prepared to present the arrival of *Scoti* in Scotland as only a partial migration in the train of the Picts. This reinforces the impression that, as far as he was concerned, *Scoti* in Scotland were in origin no more than an offshoot of *Scoti* in Ireland. The portrayal of Ireland in the 'Partholón' account as the homeland reached by *Scoti* at the end of an arduous exodus from Egypt also clearly implied that *Scoti* in Scotland were no more than an offshoot of *Scoti* in Ireland.[37]

What is particularly striking is that when the authors of the 'Partholón' and 'Éber' accounts recast the material on Scottish origins at their disposal they apparently regarded the idea of Ireland as homeland of *Scoti* as something obvious and natural. In the same way as Scots today would – without a second thought – assume that Scotland was their particular country, these thirteenth-century writers (probably somewhere in the east midlands of Scotland), as part of their vision of Scottish 'freedom', apparently regarded Ireland as their homeland. The author of γ, although rather less keen on Ireland as homeland of *Scoti*, would appear also to have emphasised that the first *Scoti* in Scotland were 'entirely of the nation of Ireland'. In short, as far as these Scottish men of letters were concerned, *Scoti* were Irish.

What aspirations and circumstances might explain the appeal of this Irish identity in the increasingly deGaelicised midlands of the thirteenth-century Scottish kingdom? As far as γ was concerned it has been suggested that its statements about the Irishness of the Scots were employed to emphasise that the Scots and their kingdom were, from the very beginning, wholly separate from the

37 Its account of the colonisation of Scotland can not be traced positively in Fordun's chronicle; it may have been the source of one of the versions of Pictish origins in XXIX, in which case it may, too, have used the legend of Picts seeking wives from *Scoti* in order to explain how *Scoti* first came to Scotland. It might be objected that this could simply be an example of the well attested phenomenon of identification with someone else's homeland. A well known example would be the adoption by English men of letters of Britain as their homeland, with the result that the ancient regnal history of the Britons expounded by Geoffrey of Monmouth became English history. Seventy-one manuscripts of the French prose *Brut* chronicle beginning with Brutus (or earlier) and including kings of England up to the twelfth century or beyond are listed in Tyson, 'Handlist', 338–41; fourteen of these terminate at some point in the thirteenth century, and two terminate in the twelfth century (1154 and 1199). This is quite different, however, from the depiction by Scottish men of letters of Ireland as homeland of *Scoti*. The English turned to British history because it related to the island and kingdom in which they actually lived. The equivalent for Scottish men of letters would have been to embrace Pictish history as their own. On the evidence of the 'Partholón' and 'Éber' accounts, however, the emphasis was on Ireland, not Pictland, as the *locus* of their ancient past and homeland. This choice would have been striking in the 'Éber' account if, like α, it included a list of Pictish kings.

Britons and the kingdom of Britain. Did Irish identity, therefore, amount to no more than a debating-point in a historiographical battle for Scottish independence?[38] The answer must be no. Not only is there no particular emphasis on not being British in what can be retrieved from the 'Éber' and 'Partholón' accounts, but their portrayal of Ireland is quite different from that in accounts of Scottish origins which can be dated specifically to sometime after Edward's challenge to Scottish independence in the 1290s.[39]

Accounts of Scottish origins in the first war of independence

There are accounts of Scottish origins in texts aimed specifically at justifying Scottish independence in the face of English counter-claims, and it is striking how in these the origin-legend was adapted to focus on Scotland rather than Ireland. The Declaration of Arbroath in 1320 included a brief summary of the exodus of *Scoti* from Scythia to Scotland which, although it featured Spain, omitted Ireland altogether.[40] It was stated there (in the recension with which late-medieval Scottish historians would have been familiar) that[41]

> . . . the Scottish nation . . . journeyed from the lands of Greece and Egypt by the Tyrrhenian Sea and the Pillars of Hercules, and stayed for many years in Spain among the fiercest of peoples, but could not be subdued anywhere by any peoples however barbaric. Coming from there one thousand and two hundred years after the Children of Israel crossed the Red Sea, it took possession of the settlements in the west which it now possesses,[42] after first driving out the Britons and totally destroying the Picts; and although often attacked by the Norwegians, Danes and English, its victories were many and its efforts innumerable, and it

38 The idea of a 'war of historiography' fought alongside the political struggle in the first war of independence has been employed to good effect particularly in Goldstein, *The Matter of Scotland*, chapters 2 and 3.

39 Including γ. See below, 128–9.

40 Fergusson, *The Declaration of Arbroath*, 9. Robert I's chancellor, Bernard de Linton, was credited as the Declaration's author until the grounds for this were challenged by A. A. M. Duncan in *RRS*, V. 164–6. Barrow, *Robert Bruce*, 3rd edn, 308, has suggested Master Alexander Kinninmonth, one of King Robert's ambassadors to the Curia, as the author. The Declaration's chief source for its brief account of Scottish origins was (ironically) Henry of Huntingdon's *Historia Anglorum*: see Brown, 'The Scottish origin-legend before Fordun', 144–5.

41 Scott and Watt, *Scotichronicon*, VII. 4–7 (based on their translation): . . . *Scotorum nacio . . . de Grecie finibus et Egipti per Mare Tirenum et Columpnas Herculis transiens, et in Hispania inter ferocissimas gentes per multa temporum curriculam residens, a nullis quantumcumque barbaricis poterat alicubi gentibus subiugari. Indeque ueniens post mille ducentos annos a transitu populi Israelitici per Mare Rubrum sibi sedes in occidente quas nunc optet* [see note below], *expulsis primo Britonibus et Pictis omnino deletis, licet per Norweigenses, Dacos et Anglicos sepius impugnata fuerat, multis tamen uictoriis et laboribus quamplurimis acquisiuit, ipsasque ab omni seruitute liberas ut prisce testantur historie semper tenuit. In quorum regno centum et tredecim reges de ipsorum regali prosapia nullo alienigena interueniente regnauerunt.*

42 Ibid. has *optet*, 'desires', but the original presumably read *optinet*; apparently a suspension-stroke for *in* has been omitted.

> has held these places always free from all servitude, as the old histories testify. One hundred and thirteen kings of their royal lineage have reigned in their kingdom, with no intrusion by a foreigner.

The first extant account of Scottish origins which cast Scotland itself as the homeland of *Scoti*, however, was Baldred Bisset's *Processus* prepared at the Curia in 1301.[43] He recounted how 'a daughter of Pharaoh king of Egypt landed in Ireland with an armed force and a very large fleet. Then after taking on board some Irishmen, she sailed to Scotland, carrying with her the royal seat' which Edward I had forcibly removed. She conquered the Picts, and took over the kingdom. 'And from this Scota the Scots and Scotland take their name. Hence the ditty: The whole of Scotland is named after the woman Scota.' Bisset closed by observing that the name of people and country had remained the same since then to the present day.[44] Bringing Scota herself to Scotland was a new idea; it is notable that Ireland itself was demoted to a mere stopping-off point to acquire reinforcements.

Skene argued that Bisset's account was the first which associated Scota with the stone of Scone.[45] The same idea is found in an Anglo-French song dated by Dominica Legge to in or soon after 1307 (and certainly after 1296),[46] and in the Life of Edward II written shortly after his death in 1327:[47] in both cases Scota was also brought to Scotland (accompanied by her husband Gaedel). Skene noted that a different account of Scottish origins appeared in a draft of the Scottish case before the Curia of which Bisset's *Processus* was the polished version. This told how '*Scoti*, so-named after a certain Scota, daughter of Pharaoh king of Egypt' first occupied Ireland; then, according to Bede, they occupied Argyll, 'the aforesaid part of Britain which lies next to Alba', noting that 'this Argyll was then and still is called after Erc son of Scota and Gaedel husband of the same Scota' by combining the names Erc and Gaedel; and finally they settled in Alba after driving out the Britons, so that 'the new name Scotland was given to that part of the island which was thus occupied by *Scoti*, from that first Scota, lady of *Scoti*, according to the verse: The whole of Scotland is named after the woman Scota'.[48] Skene plausibly

43 See also below, 198.

44 Shead, Stevenson and Watt, *Scotichronicon*, VI. 182–3 (based on their translation). *Filia namque Pharaonis regis Egipti cum armata manu et maxima classe nauium applicuit in Hibernia. Postea assumptis quibusdam Hibernicis in Scociam nauigauit, deferens secum sedile regium quod iste rex Anglie inter cetera regni Scocie insignia secum per uiolenciam de regno Scocie in Angliam asportauit. Ipsa deuicit et deiecit Pictos et regnum ipsum optinuit. Ac ab ipsa Scota Scoti et Scocia nuncupantur. Unde uersus: A muliere Scota uocitatur Scocia tota. Qui Scoti nomen et locum usque in hodiernum diem noscuntur optinere.*

45 Skene, 'The coronation stone', esp. 81–2.

46 Legge, 'La Piere d'Escoce'.

47 Denholm-Young, *Vita Edwardi Secundi*, 132.

48 Shead, Stevenson and Watt, *Scotichronicon*, VI. 142–3 (translation based on theirs). *Postquam Scotorum . . . a quadam nomine Scota filia Pharaonis regis Egipti sic uocatus descendisset de Egiptos et post occupatam per ipsos primo insulam in occeano Hiberniam . . . et secundum Bedam post occupatam ab eis secundo Ergadiam adjacentem ipsi Albanie part<e>m predicte Britannie que Ergadia ab Erk filio Scote et Gaelo eius<dem> Scote uiro, tunc duobus inde uocata Ergadia usque diem istum nominibus compositis Erk et Gayl predictorum, susequenter occupauit Albaniam . . .*

concluded that Bisset created the association between Scota and the stone of Scone (and thereby was the first to bring her to Scotland) when the draft was refashioned into a cogent and compelling presentation, and that it soon spread to England, no doubt via the English procurators at the Curia (although there is no evidence that Bisset ever delivered his pleading in public).[49] The introduction of the idea of Scotland as homeland of *Scoti* into the legend, therefore, need not be any older than 1301. The germ, however, was the ditty *a muliere Scota uocitatur Scocia tota*, which at least by 1301 had come to be regarded as applying to Scotland. The different notion that Ireland had been called *Scocia* after Scota had been repeated in α, β, δ, and in the synthesis underlying Fordun's chronicle,[50] although in γ *Scocia* and *Scoti* were deliberately associated with Scotland and the Scots; in δ, moreover, it will be recalled that there may have been an attempt to distinguish between Scots and Irish.[51] It is not until the reign of King John and the first war of independence, therefore, that there is any definite indication that Scotland was portrayed as homeland of *Scoti*; and in each case this looks like a fresh reworking, rather than simple repetition, of existing materials.

The account of Scottish origins in Liber Extrauagans *attached to Bower's* Scotichronicon

The portrayal of Scotland rather than Ireland as homeland of *Scoti* is made emphatically in a final witness of α which may be dated to sometime before 1306. The text was not simply a rewrite of α or a descendant of α, however, but was drawn from a number of sources for its version of the origin-legend. Unlike Bisset's *Processus* or the Declaration of Arbroath, this account was part of an extended treatment of Scottish history from origins to the then present day, rather than a brief statement of the legend within a more general text arguing for Scottish independence. It is traceable only as the chief source behind a body of material which Bower completed in 1447/8 as a complement to his *Scotichronicon*. No title has been given to this material in Bower's extant working-copy of *Scotichronicon*,

---

imposito ipsi parti insule sic occupate per ipsos Scotos nouo nomine Scocia a prima illa Scota Scotorum domina juxta uersum: A muliere Scota uocitatur Scocia tota. Another draft exists, edited in Hearne, *Johannis de Fordun*, III. 835–83. Hearne used only one manuscript, which can lead to obvious difficulties (for an example see Shead, Stevenson and Watt, *Scotichronicon*, VI. 276). Skene reprinted it below his text of the 'Instructions', in Skene, *Chronicles*, 232–71: the origin-legend is at 242, and has only minor variants at this point, except for mentioning Spain on the itinerary from Egypt, a point omitted in the draft (or copy of the draft) reproduced by Bower. For a discussion of these drafts prepared by the Scottish procurators at Rome see *Scotichronicon*, VI. xviii–xxi, 260–3; also Broun, 'The birth', and Goldstein, 'The Scottish mission'. Another account of Scottish origins is found in the text of the Scottish case prepared for the negotiations at Bamburgh in 1321. It is largely derived from the 'Instructions' with some knowledge also of the Declaration of Arbroath; see Linehan, 'A fourteenth-century history', esp. 113–14.

49 Shead, Stevenson and Watt, *Scotichronicon*, VI. 261.

50 There is nothing to indicate whether it had also been stated in the 'Éber' and 'Partholón' accounts.

51 See above, 111.

but in the only complete manuscript of Bower's own refashioned version of *Scotichronicon* (the 'Book of Coupar Angus') it is entitled (after a convention in canon law) *Liber Extrauagans*, 'Supplementary Book', which is the title used in the most recent edition.[52]

The 'Book of Coupar Angus', however, has only an abbreviated version of *Liber Extrauagans*; this was evidently produced by Bower in the same spirit that inspired him when remodelling *Scotichronicon* itself into the text preserved in the 'Book of Coupar Angus'. Skene considered this shorter version to represent the work's original extent, and published an edition of it from two manuscripts.[53] An edition of the fuller and earlier version of *Liber Extrauagans* has only recently been published for the first time since 1759;[54] it is also the first to include a translation and commentary.[55] My discussion of this text is based largely on this commentary.

It has been shown that *Liber Extrauagans* consists largely of three poems concerned with various aspects of the history of the Scottish kingship which were probably originally written on the same occasion, as a trilogy, sometime between Edward I's conquest of Scotland in July 1296 and Robert I's *coup* in March 1306 (perhaps more precisely sometime after the surrender to Edward I on 9 February, 1304). By far the longest of the three is a history of the Scots and their kings from origins to the first war of independence, running to 352 lines as it stands in Bower's manuscript. It can be divided into four parts: (i) an account of Scottish origins which begins with Pharoah's death in the Red Sea and the removal of Gaedel (*Gaizilglas*), a Scythian exile, from Egypt to Spain with the stone of Scone; the stone is later handed over by Míl to his son Simón Brecc whose offspring settle in Ireland, and some of Simón's descendants later reach Argyll led by *Lori* or *Lorimonie*;[56] (ii) a discussion of when *Scoti* first reached Scotland, how long they ruled before the Picts, how long the Picts ruled, and when the Picts were conquered by *Scoti* under Cinaed mac Alpín; (iii) a king-list beginning with Fergus son of Erc who brought the stone of Scone to Argyll, and continuing to Cinaed mac Alpín and beyond to the death of Alexander III (1286), the fifty-first king; and finally (iv) an account of the Great Cause (1291–2) in which it was decided that John Balliol

52 Broun and Scott, '*Liber Extravagans*'. The 'Book of Coupar Angus' itself is Edinburgh, National Library of Scotland, MS Adv. 35.1.7 (dated 'before 1480' in Watt, 'Editing Walter Bower', 168). Unfortunately its copy of *Liber Extrauagans* has suffered from the loss of folios at the end: *Liber Extrauagans* occupies fo. 350r/v and breaks off after line 108. This version of *Liber Extrauagans* is found complete in the section of the 'Book of Coupar' text of *Scotichronicon* which has been combined with MS **F** of Fordun's chronicle to form Edinburgh, National Library of Scotland, MS Acc. 10301/6: this part of the codex was written in 1509 (see fo. 199v), and the poem in *Liber Extrauagans* runs from fo. 199v – fo. 202v.

53 Skene, *Chronicles*, 332–40.

54 Goodall, *Joannis de Fordun Scotichronicon*, II. 521–37. Goodall used **E**, the latest extant manuscript, as his base.

55 Broun and Scott, '*Liber Extravagans*'.

56 *Lorimonie* is what appears in Bower's own manuscript. This might be restored to *Lori nomine* (as occurred in a copy made *c.*1455): see Broun and Scott, '*Liber Extravagans*', 68, 108–9.

rather than Robert Bruce should be king, followed by Edward I's high-handed treatment of King John and the opening years of the first war of independence.

Much of this is plainly independent of Bower's *Scotichronicon*. There is nothing in *Scotichronicon* to parallel, for instance, the description of Gaedel as a Scythian or the spelling of his name as *Gaizelglas*; *Lori/Lorimonie* as leader of the first *Scoti* in Scotland; the bringing of the stone of Scone to Argyll by Fergus son of Erc (rather than Fergus son of Ferchar); the year-totals for the Pictish kingdom and the settlement of *Scoti* which preceded it; Cinaed's seven-year reign before conquering the Picts; the list of Fergus and his successors which conforms in general with king-lists of Marjorie Anderson's X- and Y-groups[57] (unlike Bower who copied the extra kings and elongated reign-length for Fergus from Fordun's chronicle); the pro-Balliol account of the Great Cause; or the treatment of the capture of Berwick and the battle of Dunbar. There are, however, some passages which are found word-for-word in *Scotichronicon*: two sections concerning William Wallace; some lines on Robert I prophesying his destruction of the English; and some material concerning the conversion of the Scots and the advent of Fergus son of Ferchar, which appears incongruously in the middle of the king-list between Cinaed's seven-year reign before destroying the Picts and the sixteen years he ruled subsequently. Most of these passages on Robert I and William Wallace are in fact abridgements of the corresponding verses in *Scotichronicon*, so that it seems likely that Bower has added them to the poem (rather than quoting the poem in *Scotichronicon*). On this basis it is probable that Bower was in fact responsible for introducing all the material on William Wallace (and the lines which serve to link this and the passage on Robert I to the rest of the poem). Skene pointed out that the pseudo-historical matter found awkwardly between Cinaed's reigns must also be a later addition; it is less certain, however, that it has not been added by Bower.[58]

The sections under scrutiny here are the account of Scottish origins and the material on the Pictish kingdom and the Scottish settlement which preceded it. At the beginning (lines 1–22) the author declares his intention to write concerning the Scots from their very beginning, basing his account on 'ancient chronicles' and on what he himself has seen,[59] and he commences his history with the death of King Pharaoh in 1561 BC. We are then told (lines 23–36) that when Pharaoh was drowned a noble Scythian exile called Gaedel Glas (who was twenty-two generations from Japhet) left Egypt by sea taking with him the 'stone of Pharaoh'. He eventually reached Spain, guided by the stone (which was known as the 'anchor of life'), and there his progeny multiplied. The next passage (lines 37–58) concerns a king of the Spaniards 1,002 years after Pharaoh's death called Míl (*Milo*) who

57 It is discussed in detail below, 163–4.

58 It may be noted in particular that lines 115–17 are found as the first three lines of four lines of verse quoted by Fordun (book II, chapter 35): the fourth line in Fordun's verse seems to belong to the other three, which would suggest that both Fordun and *Liber Extrauagans* contain independent borrowings from a lost verse-history of the Scots which may have been the source for all the interpolated material in this part of *Liber Extrauagans* (lines 115–28).

59 Presumably referring to the detailed account of events in the 1290s: see Broun and Scott, '*Liber Extravagans*', 107.

loved one of his several sons more than the rest, Simón Brecc by name, on whom he bestowed the stone which Gaedel had brought from Egypt. Míl prophesied that Simón's descendants would reign wherever the stone was placed: Simón's offspring lived in Ireland many years before some of them colonised Argyll. This is the point where Scotland was clearly identified as the homeland of *Scoti*. The inherent link between *Scoti* and *Scocia* (which may unambiguously be translated here as 'Scots' and 'Scotland') is given some emphasis: the passage (lines 52–7) reads,

> a mighty man, *Lori* by name [or *Lorimonie*], brought to Argyll certain of them [descendants of Simón Brecc] whom he saw to be of mature age . . . Those he led there are afterwards called *Scoti*. For just as the Get takes his name from Gethia, and the Goth from Gothia, and the Scythian from Scythia, so the Scots from Scotland.

In the following section (lines 59–85) this first settlement of *Scoti* in Scotland is dated to 443 BC, and 265 years[60] and 3 months before the kingdom of the Picts. The Picts, who inhabited Alba on 'this side of Drumalban, but to a lesser extent on the far side', reigned for 1,224 years and 9 months before being destroyed by Cinaed mac Alpín in AD 844. It is then explained that the Picts had killed Cinaed's father treacherously, and Cinaed took revenge by overcoming the Picts; for seven years Cinaed had only ruled part of the kingdom (west of Drumalban), but after conquering the Picts he ruled the kingdom of Alba in its entirety, and his posterity have held sway ever since. The next passage (lines 86–97) serves to introduce the king-list by relating how the Scots lived for many generations in Argyll 'under natural law, without a king' until Fergus (son of Erc)[61] brought the aforementioned stone to Argyll and so became the first to rule the Scots. The stone thus became the royal throne, we are told, but only of Scottish kings, not foreign kings, and was in Scone 'until then' (that is, until it became the throne of a foreign king, i.e. Edward I in 1296).

The account of Scottish origins has been constructed by blending a range of sources. These would have included *Historia Brittonum* (not necessarily directly) from which the notion of a Scythian exile as progenitor of *Scoti* may ultimately have been derived, and especially the figure of 1,002 years between the death of Pharaoh and the settlement of Ireland.[62] The identification of the stone of Scone as the stone of Pharaoh, and the notion that Gaedel brought the stone from Egypt, is strongly reminiscent of the Anglo-French song discussed above and would appear to belong to the same current of legend surrounding the stone which may have originated in Baldred Bisset's *Processus* in 1301.[63] The role assigned to Simón Brecc and Fergus in the stone's history tallies with the material which would have

60 Reading *deca quinqu<ies> centibinorum*: see Broun and Scott, '*Liber Extravagans*', 110.

61 In the principal manuscript Erc is identified in the text hand in the margin as the father of Fergus.

62 The chapter attributed to *periti Scottorum*: see Dumville, *The Historia Brittonum*, III. 69–70. (The other volumes in the series have not yet been published: some idea of the place of this passage in the other recensions and editions may be gained from the concordances at ibid., 56–7.)

63 See above, 120–1.

been attributed to *legenda Sancti Congalli* in α; it is striking, however, that Fergus son of Ferchar has been merged with Fergus son of Erc, which would point particularly to δ as a source.[64] There is no known precedent for identifying Míl as the father of Simón Brecc; this can most readily be explained as a consequence of blending information derived from δ with other material, although it is impossible to say precisely which source has supplied Míl.[65] The most curious figure is *Lori/Lorimonie*, the leader of the first *Scoti* in Scotland. It is tempting to identify him with Loarn, eponym of the Cenél Loairn, who since the tenth century had been regarded as a brother of Fergus son of Erc;[66] no other account of Scottish origins, however, survives in which Loarn is given such a prominent role.[67] Perhaps Míl and Loarn (if it was he) have been derived from some lost text; if so, then the account of Scottish origins in *Liber Extrauagans* could be recognised as a skilful blend of as many as four different sources.

The use of δ is suggested not only by the conflation of Fergus son of Ferchar with Fergus son of Erc, but also by the figures given for the Pictish kingdom and the Scottish settlement which preceded it. It has been argued above that the idea of a pre-Pictish Scottish kingdom probably originated in β when the king-list consisting of kings of Dál Riata followed by Pictish kings and then Cinaed mac Alpín and his successors was taken to represent a continuous succession to a single kingship, thereby propelling Fergus son of Erc and his Dalriadic successors back in time by more than a millennium.[68] The figures given in those derivatives of β which stated the duration of the Pictish kingdom and the Scottish settlement which preceded it are as follows (only the number of years is significant). (King-lists are given in bold; bear in mind that **K** is Grey's copy of the king-list.)

	Duration of Scots before Picts	*Duration of Pictish kingdom*
K	305 years	1,237 years
D	260 years	1,061 years
Wyntoun	245 years	1,061 years
Lib. Extr.	265 years	1,224 years

(**N** is a witness only of the section from Cinaed mac Alpín)

Marjorie Anderson has deduced that the archetype of her X group of list (to which these belong) would have given an equivalent figure of 307 years for Fergus son of Erc to Alpín father of Cinaed, and that its Pictish reign-lengths would actually have totalled between 1,227 and 1,232 years, but that *mile clxxxuii* in **K** may have been a

64 Above, 109.

65 In MacQueen and MacQueen, *Scotichronicon*, I. 144, Míl as father of Simón was taken to be an original feature of *legenda Sancti Congalli*, but this runs against the manuscript evidence: see below, 22–3.

66 Bannerman, *Studies*, 118–32.

67 Although Loarn does appear as first king in the list of kings of *Scoti* in Scotland in *Duan Albanach*; see Jackson, 'The Duan Albanach', 130–1; on this text see below, 170–1.

68 See 107–9.

miscopying of *mile ccxxxuii* (from γ, therefore).[69] This suggests the following possible sequence:

Stage I The archetype of the X-group: *cccuii* and *mccxxuii*;
Stage II β: *cccuii* and *mccxxuii*;
Stage III γ: *cccu* (<*cccuii*) and *mccxxxuii* (<*mccxxuii*).
δ: *cclxu* (<*cccuii*) and *mccxxiiii* (<*mccxxuii*);
Archetype derived from δ shared by Wyn. and **D**:
cclxu and *mlxi* (fresh calculation[70]).

This would allow the figures in **K** to be explained as a copy of *cccu* and miscopying of *mccxxxuii* as *mclxxxuii* (as suggested by Marjorie Anderson); it would also allow the 1296x1306 source of *Liber Extrauagans* to have read *cclxu* and *mccxxiiii* as a copy of δ; and *ccxlu* and *cclx* in Wyntoun and **D** to be interpreted as miscopies of *cclxu*, and *mlxi* as a copy from their immediate shared archetype. Wyntoun, **D** and **K** also have a date for the beginning of the pre-Pictish Scottish kingdom: 443 BC in **D** and **K**,[71] 452 or 442 BC in Wyntoun.[72] *Liber Exrauagans* also has 443 BC.[73] The relationships between these witnesses (and also list **N**) may be represented diagramatically (with ω denoting the archetype shared by Wyntoun and **D**, and therefore also by **N**):[74]

69 Anderson, *Kings and Kingship*, 216, 220.

70 Based on a mistaken grandtotal for Dál Riata, Picts and Cinaed and successors combined: see ibid., 221–2.

71 Ibid., 264, 288; see also 64.

72 Ibid., 221 n.11; 64 n.86.

73 Lines 60–2.

74 Anderson, *Kings and Kingship*, 64, noted two errors shared by **D** and **N** (only in the section from Cinaed mac Alpín, the part of **N** belonging to Anderson's X-group); unfortunately Wyntoun also used the Verse Chronicle for his account of reigns from Cinaed mac Alpín, so it can not be concluded from the absence of these errors in Wyntoun that they were not therefore present in ω (for which see 127 below). There are equivalent pairs of figures (for the duration of the Pictish kingdom and the preceding Scottish settlement) found in texts other than king-lists; such figures have presumably also been drawn ultimately from a king-list related to those under discussion. In a passage added to Fordun (MacQueen and MacQueen, *Scotichronicon*, I. 72–3: book I, chapter 31) Bower stated that the Scots ruled 249 years before the Picts and that the Picts ruled for 1,061 years: no doubt his source was derived ultimately from ω, and may possibly have shared with Wyntoun an exemplar which misread *cclxu* as *ccxlu*. Another related pair of figures is 265 and 1,061 years found in Craigie, *The Asloan Manuscript*, II. fo.109: these are precisely the figures which I have suggested would have been given in ω, and may therefore be a direct witness of ω itself.

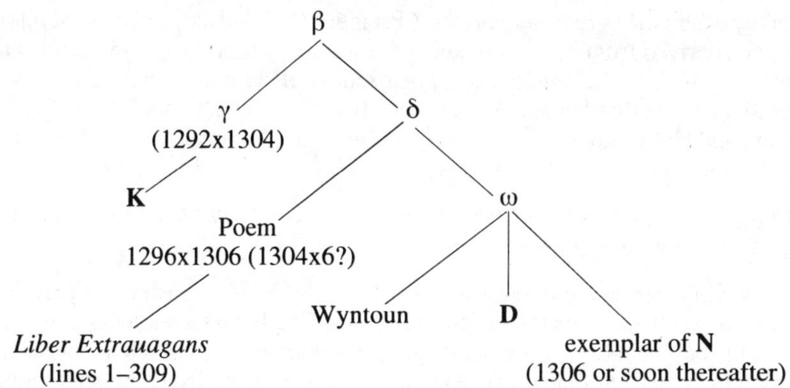

The source of lines 1–309 of *Liber Extrauagans* was not only a blend of disparate accounts of Scottish origins, however, but was also composed from more than one king-list. Its own listing of kings has been taken from a text which was not derived from the archetype of Marjorie Anderson's X-group.[75] It is also noteworthy that its author has rejected 443 BC as the date of the advent of Fergus son of Erc which he would have learnt from δ. He may have preferred what he found in his other list (which would not have included Pictish kings),[76] especially if he was familiar with the royal genealogy (which he referred to it in lines 27–8), and considered such an early date to be incompatible with Fergus's place in the pedigree.

Liber Extrauagans is the final witness of a descendant of α, and may shed some more light on the date-limits for δ in particular. Most obviously, it can help to consolidate 1306 as the *terminus ante quem*; the distance between δ and the exemplar of **N** would thus suggest *c.* 1300 as a permissible *terminus ante quem*. As for the *terminus post quem*, the potential key here is the figures for the reigns of Alexander II and Alexander III. In *Liber Extrauagans* these are 35 years and 'almost 37 years'; **N** reads 35 years and 37 years. **K** has 37 years for each, which may possibly have been *xxxiiii* in γ for Alexander II miscopied as *xxxuii*, but could equally be because Alexander III's reign-length has been attributed by accident to his father.[77] Now, Alexander II actually reigned from December 1214 to his death on 8 July 1249, and Alexander III from July 1249 to his death on 19 March 1286 ('1285' in *Liber Extrauagans*, taking Lady Day, 25 March, as marking the New Year). A comparison with other lists suggests that the rounded-up figure of 35

75 See below, 163–4. This raises the question of why it was preferred to the list in δ. Was this other king-list already in verse? There is a formal possibility that it has not been derived from δ itself but from an abridgement which omitted most of the king-list material.

76 See below, 164.

77 If '37 years' (> 34 years) for Alexander II in **K** represented an independent calculation, then this could suggest that β did not include Alexander II's reign-length, and indicate a *terminus ante quem* for β of 1249. The possibility of another explanation for **K**'s 37 years for Alexander II, however, makes this too uncertain to be useful. Unfortunately **D** terminates at Lulach mac Gilla Comgáin (1057–8).

shared by **N** and *Liber Extrauagans* for Alexander II is unusual, and may therefore have been derived from δ. Unfortunately the similarity between 37 years in **N** and 'almost 37' in *Liber Extrauagans* for Alexander III is not so compelling: it is perfectly possible that 'almost 37' has been taken from a list which actually read 36 years and 8 or 9 months.[78]

Summary of accounts of Scottish origins, 1214–1306, and their identification of the Scottish kingship with Ireland

The following stemma may serve as a summary of the relationship between lost accounts of Scottish origins in the period 1214–1306. Each Greek letter denotes a copy of the base text (the origin-legend king-list compilation) which may be characterised by some significant textual amendment(s), ranging from the reinterpretation of the king-list as a continuous succession of a single kingship in β to the rewriting of this material in the 'Éber' account (represented here by the siglum ε). It is uncertain how much of the particular detail in Wyntoun has been derived from δ itself or from ω.

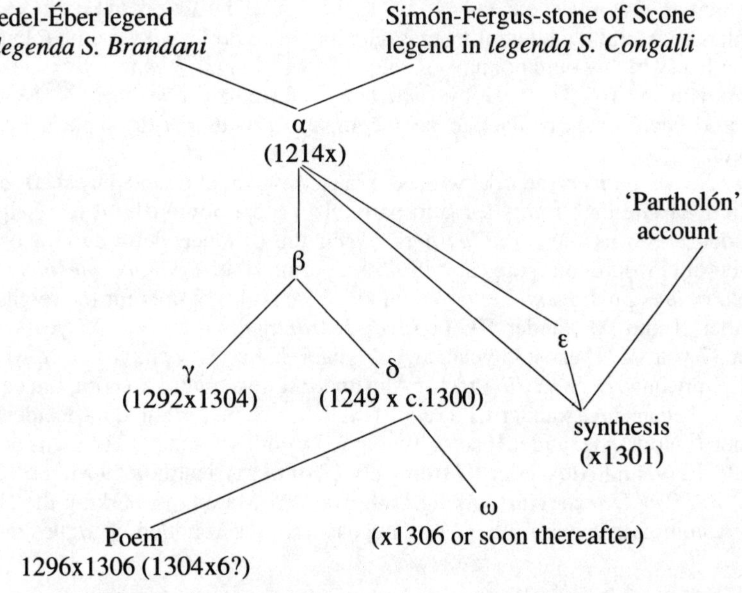

78 **F** has 34 years and 8 months for Alexander II (and terminates before Alexander III's death) while **I** has 33 years for Alexander II and 39 (> *xxxui* ?) for Alexander III (Anderson, *Kings and Kingship*, 277, 285). The equivalent figures in **G** are 32 (probably > *xxxu*) and 36; **M** has 36 years 9 months for Alexander II; and **L** has 36 years and 9 months for both Alexanders (although Skene did not report in his edition that the 9 months for Alexander II has been scored out); the 'Chronicle of Huntingdon' has 26 years for Alexander II (Skene, *Chronicles*, 303, 301, 297, 213). **H** has 35 years and **J** has 33 for Alexander II (see below, 141–3).

To conclude: the first traceable accounts of Scottish origins which identified Scotland rather than Ireland as the homeland of *Scoti* were produced during the reign of King John and first war of independence (and may, indeed, belong to the opening years of the fourteenth century). Other accounts suggest that Scottish men of letters regarded *Scoti* as Irish in the literal sense that Ireland was their homeland. This identification with Ireland was particularly pronounced in the case of the 'Éber' and 'Partholón' accounts (and to a lesser degree γ) whose authors can all be shown to have substantially remodelled their sources. It was also visible in α, β, and δ, for instance in the naming of Ireland as *Scocia* and linking the stone of Scone with Tara. In γ and possibly δ, however, there was also some attempt made to emphasise that Scots were distinct from Irish. It may be surmised that this Irish identity was current (and may have been the norm) before the 1290s, and that it was only in the 1290s (or possibly as late as *c.* 1300) that it began to be challenged.

This begs the question: why did Irish identity retain its vitality as a central element in the identity of the Scottish kingdom before the wars of independence? As indicated in the opening chapter, the notion of the inhabitants of Ireland and the Scottish kingdom forming a single people would have been readily explicable between the tenth and twelfth centuries. They belonged to a single cultural area; moreover, it would appear that men of letters in Scotland would have been accustomed to look to Ireland for the highest standard of schooling. The vitality of the umbilical link between Gaelic culture in Scotland and its parent in Ireland would have been one way, therefore, in which the notion of Ireland as homeland of *Scoti* could have had an immediate significance. This would have been all very well as long as Gaelic high culture was a major force in the Scottish kingdom. In the twelfth century, however, Gaelic came under pressure as the dominant vernacular in court and church, and in the thirteenth century retreated altogether from most of the kingdom's heartlands. The precise chronology and dynamics of Gaelic's decline are difficult to determine; a case can be made that Gaelic remained socially significant in the east midlands until the reign of Alexander II (1214–49).[79] If (as seems probable) most of the origin-legend texts discussed in previous chapters were written in the east midlands, it would seem increasingly unlikely that they were written by men of letters who could read Gaelic.

Direct evidence for knowledge or ignorance of Gaelic in these accounts is not plentiful: only two passages may be attributed to them which have a bearing on this question. It has been suggested that because *Scoti* as a mixture of Greeks and Egyptians is a central feature of XXVII.l–n this section may have been derived from the 'Éber' account in which elsewhere *Scoti* are portrayed as a combination of Greek and Egyptian nobles.[80] In XXVII.l–n we are told that the Greeks called themselves *Geythelenses* after their leader *Gaythelos* (Gaedel), while the Egyptians adopted the name *Scoti* from *Scota*; 'afterwards, and today, each people jointly gives thanks to enjoy the full benefit of this last name alone', concerning which a verse is quoted: '*Scoti* have a name from Scota and all *Scocia* from *Scoti*, after an increase has been forbidden [in the use of the name] of the leader

79 See Broun, 'Gaelic literacy'.

80 Indeed, it was suggested that the preceding section in XXVII may also have had the 'Éber' account as its source.

Gaedel.'[81] It would appear from this that the author of the 'Éber' account (if indeed he penned these lines) identified with non-Gaelic-speaking *Scoti*, and was well aware of the decline of Gaelic (and even approved of its demise). In contrast there is XXVIII which, it was argued, may have been created by the synthesist himself when he spotted Eochaid *Rothay* in his copy of the royal genealogy and regarded him as a plausible eponym of Rothesay.[82] We are also informed that the island of Rothesay is known as Bute because 'St Brendan built on it a hut, *bothe* in our language – that is, a cell.'[83] It has been suggested that *bothe* here referred to Scots *buth* (*Anglice* booth),[84] but it would appear rather to be Gaelic *both*, normally 'hut',[85] but also attested as meaning 'cell'.[86] This, therefore, would suggest that the synthesist (if indeed he wrote this) identified with Gaelic and was himself a Gaelic-speaker.[87]

The synthesist may have known Gaelic, but this would not necessarily mean that he was sufficiently literate in Gaelic to have participated in Gaelic high culture. Indeed, these accounts of Scottish origins betray an ignorance of Irish historiography which make it difficult to accept that their authors had any meaningful contact with mainstream historical texts written in Gaelic after the eleventh century. It has been noted earlier that the origin-legend material in Fordun exhibits a number of significant differences with the treatment of fundamentally the same origin-legend in the eleventh-century *Lebor Gabála* and its derivitives which dominated this aspect of Irish historiography thereafter (down to the seventeenth century).[88] It was argued that these discrepancies made it seem most unlikely that Fordun himself had any links with Irish historians.[89] Now that it can be shown that Fordun's account of Scottish origins represented a synthesis of earlier accounts which may be dated to sometime in or before 1301, these same discrepancies with *Lebor Gabála* lead inevitably to the suggestion that the authors of the accounts used in the synthesis, and the synthesist himself, were unaware of *Lebor Gabála*. Each of these divergences from the historiographical mainstream of the Gaelic world are not of the kind that could be regarded as changes within the tradition; they each subvert fundamental aspects of the historiographical canon, which suggests that they were made without knowing the literature on these matters that was widely available in Gaelic for those who could read it. The synthesist, for example, constructed his impressively careful chronological structure apparently

81 *quo solo nomine postmodum hodieque communiter utraque gens perfrui gratulatur. Unde quidam: Scoti de Scota de Scotis Scocia tota / nomen habent uetito Gaythelos ducis adaucto.*

82 Above, 71. It is unlikely to have been introduced by Fordun (as suggested in Scott, 'John of Fordun's description', 11); Fordun found a chronologically impossible alternative eponym for Rothesay (see above, 73).

83 *sanctus Brandanus in ea botham ydiomate nostro .bothe. i. cellam construxit.*

84 *DOST*, *s.v. buth*: this is the only example cited of *buth* meaning anything more general than 'booth' or 'stall'.

85 As argued in MacQueen and MacQueen, *Scotichronicon*, I. 147.

86 *DIL*, *s.v. both*[2].

87 If so, his interest in the Isle of Bute might, indeed, be taken to indicate that he belonged to a Gaelic area somewhere near the Firth of Clyde.

88 See above, 12–13.

89 Ibid.

without realising that Simón Brecc was a space-filling king of Ireland descended from Míl, or that Partholón was the first colonist in Ireland after the Flood; the author of the 'Éber' account showed no awareness that the Gaelic colonisation of Ireland was attributed in *Lebor Gabála* to sons of Míl, one of whom was named Éber; the author of the 'Partholón' account rewrote Geoffrey of Monmouth's story of Partholón without recourse to *Lebor Gabála*, in which it was made clear that Partholón settled Ireland long before the *Gaídil*; and the author of β saw fit to move Fergus son of Erc back in time by more than a millennium, apparently without realising that this would make a nonsense of the royal genealogy or of the place accorded to Fergus son of Erc in the genealogical framework devised for the royal families of the *Gaídil*. Finally, it is only possible to spare whoever wrote α from this charge of historiographical ignorance if it is maintained that his compilation of origin-legend material involved little or no judgement on his part (beyond perhaps an interest in what could be gleaned from hagiographical texts), and was simply a copy of what he found.[90]

The likelihood that the authors of most (if not all) these accounts – and certainly the 'Éber' and 'Partholón' accounts – were not literate in Gaelic suggests that Irish identity for them was not simply an expression of membership of Gaelic high culture which looked to Ireland as its source. It may be presumed that there was another aspect of Irish identity which served to sustain it among these Scottish men of letters before the wars of independence. The first place to look for this should be the texts themselves. All of those identified as definitely or probably from the thirteenth century would appear to have included the origin-legend as the first part of a history of the Scottish kingship, *regnum Scottorum*. In particular, the 'Éber' account probably included Fergus son of Ferchar as first king of *Scoti* in Scotland, and Fergus son of Erc as first king of Scotland itself, which would indicate that its author was concerned to write a history of at least the origins of Scottish kingship; he may, indeed, have included a copy of the king-list from α. As far as he was concerned the ancient freedom of *Scoti* and their kings was divinely sanctioned by the occupation of uninhabited Ireland.[91] There is no evidence that the 'Partholón' account, as part of a rewriting of Geoffrey of Monmouth from a Scottish point of view, included a king-list, but the work of which it was probably a part was evidently concerned to assert the ancient freedom of *Scoti* and their kings. Again, however, this would appear to have been established first of all when they acquired 'perpetual settlements in freedom'[92] in Ireland, which island their leader Partholón 'took possession of for himself for ever'.[93] And even although α was little more

[90] Note that I have changed my view on this issue since my doctoral thesis, which was referred to in Bannerman, 'The king's poet', 147 and nn. 4 and 5.

[91] There is no immediate reason, therefore, to suppose that the passage in Gaedel's death-bed speech about the pricelessness of freedom, 'to suffer the rule of no foreign lordship, but to enjoy of one's own accord only the distinctive power of one's own nation' (*nullius alienigene dominantis imperium pati sed successiue solummodo proprie nacionis uti spontaliter potestate*; XVI.1), has not been taken from the 'Éber' account. For further discussion see above, 81, n. 90.

[92] *perpetuas cum libertate mansiones.*

[93] *in perpetuam sibi possessionem optinuit.* In XX.2.d the hardship endured by *Scoti* in Spain leads to the striking statement that 'in all these misfortunes and hardships they could never be prevailed upon to submit to or to obey a foreign king, but on the contrary

than a compilation of origin-legends and king-list, the mere fact that its author made what proved to be such an influential combination suggests that in his mind the origin-legend material he reproduced had a direct bearing on the kingship's history. Presumably he included the legend of Simón Brecc, Fergus son of Ferchar and the stone of Scone precisely because it concerned the stone inaugural throne of Scottish kings.

It is striking, therefore, how the link with Ireland was seen to provide the kingship with a prestigious origin by relating it to an ancient people who had (according to the more expansive accounts) a divinely ordained claim to freedom. It might seem strange that this was not deemed to have been sufficiently established by the impressive roll-call of royal forebears announced in the king-list. The king-list became even more impressive in this regard when it was reinterpreted (in β) as a continuous succession to a single kingship. It was this reinterpretation which formed the basis of the claim in the Declaration of Arbroath that there had been 113 kings without a foreigner intervening. As far as the author(s) of the Declaration were concerned this amounted to such a compelling vision of ancient independence that they could afford to drop the association with Ireland altogether. If the king-list was good enough for Robert I's seasoned apologists, why would it not have been good enough for men of letters in the thirteenth century?

The answer, I will argue, is that the ample king-list which would have been found in α, not to say the much more impressive regnal succession claimed in β, was only of recent vintage. It appears that it was only sometime in the reign of Alexander II (1214–49) that Pictish kings were first combined with kings of *Scoti* to form a single king-list text; moreover, I will argue that an analysis of extant lists suggests that a list of kings of Dál Riata was joined afresh with the listing of Cinaed mac Alpín and his successors sometime during the reign of William I (1165–1214). For most of the twelfth century (and probably since the mid-tenth century, at least) the king-list had not been used as a vehicle for expressing the kingship's claim to antiquity.

A claim to antiquity was among the most powerful statements of a kingship's legitimacy, and was not something which kings, or the men of letters who identified with them, would have felt comfortable without. The two most obvious ways of making such a claim was either by a long succession of kings in a regnal list or by boasting an impressive royal ancestry; both were often combined. I will argue that Scottish kings before the reign of Alexander II looked to their Irish ancestry for the legitimising lustre of ancient royalty, and that it was chiefly because of this that Irish identity retained its vitality among men of letters who were no longer literate in Gaelic, even when new forms of king-list were developed in the thirteenth century.

---

they were always subservient and loyal under their own kings' rule and chose to lead no other life than this that was no better than the life of wild beasts, so long as they had their freedom' (*in omnibus hiis malis et angustiis nuncquam ut regi subderetur alieno uel ad obediendum flecti poterat quin pocius humilis semper et deuotus sub rege proprio cum libertate tantum hanc uitam eligeret ducere bestialem*) (translation from MacQueen and MacQueen, *Scotichronicon*, I. 53). For further discussion of possible contexts for these and similar sentiments, see above, 81 n. 90.

VII

SCOTTISH KING-LISTS 1093–1214

In order to assess the role of Irish identity in the legitimation of the kingship it is necessary to examine to what extent, if at all, king-lists were used as a way of endowing the kingship with an authenticating ancient past. This involves embarking on a detailed discussion of the development of Scottish king-lists in the century or more before the reign of Alexander II, in so far as this can be discerned from extant witnesses of regnal lists.

Very few Scottish king-lists survive in manuscripts earlier than the fourteenth century. Most witnesses, however, are copies of texts which have become frozen at some point in the thirteenth century.[1] Excavating these texts to reveal lost ancestors from before the reign of Alexander II is therefore not so daunting a prospect. This task is made very much easier by Marjorie Anderson's pioneering work on Scottish king-lists, culminating in the second chapter of her *Kings and Kingship in Early Scotland* (2nd edition, 1980).[2] She was chiefly concerned, however, with these texts as evidence for kings in Scotland between the sixth and ninth centuries, rather than as a source for how the kingship was perceived in the twelfth and early thirteenth centuries. As a result she did not need to come to definite conclusions about how the king-list developed in this period. For our purposes, therefore, it will be necessary to examine the text-history of these king-lists more closely than has been attempted hitherto. This will involve considering three copies of the king-list which were not incorporated into Marjorie Anderson's discussion (two of them were unknown to Anderson or earlier scholars and are published here for the first time; the other is in *Liber Extrauagans*, which may have been overlooked because it is not *a priori* earlier than the fifteenth century). As a result a new view of the twelfth-century ancestors of extant lists will be advanced.

Marjorie Anderson's X-group of regnal lists

Marjorie Anderson divided witnesses of the king-list into two groups, the 'X-group' and the 'Y-group'. She has shown that the archetype of the X-group (which I will refer to hereafter as ξ) was a Latin text consisting of a list of kings of Dál Riata from Fergus son of Erc to Alpín (father of Cinaed mac Alpín),[3] a Pictish

1 The earliest extant text of the king-list beginning at least with Cinaed mac Alpín is found in a compilation which has been dated 1202x14: see below, 114.

2 For her earlier studies see Anderson, 'The lists of the kings', 'The lists of the kings, II', and 'The Scottish materials'.

3 Or so this was understood: this Alpín has been moved, however, from the eighth century (see below, 148–9).

king-list, and a list of kings from Cinaed mac Alpín which, as well as the usual formula of name plus reign-length, also gave details of each king's death and (for all but a few kings) their place of burial. She published up-to-date editions of all witnesses of the X-group which included lists of kings of Dál Riata, Pictish kings and an annotated list of Cinaed mac Alpín and his successors.[4] These witnesses are:

D. Edinburgh, National Library of Scotland, MS Adv. 34.7.3, the commonplace book of James Gray, priest of the diocese of Dunblane and secretary to two archbishops of St Andrews in the late fifteenth century.[5] It is a paper manuscript. The king-list is on fos 19v–21v (pencil foliation) and has been published by Anderson in *Kings and Kingship*, 264–8. It is preceded (fos 17r–19r) by a copy of the royal genealogy (in the same colour of ink as the first part of the king-list) which starts with Adam and progresses (in the form X *cuius filius fuit* Y or X *genuit* Y) as far as Fergus son of Erc.[6] The list terminates with Lulach (1057–8), and is followed without a break by a short list of early dates in Christian history which fills the remainder of fo. 21v.[7] Another king-list follows in the same hand but in a different coloured ink (fos 22r–23r) which begins with Mael Coluim Cenn Mór (1058–93) and terminates with the coronation of James IV in 1488. This second list is slightly annotated, and there is a gap of about seven lines between 1290 and a note on William Wallace, and a change of ink after the beginning of Alexander III's reign. There is no suggestion that the list from Mael Coluim Cenn Mór has been derived from the exemplar of list **D**; **D** has clearly been truncated so as not to overlap with it. The genealogy from Adam to Fergus son of Erc and **D** may, however, have originally formed a single work; it is significant that Wyntoun (who had access to a king-list closely related to **D**) has a very similar version of the genealogy which terminated with Fergus son of Erc.[8] The combination of royal genealogy and king-list may therefore be identified as a feature of their common source. In the eyes of James Gray (the scribe as well as the owner of the manuscript), the genealogy to Fergus son of Erc, **D** (from Fergus to Lulach), and the list from Mael Coluim Cenn Mór to James IV evidently came together to form a single history which he entitled *Chronica Breuis*.

Along with **D** should be considered **N**: London, British Library, MS Harley 1808 fo. 66r/v. Marjorie Anderson dated the manuscript (which is English) to the second half of the fourteenth century.[9] Its Scottish regnal list forms part of an anti-Scottish tract, and is seriously corrupt. From Cinaed mac Alpín it belongs to Anderson's X-group; this is preceded by a Dál Riata list which belongs to Anderson's Y-group. Marjorie Anderson published an edition in *Kings and Kingship*,

4 There are witnesses which include only the annotated list from Cinaed mac Alpín, namely **G** and **N** (for which see below, 134–5, and the so-called Verse Chronicle, on which see Anderson, *Kings and Kingship*, 60–1).

5 Anderson, *Kings and Kingship*, 64. She noted (64 n.87) that the next two owners of the manuscript were officials of the diocese of Dunblane.

6 See below, 181.

7 Published in Skene, *Chronicles*, 152.

8 See below, 181–2.

9 For this account of **N** see Anderson, *Kings and Kingship*, 66–7.

290–1. The list ends with Robert I's *coup* and his killing of John Comyn in 1306; its exemplar may therefore be dated to sometime in or soon after 1306.[10] Marjorie Anderson has identified a number of features which suggest it is related to **D**.[11]

F. I will use this siglum to refer to the copy of the king-list published by Thomas Innes in 1729 as Appendix V in his *Critical Essay on the Ancient Inhabitants of the Northern Parts of Britain or Scotland*. Innes's source was a summary of material from the *registrum* of St Andrews, including copies of a few items, among them the king-list. The *registrum* itself had been lost sometime shortly after 1660. Innes acquired this material from Sir Robert Sibbald; Sibbald's own copy no longer survives, but a copy of it made in or after 1708 is London, British Library, MS Harley 4628, fos 213–242 (the king-list is on fos 219v–224r).[12] Marjorie Anderson has published an edition of **F** with variants from BL MS Harley 4628 in *Kings and Kingship*, 269–78. The copy in BL MS Harley 4628 is consistently inferior to **F**.[13]

The list witnessed by **F** was, therefore, a copy in the lost St Andrews *registrum* which can be dated to the fourteenth century;[14] its text, however, has been frozen since the mid-thirteenth century. The list concludes with the knighting of Alexander III in 1251 at York by Henry III of England; his marriage next day to Henry III's daughter; and the dismissal of the justiciar and chancellor (who have not been named) after representations had been made to King Henry. Alan and Marjorie Anderson thought these sackings referred to the change of government in 1255;[15] it would appear, however, to refer to the removal of Alan Durward as justiciar and Robert Kenleith as chancellor following Alexander III's wedding. The text of the list seems, therefore, to have reached its current extent sometime in or soon after 1251.[16]

Along with **F** should be considered the incomplete witness, **G**: London, British Library, MS Cotton Vitellius A xx, fos 44rb–45ra. This manuscript dates to the mid-fourteenth century and belonged to the priory of Tynemouth. The king-list appears in a digression within a chronicle of English affairs (running to 1347, with additions for 1347 and 1348); the digression follows the notice of the death in 1290 of Margaret granddaughter of Alexander III, and it includes two versions of the Scottish king-list – the first is **M** (see below) followed immediately by **G**. **G** is closely related to **F** as far as a *summa annorum* following the accession of Alexander II in 1214; unlike **F**, however, it consists only of the annotated list from Cinaed mac Alpín.[17] The most recent edition of **G** is in Skene, *Chronicles*, 301–3.[18]

10 See above, 112.

11 Anderson, *Kings and Kingship*, 64.

12 The above information on **F** is taken from Anderson, *Kings and Kingship*, 54–5 and nn.

13 Reference will be made only exceptionally to readings in BL MS Harley 4628, which will be denoted F (Harl).

14 On this and other possible stages in the list's transmission see ibid., 54–8.

15 Anderson, *Early Sources*, II. 562 n. 2; Anderson, *Kings and Kingship*, 54.

16 This was first suggested by Reid, 'Alexander III', 181.

17 All the above information on **G** is from Anderson, *Kings and Kingship*, 58–9 and nn.

18 Some corrections to Skene are noted in Marjorie Anderson's edition of **F**. To these may be added the following: under the reign of Illulb mac Custantín *interfectus est in* [sic] *a*

The account of Alexander II and Alexander III in **G** is independent of **F**, and it concludes with a brief eulogy of Alexander III after a note of his death (dated to the day) and burial. The exemplar of **G** may therefore have been written sometime in or soon after 1286; possibly its Pictish and Dál Riata sections were omitted when it was incorporated into the English chronicle by the scribe of BL, MS Cotton Vitellius A xx.[19] The ancestor shared by **F** and **G** can therefore be dated to the reign of Alexander II (1214–49).[20]

I. Oxford, Bodleian Library, MS Latin Misc. C. 75, fos 53v–54v (*olim* Phillips 3119). These folios have been bound into this codex and were originally independent of it. Marjorie Anderson has dated the handwriting to 'rather later' than the first quarter of the fourteenth century (the date suggested by Skene).[21] She published a fresh edition in the second edition of her *Kings and Kingship*, 279–85. After the notice of Alexander III's death and burial the list concludes with the statement: 'and the land has rested without a king for as many years as have occurred'.[22] Its exemplar may therefore be dated *c.*1290. The author of this exemplar would appear to have made a number of 'improvements' to the list; he may have been responsible for rearranging it so that the Pictish list rather than the Dál Riata list came first.[23]

K. This forms part of the king-list-plus-origin-legend text which has been discussed at length above;[24] it was incorporated by Grey into his *Scalacronica* (and in the process translated by him into French). The king-list material has been edited by Anderson, *Kings and Kingship*, 286–9. It was argued that Grey's exemplar (γ) can be dated to 1292x1304.[25]

Fordun and Wyntoun, of course, are also witnesses to lost archetypes of Marjorie Anderson's X-group in which kings of Dál Riata and Pictish kings were listed as well as the successors of Cinaed mac Alpín.[26] Anderson has also discussed king-lists belonging to her X-group which are witnesses only of the section beginning with Cinaed mac Alpín. As well as **G** and **N**, there is a version of the list in Latin elegiac couplets (known as the 'Verse Chronicle').[27] The Verse Chronicle was

---

Norwagiensibus in Innircolain (Skene printed, *interfectus est a Norwagiensibus in Innircolam*); and under Donnchad ua Maíl Choluim, *Bethoc filie Malcolmi* (Skene printed *Bethoc filie Malcom*).

19 Unless, of course, the list was already included in the exemplar of this copy of the chronicle.

20 The unusual feature shared by **F** and **G** of using arabic numerals may have been derived from this ancestor, which would solve the objections raised in Anderson, *Kings and Kingship*, 59–60, to assigning the common ancestor of **F** and **G** to 1214x49.

21 Anderson, *Kings and Kingship*, 61–2 for this and other information about the manuscript (esp. 61 n. 76).

22 *et siluit terra sine rege tot annis quot interuenerunt.*

23 Anderson, *Kings and Kingship*, 62–3.

24 See above, 91–5.

25 Above, 84–5, 95; see also Anderson, *Kings and Kingship*, 66.

26 See above, 104–8.

27 For what follows, see Anderson, *Kings and Kingship*, 60–1.

inserted piecemeal into the Chronicle of Melrose (not later probably than 1264),[28] Wyntoun's chronicle, and Bower's *Scotichronicon*; there is only one manuscript in which the text is preserved as a single entity (Oxford, Bodleian Library, MS 302, fo. 138 r/v).[29] Only in Bower and the Bodleian manuscript is the text complete; Bower's exemplar evidently concluded with the beginning of Alexander II's reign (1214–49), while in the Bodleian manuscript the text is continued to the beginning of Alexander III's reign (1249–86).

The earliest extant text derived from ξ which Anderson identified was the version of the Verse Chronicle which concluded with Alexander II as the reigning king;[30] the existence of ξ in Alexander II's reign can also be vouchsafed by the common ancestor of **F** and **G**. She noted that all members of the X-group have an erroneous 50-year reign-length (or more[31]) for William I (who actually reigned for just under 49 years); she deduced that this was most unlikely to have arisen independently as a scribal accident and was, therefore, no doubt an original feature of ξ. She concluded that the archetype of the X-group (ξ) may be dated to sometime during the reign of Alexander II (1214–49).[32]

Anderson's Y-group of regnal lists beginning with Cinaed mac Alpín

Marjorie Anderson's Y-group presents more difficulties. She argued that they were all derived from a plain list (recording the usual name plus reign-length) which began with Fergus son of Erc and continued through to Mael Coluim IV (1153–65), and that the archetype of this group was therefore composed sometime during the reign of Mael Coluim's successor William I (1165–1214).[33] The Y-group, however, is not as homogenous as her X-group. It can usefully be broken down into two smaller groups: those beginning with Cinaed mac Alpín, and those which include kings of Dál Riata and so begin with Fergus son of Erc.[34] Those beginning with Cinaed mac Alpín are as follows:

28 The text has been reassembled and published in Anderson and Anderson, *The Chronicle of Melrose*, xxv–xxvi; for discussion, see xxiv–xxv.

29 Dated in Anderson, *Kings and Kingship*, 60, to 'the fourteenth century or later'. It was published in Skene, *Chronicles*, 177–82, under the title *Chronicon Elegiacum*.

30 Anderson, *Kings and Kingship*, 60–1. Her contention (at 60) that the Verse Chronicle and List **I** share an error in the rendering of the name of the killer of Cuilén mac Illuilb seems to be wrong: *Radharc* (**I**) and *Radhardus* (Verse Chronicle) presumably refer correctly to a Briton named Rhydderch (as pointed out in Jackson, review of Anderson, *Kings and Kingship*); *Amdarch* (**D**), *Andarch* (**F**), *Amdrach* (**G**) and *Amthar* (**K**) look like no known name, and would appear to be corrupt. The only reason to see the Verse Chronicle as derived from ξ, therefore, is its fifty-year reign-length for William I: the existence of a witness to what was probably a pre-1214 stage of the annotated list from Cinaed mac Alpín (see below, 161–4) serves to reinforce this point.

31 William I is given 52 years in **G**.

32 Anderson, *Kings and Kingship*, 52.

33 Ibid. Her *terminus ante quem* would have been governed by her view that the exemplar of **E** may be dated to sometime in or before 1184; it should, however, be dated 1202x14 (see below).

34 It may be noted that (with the exception of the Verse Chronicle, which may not indeed

L. London, British Library, MS Cotton Claudius D vii, fo. 8r (pencil foliation); part of a collection of material prefixed to the Chronicle of Lanercost. The handwriting of the chronicle has been dated to the second half of the fourteenth century (the chronicle itself runs up to 1346). The list (like **M** below) represents a partial collation of a Y-type list with a copy of the Verse Chronicle (or a related list). Its most recent edition is in Skene, *Chronicles*, 295–7. It terminates with the second reign of Edward Balliol (a blank is left where its length would be indicated) and the last event noted is the cession of Scotland's southern counties to Edward III of England in 1334. The exemplar of **L** may therefore be dated to sometime in or shortly after 1334.[35]

M. London, British Library, MS Cotton Vitellius A xx, fos 43vb-44rb; for the manuscript see **G**, above. The most recent edition of **M** is in Skene, *Chronicles*, 299–301. It evidently shared with **L** an ancestor in which a partial collation was made with a list related to the Verse Chronicle. Its final king is Alexander III, and it finishes with a reference to Margaret granddaughter of Alexander III as if she was already dead (she died in 1290). Its exemplar may therefore be dated 1290x2; it may have been written in connexion with Edward I's appeal for historical material relating to Scotland.[36]

There is also London, Public Record Office, E 39/100 no. 170, which is the return made by the canons of St Mary's, Huntingdon, to Edward I in 1291 (referred to by Anderson as 'Hunt.'). This is written on the smooth side of a single, large piece of vellum; the script is of high quality and the text is beautifully laid out and decorated. Unfortunately the writing itself has deteriorated alarmingly: letters have fallen off and some have become fixed again out of position. The situation has obviously worsened considerably since Skene's day: his edition (*Chronicles*, 209–13) is therefore an invaluable witness of the text. Hunt. is much more than a simple king-list; the king-list which has been used to provide its basic framework is related to **L** and **M**.[37]

Note must also be made of the account of Mael Coluim Cenn Mór and his successors found in 'inserted folio 13' of the Chronicle of Melrose. This is the end of a roll which has been bound into the Chronicle of Melrose;[38] its provenance,

---

derive from ξ) those witnesses in the X-group which include only the annotated list from Cinaed mac Alpín have been written by English scribes who either showed a clear tendancy to abbreviation (as in **N**) or had cause to shorten the text because it was being incorporated as part of a larger work (as in the case of **G**). The relationship of **N** with **D** and **G** with **F** allows little doubt that in both cases **G** and **N** derive from complete copies of X-type lists.

35 For this account of **L** see Anderson, *Kings and Kingship*, 73–4.

36 See ibid., 71, 74–5, for this account of **M**.

37 The common ancestor of Hunt. **L** and **M** (which Marjorie Anderson argued may be dated sometime in or after 1286) was probably earlier than the collation with a list akin to the Verse Chronicle shared by **L** and **M**: ibid., 71–2.

38 Anderson and Anderson, *The Chronicle of Melrose*, 25–6; xl. See also Anderson, *Kings and Kingship*, 75. I am much less inclined than is Marjorie Anderson to allow that the

however, is unknown. It originally concluded with a notice of the birth of Alexander II in 1198, and it was presumably written 1198x1214 before being continued in more than one hand up to 1263.[39]

We now come to two lists which neither Marjorie Anderson nor Skene edited, and which are edited anew or for the first time below:

H. Cambridge, Corpus Christi College, MS 92, a copy of the St Edmundsbury chronicle made at Peterborough in the early fourteenth century.[40] King-list **H** (fo. 197vb9–43) is part of a collection of pieces which disturbs the chronological flow of the chronicle following the notice of events in 1291. The whole collection consists of an account of Northumbrian history from the Anglian settlement to Earl Waltheof (executed 1075) (fo. 197rb/vb); list **H**; and then various pieces relating to Anglo-Scottish relations (fos 197vb–199vb). Marjorie Anderson has remarked that **H** and the following pieces may have been collected at Peterborough in response to Edward I's demand in 1291 for historical information relating to English sovereignty over Scotland.[41] An edition of **H** was published by Benjamin Thorpe in 1849.[42]

A previously undiscussed list closely related to **H** is to be found in London, British Library, MS Additional 47214, fo. 22v, where it appears after a collection of king-lists relating to Anglo-Saxon kingdoms (fos 20v–22v).[43] The manuscript has been described in detail by Antonia Gransden.[44] She noted that all the contents in this mid-fourteenth-century commonplace book of 48 paper leaves, bar the chronicle of the Grey Friars at Lynn itself, have been written in one hand, and she suggested that it may have been 'compiled for some East Anglian lawyer who took an interest in Scottish affairs'.[45] The king-list is very like **H**, but is rather reduced: patronymics have been omitted, and reign-lengths reckoned in **H** in both years and months have been given only in years (although occasionally a half-year has been retained). The chief reason for supposing that this is not simply a copy of **H** is that Donnchad ua Maíl Choluim (1034–40) appears as *Dunetus*, rather than *Duncus* as in **H**; in the related king-list in inserted folio 13 of the Chronicle of Melrose Donnchad appears as *Dunec* with suspension-stroke above the *c* (i.e. *Dunecanus*).

---

roll may have originally contained material relating to the succession before Mael Coluim Cenn Mór which has been cut away; there is no indication on the roll itself that it is acephelous.

39 It finishes with a series of calculations made in 1263: see Anderson, *Early Sources*, II. 560–1 and nn.

40 See James, *Descriptive Catalogue*, I. 177–9; Anderson, *Kings and Kingship*, 75 and refs cited in n. 129.

41 Anderson, *Kings and Kingship*, 76; she notes that there is no evidence that Edward I actually received information from Peterborough.

42 Thorpe, *Florentii Wigorniensis*, II. 252–3.

43 Northumbria (to 830); Mercia (to 874); Wessex (to 788); East Anglia (to 714); summary of Essex (to 870); and Kent (to 823). The Kentish list finishes on fo. 21v; the remains of fo. 21v and all of fo. 22r are blank; the Scottish list begins on fo. 22v.

44 Gransden, 'A fourteenth-century chronicle', 270–2.

45 Ibid., 271.

It may be supposed that the common source of **H** and BL, Add. MS 47214 read *Dunecus* (which may in turn have been derived from *Dunec* with suspension-stroke over *c*). The close relationship between **H** and BL, MS Add. 47214, however, suggests that they probably shared a common exemplar (hereafter ***H**). The provenance of both manuscripts is near the earldom of Huntingdon, held by kings of Scots or their close relatives for most of the twelfth and thirteenth centuries. It is possible, therefore, that ***H** was written in a church associated with the earldom. A new edition of **H** is given below, followed by an edition of the king-list in BL, MS Add. 47214 fo. 22v.

List **H** *(CCCC, MS 92, fo. 197vb9–43)*

(Capitals editorial; layout and punctuation as in the manuscript; Thorpe's edition[46] will be referred to as 'Thorpe'.)

Et notand*um* quod hec sunt no*min*a regum Scoc*ie* qui regnaue*ru*nt in Scoc*ia* post Pictos.

Kynet macke[47] Alphin p*rimus* p*ost* Pictos .*regnauit*.[48] xvi. a*nnis*.
Douenald macke Alpin. regn*auit*. — iij. ann*is*.
Constantinus macke Kynet .*regnauit*. — xix. ann*is*.
Kyneth macke Kynet. regn*auit*. — .j. ann*o*.
Tirged macke Dugal. regn*auit*. — xij. ann*is*.
Douenald*us* macke Constantini — xi. ann*is*.
Constantin*us* macke Beth. — xlv. ann*is*.
Malcolm*us* macke Douenalde. — ix. ann*is*.
Indolf macke Constantin.[49] — ix. ann*is*.
Duf. macke Malcolmi — iij. a*nnis et*[50] vi. mens*ibus*.
Culen mack Indolf. — iiij.[51] *annis* vi mens*ibus*.
Kineth mack Malcolm. — xxij. a*nnis et* ij. mens*ibus*.
Constantin*us* mack Culen. — .j. a*nno*. *et* Dimidi*o*.
Kyneth mack Duf. — .j. a*nno*. iij. mens*ibus*.
Malcolm*us* mack Kyneth. — xxx. ann*is*.
Duncus nepos eius.[52] — .v. a*nnis*. ix. mens*ibus*.
Macbet[53] mack Finleth.[54] — xvij. ann*is*.
Lusach regn*auit*. — .iiii. ann*is et* dim*idio*.

46 Thorpe, *Florentii Wigorniensis*, II. 252–3.

47 *.i. filius* added above as interlinear gloss. Thorpe rendered *macke* and *mack* as *mack-* in all instances.

48 Thorpe omitted every instance of *regnauit* before Mael Coluim Cenn Mór mac Donnchada (*Malcolmus mack Dunkan*).

49 Thorpe has *Constantini*.

50 *et* om. Thorpe

51 Thorpe has *iv* for *iiij* both here and for the reign of Lulach (*Lusach*).

52 Thorpe has *Enis* for *eius*.

53 *Machet* Thorpe.

54 *Fineleth* MS, with *punctum delens* under the first *e*. Thorpe has *Fineleth*.

Malcolm*us* mack Dunkan[55] accepit i*n* uxorem
s*anct*am Margaret*am* reg*inam et*[56] *regnauit* xxxvij. ann*is*.
Douenald*us* frat*er* ei*us* regn*um* inuasit. iij. ann*is*.
Duncan*us* fil*ius* Malcolmi nothus. j. a*nno et* dimid*io*.
Edgar*us* fil*ius* Malcolmi et Margarete. ix. ann*is*.
Alexander frat*er* eius. xvii. a*nnis*. *et* iii me*nsibus*.
Dauid glor*io*sissim*us* eo*rund*e*m* frat*er*. xx.ix. ann*is*. *et*
genuit Henricu*m* comite*m* de Huntigton[a].
Malcolm*us* fil*ius* Henr*ici* comit*is*. xij. a*nnis*. *et* dimid*io*.
Will*elmus* fil*ius* Henr*ici* p*redict*i comit*is*. xl.ix. ann*is*.
Alexander fil*ius* p*redict*i Will*elm*i. xxxv. ann*is*.
Alexander fil*ius* Alexandri. Hic accepit in
uxorem Margareta<m>[57] filia*m* Henr*ici*. Regis
Angl*ie*. *et* genuit Margaretam reginam
Norwegie.

King-list in BL, MS Add. 47214, fo. 22v

(Capitals editorial; layout and punctuation as in MS.)

Nomina regu*m* Scocie post Pictos

Kineth *et* makehalpi*n r*e*gnauit* .xvj. ann*is*.
Dunewald r*egnauit* .iij. ann*is*.
Co*n*stantin*us* r*egnauit* .xix. ann*is*.
Kinech r*egnauit* .j. ann*is*.
Tirgec r*egnauit* .xij. ann*is*
Dunewald r*egnauit* .xj. ann*is*.
Co*n*stantin*us* r*egnauit* .xlv. ann*is*.
Malcolm*us* r*egnauit* .ix. ann*is*.
Indolfus r*egnauit* .ix. ann*is*.
Duf r*egnauit* .iij. ann*is*.
Kulen r*egnauit* .iiij. ann*is*.
Kineth r*egnauit* .xxij. ann*is*.
Constant<in>*us*[58] r*egnauit* .j. ann*is*.
Kineth r*egnauit* .j. ann*is*.
Malcolm*us* r*egnauit* .xxx. ann*is*.
Dunet*us* r*egnauit* .v. ann*is*.
Maketh r*egnauit* .xvij. ann*is*.
Kisach r*egnauit* .iiij. ann*is* di*midio*.
Malcolm*us* r*egnauit* .xxxvij. ann*is*.
Dunewald r*egnauit* .iij. ann*is*.

55 *Duncan* Thorpe.
56 *reginam et* om. Thorpe.
57 *Margareta* MS. Thorpe has *Margaretam*.
58 *Constantus* MS

Dunekanu*us* r*egnauit* .xvij. ann*is*. di*midio*.
Edgar*us* r*egnauit* .ix. ann*is*.
Alexander r*egnauit* .xvij. ann*is*.
Dauid f*rate*r ei*us* r*egnauit* .xxix ann*is*.
Malcolm*us* r*egnauit* .xij. ann*is* di*midio*.
Will*elmus* f*rate*r ei*us* r*egnauit* .xlix ann*is*
Alexander fil*ius* ei*us* r*egnauit* .xxxv. ann*is*.
Alexander fil*ius* ei*us* r*egnauit*.
Iste Alexander accep*it* Margareta*m* fil*iam* Reg*is* Henr*ici* in ux*or*em et genuit una*m* filia*m* q*uam* defu*n*cta<m>[59] s*ine* h*erede*.[60]

J. British Library, MS Arundel 202, a vellum manuscript of 79 folios which has a previously unnoted copy of the Scottish king-list on its final folio. The manuscript consists chiefly of the chronicle of popes by Martinus Polonus (fos 1r–58v), continued in more than one hand with a list of popes on each verso, and emperors on each recto. This is followed by French and Scottish king-lists on fos 78 and 79; both these folios are of uneven size in relation to the rest of the book, and are coarser and lack the distinctive horizontal ruling found throughout the book. The first item (fo. 78r/v) is a list of French monarchs (in the same hand as fos 61v–76v) as far as Charles Valois who (we are told) was 'reigning AD 1380'. The Scottish king-list comes next (fo. 79r/v) (possibly in the same hand as the French list, but using a sharper point), ending with Robert II (1371–90). The Scottish list can therefore be dated 1380x90. Reign-lengths, however, are given only as far as Alexander II (1214–49), so the archetype of the Scottish list may therefore be assigned to the reign of Alexander III (1249–86).

(The capitals, punctuation and lay-out are as in the MS.)

/fo. 79r/[61]Post Aduentu*m* Picto*rum* i*n* Scocia*m*, Prim*us* r*egnauit*
Kynad mac Alpin .xv. annis.
Addoc mac Kynad r*egnauit* .j. anno.
Grig mac Dougil r*egnauit* .xv. annis.
Douenald mac Alpyn r*egnauit* .iiij. annis.
Constantin mac Kymad r*egnauit* .xx. annis.
Douenald mac Co*n*stantin r*egnauit* .xj. annis
Constantin mac Seth. r*egnauit* .xlv. annis.
Malcolm mac Douenald r*egnauit*. r*egnauit*[62] .xx. annis.
Indolf mac Co*n*stantin r*egnauit* .ix. annis.
Duf mac Malcolm r*egnauit* .iiij. annis *et* vj. mensib*us*.
Kynad mac Duf r*egnauit* .j. anno *et* iiij. mensib*us*.
Colan mac Indolf r*egnauit* .iiij. annis. *et* vj. mensib*us*.

59 *defuncta* MS
60 Continues with account of Edward I's judgement, as Lord Superior of the kingdom of Scotland, that John Balliol was the legitimate heir of Alexander III.
61 The initial P is four lines deep.
62 sic

Malcolm mac[63] Kynad r*egnauit* .xxx. annis
Donecan nepos ei*us* r*egnauit* .v. annis *et* ix. mensib*us*.
Macbeth mac Forilegh[64] r*e*gnauit .xvij. annis.
Loulac r*e*gnauit .iij. mensib*us et* dimid*io*.
Malcolm mac Donecan. r*egnauit* .xxx. ann*is et* dj*midio*. *et* iiij. mensib*us*.
Douenal frat*er* ei*us* regnauit .ix. annis. *et* vj. mensib*us*.
Duncan fili*us* Malcolm r*e*gnauit .dj*midio*. anno.
Edgar fr*ater* ei*us* r*egnauit* .ix. annis.
Alexander fr*ater* ei*us* r*e*gnauit.[65] vj. annis.
Dauid fr*ater* ei*us* r*e*gnauit .l. annis et vltra
Malcolm fili*us* Henr*ici* co*m*itis filij Dauid r*egnauit* .xij. annis *et* dj*midio*.
Will*el*mus f*rate*r ei*us* r*egnauit* .l. annis et vltra.
Alexander fili*us* ei*us* r*e*gnauit .xxxiij. annis
Alexander filius eius r*e*gnauit
Edward*us* Rex Anglor*um* p*rimus* post co*n*questu*m* r*e*gnauit .xj. ann*is*.
Joh*ann*es Baliolf. r*e*gn*auit*.
/fo. 79v/Robert*us* Brus r*e*gnauit
Dauid Brus fili*us* Rob*er*ti. r*e*gnauit.
Robert*us* Stiward. r*e*gnauit.

Marjorie Anderson pointed out that **L**, **M** and Hunt. share a number of errors: Mael Coluim mac Domnaill has been given twenty years (rather than the usual nine), Cinaed mac Maíl Choluim and Custantín mac Cuiléin have been omitted, and Cinaed mac Duib and Cuilén mac Illuilb have been transposed.[66] All these errors are also found in **J**.[67] It appears, however, that **J** has not been derived from the common ancestor of **L**, **M** and Hunt. because it does not share their naming of the father of Giric mac Dúngaile as Domnall. Even more significant is **J**'s reign-length of '50-or-more years' for William I as opposed to the 49 years given in the others. This suggests that the common ancestor shared by **J** and **L**, **M** and Hunt. was in existence before the addition of William I's reign-length, and may be dated therefore to sometime in or before 1214.

List ***H** had none of the errors noted above shared by **J**, **L**, **M** and the Huntingdon Chronicle. It did, however, have an error which is otherwise found only in inserted folio 13 in the Chronicle of Melrose: the reign of Donnchad mac Maíl Choluim has been increased from six months to a year-and-a-half. ***H** may be dated to sometime after the death of Alexander II in 1249, whose reign-length would have been the last recorded in the list.

63 There is a significant gap at this point; there appears to be an erasure here, with *mac* written over part of it.

64 There is a horizontal suspension-stroke above *gh*.

65 Followed by a gap here.

66 Anderson, *Kings and Kingship*, 71.

67 Its exemplar may also have shared the erroneous *xxxix* years for David I (*xxix* years is given correctly in ***H**, inserted fo. 13 in the Chronicle of Melrose, and in X-group lists); unfortunately in **J** David I's reign-length has been mistakenly replaced by William I's.

The relationships between these lists may be summarised:

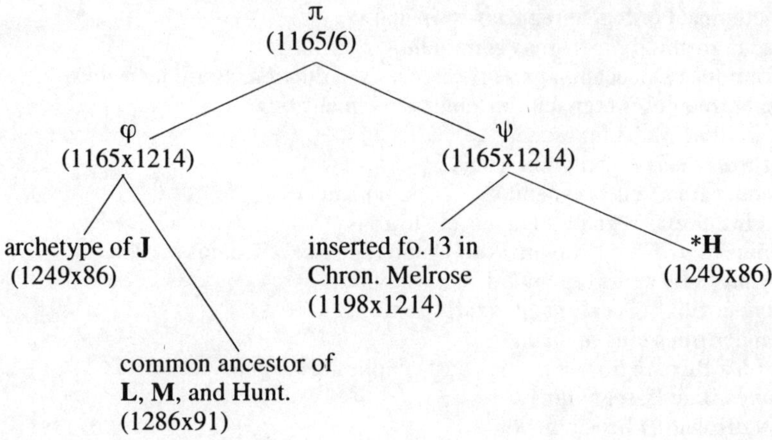

Anderson's Y-group regnal lists which include kings of Dál Riata

The next group of witnesses which Marjorie Anderson also classified as part of her Y-group consist of the following:

E. Paris, Bibliothèque Nationale, MS latin 4126, fos 29v-30v. This is the fifth item in the collection of historical pieces which survives uniquely in this manuscript, produced in York for a Roger of Poppleton *c*.1360.[68] The collection has been edited in Anderson, *Kings and Kingship*, 240–60: **E** is at 253–6. Anderson was inclined to date the collection itself to 1165x84;[69] a cogent case has been made, however, for dating it 1202x14.[70] The latter stages of the list include two lengthy insertions which have been dated respectively to 1118x52 and sometime in or after 1153; these may have been incorporated into the list before the collection of pieces was made 1202x14.[71]

A list similar to **E** was used (probably 1240x64) to enter notes on the succession of kings of Dál Riata in the margin of the Chronicle of Melrose (therefore only from the chronicle's beginning in 731). The exemplar may not have included patronymics (like **N** below).[72]

68 For discussion, see Anderson, 'The Scottish materials'; Anderson, *Kings and Kingship*, 235–40; Cowan, 'The Scottish chronicle'; Miller, 'Matriliny by treaty', 138–42; Crick, *The Historia Regum Britannie*, III. 256–61.

69 Anderson, 'The Scottish materials', 34, 40; *Kings and Kingship*, 68.

70 Miller, 'Matriliny by treaty', 138–42, esp. 138.

71 Anderson, *Kings and Kingship*, 69.

72 Ibid., 70–1.

N. London, British Library, MS Harley 1808 fo. 66r/v.[73] Only the Dál Riata part of this list belongs to Anderson's Y-group. At some stage patronymics have been discarded in this section.[74]

The feature which distinguishes this group from the other lists in Anderson's Y-group is the inclusion of a list of kings of Dál Riata. The archetype of these three lists (which I will refer to as η) may be dated to sometime during the reign of William I; it would have consisted of a succession of Scottish kings beginning with Fergus son of Erc through Cinaed mac Alpín to William I, and would have given the reign-length of William's predecessor Mael Coluim to the exact day, as in π.

Another notable characteristic of η is that its author made a determined effort to translate Gaelic words into Latin.[75] It is apparent from both ***H** and **J** that ψ and φ used *mac* rather than *filius* (as far as Mael Coluim Cenn Mór mac Donnchada); this must also, therefore, have been a feature of π. In η, however, *filius* was used throughout. It is also apparent that eponyms of kings of Dál Riata have been translated.[76] Seven kings had epithets and the original Gaelic has been preserved in lists of the X-group, although not in Gaelic orthography. In six cases the Gaelic word can be recovered and can be matched convincingly with their translation into Latin in η:

Readings in X-group lists:

D	*bud*	*kere*	*brek*	*foda*	*fyne*	*annune*
F	*bude*[77]	*kerr*[78]	*brec*[79]	*foda*	*fin*	*annuine*[80]
I	*bude*	*ker*	*brec*	*fode*	*fin*	*anuine*
K	*brid*	*er*	*brec*[81]	*fod*	*fin*	(omitted)
Gaelic:	buide	cerr	brecc	fota	finn	an-nimnech[82]
Latin in η: (as witnessed in **E**)	flauus	sinistralis	uarius	longus	albus	uenenosus

73 See above, 134–5.

74 Anderson, *Kings and Kingship*, 71.

75 He has also gone further than other king-list scribes in the transliteration of Gaelic names into an orthography which had become familiar in Latin documents in eastern Scotland in the twelfth-century: thus he rendered Eogan (genitive: Eogain) as *Ewen*, representing the intervocalic vocalised *gh* with *w* instead of retaining the *g* of Gaelic orthography found in other witnesses.

76 Only **E** has all the epithets. Most have been omitted in **N** (which has only *aldus*, i.e. *albus*), and also in the material entered into the margins of the Chronicle of Melrose (which has *albus* and *uenenosus*): see Anderson, *Kings and Kingship*, 70–1.

77 *bad* F (Harl.)

78 *ker* F (Harl.)

79 *breck* and *brek* F (Harl.)

80 *annine* F (Harl.)

81 Also *brech* and *bret*.

82 See next note.

The only epithet which is especially remarkable is the one represented by *anuine/annuine*. Whatever this may have been originally it has evidently been taken by the author of η to represent *nimnech* 'poisonous' preceded by the intensive prefix *an*, hence *uenenosus*, 'very poisonous'.[83] This in particular suggests that the author of η had a good knowledge of Gaelic.[84] The only epithet which is difficult to reconstruct is the one which was translated as *habens curruum nasum*, 'having a hooked nose': the original word has been rendered haphazardly in witnesses of the X-group, with **D** reading *monanle* and *ranual*, **F** reading *rinnavel* or *monanel* (F (Harl) has *rinnevale* or *ramele*), **I** *rounauel* and *miniele*, and **K** has *inen Danel* (once only). The problem is made worse by the likelihood that the word was not originally an epithet at all, but represented the garbled remnant of a king called Fiannamail (d.700).[85] The eye of faith can discern *srón*, 'nose', as the way the author of η interpreted the first syllable, but the rest is hopelessly obscure.

There is one notable error which would have been shared by η and π: the witnesses of both give Cinaed mac Duib a reign of only a year-and-a-half rather than eight years;[86] the translation of *mac* (from Cinaed mac Alpín onwards) into *filius* in η indicates that η was derived from π (rather than the other way round).

The author of η was presumably a Gaelic-speaker writing probably for a non-Gaelic audience (such as the Anglo-French churchmen who came to prominence in the east and south of the kingdom during the twelfth century). The translation from *mac* to *filius* suggests that η was written in Scotland (which in turn makes it likely that π was also written within the Scottish kingdom).

The addition of the Dál Riata regnal list (1165x1214)

It is apparent that the X-group of king-lists are witnesses to a stage in the development of the Dál Riata king-list in which epithets were left untranslated, and must therefore be derived ultimately from a source of η; this source of η is represented hereafter by the siglum ϱ. These relationships may be summarised diagrammatically (remembering that the archetype of the X-group is denoted as ξ):

83 If lenited *m* was represented as *u* in the X-group lists, then *an-nimnech* would have required nine minims, as in **F** (Innes). The final consonant (if it was ever present) could have been written as *c* and may have been lost in the archetype of the X-group.

84 It is possible, therefore, that errors in the rendering of Gaelic names noted by Marjorie Anderson (*Kings and Kingship*, 68) – final *l* for final *d* in Eochaid; metathesis in rendering of Muiredach – should be attributed to a copy of η. Either at this later stage or with η itself Mael Dúin son of Conall Crandomna has been omitted.

85 Anderson, *Kings and Kingship*, 68 n. 102 (where *rindamail*, 'acute, piercing' or *rïanamail*, 'well-disposed, orderly' was suggested) and 105.

86 Anderson, *Kings and Kingship*, 68. X-group lists erroneously have a Giric son of Cinaed rather than Cinaed mac Duib himself. That Cinaed mac Duib ruled for eight years (997–1005) is confirmed by the continuation of *SL*2 to Mael Coluim Cenn Mór (see e.g. List **B** in Anderson, *Kings and Kingship*, 263). On *SL*2 see further below, 168–70.

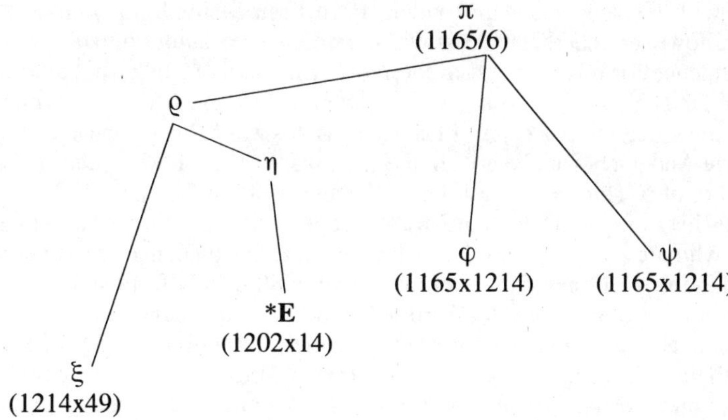

The proposition that π was therefore an ancestor of ξ will be discussed in due course.

In the absence of any evidence that π included a listing of kings of Dál Riata it would be natural to conclude that the Dalriadic king-list in ϱ was a new feature. This would not, however, fit into Marjorie Anderson's understanding of how the king-list developed in Scotland in this period. Before examining Anderson's scheme in more detail it will be useful to assemble the evidence which points to ϱ as the earliest archetype of extant Scottish lists which included the Dál Riata king-list.

Marjorie Anderson pointed out that Cinaed mac Alpín is described in **E** (the only certain witness of how Cinaed mac Alpín may have been treated in η) as *primus rex Scottorum*, despite the fact that **E** is a continuous list from Fergus son of Erc to William I which is otherwise unannotated up to the eleventh century.[87] She compared this with the description of Cinaed as *primus* or *primus rex* in witnesses of π. This would appear to reinforce the impression that **E** was descended from an archetype (ϱ) in which a list of kings of Dál Riata had been tacked on in front of a list of Cinaed mac Alpín and his successors. In ξ, for its part, there is a clear difference in character between its listing of Cinaed mac Alpín and his successors, which included details of their death and burial, and its plain unannotated listing of kings of Dál Riata; this also coincided with a change from *filius* (in the Dál Riata list) to *mac* (from Cinaed mac Alpín).[88] Again, this would appear to reinforce the impression that these were once seperate lists, so that the Dál Riata king-list has been added at some stage to the list from Cinaed mac Alpín. A proper understanding of how this may have occurred must, however, await a discussion of the relationship between ξ and π.

It might be imagined that adding a Dál Riata king-list to a list like π which

87 Anderson, *Kings and Kingship*, 71 and n.116: she also noted that Cinaed is described as *primus rex Scottorum* in **N**, although at this point **N** is otherwise a member of the X-group.

88 From Cinaed to Mael Coluim Cenn Mór π also used *mac* rather than *filius* in patronymics (witnessed by **H** and **J**); there is no evidence that the Dál Riata list in ϱ used *mac*. See 156–60, below.

began with Cinaed mac Alpín would have been a simple operation. It would appear, however, that this process was regarded by the author of ϱ as problematic. The evidence for this is found in the most remarkable feature unique to Scottish texts of the Dál Riata king-list. We can begin with figure 1 (below), which details part of the succession of kings of Dál Riata as this would have appeared (following Marjorie Anderson's analysis)[89] in the exemplar of the Dál Riata king-list used by the author of ϱ. This would have been the same as the archetype of all witnesses of the king-list (both Irish and Scottish),[90] except for the inclusion of two kings called Eogan who are found only in Scottish witnesses. The evidence of Irish chronicles (which in this section derived their information ultimately from an Iona chronicle which was contemporary at least from the 680s to 740)[91] suggests that the succession delineated in figure 1 represents the actual succession of kings of Dál Riata, but with the following exceptions: (i) the transposition of Dúngal mac Selbaig and Eochaid mac Echdach (ii) the omission of Fiannamail ua Dúnchado, and (iii) the addition of the two kings called Eogan attested only in Scottish witnesses. If figure 1 is compared with figure 2 it is apparent that the succession in ϱ has suffered serious disruption. A group of four kings has been transposed *en bloc* from their original position in the early eighth century (preceding Muiredach mac Ainbcellaig, d.736) so that they now appeared as successors of Fergus mac Echdach (778–81). The patronymics of some in the group have evidently been altered according to their new position in the list, no doubt to safeguard the credibility of their place as successors of Fergus mac Echdach. It is also notable that there is no sign of the successors of Fergus mac Echdach attested in Irish witnesses of the list (and occasionally in Irish chronicles) in the sixty-or-more years between the death of Fergus in 781 and the sixteen-year reign attributed in nearly all lists to Cinaed mac Alpín (d.858).[92]

89 Conveniently summarised in Anderson, *Kings and Kingship*, 228–9.

90 For the Irish witnesses, see below, 168–72.

91 See esp. Bannerman, 'Notes on the Scottish entries'; and in general, Herbert, *Iona, Kells and Derry*, 22–3.

92 The only king given the title 'king of Dál Riata' in this period in contemporary record is Donncoirce (AU 792.4). At least three other kings in the king-list are found in contemporary chronicles: Conall mac Taidg and Conall mac Aedáin (AU 807.3; cf. AI 807.2), and Aed mac Boanta (AU 839.9). Not all the kings in the Dál Riata king-list were necessarily kings of Dál Riata at all; see Broun, 'Pictish kings 761–839'.

Figure 1. Probable succession of kings of Dál Riata (from 697) in exemplar used by author of ϱ

(excluding Fiannamail ua Dúnchado, d.700, who may already have been lost/garbled at this stage)

(Dates of historical reign of each king are given, if known.)

1.	Eochaid mac Domangairt	(697)
2.	Ainbcellach mac Ferchair	(697–8)
3.	Eogan mac Ferchair[93]	
4.	Selbach mac Ferchair	(c.700–723)
5.	Eochaid mac Echdach	(726–33)
6.	Dúngal mac Selbaig	(? –726)
7.	Alpín	(–?736)
8.	Muiredach mac Ainbcellaig	(–?736)
9.	Eogan mac Muiredaig[94]	
10.	Aed Find mac Echdach	(–778)
11.	Fergus mac Echdach	(778–81)
	↓	
	(6 kings)	
	↓	
18.	Alpín mac Echdach (father of Cinaed mac Alpín)	(–?842)

Figure 2. Succession as it would have appeared in ϱ

bold denotes transposed kings; → marks place from where they were transposed; * denotes king in royal genealogy. Spelling of names has been standardised. Numbering relates to figure 1, above.

1.	*Eochaid 'son of *Domangart son of *Domnall Brecc'
2.	Ainbcellach son of Ferchar
3.	Eogan son of Ferchar
	→
8.	Muiredach son of Ainbcellach
9.	Eogan son of Muiredach
10.	*Aed Find son of *Eochaid
11.	Fergus 'son of *Aed Find'
4.	**Selbach** 'son of Eogan'
5.	***Eochaid** 'son of *Aed Find'
6.	**Dúngal** son of **Selbach**
7.	***Alpín** 'son of ***Eochaid**'

93 In Scottish witnesses only.

94 In Scottish witnesses only.

Marjorie Anderson sought to explain both the transposition of the group of four kings and the absence of successors of Fergus mac Echdach as the result of scribal error. She described the Scottish witnesses of the Dalriadic king-list as representing a 'corrupt version' which 'had been very carelessly transmitted'.[95] She suggested that, at some stage after the four kings had been misplaced, the eye of a copyist may have jumped from Alpín (the last in the transposed group) to Alpín mac Echdach (father of Cinaed mac Alpín) so that all intermediate kings were omitted; alternatively the connexion between Alpín in the list and Cinaed's father may have been made consciously, with the same result.[96]

Scribal accident is certainly the most natural explanation of transposition and omission in a king-list. Nevertheless, the transposition of this group of four kings has an interesting outcome which is unlikely to be coincidental. Moreover, there are also a couple of indications that successors of Fergus mac Echdach have not been lost at some stage after the transposition, but were absent from the source of ϱ itself. I will argue that the transposition was in fact deliberate, and that it was an attempt by someone who placed great store by the royal genealogy to make a king-list terminating with Fergus mac Echdach run convincingly on to a list beginning with Cinaed mac Alpín.

A remarkable feature of the list as it would have appeared in ϱ is that, despite the transposition of the group of four kings and the absence of any historical successor of Fergus mac Echdach, its account of the kingship of Dál Riata nevertheless tallied with the comparable section of the pedigree of kings of Scots. As can be seen from comparing figures 3 and 4 (below), it is possible to trace the royal genealogy back from Cinaed through to Domnall Brecc (and thus back in time to Fergus son of Erc through the rest of the list). Had the transposition and omission of kings been simply a careless error, it is unlikely that such good order would have resulted. Moreover, a knowledge of the royal pedigree can be corroborated by the description of Eochaid (d.697) as 'son of Domangart son of Domnall Brecc'. It would have been impossible to know from the source of ϱ, or indeed from the archetype of all extant lists (both Irish and Scottish), that Eochaid's grandfather was Domnall Brecc; this was because in the archetype itself Domangart mac Domnaill Bricc had been omitted due to a scribal accident.[97] The most likely source of this information, therefore, would have been the royal pedigree. It is also notable that Eochaid would have been the only king in ϱ described as 'son of X son of Y' (rather than just 'son of X'), and that the relationship between his father Domangart and grandfather Domnall Brecc would have been the only link in the royal pedigree which would not have been visible by the usual practice of referring to a king simply as 'son of X'. This is further evidence, therefore, that a deliberate effort has been made to make sure that the royal genealogy could be traced through the king-list.

95 Anderson, *Kings and Kingship*, 46.

96 Ibid.

97 Ibid., 46. She suggested (46 n. 8) that this may have occurred at the same time as, or possibly as a consequence of, the reversal of Domangart's successors, Mael Dúin and Domnall Donn. The obits of these three kings are noted in AU 673.1, 689.6 and 696.1 and AT 673.2, 689.4 (in which material corresponding to AU 689.4–6 has been conflated) and 696.1*a*.

Figure 3. Section of royal pedigree visible in ϱ

(Numbers refer to the order of succession of each king in figure 1, above.)

Cinaed
son of Alpín (7)
son of Eochaid (5)
son of Aed Find (10)
son of Eochaid (1)
son of Domangart
son of Domnall Brecc

Figure 4.[98] *The earliest extant text of the royal genealogy: the pedigree of Custantín mac Cuiléin (995–7) in* Genelaig Albanensium[99]

underlining denotes the part corresponding to figure 3, above.

Causantin
m*ac* Culiuin
m*eic* Ilduib
m*eic* Causanti*n*
m*eic* Aeda m*eic* Cinaeda
m*eic* Alpín m*eic* Echach
m*eic* Aeda Find
m*eic* Echach
m*eic* Domang*airt*
m*eic* Domnaill B*ricc*
m*eic* Echa*ch* Buide
m*eic* Aedáin
m*eic* Gabráin
m*eic* Domang*airt*
m*eic* Fergusa
m*eic* Eirc
[*continues for 30 more generations*]

98 This is not the earliest manuscript witness (which is the genealogy of Mael Coluim mac Cinaeda in Rawl. B.502, *c.*1130) but it is the earliest extant text, and may be dated 995x7: see below, 174. It should be noted that other witnesses give a slightly different account of the section between Aed Find mac Echdach and Domangart mac Domnaill Bricc, and that it would appear that the copy here has omitted a generation: see Anderson, *Kings and Kingship*, 239. It is possible, therefore, that the author of ϱ used a copy related to the one presented here from *Genelaig Albanensium.*

99 Edited from Dublin, Trinity College, MS H.2.7. col. 89a (xiv^{med}) (see Bannerman, *Studies*, 28–31, and 65–6 for edition of complete *Genelaig* in this manuscript). The other late-medieval witnesses are BB (beginning at 148c41) and Lec (beginning at 109vb34). In the extract quoted here they erroneously have 'Colum' instead of Cuilén as the father of Custantín (see Bannerman, *Studies*, 67).

Could a desire to make the king-list consistent with the genealogy have provoked the transposition of the four kings? The answer is yes, if the source of ϱ terminated with Fergus mac Echdach. One problem which would have arisen if Cinaed mac Alpín had simply been added as the immediate successor of Fergus mac Echdach would have been the omission of Cinaed's grandfather Eochaid son of Aed Find, which would have broken the thread of the royal genealogy running through the king-list. A simple solution, however, would have been to give two generations of Alpín's ancestry in the same way as Eochaid (d.697) was described as son of Domangart son of Domnall Brecc. A more pressing problem for a scholar conscious of the royal pedigree, however, could have been that such a list would have separated Cinaed's accession from the death of his great-grandfather Aed Find by only three years (the duration of the reign ascribed to Aed's successor Fergus mac Echdach). This would have required the more drastic solution of rearranging the list in order to create more space between Aed Find and Cinaed mac Alpín. This would have seemed all the more attractive once it was realised that the transposition of early-eighth-century kings into successors of Fergus mac Echdach would actually make the list conform more exactly to the royal pedigree (at least as this is witnessed in figure 4).

This may be corroborated by two other details which would have been present in ϱ. The first is the only widely inaccurate reign-length in ϱ: Eochaid in the transposed group has been given thirty years, instead of the seven years that would appear to have been his due.[100] It is difficult to see how *uii* could have been miscopied accidentally as *xxx*. It must be suspected that this was deliberate. Because this has occurred to one of the transposed kings, it may be supposed that this was part of the process of creating space between Cinaed mac Alpín and Fergus mac Echdach which inspired the kings' transposition.[101]

It is not unknown for the figure of thirty years to be used merely to denote a long reign.[102] Marjorie Anderson, however, has drawn attention to an extraordinary facet of Eochaid's thirty-year reign: the extra twenty-three years would seem to have been the exact number lost by the omission of Conall Crandomna, Dúnchad and Domnall Donn at some stage between ϱ and the archetype of all extant witnesses of the Dál Riata king-list.[103] It would appear, therefore, that this discrepancy has been noted by someone who added up the reign-lengths in his source and compared it with a year-total for the kingdom of Dál Riata stated in his source. Instead of revising the year-total for the kingdom, however, he would have added the missing twenty-three years to the reign-length of Eochaid in the transposed group of kings. The year-total stated in the source would, therefore, have been the 315 years given in ϱ[104] – a figure which could only have been arrived at in a list which lacked the successors of Fergus mac Echdach. This may serve, therefore, to

100 Anderson, *Kings and Kingship*, 112.

101 The result is that the chronological gap in the list between Cinaed mac Alpín and Fergus mac Echdach is nearly the same as it would have been in real life (see Anderson, *Kings and Kingship*, 113). This was probably accidental: see below.

102 See Dumville, 'The West Saxon', 39–40, 40 n. 47, also 58–9; Swanton, 'A fragmentary life', 24 n. 37.

103 Anderson, *Kings and Kingship*, 113; see also 47.

104 See below, 164.

corroborate that the source of ϱ (as suspected already) terminated with Fergus mac Echdach.

All the peculiar features which would have been found in ϱ can therefore be explained as the result of a conscious effort to create a king-list running from Fergus son of Erc through Cinaed mac Alpín and on to the twelfth century in which it was possible to trace every generation of the royal pedigree.[105] The most eccentric aspects of ϱ – the four transposed kings, the absence of successors of Fergus mac Echdach attested in Irish versions of the list, and the curious thirty-year reign-length of Eochaid in the transposed group – can all be seen, moreover, as products of a determination to make the king-list compatible with the genealogy, and in particular to fill a chronological hole between Cinaed mac Alpín and his great-grandfather Aed Find which would have arisen from making the list of Cinaed mac Alpín and his successors follow directly from a king-list terminating with Fergus mac Echdach. Such effort and ingenuity, moreover, would appear to be striking testimony not only to the character of ϱ as a new combination of the Dál Riata king-list with the list from Cinaed mac Alpín, but also to how unusual such a list would seem to have been for a significant period prior to the creation of ϱ. Had a version of the list been known which included a succession of kings between Fergus mac Echdach and Cinaed mac Alpín – similar to the one witnessed in Ireland – then the author of ϱ would presumably not have been forced to undertake his impressive work.[106]

Anderson's discussion of Scottish regnal lists 1094–1214

The discussion so far of ancestors of extant Scottish king-lists has already made a number of significant departures from Marjorie Anderson analysis of their development in the period 1094–1214. It would be appropriate at this point, therefore, to examine her scheme in the light of what has been argued above and consider if further changes may be in order.

Anderson proposed[107] tentatively that all witnesses, both Irish and Scottish,

105 With the exception of Eochaid mac Echdach, who is found, however, in only one witness of the pedigree, and may not therefore have been present in the text used by the author of ϱ: see n. 98 and Anderson, *Kings and Kingship*, 239.

106 The combination of a list of Dál Riata kings and a list of Cinaed and his successors in Irish witnesses datable to the late eleventh and early twelfth centuries may indeed be explained as an independent joining-together of the two elements. In the *Comaimsera* (on which see below, 170–2) there is striking error where the join occurs: in the chronological chunk defined by the deaths of Aed Alláin (743) and Aed Findliath (879) the listing of 'kings of Alba' runs up to Cinaed mac Alpín (d.858), while in the next chronological chunk, defined by the deaths of Aed Findliath (879) and Brian Boruma (1014), the 'kings of Alba' begin with Domnall mac Alpín (d.862) (see Boyle, 'The Edinburgh Synchronisms', 176–9; Thurneysen, 'Synchronismen', 90–3, where Cinaed mac Alpín has been conflated in the text with his father). This mistaken division of 'kings of Alba' at Cinaed mac Alpín may have been influenced by knowledge that the kings before and after Cinaed represented two originally distinct lists. For the designation of kings before Cinaed as kings of Alba, see Broun, 'Pictish kings, 761–839'.

107 For what follows see esp. Anderson, *Kings and Kingship*, 48–52. The stemma at 234 is

descended from a list which consisted of kings of Dál Riata followed by Cinaed mac Alpín and his successors; notes on the death and burial of Cinaed and his successors were then added sometime between *c.*1105 and 1165. The common source of both her X- and Y-groups included the precise reckoning to the day of the reign of Mael Coluim IV, so she therefore dated it to 1165/6. She argued, however, that the notes on royal deaths and burials were jettisoned in the archetype of her Y-group; she also envisaged, it would appear, that the list of Dál Riata kings was subsequently jettisoned independently in an ancestor of **H** and again in the common source of **L**, **M** and the Huntingdon Chronicle.[108] Finally, a Pictish king-list was added to create the archetype of her X-group (1214x49). Her scheme can be summarised as follows (but using the sigla which I have adopted):

Marjorie Anderson's scheme
of how the king-list may have developed

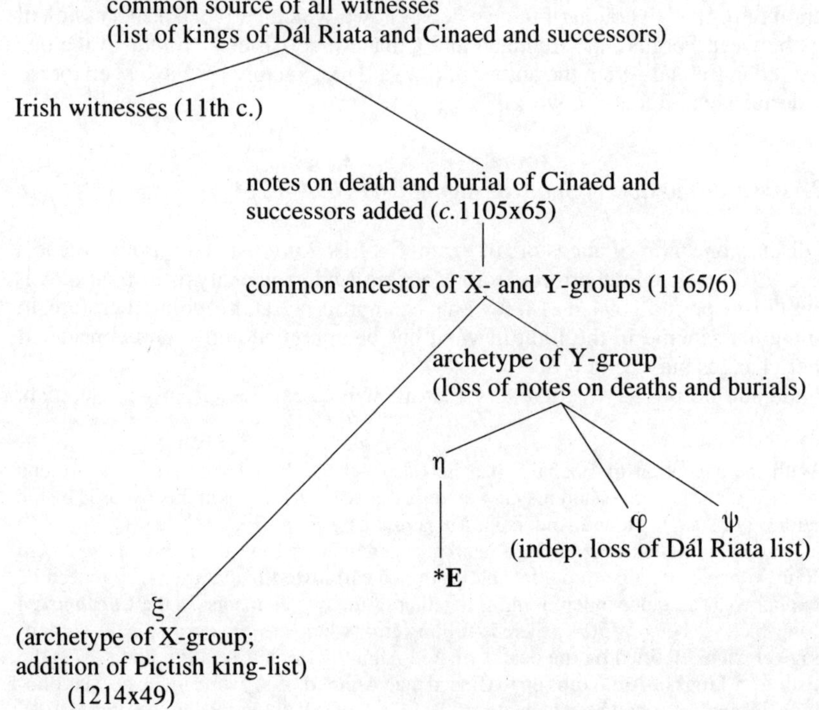

not clear for these stages: it would appear from it that she suggested that the archetype of her Y-group, as well as the common ancestor of both Y- and X-groups, may be dated 1165/6.

108 Ibid., 71.

There are two aspects of this which are problematic. One is the independent loss of the Dál Riata list on two occasions. It would be more natural to take the existence of lists beginning with Cinaed mac Alpín in different branches of her Y-group, and the restriction of details of royal deaths and burials to Cinaed mac Alpín and his successors, as evidence that the Dál Riata list was not an original feature of the common source of her Y-group lists. This would tally, moreover, with my proposition that η has been derived from a text (ϱ) in which a list of Cinaed mac Alpín and his successors was joined with a Dál Riata king-list, and that the transposition of four kings was deliberate and not simply the result of careless copying. The other awkward aspect is the apparent complete loss of the material on royal deaths and burials (but nothing else) in the archetype of her Y-group. Such comprehensive and uncannily precise excision of this material seems improbable.

Marjorie Anderson's scheme hinges on one impressive feature found in lists of both her X- and Y-groups: the remarkably detailed reign-length ascribed to Mael Coluim IV. It was this which forced her to conclude that the archetypes of both groups must share a common ancestor datable to 1165/6. Because the material on royal deaths and burials must be older than this, it followed that it had been jettisoned in the archetype of her Y-group; moreover, because the Dál Riata king-list was present in members of both her X- and Y-groups, it seemed that it, too, was present in their common source. If an alternative scheme is to carry conviction, therefore, it must not only find a more plausible explanation of how different branches of Anderson's Y-group begin only with Cinaed mac Alpín, why the material on royal deaths and burial is confined to Cinaed and his successors, and why there is no trace of this material in Y-group lists, but it must also explain how both X- and Y-group lists both give the reign-length of Mael Coluim IV in unprecedented detail.

A new scheme for the development of Scottish regnal lists 1094–1214

In reconstructing the development of Scottish king-lists in this period, we may note that Anderson's X- and Y-groups all share a significant error in assigning 37 years (and some months) to the reign of Mael Coluim Cenn Mór mac Donnchada (1058–93); he actually reigned for 35 years and just under 8 months.[109] An ancestral list consisting only of Cinaed and his successors may be traced back, therefore, at least to sometime in or after 1093.[110] A common ancestor (π) may (as noted already) be recognised for φ and ψ, which would have shared an erroneous reign-length for Cinaed mac Duib (a year and a few months rather than eight years).[111] This would then suggest that the addition of the Dál Riata king-list occurred sometime later than π; as noted already, π may be dated to 1165/6 due to the precise reckoning of the reign of Mael Coluim IV found in its witnesses. This may be summarised:

109 Anderson, *Kings and Kingship*, 49. It is apparent, however, that the number of months was recorded differently in π and ξ: the latter had '8 months', the former had 'half a year and 4 months' (so **E** and **H**; this had evidently been reduced to '4 months' in φ).

110 Probably earlier, in fact: see below, 165–70.

111 Anderson, *Kings and Kingship*, 68.

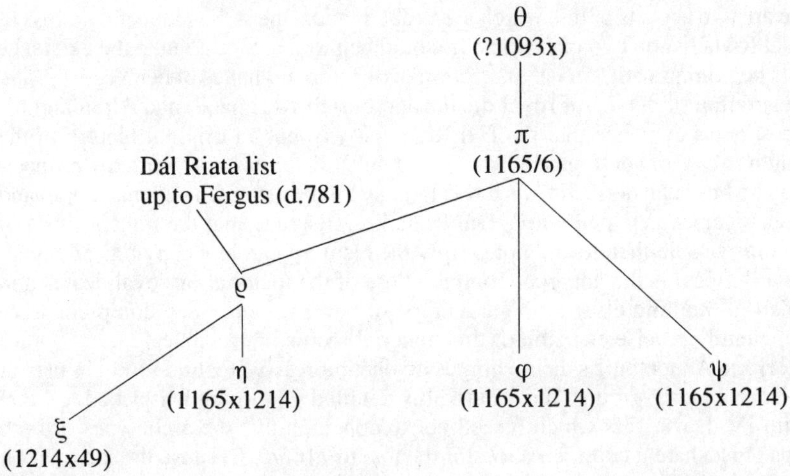

This cannot be the whole story, however. The archetype of Anderson's X-group (ξ) did not share the erroneous reign-length given in π to Cinaed mac Duib.[112] There is evidence, indeed, that the list of Cinaed mac Alpín and his successors found in ξ was derived from θ independently of π. Edgar's reign-length was given in ξ as 9 years and 3 months, Alexander I's as 17 years 3½ months and David I's as 29 years and 3 months;[113] the equivalent figures in π were less detailed – 9 years, 17 years 3 months and 29 years.[114] The detail given in π for the reign-length of Mael Coluim IV shows that it was not written by someone who may have been disinclined to preserve a precise reckoning for Edgar, Alexander I or David I; it may be concluded, therefore, that these details in ξ were derived from an independent source, such as another continuation of θ in which the very precise reign-length for Alexander I was doubtless recorded soon after his death; this may have been updated soon after David I's death (especially if the figure originally read '3

112 Indeed, in ξ Giric son of Cinaed mac Duib (whose existence is otherwise unattested) appeared instead of Cinaed mac Duib himself: this may simply have been a copyist's error (as suggested in Anderson, *Kings and Kingship*, 52).

113 See text edited below for these figures.

114 For **H** see above; the reign-lengths for Alexander I and David I in **J** are corrupt; for **E** see Anderson, *Kings and Kingship*, 255; for **L**, **M** and the Huntingdon Chronicle (whose common ancestor gave David I 39 years) see Skene, *Chronicles*, 296, 300 and 212 respectively; for inserted fo. 13 in the Chronicle of Melrose, see *Chronicle of Melrose* facsimile edn, 25 (though it is rather more than a plain king-list and supplies exact dates for the deaths of these kings). The beginning of Edgar's reign is difficult to establish; the period between Edgar's death and Alexander's death was probably 17 years 3 months and 16 days. The period between Alexander's death and David I's, however, was 29 years and 1 month, which can not readily be reconciled with the figure in ξ, unless it may be assumed that '3 weeks' was intended rather than '3 months' and that the reign may have been calculated from David I's inauguration – although the exact date of this is unfortunately unknown.

weeks').[115] The relationship this suggests between the archetypes may be summarised diagrammatically:

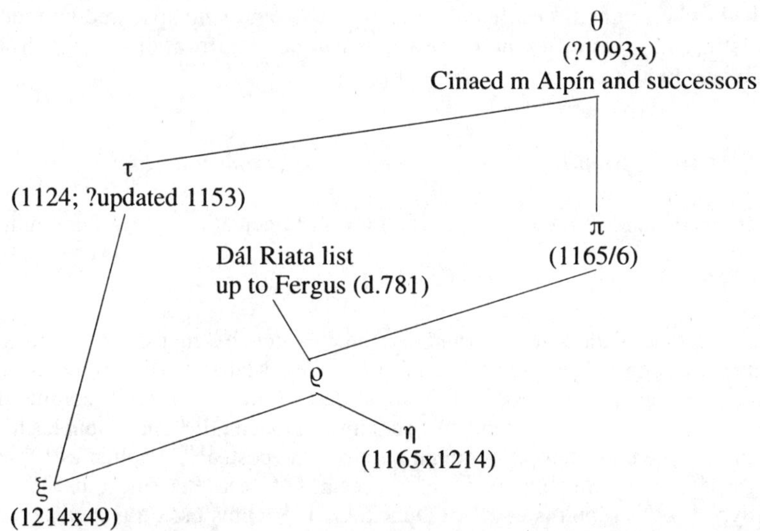

A particular attraction of the independent ancestry of ξ and π from θ is that it would allow the notes on each king's death and burial to have been added at the stage represented by τ, rather than suppose (with Marjorie Anderson) that these had been jettisoned by the archetype of her Y-group. Anderson took this view because she was inclined to regard patronymics in *mac* found in members of both her X- and Y-groups from Cinaed mac Alpín to Mael Coluim Cenn Mór as derived from the same source as the annotated list.[116] She may have been influenced by the use of Gaelic forms of place-names in the notes (notably *Inueraldan* for Alnwick). The use of *mac* rather than *filius* in the notes does not, however, correspond with the use of *mac* in the list proper (as represented for instance by **H** and **J**). The notes do not show an exclusive preference for *mac*: Giric mac Dúngaile, Rhydderch ap Dyfnwal and Cinaed mac Duib[117] all appear with patronymics in *filius*; the first instance of *mac* in this context is Mac Bethad mac Findlaích.[118]

It is notable, moreover, that the appearance of *mac* in π and ξ would not have

115 There is no way of knowing, of course, if its reckoning of Edgar's reign was notably precise; if it was, then this too would be likely to have been written down soon after Edgar's death.

116 Anderson, *Kings and Kingship*, 50–1; the first use of *filius* rather than *mac* in the list proper (but not the notes) was for Mael Coluim IV, which suggested to her a *terminus ante quem* for the notes of 1165/6 (ibid., 52), but see below, 157–9.

117 Mistakenly described as son of Mael Coluim; Anderson, *Kings and Kingship*, 267, 275, 284, 288.

118 This pattern is attested by **D**, **F** and **K** (in French, in which *filius* has been translated into *fitz*, but *mac* has been retained); *mac* has generally been translated into *filius* by the author of **I** (or its exemplar).

tallied in the list proper itself. **H** and **J** show clearly that in π *mac* rather than *filius* was used as far as Mael Coluim Cenn Mór; Mael Coluim's brother Domnall Bán was identified as *frater eius*, and *filius* was first used for Mael Coluim's son Donnchad (who reigned for a few months in 1094), and *mac* appeared no more. The situation in ξ was different, however, as can be seen from this extract from Domnall Bán to David I.

*Extract from List **G** (with variants noted from **F** and **I**)*[119]

Contractions expanded silently; capitals editorial. Punctuation follows that in the MS.

/fo. 44vb/
Douenald[120] mac Dunchath[121] prius regnauit[122] .<6>.[123] mensibus, et postea expulsus est a regno,[124] et tunc[125] Dunckach[126] mac Malcolm(i)[127] .6. mensibus regnauit,[128] et interfectus est[129] a Malped<e>r[130] mac Loren,[131] comite de Meorne,[132] <in>[133] Monethefoen,[134] et rursum[135] Douenald[136] mac Dunekach[137] [138].3. annis (predicto tempore connumerato,) et postea[139] captus est[140] ab Ea<d>gar,[141] mac Malcolm(i),[142] et[143] cecatus[144] est <et mortuus>[145] in Roscolbyn,[146] et[147] sepultus est[148] in Dunekeldyn,[149] cuius ossa translata sunt[150] <in Ioua insula>.[151]

119 **G** has been preferred as one of the earliest manuscripts with a reasonably accurate text. The text of **G** has been taken from the MS; the readings of **F** and **I** have been taken from the edition in Anderson, *Kings and Kingship*, 276–7 and 284 (**F** = Innes's copy). Of the other lists derived from ξ, **D** terminates before this point; **K** is in French (and is in any event erratic); **F** (Harl), the alternative copy of ***F**, is notably inferior to Innes's transcription; **N** is shortened and corrupt.

120 G; *Donald* F; *Douuenald* I

121 *mac Dunchath* G; *Mac-Donechat* F; *filius Doncath* I

122 *prius regnauit* FG; om. I

123 *6* F; *7* G; *vi* I

124 *a regno* GI; om. F

125 GI; om. F

126 G (read *Dunekach*?); *Donekan* F; *Doncath* I

127 G; *Mac-Malcolm* F; *filius Malcolin* I

128 *6 mensibus regnauit* G; *regnavit 6 mensibus* F; *vi mensibus* I

129 *et interfectus est* G; *hoc interfecto* F; *et interfectus* I

130 *Malpedir* G; *Malpeder* FI

131 G; *Macloen* F; *filio Lorin* I

132 G; *Moerns* F; *Mar* I

133 *in* F; *tamen* G; om. I

134 G; *Monachedin* F; om. I

135 FG; *rursus* I

136 G; *Donald* F; *Douuenald* I

137 G; *Mac-Donechat* F; *filius Doncath* I

138 *regnavit* add F

139 *predicto tempore connumerato et postea* G; *hic* F; *et postea* I

140 FG; om. I

141 *Eagar* G; *Edgar* FI

142 G; *Mac-Malcolm* F; *filio Malcolin* I

143 GI; om. F

144 FG; *secatus* I

145 *et mortuus* FI; om.G

146 G; *Roscolpin* F; *Roscolbin* I

147 GI; om. F

148 G; om. FI

149 G; *Dunkelden* F; *Dunfermlin* I

150 *cuius ossa translata sunt* GI; *hinc translata ossa* F

151 *ad Hyonam insulam* G; *in Iona* F; *in Ioua insula* I

/fo. 45ra/ Eadgar[152] .9. annis regnauit, et .3. mensibus, et[153] mortuus est[154] in Dunedenn[155] et sepultus est[156] in Dunfermelyn.[157]
Alexander[158] .17. annis, et .3. mensibus et dimidio regnauit,[159] et[160] mortuus est[161] in Cruflet,[162] et[163] sepultus in Dunfermelyn.[164]
Dauid[165] .29. annis et .3. mensibus regnauit, et mortuus est[166] in Karliolo,[167] et sepultus est[168] in Dunfermely<n>.[169]
Malcolm(i)[170] filius Henrici, filii .Dauid. regis.[171] .12. annis, et .6. mensibus, et .20. diebus regnauit[172] et[173] mortuus est[174] apud[175] Gedworth,[176] et[177] sepultus est[178] apud[179] Dunfermelyn.[180]

The patronymics of Domnall Bán, Donnchad son of Mael Coluim Cenn Mór and (in the notes) Edgar son of Mael Coluim Cenn Mór have been rendered using *mac* rather than *filius*; moreover *filius* is not to be found until Mael Coluim IV. This could be taken as evidence that θ (the common source of ξ and π) terminated with the death of Mael Coluim Cenn Mór.[181] As for τ (the archetype of the list with notes on each king's death), it is notable that Edinburgh, the place where Edgar died, was rendered in Gaelic. The probable date-range for τ is therefore sometime after Edgar's death and soon after David I's (the precision in calculating Alexander I's reign-length has already been noted as suggesting 1124).[182]

The final piece of this particular jigsaw is the exact reign-length for Mael Coluim IV shared by both π and ξ: in π this would appear to have read 12 years 6 months and 16 or 13 days,[183] and in ξ 12 years 6 months and 20 days. Marjorie

152 G; *Edgar* FI
153 *regnauit et 3 mensibus et* G; om. F; *et tribus mensibus et* I
154 G; om. FI
155 G; *Dunedin* F; *Dunde* I
156 G; om. FI
157 G; *Dunfermling* F; *Dunfermlin* I
158 *.f.ma.* (read *filius Malcolin*) added superscript in I: see Anderson, *Kings and Kingship*, 284 n.120.
159 G; om. FI
160 GI; om. F
161 G; om. FI
162 Possibly *Eruflet* or *Gruflet* G (see also Anderson, *Kings and Kingship*, 277 n. 86); *Crasleti* F (*Crufleth* Harl.); *Strafleth* I
163 GI; om. F
164 G; *Dunfermling* F; *Dunfermlin* I
165 *filius Malcolin* add I
166 G; om. FI
167 G; *Carleolo* F; *Karleil* I
168 G; om. FI
169 *Dunfermely* G; *Dunfermling* F; *Dunfermlin* I
170 *Malcolmi* G; *Malcolm* F; *Malcolin* I
171 GI; om. F
172 G; om. FI
173 GI; om. F
174 G; om. FI
175 FG; *in* I
176 G; *Jedword* F; *Gedwrd* I
177 GI; om. F
178 G; om. FI
179 G; *in* FI
180 G; *Dunfermling* F; *Dunfermlin cum predictis regibus* I

181 The situation is more complicated, however: see below, 165–7.
182 This could be stated more clearly if the status of Edgar's reign-length was not such an unknown quantity.
183 **E** reads 12 years 6 months and 13 days; **L** and **M** both read 12½ years and 3 days; the Huntingdon Chronicle gives 12½ years and 3 months and 14 days; **H**, **J** and inserted folio 13 in the Chronicle of Melrose give merely 12½ years. Marjorie Anderson (*Kings and Kingship*, 52) suggested that the archetype of her Y group (i.e. π) gave the number

Anderson was doubtless right to infer that such detail to the day was unlikely to be independent.[184] The exact number of days should either have been 16 or possibly 13;[185] the reading in ξ may therefore be interpreted as a miscopying of *xiii* or *xui* as *xx*. If so this would be evidence that ξ, although essentially a copy of τ, also included information from π: a likely scenario would be that an ancestor of ξ was updated to include Mael Coluim's reign using a derivitive of π. It has already been suggested that the Dál Riata king-list in ξ was derived from ϱ, which (from Cinaed mac Alpín) was in turn derived from π. The most likely occasion when Mael Coluim IV's exact reign-length was incorporated into an ancestor of ξ therefore would have been the addition of a Dál Riata king-list from ϱ to an annotated king-list from Cinaed mac Alpín copied from τ. These relationships may be summarised diagrammatically:

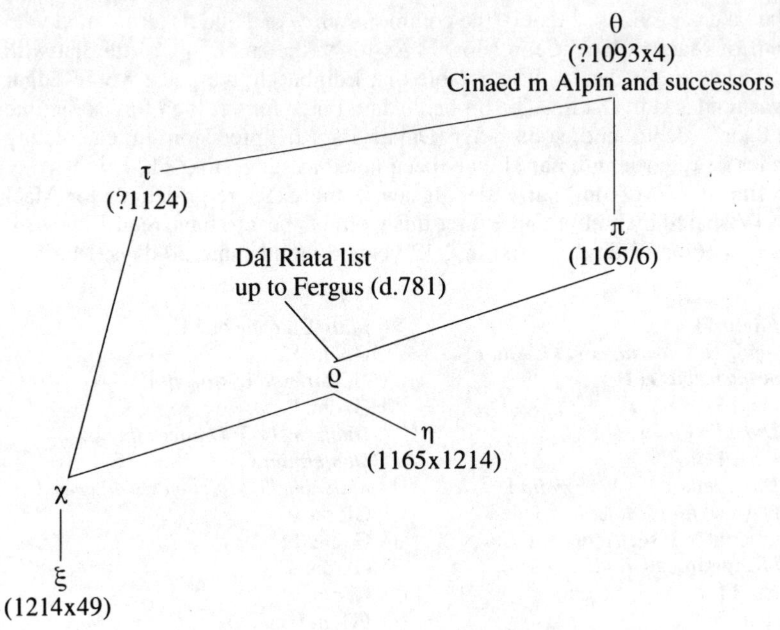

of days as 13, although Mael Coluim reigned for 12 years, 6 months and 16 days. It is possible that the calculation was made from his inauguration rather than the death of David I (in the circumstances no time would have been lost in establishing Mael Coluim as king); it is also conceivable that *xui* was misread independently as *xiii* in two descendants of π.

184 Anderson, *Kings and Kingship*, 52.

185 Depending on whether it was calculated from David I's death or the inauguration of Mael Coluim at an unknown date (almost certainly only a couple of days later, and doubtless before the burial of David I: the inauguration of Alexander II before William's burial would be an appropriate parallel; see Scott, 'Fordun's description of the inauguration').

One final problem remains to be tackled. ξ consisted not only of a combination of the annotated list from Cinaed mac Alpín and the Dál Riata list, but also a Pictish king-list. On the evidence of the lists discussed by Marjorie Anderson it cannot be ascertained whether this was a two-stage process – the list from Cinaed and the Dál Riata list brought together first (to create a text represented above as χ), and then the Pictish list added later (to create ξ itself) – or whether all three lists were brought together at the same time. Moreover, if all three were brought together on the same occasion, it would be conceivable that this occurred earlier than ξ itself (sometime between 1165/6 and 1214). The answer to this uncertainty lies in the king-list which forms part of the first and longest poem in the trilogy composed 1296x1306 (possibly 1304x6) preserved in *Liber Extrauagans* attached to Bower's *Scotichronicon*, a text we have met already.[186] The list may be summarised:

The king-list in Liber Extrauagans[187]

Fergus[188]	3 [years]
Donegard	5 years
Congal	[*quater oct*]*o b*[*inis*] (i.e. 34 years)
Gouren	22 years
Conal	14 years
Edham	*quatuor et deca bis* (i.e. 24 years)
Eogledbod	16 years[189]
Kinath Ker	3 months
Ferqwhart	16 years
Douenald	14 years
Mald[*oinn*]	16 [years]
Ferard	21 years
Eoge[*d*]	13 years
Arinkelleth[190]	1 year
Eoga[*n*]	13 years
Mordahu	3 years
Neagau	3 years
Hetfin	30 years
Fergus	3 years
Sealanban	24 years
Eoged Anyn	30 years

186 See above, 121–8. It was not included in Marjorie Anderson's discussion of king-lists.

187 Brackets denote lacuna in S (see above, 26–7, for manuscript); reading supplied from Donibristle MS (hereafter D). See Broun and Scott, '*Liber Extravagans*', 70–9, for text, apparatus and translation.

188 *Primus in Ergadia Fergus rexit tribus annis*

189 *sed se*[*x*?] in S, corrected later in darker ink to *x sex*. The other manuscripts read *x sex*.

190 S, corrected later in darker ink to *Armkelleth* (*Armkelleth* is the reading in the other manuscripts).

Dugal	7 years
Alpinus	3 years
Kenedus filius Alpyn	7 years[191]

'These ruled side-by-side with the aforesaid Picts in their time.
This period comprises 312 years,
but you ought to add three months to these years.'[192]

. . .

'After this *Kened* had driven out the Picts completely
he continued reigning for 16 years'[193]

Douenald McAlpin	4 years
Constantinus	16 years[194]
Ed	1 year
Greg	12 years
Douenald	11 years
Constantin	40 years
[*Malcomus primus*]	[9 years]
[*Indolf*]	[9 years]
Duff	[4 years and 6 months]
Culen	the same length of time
[*Kened*]	[24 years and 2] months
[*Constantinus*]	[1 year and 6] months
[*Gred*]	[8 years]
Malcolm	[30 years]
[*Du<n>can*][195]	[6 years]
Macbeth	[17 years]
[*Lahoulan*]	[4 months]
Malcol[*m Kenremor*]	[37 years and 8 months]
[*Donenaldus*]	3 years
[*Duncan*]	6 months in the middle of Domnall's reign[196]
[*Edgar*]	9 years [and 3 months]
Alexander	[17 years], 3 months [and two weeks].
Dauid	2[9] years and 3 months
M[*alcolm filius Henri*]	12 years and a half.
Willelmus	49 years

. . .

191 The account of Cinaed's rule before his takeover of the Picts has probably been derived from a source other than the king-list: see Broun and Scott, '*Liber Extravagans*', 112.

192
Hii cum predictis regnauerunt tempore Pictis.
Quod tricentenos quater octoque continet annos;
hiis annis sed tres debetis iungere menses.

193
Hic postquam Kened Pictos omnino fugauit,
annos octos bis regnando continuauit.

194 *sed* in all manuscripts; Skene was surely correct to read *sedecim* (Skene, *Chronicles*, 336).

195 *Ducan*, D

196 *Duncan medio sex menses tempore uixit*

'Up to this point I have learned everything I have mentioned from written chronicles;
from now on it is my intention to put down in writing what I myself have learned.'[197]

[*Alter Alexander*] [35 years]
Ternus Alexander[198] nearly 37 years.

'For almost seven years the Scots mourned
because they had no king for as many harvests.'[199]
. . .
'On St Andrew's Day
AD 1292, in observance of custom,
he who was fifty-second in the sequence of kings
took up the honour of king on his own account.'[200]

This king-list is remarkable for exhibiting features regarded as characteristic of Marjorie Anderson's X-group and also other features associated with her Y-group (or to be more precise, ϱ). For instance, it shares with X-group lists the replacement of Cinaed mac Duib with his erstwhile son Giric, and gives an eight-year reign-length at this point (as against a year and some months in ϱ); Custantín mac Aeda is accorded 40 years (as against 45 years in ϱ); and the reigns of Edgar, Alexander I and David I are given in the same detail as would have been found in ξ.[201] It has a reign of 49 years for William I, however, as against the diagnostic 50-year reign which would have appeared in ξ. In the Dál Riata section the Gaelic epithets have largely been retained, and are untranslated: *Eogledbod* (Eochaid Buide), *Kinath Ker* (Connad Cerr), *Hetfyn* (Aed Find), *Eoged Anyn* (Eochaid 'An-nimnech'). Moreover, its 34 years for Comgall mac Domangairt compares with 33 years in **E** (the only witness of η at this point) and chronicle-references to Comgall dying in the thirty-fifth year of his reign, as against witnesses of ξ which all exhibit a loss of an *x* in their figure.[202] Also, it agrees with **E** in the 13-year

197 *Actenus hec dicta sciui per cronica scripta.*
Amodo que noui scriptis describere uoui.

198 Described as 'fifty-first in the succession of kings' (*quinquagenus regum fuit ordine primus*).

199 *post annis fere septem Scoti doluere,*
quod regem uere tot aristis non habuere.

200 *Andree festo Domini post mille ducentos*
atque decem nouies, cum binis insimul annis,
seruando morem sibi sumpsit regis honorem,
quem quinquagenum regum facit ordo secundum.
This refers to the inauguration of King John on 30 November 1292.

201 Indeed, where ξ evidently read half a month in Alexander's reign-length, *Liber Extrauagans* has two weeks: in view of what follows this may have been the original reading, which would suggest even more notable precision than might be inferred from 'half a month'.

202 Anderson, *Kings and Kingship*, 253 and n.166. AT 538.2 reads *Comgall mac Domanguirt. ri Alban obit .xxxu. anno reigni súi*; AU 538.3 similarly reads *Mors Comgaill mc. Domangairt .xxx^o. u^o. anno regni*. This would appear to have been derived from the Chronicle of Ireland, and therefore would have a text-history older than 911. The

reign-length for Eogan son of Ferchar Fota, as against witnesses of ξ which have 16 years.[203] If (as seems likely) its reign-lengths for Comgall and Eogan were found in ϱ, then this would suggest that the year-total for Dál Riata in ϱ would have been 315 years (and 3 months); the figure in *Liber Extrauagans* of 312 years may be a simple misreading of *cccxu* as *cccxii*, and would therefore be closer to ϱ than the 314 years stated in **E** or the 307 given in ξ.[204] This mix of features which would have been found in ϱ and ξ, and the probability that some readings are older than any other extant king-list, suggests that the archetype of the king-list in *Liber Extrauagans* represented a stage in the transmission and development of the king-list between ϱ and ξ. According to the scheme advanced so far this would mean that this archetype was derived from ϱ and ancestral to ξ. This archetype would therefore have been χ in the stemma above. It may be noted that when the author of the poem (written 1296x1306 (?1304x6)) preserved in *Liber Exrauagans* reached the reign of Alexander II he stated that up to this point he had drawn his information from written sources, in contrast to what followed which he wrote from 'what I myself have learned'.[205] If, therefore, his king-list terminated with William I's 49-year reign-length, then it is possible that it was a copy of χ updated to 1214. It may be presumed that the poem's author decided against reproducing the patronymics and notes on royal deaths and burials found in his exemplar; perhaps he regarded the effort of converting a king-list into verse as sufficiently onerous without having to include detail that was not necessary for a chronological account of the royal succession.

It has been noted previously that the author of this poem in *Liber Extrauagans* had recourse to a much later text of the king-list for his information on the Picts. It may be inferred from this that the copy of χ at his disposal did not itself include the Picts. This would suggest that the combination found in ξ of Cinaed mac Alpín and his successors, Dál Riata and Pictish lists was a two-stage process: first the list from Cinaed and the Dál Riata list derived from ϱ were brought together to form χ, and subsequently a Pictish list was added to this to create ξ.

---

statement that Comgall died in the thirty-fifth year of his reign could have originally been derived from a king-list.

203 Anderson, *Kings and Kingship*, 216.

204 Ibid.

205 Broun and Scott, '*Liber Extravagans*', 107, 114.

VIII

ROYAL HISTORY AND THE LEGITIMATION OF THE SCOTTISH KINGSHIP *c.*950–1249

During the twelfth and thirteenth centuries it was only sometime in the reign of Alexander II (1214–49) that a Pictish king-list was incorporated into a regnal list culminating with the currently reigning monarch. Moreover, it would appear that, until sometime during the reign of Alexander II's father William (1165–1214), the royal succession had been portrayed simply as a list of successors of Cinaed mac Alpín. I have suggested that extant Scottish texts of the king-list may all have been derived from an archetype datable to sometime in or soon after 1093. The situation, however, is more complicated.

Scottish regnal lists c.*950–1093*

It is apparent from witnesses of π that its reign-lengths for eleventh-century kings were given with greater precision than in ξ. After the 30-year reign attributed to Mael Coluim mac Cinaeda (1005–34), Donnchad ua Maíl Choluim (1034–40) was accorded 5 years and 9 months, Mac Bethad mac Findlaích (1040–57) 17 years (which was, indeed, the exact span of his reign),[1] and Lulach mac Gilla Comgáin (1057–8) 4½ months.[2] This compares with witnesses of ξ which have 6 years for Donnchad ua Maíl Choluim and 4 months for Lulach. Logically there are two explanations for this: either these figures represent independent calculations, or the figures have been rounded by the author of ξ (or of one of its ancestors derived from θ). This latter option can be swiftly disposed of. Not only were twelfth-century reign-lengths in ξ given without such rounding up or down,[3] but some tenth-century reign-lengths were reckoned to the nearest month: 4 years and 6 months for the reign of Dub mac Maíl Choluim (962–6), 4 years and 6 months for Cuilén mac Illuilb (966–71), 24 years and 2 months for Cinaed mac Maíl Choluim (971–95) and 1 year 6 months for Custantín mac Cuiléin (995–7). It would appear, therefore, that π and ξ were heirs of independent traditions of maintaining the king-list.

1 Either 15 Aug. 1040 to 15 Aug. 1057, or 8 Sept. 1040 to 8 Sept. 1057; see Anderson, *Early Sources*, I. 579 and nn. 7 and 8, and 602 and n. 1, for discussion.

2 These figures are attested in all witnesses, with the following exceptions: Donnchad ua Maíle Choluim has been omitted in **E**, φ evidently read 3½ months for Lulach (4½ months in π is vouchsafed by **E** and **H**; **H** mistakenly has years rather than months); Hunt. has 15 years for Mac Bethad and does not include Lulach.

3 See above, 156–60.

This demands a fresh consideration of their common error in the reign-length of Mael Coluim Cenn Mór: as noted earlier, he was assigned 37 years (and a number of months) in both, rather than the 35 years since the death of his short-reigned predecessor Lulach (1057–8).[4] The coincidence between π and ξ was not exact, however: in π the span was stated as 37½ years and 4 months,[5] while in ξ it was 37 years and 8 months. The discrepancy may mean that this was calculated independently; the probability remains, however, that an exchange of information underlies the shared error of 37 years. On its own this would not be enough to deny that π and ξ were in all other respects derived from different archetypes older than 1093x4. A parallel could be found in the precise reckoning of Mael Coluim IV's reign shared by both χ and π, although χ was otherwise derived from τ rather than π.[6]

The common ancestor of π and ξ (which will still be denoted as θ) should therefore be pushed back at least to sometime during the reign of Donnchad ua Maíl Choluim (1034–40). Not only was Mael Coluim mac Cinaeda credited in both with a thirty-year reign-length, although he actually reigned for less than thirty years (1005–34), but the exact reckonings for late-tenth-century kings attested in ξ would also have been found in π: 4 years and 6 months each for Dub and Cuilén, 22 years 2 months for Cinaed mac Maíl Choluim ('22' in error for '24'), and 1½ years for Custantín mac Cuiléin.[7] These precise reign-lengths look like a series of contemporary calculations, which would suggest that θ, datable 1034x40, was a copy of an earlier list (hereafter σ) which had been maintained at least between 966 or soon thereafter (say, *c*.970)[8] and sometime in or after 997.[9] The ascertainable development of the list may be summarised thus:

4 Given the power-struggle which may have begun with the return of Mael Coluim from exile in 1054, and his eventual climb to the throne in the following years, it is conceivable that there was a convention that Mael Coluim became king in 1056 (as joint-king with Mac Bethad and then Lulach?).

5 Attested by **E** and **H**; in φ this had evidently been reduced to 37 years and four months.

6 See above, 155–60.

7 These figures are attested by **E** and **H**; Cinaed and Custantín were omitted in φ.

8 It should be noted that the exact coincidence between Dub and Cuilén's reign-lengths may have been due to some textual mishap, which would push the *terminus post quem* forward to 971.

9 Unfortunately there was confusion in both ξ and π concerning the next reign (Cinaed mac Duib, 997–1005): in ξ 8 years was assigned to a Giric son of Cinaed (who was probably the result of a scribal error, as suggested in Anderson, *Kings and Kingship*, 52), while in π Cinaed mac Duib evidently had only one year and three or four months (probably by assimilation with the reign-length of Custantín mac Cuiléin, with *ui* being in due course misread as *iii*). It is likely, therefore, that θ would have read 'Cinaed mac Duib reigned for eight years.'

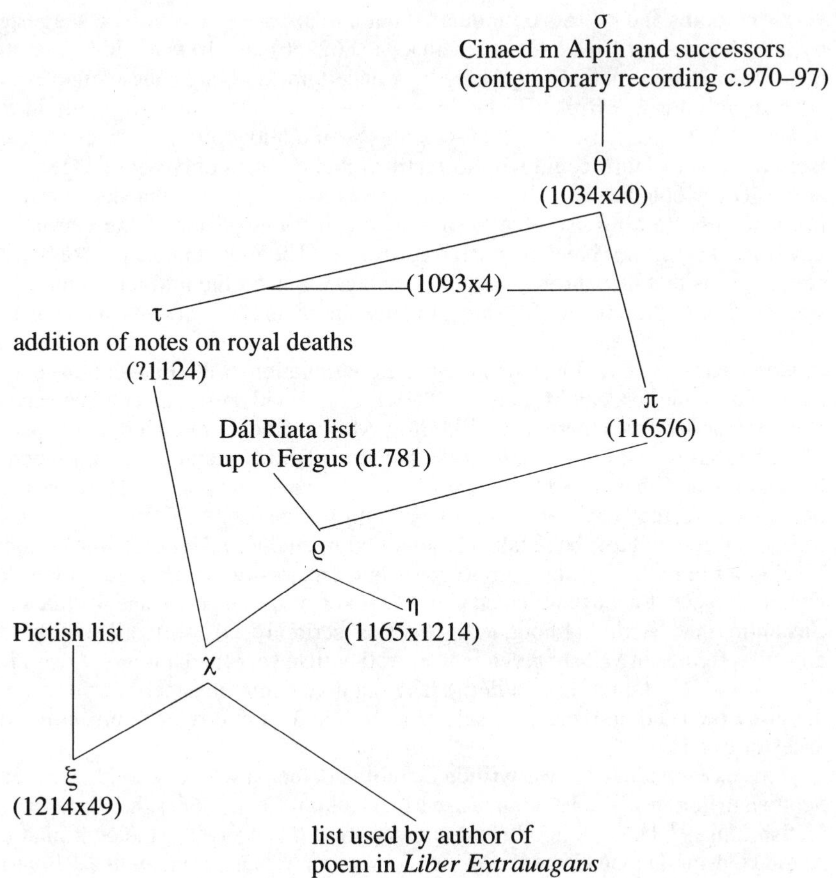

It may be no more than a supposition to state that σ was simply a list of Cinaed mac Alpín and his successors, rather than a longer list (of kings of Picts or Dál Riata) which would therefore have been truncated in θ. The matter requires closer examination. A relationship between lists descended from σ and the Chronicle of the Kings of Alba has been suggested by Edward Cowan.[10] The Chronicle, probably written originally during the reign of Illulb (954–62) and continued to the reign of Cinaed mac Maíl Choluim (971–95), is a history of Cinaed mac Alpín and his successors written as an annotated king-list.[11] The link between the Chronicle and the lists breaks down, however, as far as the reigns of Illulb, Dub and Cuilén are concerned (the Chronicle has 8, 5 and 5 years as against the lists' 9 years, 4

10 Cowan, 'The Scottish chronicle', 6; unfortunately the figures quoted there for Mael Coluim, Dub and Culén in the lists are inaccurate, and Illulb has been omitted.

11 Broun, 'The birth', 5; Cowan, 'The Scottish chronicle', 18, dated the work to 'shortly before 995'; Hudson, 'Historical literature', 145–6 dated the chronicle to '*circa* 973'. Dr Hudson has prepared a new edition which will appear shortly in *SHR*.

years 6 months and 4 years 6 months),[12] but a relationship may still be suggested by the 16 years for Custantín mac Cinaeda (862–76) and 40 years for Custantín mac Aeda (whose actual reign-length is uncertain), although these figures are attested only for ξ.[13] If the Chronicle was, as suggested, written originally in the reign of Illulb mac Custantín (954–62), this would allow σ to have been derived from it, which in turn could help to confirm that σ began only with Cinaed mac Alpín. This would be difficult to sustain, however. It is possible that the Chronicle itself has used a king-list as its source; even if σ was related to the Chronicle, therefore, it need not have been derived from it. The most that can be said with conviction is that the Chronicle itself is evidence that by the mid-tenth century it was possible to present the kingship's history simply in terms of Cinaed mac Alpín and his successors.

Consideration should also be given to a continuation of the Pictish king-list as far as Mael Coluim Cenn Mór (1058–93) which is found only in a version of *Lebor Bretnach* or derivities thereof (I will follow Molly Miller in referring to this list as *SL*2).[14] It has been pointed out that the list reads 'and Custantín' when it reaches Custantín mac Cinaeda (862–76), as if it once ended at that point.[15] The continuation, therefore, may have begun with Custantín's reign-length. There is some indication that it may have been taken from a text related to θ. Not only does it have Mael Coluim mac Cinaeda with 30 years but it shares two curious reign-lengths with π: 20 years for Custantín mac Cinaeda (in error for 16 years) and 45 years for Custantín mac Aeda (although this is less certainly erroneous).[16] Unlike π, however, figures in *SL*2 are given in years rather than years and months (except for 1½ years for Custantín mac Cuiléin). The putative common ancestor with π may therefore be dated no more precisely than 1034x93. (I will refer to this common ancestor as ι.)

If the exemplar of *SL*2 was written in Scotland, then it would be evidence that a Scottish historian wished to emphasise Mael Coluim Cenn Mór as the successor of Pictish kings.[17] There is good reason to suppose, however, that the continuation beyond Custantín mac Cinaeda was the work of an Irish historian with a scholarly interest in the Pictish past. It can be shown that *SL*2 (or an ancestor of it) lay behind reckonings that there were seventy Pictish kings 'from Cathluan to Custantín'.[18]

12 The Chronicle's 11 years for Mael Coluim mac Domnaill is not so different from the lists' 9 years: *xi* and *ix* are readily interchangeable.

13 In π these reigns were evidently 20 years and 45 years.

14 Van Hamel, *Lebor Bretnach*, 82–7; Anderson, *Kings and Kingship*, 77–8, 261–3; Miller, 'Matriliny by treaty', 159–60; see also Dumville, 'The textual history', 266. The earliest extant manuscript of *SL*2 is *Leabhar Ua Maine*, which may be assigned (roughly) to the second half of the fourteenth century; see Dumville, 'The textual history', 260–3.

15 Anderson, *Kings and Kingship*, 78–9.

16 The evidence is reviewed in Broun, 'Dunkeld', 124 n. 56.

17 As argued in Hudson, 'Historical literature'.

18 This figure is found in *Duan Albanach* (see n. 22, below for edition) and in a tract on the Picts which was incorporated into a version of *Lebor Bretnach* (van Hamel, *Lebor Bretnach*, 8–9) and *Lebor Gabála*: see Anderson, *Kings and Kingship*, 78–9; Miller, Matriliny by treaty', 146–7; Mac Eoin, 'On the Irish legend', 142–3; Scowcroft, '*Leabhar Gabhála* Part I', 116–18.

According to *SL*2, the seventieth king after Cathluan would have been Custantín mac Cinaeda (862–76).[19] This calculation of seventy kings, however, would have been possible only after the miscopying of a phrase which resulted in the addition of four kings called Gartnait (the original reading has been preserved in *SL*1).[20] Whoever counted the seventy kings from Cathluan to Custantín was, therefore, presumably looking at a list like *SL*2 *before* it had been updated to Mael Coluim Cenn Mór. Another figure for the number of Pictish kings was known in Ireland, morever: sixty-six kings, which was presumably derived from a list like *SL*2 terminating with Custantín mac Cinaeda but which had yet to suffer the miscopying which produced the four extra kings called Gartnait.[21] This suggests the following stages in the ancestry of *SL*2:

(i) a copy of *SL* terminating with Custantín mac Cinaeda reached Ireland; this yielded the figure of sixty-six Pictish kings;

(ii) it was copied, but an error resulted in the addition of four kings called Gartnait; this yielded the figure of seventy kings 'from Cathluan to Custantín';

(iii) it was subsequently updated to Mael Coluim Cenn Mór (presumably sometime during his reign); either at this stage or later it was added to *Lebor Bretnach*.

Because stages (i) and (ii) are witnessed in Irish texts, and *SL*2 itself is found only in *Lebor Bretnach* (or derivitives thereof), it is likely that (iii) occurred in Ireland.

The relationships suggested above may be summarised:

19 Anderson, *Kings and Kingship*, 78 (which supersedes the explanation offered in Jackson, 'The Duan Albanach', 135).

20 Miller, 'Matriliny by treaty', 154.

21 The figure appears in the final stanza of the poem *Cruithnig cid dosfarclam* found in BB's copy of *Lebor Bretnach* (which has two more stanzas at the end than the cognate copy in Lec.): van Hamel, *Lebor Bretnach*, 14. On the status of these final stanzas in BB see comments in Mac Eoin, 'On the Irish legend', 139.

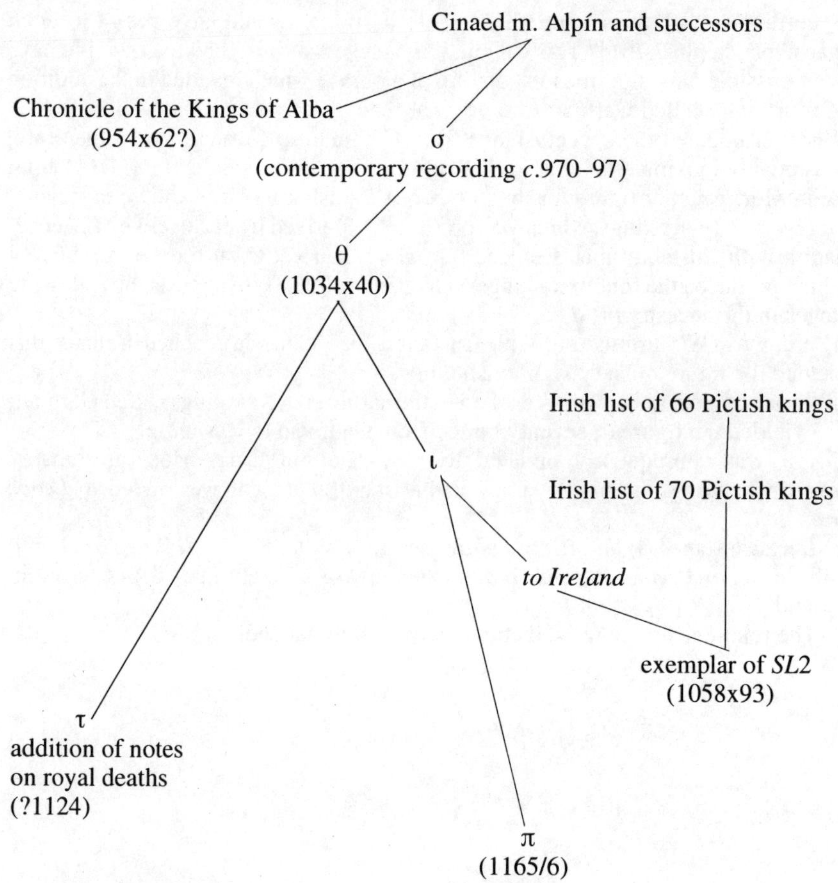

Cinaed mac Alpín as founder of the Scottish kingship

So far in this analysis no king-list written in Scotland before 1165x1214 has been identified which portrayed the currently reigning king as the latest in a succession beginning before Cinaed mac Alpín. The discussion, however, has been based largely on examining the internal evidence of texts which, in their extant form, cannot be dated earlier than the twelfth or thirteenth centuries. It would be difficult to argue that no attempt was made in the late tenth or eleventh centuries to construct a list of kings of Alba which extended earlier than Cinaed mac Alpín. There are, indeed, two texts which indicate that a list beginning with Fergus Mór, the reputed first king of Dál Riata, existed in the eleventh century. One of these is *Duan Albanach*, 'Scottish Poem', in which an account of the colonisations of Alba is followed by a list of kings from Loarn and Fergus sons of Erc through Cinaed mac Alpín to Mael Coluim Cenn Mór.[22] The second is *Comaimsera Ríg nÉrenn*

22 Jackson, 'The poem *A eolcha Alban uile*'; idem, 'The Duan Albanach'. Jackson's

ocus Ríg na Cóiced iar Creitim, a synchronism of Irish kings written in or shortly after 1119[23] whose author included Scottish kings from a list akin to that used in *Duan Albanach*. Marjorie Anderson has shown that the Dál Riata section of the common source of *Duan Albanach* and *Comaimsera* was related to Scottish witnesses (that is, descendants of the list ending with Fergus mac Echdach used by the author of ϱ).[24] Moreover, there is some indication that this list may have been derived from ι. This depends on examining reign-lengths, and unfortunately these are given only in *Duan Albanach*, where they seem to have suffered from more than average corruption.[25] It may be noted, however, that *Duan Albanach* has 30 years for Custantín mac Cinaeda, which could have been derived from '20 years' (by the loss of an *x*), and 46 years for Custantín mac Aeda which may be an error for '45' (by the addition of a minim); both '20' and '45' would have been characteristic of ι. If the common source of *Duan Albanach* and *Comaimsera* was derived from ι, then it could be dated 1034x93. Marjorie Anderson has also pointed out that Dub mac Maíl Choluim has been given 7 years (rather than 4½) in both *SL2* and *Duan Albanach*.[26] This could indicate a relationship between the exemplar of *SL2* and the common source of *Duan Albanach* and *Comaimsera*, although the misreading of *iiii* as *uii* is too easy to be regarded on its own as diagnostic.

---

argument for Irish authorship has been challenged by Hudson, 'Historical literature', 148 n. 31; an analysis of the opening pseudo-historical section, however, can confirm Jackson's view. (I have discussed this in a paper on Irish pseudo-historians and the Scottish kingship *c.*1050–*c.*1150 which I have given to the Conference of Irish medievalists at St Patrick's College, Maynooth, in July 1996, and to EMERGE at the Open University, Edinburgh, in April 1997.)

23 There are two versions of this text; the longer (edited Thurneysen, 'Synchronismen', and dated by him in or after 1119), and the shorter (edited Boyle, 'The Edinburgh synchronisms'), which breaks off in the early eleventh century. Boyle (170) raised the possibility of a Scottish authorship because kings of Alba appear in the text ahead of provincial Irish kings, but this is almost certainly because of the geographically clockwise arrangement of the sequence of kingships, starting in the north, and need not be regarded, therefore, as indicative of any special interest in Alba. It has also been understood (Anderson, *Kings and Kingship*, 45; Miller, 'The last century', 43) that the longer version was simply a continuation of the shorter version. No reason has been adduced for this beyond the fact that one version is shorter than the other. The shorter version, however, breaks off abruptly halfway through one of the text's characteristic chronological chunks, almost certainly due to the loss of the remaining text. The longer version would therefore represent the surviving text's original extent. An earlier core, datable to the mid-eleventh century, can also be detected, but it may not have included Scottish kings; see Scowcroft, '*Leabhar Gabála* Part I', 130–1.

24 Anderson, *Kings and Kingship*, 46.

25 The earliest witness of the text is from the seventeenth century; see Jackson, 'The poem *A eolcha Alban uile*', 149–59. Note, however, the comment in Anderson, 'Dalriada and the creation', 107, that up to Fergus mac Echdach (the extent of the Dál Riata list in ϱ) 'the author of the *Duan* was pretty faithful to his list-source, and that the source was not corrupt beyond the limits of obvious emendation'.

26 Anderson, *Kings and Kingship*, 49, where she also observed that in all these texts and the Scottish witnesses (descended from σ) Mael Coluim mac Domnaill has been given 9 years rather than (a probably more correct) 11 years, but she remarked that 'the mistake is an easy one which could have been made more than once'.

Moreover, their common list-source may have been designed to portray the kings of Dál Riata not simply as a prelude to Cinaed mac Alpín and his successors, but as Cinaed's predecessors as king of Alba. This is certainly how the entire series is presented in both texts. It is possible, therefore, that both *Duan Albanach* and *Comaimsera* have been derived from a self-conscious attempt to create a more impressive succession of kings than merely a list beginning with Cinaed mac Alpín. Although both these texts were written in Ireland, the possibility cannot be ruled out that their common list-source originated in Scotland.[27] Equally, however, *Duan Albanach* is a striking monument to Irish interest in Scottish history in this period, so that Irish authorship for the exemplar of its king-list cannot be ruled out either. Indeed, given the likelihood of close connections between men of letters across the Gaelic world at the time when *Duan Albanach* and *Comaimsera* were being written, the validity of drawing too sharp a distinction between Scottish and Irish authorship may be called into question.

As far as the link with Cinaed's Pictish antecedents was concerned, we may be more certain that in king-list terms this was decisively rejected by the mid- to late tenth century. In the Chronicle of the Kings of Alba it was stated that Cinaed came to Pictland after ruling in Dál Riata for two years and destroyed the Picts.[28] In ξ Cinaed reigned 'after the Picts had been destroyed',[29] while in π he was the first king who reigned 'after the Picts'.[30] A clear break was intended between the Picts and the kingship of Cinaed and his successors. At an earlier stage, however, Cinaed and his sons had been regarded as Pictish kings. This is suggested not only by the probable existence of an ancestor of *SL*2 terminating with Custantín mac Cinaeda, but also by the use of the title *rex Pictorum* in Irish chronicles for Cinaed, his brother Domnall, Custantín and Custantín's brother Aed (876–8), which is likely to reflect contemporary usage.[31] The rejection of the kingdom's Pictish antecedents may be dated, therefore, to anytime between the end of the ninth century and the mid- to late tenth century. The determination *not* to present Cinaed's successors as the latest in a series of kings which began with the Picts did not mean that the Pictish king-list itself was necessarily forgotten; as long as Pictish kings featured in foundation-legends of important churches there would have been some reason to take an interest in a Pictish king-list.[32]

27 This would be particularly likely if it were accepted that three kings of Fortriu associated closely with Dunkeld and St Andrews have been interpolated into the list; see Broun, 'Pictish kings 761–839'.

28 *Kinadius igitur filius Alpini primus Scottorum rexit feliciter istam annis xui. Pictauiam. Pictauia autem a Pictis est nominata quos ut diximus Cinadius deleuit. . . . Ist<e> uero biennio antequam ueniret Pictauiam Dalriete regnum suscepit* (Anderson, *Kings and Kingship*, 249–50; the chronicle's account of Cinaed's destruction of the Picts has not survived (although see the suggestion in Cowan, 'The Scottish chronicle', 12–14, that it may be represented in some way in Hunt.).

29 *Destructis Pictis*: **DFGIN** (*Les Picys destruytz . . .*, **K**).

30 *Post Pictos*: **HJLM** (an elaborate account of the Picts' fate is given in Hunt.: see Skene, *Chronicles*, 209).

31 See Broun, 'The origin of Scottish identity', 40–5, Dumville, 'Ireland and Britain', 182, and Broun, 'Dunkeld', for how this usage may have been derived from a Scottish source.

32 Pictish kings played a prominent role in the foundation-legends of Cenn Rígmonaid (St Andrews), Abernethy and Loch Leven (but not, of course, Deer, as stated in Broun, 'The

From at least the late tenth century until sometime in the reign of Alexander II (1214–49), therefore, Scottish historians repeatedly maintained that the current political order had been founded by Cinaed mac Alpín who conquered and destroyed the Picts. Such stories of conquest frequently included some device which enabled an important element of continuity to be presented (such as the conqueror marrying into the conquered population, or the conqueror as a returning exile related by blood with the people over whom he took power).[33] Nothing of the sort is apparent in this case, however; indeed, the annihilation of the Picts made the break unambiguously decisive.[34]

This vivid portrayal of Cinaed as founder can readily be explained by the fact that his descendants monopolised the kingship; between 889 and 1034 the kingship was held by lineages sprung from Cinaed's sons Custantín and Aed. Cinaed, therefore, was the nearest ancestor who all members of the royal dynasty had in common. He was ideally suited to the role of definitive ancestor of kings of Alba, whose presence in an individual's pedigree would have been deemed to be a necessary ingredient to their claim to the kingship. In the annotated genealogy of David I preserved in the Books of Ballymote and Lecan reference is made to *in rígrad .i. Clann Cinaeda meic Alpín*, 'the royal dynasty, that is, the descendants of Cinaed mac Alpín'.[35] This view of Cinaed may have been challenged, however, by the accession of Mac Bethad mac Findlaích in 1040, who is portrayed in his extant pedigree as a descendant of Loarn, brother of Fergus Mór and eponym of Cenél Loairn.[36] The importance of descent from Cinaed was strikingly reasserted,

birth', 8 n.18, which featured a Pictish *mormaer*). Both extant versions of the Pictish king-list (Molly Miller's *SB* and *SL*) included information on the foundation of Dunkeld and Cenn Rígmonaid (in *SB*) and Abernethy (in *SL*).

33 This is discussed in Thornton, 'Power, Politics and Status', 18–22.

34 In the Chronicle of the Kings of Alba Cinaed is described as king of *Pictauia*; even this connexion between the territory of the Picts and the kingdom ruled by Cinaed's successors became obscured: see Broun, 'The birth', 6.

35 BB.149a31–2; Lec.110r39–41. On this text see Broun, 'The birth', 6–7 and nn. 13, 14; it may be as old as the late tenth or early eleventh century. Note also that in *Comaimsera* the role of Cinaed mac Alpín as founder of the current political order is emphasised by the description of him as 'the first of the Irish to take the kingdom of Scone', *in cétríg rogab ríge Sgóinde do Gaidhelaib*: Boyle, 'The Edinburgh synchronisms', 177; Thurneysen, 'Synchronismen', 91 (where the comment is made of Cinaed's father Alpín, no doubt because Cinaed himself has been omitted by a copyist).

36 *CGH*, I. 329–30 and nn., 426. This pedigree can be shown, however, to have been concocted, although probably by an Irish scholar who considered the rulers of Moray to be Cenél Loairn (I discussed this in a paper, 'The genealogy of Mael Snechta mac Lulaig, ruler of Moray, d.1085', given at the Conference of Irish Medievalists, St Patrick's College, Maynooth, in June 1994). The common source of *Duan Albanach* and *Comaimsera* (with a suggested date of 1034x93) may conceivably have been written with such a challenge in mind. This, at least, might explain a remarkable feature of *Duan Albanach*: it alone of all Dál Riata regnal lists has Loarn as the first king rather than Fergus Mór, who is demoted to become Loarn's successor. (If this was so it would not be surprising that no trace of the common source of *Duan Albanach* and *Comaimsera* can be found in Scottish texts of the twelfth and thirteenth centuries, especially if these texts originated in the heartland of the realm which the family of Mael Coluim Cenn Mór,

however, in the pedigree of twelfth-century kings of Scots,[37] in which the almost unprecedented step (in a Gaelic context) was taken of tracing their descent through a female (Bethoc, daughter of Mael Coluim mac Cinaeda, who was mother of Donnchad the father of Mael Coluim Cenn Mór).

It would appear, therefore, that Scottish king-lists since the mid- to late tenth century had been written (with at least one probable exception)[38] as simply a listing of successors of the dynastic founder Cinaed mac Alpín.[39] It might be expected, however, that some attempt was made to furnish the kingship with a past which would have served to express its legitimacy as an institution with ancient roots. The possibility of using the Pictish king-list for this purpose had evidently been rejected. The most obvious alternative was genealogy.

Twelfth- and thirteenth-century texts of the genealogy of the kings of Scots

The earliest extant text of the royal genealogy has already been met: it is headed by Custantín mac Cuiléin (995–7) and is found in the genealogical appendix to *Senchus Fer nAlban* which (in its earliest witness) has the bilingual title *Genelaig Albanensium*, 'Genealogies of the Scots'.[40] The same path of descent is followed in later texts.[41] An important aspect of the argument which can be advanced for the continuing vitality of Irish identity vis-à-vis the Scottish kingship is that the royal genealogy remained a significant element in defining Scottish kingship throughout

---

Mac Bethad's rival, had dominated since the accession of Mael Coluim Cenn Mór in 1058.) This would require that the list in *Comaimsera* must have been altered to replace Loarn with Fergus Mór as the first king; it may be significant, therefore, that *Comaimsera* also has a curious feature: it alone has Oengus, brother of Fergus and Loarn, as king. In the longer version of the text Oengus is simply the successor of Fergus Mór, but in the shorter version he is joint-king (*<F>ergus Mor mac Erce ⁊ Aengus <mac> Eirce a c<o>m<f>laitius* {illeg.} *fri*; Boyle, 'The Edinburgh synchronisms', 173). Perhaps Fergus and his brothers were portrayed as joint-kings in the common source, and that this has been partially retained (or reinterpreted) in *Comaimsera* and *Duan Albanach*. A historiographical context for this vision of Fergus Mór and his brothers as founders of Alba will be discussed in due course.

37 See below, 175–82.

38 The common source of *Comaimsera* and *Duan Albanach*, if this was indeed written in Scotland rather than Ireland. It is possible that the designation in *Comaimsera* of Cinaed mac Alpín as the first of the Irish to rule in Scone was also in the common source (although this would be difficult to square with the proposition outlined above, n. 36).

39 It may be recalled that the only king-lists of the twelfth and thirteenth centuries that include kings of Dál Riata were ultimately derived from π (datable to 1165x1214) written using a Dál Riata list terminating with Fergus mac Echdach (d.781); this need only have been distantly related to the Dál Riata list employed in the common source of *Comaimsera* and *Duan Albanach*.

40 See above, 151.

41 The only significant divergence is in the generations between Eochaid Riata (a.k.a. Coirpre Rigfota) and Eochaid Munremor. It is possible that this was rewritten in the early eleventh century to provide names which would reflect kingly qualities: see Brown, 'The Scottish origin-legend', 354–70.

most of the twelfth and thirteenth centuries. I will concentrate on texts datable to those centuries which originated in Scotland.

There are a number of copies of the royal genealogy which can with various degrees of confidence be shown to have been derived ultimately from Scottish exemplars in this period. There are two whose orthography is Gaelic: the pedigree of David I in the Book of Leinster, which may have been copied from a Scottish exemplar,[42] and the pedigree of William I extending back to 'Adam son of the living God' which forms the sixth item in a collection of Scottish historical pieces compiled 1202x1214.[43] This last is ostensibly in Latin, using *filius* rather than *mac*; only William and his father Henry, however, are rendered in Latin, and the names are otherwise in a recognisably Gaelic form.[44] It probably derives from a Gaelic genealogy of David I. It has been edited by Marjorie Anderson in *Kings and Kingship*, 256–8, but without attempting to restore name forms that have suffered even slight garbling.[45] In the critical edition which follows I have produced (as far as Míl Espáine) a partially restored text in which errors of transcription evidenced elsewhere in the 'Poppleton' collection of Scottish historical pieces have been corrected: these errors are confusion between *c* and *t*, *c* and *e*, *i* and *r*, and in the analysis of minims.[46] My corrections of these errors have been indicated by angled brackets. I have also divided names and epithets where these have been run together, and I have restored epithets to names where these have mistakenly become separate generations. In one case I have restored a name which spawned two extra generations by repetition. I have noted the manuscript reading in every instance where I have made these amendments. The text which results from these minimal corrections may, however, only be said to be partially restored; it cannot claim to be certainly the text as it would originally have appeared in the collection in 1202x14. Some idiosyncratic spellings remain, and it is impossible to discern to what extent these represent miscopyings of the genealogy by whoever made the collection of historical pieces 1202x14, or by one or more copyist of the collection itself. Moreover, some spellings which are not entirely orthodox in a Gaelic context do have parallels in Gaelic writing, and may not be regarded simply as arising from errors in transcription.

No attempt will be made to amend names beyond the parameters of the restoration outlined above. In those cases where the spelling of a name remains unorthodox some attempt will be made to indicate if there are known parallels; it may be deduced from this to what extent the unusual form of a name may be the result of miscopying. The collection survives only in Paris, Bibliothèque Nationale, MS

42 LL 336b38–c26 (O'Sullivan, *The Book of Leinster*, VI. 1471). See below for its possible connection with an extant Scottish text.

43 Anderson, *Kings and Kingship*, 240–60, at 256–8; for the dating of the collection see Miller, 'Matriliny by treaty, 138–42. On the unique manuscript, see n. 47, below.

44 Broun, 'Gaelic literacy', 189.

45 I am very grateful to Dr Anderson for allowing me access to the microfilm of this manuscript in her possession. My readings differ from hers only in a very few cases (as indicated below).

46 In one instance *is* is re-analysed as two minims.

latin 4126, produced in York *c.*1360 for a Roger of Poppleton;[47] the genealogy runs from fos 30vb to 31ra.

The 'Poppleton' text of the royal genealogy (as far as Míl Espáine)

Contractions have been expanded silently.

Willelmus rex rufus
filius Henrici
filii Dauid
fili[48] Maelcolaim
filii Donnchada que[49] fuit
nepos Malcolaim[50]
filii Cinada
filii Maelcolaim
filii et[51] Domnaill
filii Constantin
filii <Ci>na<t>ha[52]
filii Alpin
filii Echach
filii Eda Find[53]
filii Echadach[54]
filii Echach
filii Domongrat[55]
filii Domnail Bri<c>[56]
filii Echach Buide[57]
filii Edan[58]

47 Anderson, *Kings and Kingship*, 235–40; Cowan, 'The Scottish chronicle'; Miller, 'Matriliny by treaty', 138–42; Crick, *The Historia Regum Britannie*, 256–61.

48 read *filii*

49 read *qui*

50 For *Mal* as a spelling of Mael, compare *Cinada* for Cinaeda in the name below; see Jackson, *The Gaelic Notes*, 135.

51 7 preceded with *f'* superscript (and a caret sign below *f'*). Anderson, *Kings and Kingship*, 256 n. 200, has suggested plausibly that 7 was probably initially written by mistake for *f'*.

52 *Ernacha* MS

53 *Edafind* MS. For *Eda* as a spelling of Aeda, see Jackson, *The Gaelic Notes*, 134.

54 This represents Echdach, genitive of Eochaid. Another example of an unusual extra vowel is *Arandil*, below.

55 Written *Domograt* with suspension marks above each *o*. This should represent Domongairt (genitive of Domongart). The metathesis in the final syllable is also found in the rendering of Domongairt, below; this may, therefore, have been an original feature of the text.

56 *Domnailbrie* MS

57 *Echachbuide* MS

58 This represents Aedán: compare with *Eda* for Aeda, above.

filii Gabran
filii Dom<un>grat[59]
filii Fergusa
filii Eir<c>[60]
filii Echach Muinremuir
filii Oengusa Phir[61]
filii Fedil<m>the[62] Aislingig
filii Oengusa Buid<ni>g[63]
filii Fedil<m>the Ruamnaich[64]
filii Senchormaic
filii Cruitluide
filii Find Fece
filii Achir Cir[65]
filii Achach Antoit[66]
filii Fia<c>rach Cathmail[67]
filii Echdach Riada[68]
filii Conore[69]
filii Moga Landa[70]
filii Luigdig Ellatig[71]
filii Corpre Crumpchi<nn>[72]
filii Dare Dornmoir

59 Written *Domungrat*, with suspension mark above the *o*. (Anderson suggested *Domminigrat*.) See n. 55, above.

60 *Erie* MS

61 *Oengusaphir* MS

62 *Fedilinthe* MS. For *Fedilmthe* as a genitive of Fedelmid cf. *Feidilmthi*, Rawl.B.502 317c2 (*CGH*, I.353).

63 *Oengusabuiding* MS

64 *Fedilintheruamnaich* MS (Anderson has *Fedilinther Uamnach*). For the epithet, see the comment on a late-medieval Scottish attestation of this word in Thomson, 'The Harlaw Brosnachadh', 162: '*ruaimneach* does not seem to be attested in Irish, although it may be connected with *rúam*, "fame, glory (?)". This may be regarded as a Scotticism . . .'. Diss (and cognate texts: see below, 185 and n. 166) have *Romaich*.

65 *Achircir* MS

66 *Achachantoit* MS. *Achach* represents Echach (genitive of Eochu); perhaps this is an error provoked by the previous name, Achir. See, however, *Arann* for Érann, below.

67 *Fiaerachcathmail* MS (Anderson has *Fiacrachcathmail*).

68 *Echdachriada* MS

69 This represents Conaire; conceivably this may have originally read *Conoire* (cf. Jackson, *The Gaelic Notes*, 132).

70 *Mogalanda* MS. *Landa* represents Lama; *nd* for 'm' does not appear to be a simple copyist's error, and perhaps may be explained by a scribe mistakenly hearing 'm' as 'nn' (for which *nd* would be a possible spelling).

71 *Luigdig f' Ellatig* MS. *Luigdig* is an unconventional rendering of Lugdach (genitive of Lugaid). *Ellatig* represents Allathaig (cf. BB 140cb34–5); for the first syllable, cf. the spelling of this word in Diss as *Etholach*. (For Diss, see below, 186 n. 180.)

72 *Corpre Crupchimi* MS, with suspension mark over the *u*.

filii <C>orbre Admoir[73]
filii Cona<i>re Moir[74]
filii Etersceuil
filii Eoga<in>[75]
filii Elela[76]
filii Iair
filii Dedaid
filii Si<n>[77]
filii Rosi<n>[78]
filii Their
filii Rothir
filii Ro<in>[79]
filii Arandil[80]
filii Maine[81]
filii Forgo
filii Feradaig[82]
filii Elela Ara<nn>[83]
filii Fiachra Fir Mara[84]
filii Oengusa Tur<mi>g[85]
filii Fir Ce<t>hairroid[86]
filii Fer Roid[87]
filii Fir Anroid[88]

73 *Eorbre f' Admoir* MS. *Admoir* represents Findmoir; the 'fi' of Find has apparently been misinterpreted as filii.

74 *Conarremoir* MS

75 *Eogami* MS

76 This represents Ailella (genitive of Ailill); see Jackson, *The Gaelic Notes*, 128 for a possible parallel for the use of *e* in the first syllable here.

77 *Siu* MS

78 *Rosiu* MS

79 *Rom* MS. This represents Rogein (genitive of Rogen). Possibly the intervocallic *gh* has been vocalised (cf. *Rowein* in Diss; for Diss, see below, 186 n. 195).

80 This represents Arndil; the unusual extra vowel would appear to be confirmed by *Arindil* in Diss.

81 *Maine* MS, with suspension mark over the *a*.

82 The *i* is superscript.

83 *Elela Arami* MS. *Arann* represents Érann. For *Elela*, see n. 76, above.

84 *Fiachra f' Firmara* MS

85 *Oengusaturuug* MS

86 *Fircechairroid* MS. *Cethairroid* represents Cetharraid; for the *oi* spelling of the final syllable, cf. Jackson, *The Gaelic Notes*, 132.

87 *Ferroid* MS. Represents Fir Raith; *Fer* may be an error made at an early stage (nominative for genitive). For the spelling of the vowel in *Roid*, see Jackson, *The Gaelic Notes*, 132.

88 *Firanroid* MS. This should represent Fir Anaraith. Diss has simply *An Roth.* Perhaps Anaraith had become *Anraith/Anroid* at a stage ancestral to both Diss and Poppleton texts (for Diss and the relationship between Diss and Poppleton, see below, 181, 186 n. 197).

filii Fir Aibrig[89]
filii Labchore
filii Echach Altle<t>hin[90]
filii Elela Casiaclaig
filii Conlai<t>h[91]
filii Erero[92]
filii Moalgi[93]
filii Cobthaig Coelbreg
filii Ugaine[94] Moir
filii Ecdaig Buadaig[95]
filii Duach Lograich[96]
filii Fiachraig Tollgreich[97]
filii Muredaich Bollgreich[98]
filii Semoin Bricc[99]
filii Eun D<ui>b[100]
filii Edo<in> Glais[101]
filii Nuadat Fail
filii Elchada Olchaim[102]
filii Sirna
filii De<in>[103]
filii Demail
filii Rodchada[104]
filii Ogmaich[105]

89 *Firaibrig* MS. *Aibrig* represents Almaig.

90 *Echachaltlechin* MS

91 *Conlaich* MS; the *i* is superscript.

92 This represents Irero (sometimes Eirora, e.g. *CGH*, I. 668; or Irereo, see below, 191 n. 232).

93 This represents Meilge.

94 The first syllable was originally written as *iu*, but the third minim has been erased.

95 *Ecdaigbuadaig* MS

96 *Duachlograich* /fo. 31ra/ *f' Fiach^{r}aig Duadach f' Duachlograich* MS. The confusion here coincides with a move from one folio to another, and may therefore have been produced by the scribe of this MS itself. *Lograich* represents Ladrach.

97 This represents Fiachrach Tollgraich. *Fiachraig* for Fiachrach may be compared with *Lugdig* for Lugdach, above.

98 This represents Muiredaig Bolgraich.

99 *Semoin f' Bricc* MS

100 *Eundib* MS (with suspension mark above the *i*). Cf. *Eon Duf* in Diss (for Diss, see below, 186 n. 197).

101 *Edom f' Glais* MS. *Edoin* represents Aedáin. See Jackson, *The Gaelic Notes*, 134–5.

102 Two names (Giallchada and Ailella Ólchain, genitives of Giallchad and Ailill Ólchan) have collapsed into one. Possibly, at a stage when *mac* rather than *filius* was used, the G' of Giallchada has been lost by assimilation with *c* of *meic*; perhaps this is another indication of spelling by ear (cf. *Arandil* and *Moga Landa*, above).

103 *Dem* MS

104 This represents Rothechtada (also Rechtada).

105 This representes Ogmain (also Ogamain, or simply Main).

filii Oeng<u>ssa Olmochada[106]
filii Fiachrach Laibrinne[107]
filii S<m>erg<n>aid[108]
filii Smereta[109]
filii Enmo<t>ha[110]
filii Tigernaig[111]
filii Fallaig
filii Etheoir[112]
filii Iair[113]
filii hErmeo<in>[114]
filii Meled Espa<in>[115]

Three texts of the genealogy are likely to have derived from a rather different kind of text of David I's genealogy. These are the genealogy of William I extending back to Noah in Ralph of Diss's *Imagines Historiarum* (his own manuscript, begun in 1188, still survives);[116] the genealogy of David I in chapter 50 of book V of Fordun's chronicle which Fordun obtained from Walter Wardlaw (d.1387);[117] and the genealogy of Alexander III in the account of Alexander's

106 *Oengisssa* (Anderson has *Oengussa*) *f' Olmochada* MS (with letter erased before initial *o* of *Olmochada*).

107 *Fiachrachlaibrinne* MS. *Laibrinne* represents Labrainne; cf. *Labrinni*, Rawl.B.502 117g24–5 (*CGH*, I.17).

108 *Sinerguaid* MS (Anderson has *Sinergnaid*). This represents the genitive of Smirgnath (cf. Rawl.B.502 115b40; *CGH*, I.3). Smirguill (genitive of Smirgoll) is usually found here.

109 This represents Smretha. The extra vowel is not confirmed by Diss, who has *Sinrecha* (a simple misreading of Smretha). (For Diss, see below, 186 n. 197.)

110 *Enmocha* MS. *Enmotha* represents Enbotha.

111 This is genitive of Tigernach, although Tigernmais (genitive of Tigernmas) would be expected here. Cf., however, *Thiernai* in Diss (i.e. Tigernaig, with vocalisation of *gh*). It would appear that Tigernaig had replaced Tigernmais at a stage ancestral to the exemplars of both Diss and Poppleton (on the relationship between these texts, see below, 181).

112 Ethriel or Etherel would be expected here. Cf., however, Ether (nominative), Rawl.B.502 115b41 (*CGH*, I.4).

113 This represents Iaréoil (genitive of Iarél); he is often given an epithet, Fáith. In Diss this name is rendered *Iair Olfatha*, which suggests that the second syllable has become attached to the epithet at some stage ancestral to Diss and Poppleton, and then the epithet has been dropped at some stage in the Poppleton text (for the relationship between Diss and Poppleton, see 181, below).

114 *Hermeom* MS. The *h* is not clear; Anderson points out that it has originally been written *b* (possibly *d*, it seems to me), and has been corrected to *h* at the time of writing. This represents hÉremeoin (genitive of Éremón).

115 *Meledespam* MS. *Meled* represents Míled (genitive of Míl).

116 London, Lambeth Palace MS 8 (the genealogy is at fo. 107va32–b28); a copy begun two years later is London, British Library Cotton MS Claudius E.iii (the genealogy is at fo. 116rb26–va29). The relationship of these MSS is discussed in Stubbs, *Radulfi de Diceto*, I.xciiiff. The genealogy is published in ibid., II.35.

117 Skene, *Johannis de Fordun Chronica*, 251–2. Fordun referred readers to Book IV

inauguration (1249) given in the so-called *Gesta Annalia*.[118] The genealogy of Simón Brecc given in Fordun's account of Scottish origins (XXVI.c) was probably also derived from a related text of the royal genealogy. Their common ancestor (to which Diss is clearly the best witness) was written using an orthography which departs from Gaelic spelling-conventions in a number of respects, most obviously in the use of *k* and *w* and a greater willingness to reflect actual pronunciation.[119] Some Gaelic spelling-conventions have still been observed, however: this is especially evident in the treatment of *bh* (rendered with *b* and once with *f*) and *mh* (rendered with *m* and occasionally with *u*).[120] It would be wrong, therefore, to regard the text as the work of someone struggling with unfamiliar sounds. Its orthography could more readily be explained if the text was conceived as a Latin rather than a Gaelic document, written by a Gaelic man of letters in a situation where it would not have been assumed that all those who could read Latin would also have been literate in Gaelic. Moreover, there are errors which are found also in the Poppleton text, which suggests that the archetype shared by Diss, Fordun and *Gesta Annalia* was copied from a text ancestral to that in the Poppleton compilation, which would presumably have been in Gaelic.[121]

Finally, there are two fifteenth-century texts which have suffered much decay but which appear to derive ultimately from a text related to those in Diss and Fordun. These are found in Wyntoun's chronicle and (in an even more debased state) in the *Chronica Breuis* in John Gray's commonplace book.[122] Their common ancestor shared with the common ancestor of Diss and Fordun the error of merging Fiachra Tolgach with his father Muiredach Bolgrach to produce *Fyakak-Bolgeg* (in Wyntoun; *Fiechachch Bolgai* in Diss); rendering Nema as *Neande* (as in both Wyntoun and Diss; *Neandus* in Gray); and misreading Sem as *Reyne* (in Wyntoun, *Reynn* in Gray; *Rein* in Diss). What is remarkable, however, is that it is possible to detect Gaelic spelling conventions in places where they were not used in the common ancestor of Diss, Fordun and *Gesta Annalia*. For instance,

---

chapter 8 for the section between Cinaed mac Alpín and Fergus mac Eirc. The genealogy in Book IV, chapter 8, however, has been constructed from the account of the royal succession in Fordun's chronicle itself: this is evident from the appearance of Eugenius son of Findan (who corresponds to a king found only in X-group king-lists: see Anderson, *Kings and Kingship*, 52), and the use of *Eugenius* as a Latin form of Eochaid (thus *Eugenius Buyd* for Eochaid Buide; on this see Broun, 'The birth', 18–20). The section quoted in Book IV chapter 8 has not therefore been derived from Wardlaw's text (as suggested in Anderson, *Kings and Kingship*, 214 n. 14).

118 See below for new edition. The relationship of these three texts is established for example by their sharing idiosyncratic spellings, e.g. Achir Chir has been rendered *Akirkirre*, Fir as *fith* or *fich*, Rothir as *Rether*.

119 As in the frequent discarding of *g* for final palatal *gh*; vocalisation of internal *gh* in *Ewein* and *Owan* for Eogain and *Rowein* for Rogein; and an epenthetic vowel between *n* and *g* in *Enegussa* (for Gaelic Oengussa): see Broun, 'Gaelic literacy', 190.

120 Ibid., 90–1.

121 The shared errors between Poppleton and Diss are noted above, nn. 88, 111, 113.

122 The genealogy in Wyntoun's chronicle has been published in Amours, *Chronicle of Andrew of Wyntoun*, II. 114–17, 210–13, 349, 351; Laing, *Androw of Wyntoun*, I.55–6, 102–3, 169–70. Gray's commonplace book is Edinburgh, National Library of Scotland MS Adv. 34.7.3 (the genealogy is at fos 17v–19r).

d can often be found for *dh* where the common ancestor of Diss and Fordun and *Gesta Annalia* had *th*,[123] and where the common ancestor of Diss and Fordun and *Gesta Annalia* used *w* for intervocalic *gh*, Wyntoun (and Gray once) have *g*.[124] It is possible, moreover, to identify in Wyntoun (and less easily in Gray) the detritus of a comment in Gaelic added to the genealogy: where Diss (and Fordun) have *filii Ecddach Riede* ('son of Eochaid Riata', eponym of Dál Riata), Wyntoun has *Eadak Rydesedek Corbre Rygada*, which may be unscrambled to read *Echdach Riade sede Corbre Rigada* – a note that Eochaid Riata was also called Corpre Rígfata.[125] A similar note is also found in the pedigree of David I in the Book of Leinster: *Eochaid Riata is é side Coirpe Rígfota.*[126] This phrase does not appear in any other extant text of the genealogy, so this may suggest some relationship between David I's pedigree in the Book of Leinster and the common ancestor of Wyntoun and Gray. There are a number of indications, therefore, that the common ancestor of Diss, Fordun, *Gesta Annalia*, Gray and Wyntoun may have been a Gaelic text of the royal genealogy (possibly headed by David I). These relationships may be summarised diagramatically:

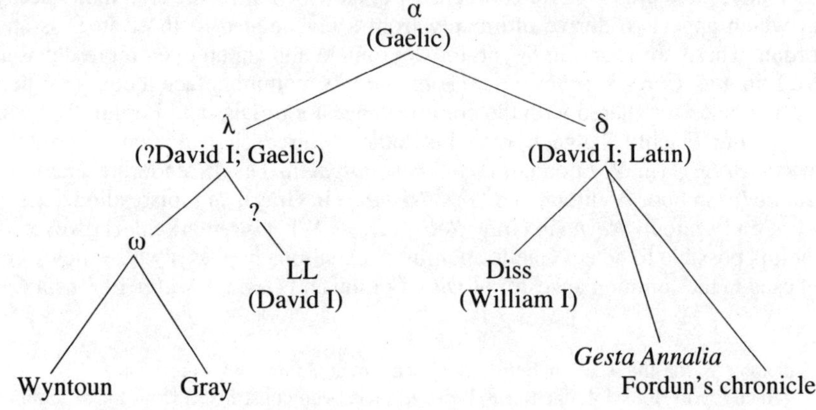

123 E.g. for Dedaid Wyntoun has *Dedaa* and Gray has *Dedoa* as against *Dethath* in Diss; for Giallchada Wyntoun has *Elkada*, Gray *Ekkadus* but Diss has *Elchatha*; and for Erchada Wyntoun has *Erkada*, Gray *Ergadus* but Diss *Erchatha*; Broun, 'Gaelic literacy', 192.

124 Thus for Eogain Wyntoun has *Eogen* and *Cogyne*, Gray has *Ewgenn* but also *Ewan*, and Diss has *Ewein* and *Owan*; Broun, 'Gaelic literacy' 192.

125 See Broun, 'Gaelic literacy', 193 and also 200 n. 34, where another possible note of this kind is discussed. Where Wyntoun has *Eadak Rydesedek Corbre Rygada*, Gray reads *Eodag Rither quem Beda Reudam vocat a quo Riddisdale cuius filius Ergada*. If *quem . . . cuius filius* is omitted we are left with *Eodag Rither Ergada*; *Ergada* is otherwise unexplained, and so may therefore be the remains of what Wyntoun rendered as *Rygada*.

126 Broun, 'Gaelic literacy', 193.

A number of texts of the royal genealogy, therefore, were in circulation; it is particularly noteworthy that a version existed which would have been accessible to men of letters who were not themselves literate in Gaelic. As an example of one of these texts, a fresh edition is offered of the genealogy of Alexander III in the so-called *Gesta Annalia* appended to Fordun's chronicle. The genealogy is found in an account of Alexander III's inauguration which would appear to be contemporary;[127] it cannot be demonstrated, however, that the text of the genealogy was originally part of it. Its exemplar need not, therefore, have been headed by Alexander III. This text of the genealogy must have been in circulation sometime in or after 1249 to have been included here in *Gesta Annalia* at all, which (as it stands) must date to sometime after 1363.[128]

Gesta Annalia is found (in whole or part) in five manuscripts.[129] The genealogy has been omitted, however, from **D**. The testimony of **A** has been discarded because it is no more than a copy of **G**, and information relating to Skene's treatment of his base manuscript has been adequately provided in the those parts of Fordun's account of Scottish origins edited above.[130] For the same reasons as in the edited extracts of Fordun's chronicle, I have not nominated one witness as a base,[131] but I have selected the best reading from the witnesses, taking into consideration the testimony of Diss. All variant readings in **C**, **G**, **I** and **S** have been noted.[132] Reference will occasionally be made to manuscript-readings in the genealogy of William I in the collection dated 1202x14 (the 'Poppleton collection') (see above, 176–8, for the text).

Genealogy of Alexander III in Gesta Annalia

C: fo. 162v (second series in foliation)
G: fos 182v–183r
I: fos 136r–v
S: fo. 206v

Salue rex Albanorum[133] Alexander

[127] Bannerman, 'The king's poet'; Duncan, *Scotland*, 555–6. See also discussion in Taylor and Watt, *Scotichronicon*, V. 435–41. It may be noted that Bishop Geoffrey of Dunkeld, who died in November that year, is said to have been present.

[128] See above, 21, 24. This section of *Gesta Annalia* may, however, be dated to 1285; see Broun, 'Searching for Scottish histories'.

[129] For an account of the manuscripts see above, 20–1, 23–4, 26.

[130] Skene's edition of the genealogy (Skene, *Johannis de Fordun Chronica*, 294–5) also shows the same potential for incorporating Hearne's mistranscriptions of **C** as if they were **C**'s readings: for example, he stated (294 n. 12) that four generations were mistakenly repeated in **C**, when in fact the mistake was made only in Hearne's edition of **C** (Hearne, *Johannis de Fordun Scotichronicon*, III. 759); see Taylor and Watt, *Scotichronicon*, V. 441, where Skene's 'blind' dependence on Hearne is noted.

[131] See above, 31.

[132] Although there are occasions where it is difficult to distinguish between *c* and *t* or *n* and *u* (and other combinations of minims). For **S**, see 30–1, above.

[133] A Latin translation of *Benach de re Albane* (*Alben* C) 'Bennacht Dé, rí Alban<ach>' in the Gaelic extract which precedes the Latin genealogy.

filii Alexandri
filii Willelmi
filii Henrici
filii Dauid
filii Malcolmi
filii Duncani
filii Beatricis[134]
filie Malcolmi[135]
filii Kenath[136]
[137]filii Malcolmi[138]
filii Donaldi[139]
filii Constantini[140]
filii Kenath[141]
filii Alpini[142]
filii Echachi[143]
filii Ethafind[144]
filii Echdachi[145]
filii Donaldi[146] Brek
filii Ecchae[147] Vuid[148]
filii Edaim[149]
filii Cobram[150]
filii Donengard[151]

134 Up to this point the names in Diss are Latin. Instead of *Beatricis*, however, Diss has Gaelic *Bethoc*.

135 Diss also consistently has *Malcolmi* for Maíl Choluim.

136 CGS; *Keneth* I. Diss has *Kinath*.

137 Lines 11–14 (*filii Malcolmi filii Donaldi filii Constantini filii Kenath*) om. S

138 CG; *Keneth filii Alpini filii* I

139 Diss has *Duuenald*.

140 Diss also has *Constantini*.

141 CG; *Keneth* I. Diss has *Kinath*.

142 Diss has *Elpini*.

143 *Echachi* GS (and probably I, though not readily legible); *Ethachi* C. Diss has *Echach*.

144 CS; *Echafind* GI. Diss has *Ethafind*.

145 CGS; *Echdathi* I. Diss has *Echdach*. At least one and possibly two names have been omitted here (and in Diss) after *Echdachi*.

146 CGI; *Donenaldi* S: The author of *Gesta Annalia* may have written *Douenaldi*. Diss has *Duuenald*.

147 CGS; *Echae* I. Diss has *Ecchach*.

148 C; *Vind* GS; *Buid* I. Diss has *Buide*. The Gaelic epithet is Buide. Unfortunately *b* and *v* can be confused in cursive fifteenth-century script, so it would be rash to come to a firm conclusion about whether the author of *Gesta Annalia* wrote *Vuid* or *Buid*. Moreover, I is not a reliable witness.

149 Diss also has *Edaim*.

150 Diss also has *Cobram*.

151 Diss has *Douengart*, which is better: the Gaelic is Domangairt (genitive of Domangart).

filii Fergusii [152]Magni[153]
filii Erch[154]
filii Ecehac[155] Munremor[156]
filii Engusafith[157]
filii Fethelmech[158] [159]Aslingich[160]
filii[161] Enegussa[162] Buchin[163]
filii Fechelmeth[164] [165]Romaich[166]
filii Sencormach[167]
filii Cruithlinth[168]
filii Findachai[169]
filii Akirkirre[170]
filii Ecchach[171] Andoth[172]
filii Fiachrach[173] Catmail[174]
filii Ecddach[175] Ried[176]
filii Coner[177]

152 *filii* add I

153 Diss has *Fergus Mor* for the Latin here (the Gaelic is Fergusa Móir, genitive of Fergus Mór)

154 *Erth* CGS; *Erch* I. Diss has *Erch*. The name is Erc (genitive Eirc). The author of *Gesta Annalia* probably wrote *Erch*, with *c* readily misread as *t*.

155 CGS (S possibly *Ecahat*); *Ecehic* I. Diss has *Ecchac*. This is *Echach*, genitive of *Eochu*. It would appear that the second *c* has been misread as *a* (perhaps by the author of *Gesta Annalia* himself).

156 CG; *Inmemor* I; *Minremor* S. Diss has *Munremor*.

157 CGS; *Engusaphich* I. Diss has *Engusafith*. The Gaelic is Oengusa Fir.

158 *Fechelmech* CG; *Fecelinch* I; *Fethelmech* S. Diss has *Fethelmech*. The Gaelic is Fedelmid: it would appear that 'd' (for *dh*) has originally been represented *th*.

159 *filii* add S, underlined for deletion.

160 *As lingich* C; *Aslingith* GS; *Ablingych* I. Diss has *Aslingich*.

161 CGS; om. I.

162 CGS; *Enagussa* I. Diss has *Enegussa* (the Gaelic is Oengusa).

163 CGS; *Brichin* I. Diss has *Buthini*. The Gaelic was probably Buidnig (cf. Poppleton's *buiding*).

164 CG; *Fechelnech* I; *Fechelmech* S. Diss has *Fethelmeth*.

165 *filii* add I

166 CS; *Ramaich* G; *Romarch* I. Diss has *Romaich*.

167 C; *Secormath* G; *Sioncorneach* I; *Sencormath* S. Diss has *Sencormach*.

168 CS; *Crinchlinch* G; *Cruithiluch* (with suspension-stroke above first *i*) I. Diss has *Cruithlinthe*.

169 CGS; *Findachar* I. Diss has *Findachai*.

170 CS; *Akyrkirre* G; *Akyrkyre* I. Diss has *Akirkirre*.

171 CS; *Acchach* G; *Eccach* I. Diss has *Ecchach*.

172 *Andoch* CGI; *Andoth* S. Diss has *Andoth*. The Gaelic is Antóit (see LL 336b4 and Poppleton).

173 CGS; *Frachroch* I. Diss has *Fiachrach*.

174 CGS; *filii Catamal* I. Diss has *Catinail*. The Gaelic is Cathmaíl (as in Poppleton).

175 CGS; *Ecddaych* I. Diss has *Ecddach*.

176 CGS; *Red* I. Diss has *Riede*. The Gaelic is Riata(i) (Poppleton has *riada*).

177 CGIS; Diss has *Conere*. The Gaelic is Conaire (Poppleton has *Conore*).

filii Mogalama[178]
filii Lugthag[179] Etholach[180]
filii Corbre[181] Crumgring[182]
filii Daredromor[183]
filii Corbre Findmor[184]
filii Coneremor[185]
filii Ederskeol[186]
filii Eweni[187]
filii Ellela[188]
filii Iair[189]
filii Dethath[190]
filii Sin[191]
filii Rosin[192]
filii Ther[193]
filii Rether[194]
filii Rowein[195]
filii Arindil[196]
filii Mane[197]

178 CG; *Morgavania* I; *Mogolama* S. Diss has *Mogalama*.

179 CG; *Lugchag* IS. Diss has *Lugthag*.

180 Diss also has *Etholach*.

181 Diss also has *Corbre*.

182 CG; *Crumgring* (with suspension-stroke over *n*) I; *Cramgring* S. Diss has *Crungring* (the first n written as a suspension-stroke).

183 *Darediomore* CS; *Darediomor* G; *Daredromor* I. Diss has *Daredromor*.

184 illegible in I. Name and epithet are run together in Diss: *Corbrefindmor*.

185 *Coneremore* C; *Coneremor* IS; *Coueremor* G. Diss has *Conere Mor*.

186 CGS; second syllable almost illegible in I: possibly *Edre*[ ]*keol*. Diss has *Eders Keol*.

187 C; *Ewem* G; *Ewyn* I; *Ewen* S. Diss has *Ewein*.

188 C; *Eliela* GS; *Elyela* I. Diss has *Ellela*.

189 Diss also has *Iair*.

190 *Dethach* CG; *Dethath* G; cut away in I. Diss has *Dethath*. The Gaelic is Dedaid (as in Poppleton): *d* has been represented as *th*.

191 CGS; *Syn* I. Diss has *Sin*.

192 CGS; *Rosyn* I. Diss has *Rosin*.

193 *There* C; *Ther* GS; *Teyr* I. Diss has *Ther*.

194 CGS; *Reych* I. Diss has *Rether*.

195 *Roweni* CS; *Rowym* I; *Rowein* G. Diss has *Rowein*. The Gaelic is Rogein.

196 *Armdi* C; *Arindil* G; *Arnidal* I; *Armdil* S. Diss has *Arindil*.

197 Cut away in I. Diss continues after *Mane*: *filii Forgso filii Feredach filii Ellela Earin filii Fiachac Fimmora filii Enegussa Turbinig filii Firketharocht filii Fir Rocht filii Anroth filii Firalmai filii Lamchure* (*filii Liethan* underlined for deletion) *filii Ecchach Aldethan filii Elela Casieclai filii Conletha filii Iretro filii Melge filii Cobthai Cailbrech filii Hugune Mor filii Ecchach Rothai filii Duach Lotherai filii Fiechachch Bolgai filii Sinonbricht filii Eon Duf filii Etheon filii Glachs filii Noethath Fail filii Elchatha Olchaim filii Sirne filii Dein filii Demail filii Rothotha filii Ogmain filii Enegus Olmucatha filii Fiachach Labrain filii Smirnai filii Sinrecha filii Embatha filii Thiernai filii Faleg filii Etheor filii Iair Olfatha filii Ermon filii Micel Espaine filii Bile filii Neande filii Brige filii Bregain filii Bratha filii Deatha filii Erchatha filii Aldoith filii*

filii Fergusii primi Scotorum regis in Albania. Qui quoque[198] Fergusius fuit filius Feredach,[199] quamuis a quibusdam dicitur filius Ferechar,[200] parum tamen discrepant in sono. Hec discrepantia forte scriptoris constat uicio propter difficultatem[201] loquele. Deinde dictam genealogiam idem Scotus[202] ab homine in hominem continuando perlegit donec ad primum Scotum[203] uidelicet Iber[204] Scot peruenit. Qui quidem[205] Iber[206] fuit filius Gaithel[207] Glas filii Neoili[208] regis quondam[209] Athene[210] genitus ex Scota filia regis Egipci Centhres Pharaonis.[211]

The significance of the royal genealogy

Alexander III is here presented as the fifty-seventh in line from Fergus son of Ferchar, 'the first king of Scots in Alba' (according to the scheme developed by the synthesist responsible for so much of Fordun's account of Scottish origins); he was more than fifty generations further removed from Éber Scot son of Gaedel Glas and Scota (as in Diss's text). Alexander III's descent from the eponyms of the *Gaídil*, both in Gaelic and Latin, was thus announced at his inauguration. The author of *Gesta Annalia*, moreover, gives a striking affirmation of Alexander III's Irish identity when he stated that the 'first Scot' was the son of Gaedel and Scota who, according to the synthesis used by Fordun in his chronicle, was the first *Scotus* to colonise Ireland.[212] This contrasts with the author of *Liber Extrauagans* who insisted that *Scoti* as a name was adopted first by those of Gaedel's descendants who settled in Scotland. The genealogy was not, however, concerned chiefly with the origin-legend itself, but was designed to show each step in the king's patrilinear ancestry.[213] It has been observed that 'it was Alexander's legal title to

Node filii Nonael filii Eber Scot filii Geithel Glas filii Neoil and for a further twenty-two generations back to Noah.

198 CGI; *quidem* S

199 CGS; *Heredach* I

200 *Ferechar* S; *Ferechar* G (with flourish which may have denoted a final *e*); *Ferechare* C; *Ferech*[I.

201 CGS; *diffacultatem* I

202 CGS; om. I

203 CGS; om. I

204 CG; *Ikeyr* I; *Hiber* S

205 CGI; om. S

206 CGS; *Ikeyr* I (the *k* has been written over subsequently by a later hand, and is difficult to read).

207 *Gaithell* C; *Gaithel* GS; *Gattel* I (altered by different hand to *Gattelos*); cf. Diss's *Geithel.*

208 CGS; *Neoli* I

209 CGS; *quandam* I

210 CG; *Ethene* I (with *Grecorum* added above line); *Athenensis* S

211 CGS; *Pharonis* I (corrected to *Pharaonis*)

212 XVII.1; for discussion, see above, 64–8.

213 With the exception of Bethoc, mother of Donnchad ua Mail Choluim (1034–40); see above, 174.

rule which was being recited as part of the inauguration ceremony',[214] What was the significance of all these names, however? It may be suspected that it was not simply Alexander's own right to the throne which was being pronounced, but also the credentials of the kingship itself which were being publicly proclaimed and reaffirmed.

Every genealogy consists of a number of key ancestors who are separated by a number of space-filling generations; typically the significance of the most important ancestors would have been celebrated in literature. The most fruitful way of reading a genealogy, therefore, is to focus on the key ancestors. It has been pointed out by David Thornton that as far as Irish kingships were concerned a distinction was often made between a dynastic founder, from whom any individual king would have claimed descent, and a founding-figure for the kingship itself who was an ancestor of the dynastic founder. A king's pedigree, therefore, would typically include the (often eponymous) dynastic founder and, further back, the founding-figure of the kingship over which the dynasty claimed a monopoly; in the pedigree of a ruler of Uí Néill, therefore, the dynastic founder was Niall Noígiallach, and the founding-figure for the kingship itself was Conn Cétchathach, founding-figure of Leth Cuinn, the northern 'half' of Ireland.[215]

The role of Cinaed mac Alpin as dynastic founder has already been discussed.[216] As far as the kingship of Alba itself was concerned the founding-figures according to this genealogical scheme were evidently Fergus Mór son of Erc and his brothers Loarn and Oengus (eponyms of Cenél Loairn and Cenél nOengusa). John Bannerman has argued that the genealogical scheme in *Senchus Fer nAlban*, whereby Loarn and Oengus are presented as brothers of Fergus son of Erc, was engineered by an editor of the text in the tenth century.[217] In the same text it is stated that Fergus and his brothers 'took Alba'.[218] In this way the tenth-century kingdom of *Alba* was baldly presented as the successor of the domain ruled by Fergus Mór and his family. It would appear, therefore, that Fergus and his brothers were fashioned into founding-figures of the kingship to correspond with Cinaed as founder of the ruling family.[219] Fergus, Loarn and Oengus were also portrayed as precursors of Cinaed's dynasty in the annotated king-list from Cinaed mac Alpín in ξ, where it was stated (with obvious anachronism) that Cinaed was buried on Iona 'where the three sons of Erc, that is, Fergus, Loarn and Oengus had been

214 Dumville, 'Kingship', 73; see also Ó Corráin, *Ireland*, 36, where he observed that 'the royal and dynastic genealogy, as we know from other sources, was the equivalent of a charter of right and was proof of the king's title to rule'.

215 Thornton, 'Power, Politics and Status', 27–9.

216 See above, 170–4. One literary celebration of Cinaed's role was the lost saga (*Braflang Scóine*), on which see Mac Cana, *The Learned Tales*, 142–5.

217 Bannerman, *Studies*, 118-32.

218 *sé díb gabsat Albain .i. dá Laornd . . . dá Mac Nisse . . . dá Fergus*: 'six of them [sons of Erc] took *Alba*, that is two Loarns . . . two Mac Nisses . . . two Ferguses': Bannerman, *Studies*, 41; comment, 118–19.

219 Fergus would already have been a figure of historiographical significance (see Bannerman, *Studies*, 119–21); he was probably regarded as first king of Dál Riata by this stage.

buried'.[220] It was insisted in the same list that nearly all kings between Cinaed mac Alpín and Lulach had been buried in Iona; Fergus and his brothers as founding-figures of the kingship were thus, it seems, being pressed into service as founding-figures for Iona's claim to be the kingship's mausoleum.[221] It is also possible that Fergus and his brothers were portrayed as founding-figures of Alba in the common source of *Comaimsera* and *Duan Albanach* (probably 1034x93), although this is incapable of proof.[222]

Fergus Mór and his brothers, Loarn and Oengus, may thus be recognised as the ancestors who epitomised the kingship. Their descent through their father, Erc, therefore provided a means for expressing the kingship's royal credentials and for establishing its status in relation to other kingships. In *Senchus Fer nAlban* Fergus and his brothers were portrayed as colonists from Ireland, an idea which (as we have seen) retained its vitality in later accounts of Scottish origins. The kingships with which the kingdom of Alba was most immediately associated, therefore, were Irish kingships. In this regard the key ancestors in the Scottish royal genealogy in the text shared by Diss, Fordun and *Gesta Annalia* were Conaire Mór, father of eponyms of the Érainn population-groups Corco Duibne, Corco Baiscind and Múscraige (who were all in Munster); Fiachu Fer Mara, ancestor of Dál Fiatach kings of Ulaid; Oengus Tuirmech, ancestor of kings of Uí Néill; Úgaine Már, ancestor of all leading royal kindreds (with the exception of Eoganachta); and Míl Espáine, ancestor-figure of the Irish.

The royal genealogy would, in particular, have proclaimed the Scottish king's descent from kings of Ireland in the deep past. Some of these ancient Irish royal ancestors would have been well known in Gaelic literature as kings of Tara, notably Conaire[223] and his father Eterscél, and Úgaine Már.[224] Conaire, for example, was as king of Tara the central figure in *Togail Bruidne Da*

220 *sepultus in Yona insula, ubi tres filii Erc, scilicet Fergus, Loarn et Enegus sepulti fuerant*: so **F** (also **DGI**, with minor misspellings; **K** is slightly garbled).

221 No doubt this idea was older than ξ; it may have been associated with the translation of the remains of Domnall Bán from Dunkeld to Iona (whenever that was) which was mentioned in ξ, and may have been an original part of the archetype of the annotated list (τ) which I have suggested may be dated 1124. On the idea of Iona as a royal mausoleum see also Cowan, 'The Scottish chronicle', 7.

222 See above, 171.

223 Also known as Conaire mac Moga Lama, who appears in the genealogy as a descendant of Conaire mac Eterscéla; see above, 177–8.

224 For Conaire, see *Togail Bruidne Da Derga*, below (in which his father Eterscél also appears as king of Tara). An example of Úgaine Már as ruler of Ireland is the poem *Úgaine uallach amra* by Eochaid ua Flannacáin/ ua Flainn (d.1004) (*LG*, V. poem CIX); or the opening of the tale *Fled Dúin na nGéd*, in which Úgaine Már obtains an oath that his descendants will be 'in the kingship of Ireland for ever', *im rígi nÉrenn . . . co bráth* (Lehmann, *Fled Dúin na nGéd*, lines 5–8. The tale may be dated to shortly after the battle of Mag Coba, 1103: see Herbert, '*Fled Dúim na nGéd*', 84–6). Note also the tale *Orgain Denna Ríg*, in which a key part of the plot is the jealousy of Cobthach Coel Breg (ancestor of kings of Scots) of his brother, Loegaire Lorc, over possession of the kingship of Ireland which Loegaire had acquired on the death of their father, Úgaine Már; the tale is found in the two twelfth-century codices, LL and Rawl. B. 502 (for edition and translation see Stokes, 'The Destruction').

Derga,[225] a saga which, it has been argued, survives as an eleventh-century compilation of two different versions dating to the ninth century.[226] There can be little doubt that it would have been known to Gaelic men of letters in Scotland; indeed, there were two associated tales (*De Síl Chonairi Móir* and *De Maccaib Conaire*) which directly concerned Coirpre Rígfota/Riata, eponym of Dál Riata, the Gaelic forbears in Scotland of the kings of Scots.[227]

There was a sense in *Togail Bruidne Da Derga* (and other early literature) in which the kingship of Tara represented the kingship of Ireland.[228] By the eleventh century, however, the idea of an ancient kingship of Ireland was given concrete expression in a detailed listing of kings of Ireland back to Éremón and Éber, sons of Míl, and indeed beyond to the Fir Bolg and Tuatha Dé Danann who were represented as pre-Gaelic inhabitants of Ireland. The earliest extant detailed exposition of this scheme would appear to be a sequence of three poems (*Érimón is Éber árd*, *Ríg Temra dia tesband tnú*, and *Ríg Temra taebaige iartain*) datable to the mid-eleventh century which bring the succession up to Mael Sechnaill mac Domnaill, the latest king of Ireland 'without opposition' (d.1022); the second and third poems are attributed to Flann Mainistrech (d.1056), and the first may have been his work, although it only survives in a confused form.[229] The earliest intact extant

225 Knott, *Togail*.

226 Thurneysen, *Die irische Helden- und Königsage*, 623–7; See also Gwynn, 'The recensions'. There is also extant a much briefer version of the saga, *Orgain Brudne Uí Dergae*, derived from *Cín Dromma Snechta*: see esp. Ó Cathasaigh, 'On the *Cín Dromma Snechta* version' (in which a convincing assessment of the relationship between *Cín Dromma Snechta* and the witnesses of this text is advanced against Ó Concheanainn, 'A Connacht medieval literary heritage'; see also the criticism of Ó Concheanainn in West, 'Leabhar na hUidhre's position', esp. 62–84). The dating of *Cín Dromma Snechta* to the first half of the eighth century (Thurneysen, *Die irische Helden- und Königsage*, 15–18) has been challenged by Mac Mathúna, *Immram Brain*, 421–69, who has suggested (at 443) that it was 'not later than the late ninth or tenth century', and possibly even later. Carey, 'On the interrelationships', 86–9, has made a compelling case for regarding *Orgain Brudne Uí Dergae* (his 'précis *Togail Bruidne Uí Dergae*') as a member of a group of *Cín Dromma Snechta* texts with a midland focus which may be dated to the reign of Fínnechta Fledach mac Dúnchada (675–95), perhaps specifically 688–9 when Fínnechta retired briefly from the kingship and took up holy orders.

227 Gwynn, '*De Síl Chonairi Móir*', and idem, '*De Maccaib Conaire*'.

228 Bhreathnach, *Tara*, 10–15. Tara is equated explicitly with the kingship of Ireland when Conaire becomes king (see esp. Knott, *Togail*, lines 165–6), and implicitly when Conaire's reign is said to bring peace and prosperity throughout Ireland (see Knott, *Togail*, lines 186–7, and line 229). It may also be noted that independent witnesses have the comment that the destroyers of *Bruden Uí Dergae* 'went to *Alba* to perform their marauding there, for Conaire's power did not allow them to do it in Ireland': see Ó Cathasaigh, 'On the *Cín Dromma Snechta* version', 110–13; West, 'Leabhar na hUidhre's position', 70–1. It would appear, therefore, that this equation of Conaire's realm with Ireland may have been present in the earliest version of the tale.

229 They were not published by Macalister in *LG*. The sequence of all three poems is found in Mulchrone, *The Book of Lecan*, 14vb43–15vb7, 15vb10–16ra34, and 16ra36–16va39; the second and third are also in Best and O'Brien, *The Book of Leinster*, III. 504–15. The poems are discussed in Scowcroft, '*Leabhar Gabhála*. Part I', 131–2; see

text which gives a comprehensive list of these kings would appear, therefore, to be the poem *Ériu árd, inis na ríg* by Gilla Coemáin (*fl.*1072).[230] The earliest kings (the precursors of Éremón and Éber and early generations of their successors) are, however, already enumerated in the poem *Éistet, aes écnai oíbind* by Eochaid ua Flannacáin (or ua Flainn) (d.1004).[231] The raw material for much of this was the elaborate genealogical scheme already mentioned; the result was that kings of Scots could boast more than twenty kings of Ireland in their pedigree.[232] Again, there can be little doubt that this was known to Gaelic men of letters in Scotland. It

---

also 96–7, 118–19, 130, 132–3, for the king-list scheme in general and the related prose *Réim Rígraide*. The scheme was subsequently updated to kings reigning in the twelfth century (ibid., 97, 130, 132–3).

230 Published as poem CXV in *LG*, V. 486–531.

231 Published as poem LXV in *LG*, IV. 252–83. For the identification of Eochaid ua Flannacáin with Eochaid ua Flainn (first suggested by Thurneysen), see Carey, *The Irish National Origin-Legend*, 18 n. 41; but see below, 192 n. 234. It is a matter of debate how the poems relate to the prose associated with them in recensions of *Lebar Gabála*; the poems are regarded as anterior in Carey, *The Irish National Orign-Legend*, esp. 17 n. 35, as opposed to Scowcroft, '*Leabhar Gabhála* – part II', 4–5, who has suggested that the poems were written to accompany the prose.

232 The kings of Ireland in the Scottish king's ancestry after Éremón and preceding Conaire and his father Éterscél can be identified in the above-mentioned poems: I will refer to *Éistet, aes écnai oíbind* and *Ériu árd, inis na ríg* as LXV and CXV respectively, and give references in Lec. (Mulchrone, *The Book of Lecan*) for *Érimón is Éber árd*. The kings are:

Iriel Fáid mac Éremóin (LXV §§36–9; CXV §36; Lec.14vb49–50) (Iriel Fáid appears elsewhere as Iarél Fáith); *Iair* is the genitive form found in the 'Poppleton' text of the Scottish royal genealogy (edited above, 176–80: all references to this text will be to the partially restored forms in the edition).

Eitherel (LXV §§40–2; CXV §37; Lec.15ra1–2) (known also as Ether or Ethriel); *Etheoir* (gen.) in Poppleton.

Tigernmas (LXV §§46–9; CXV §39; Lec.15ra7–8); *Tigernaig* (gen.) in Poppleton.

Fiachu Labrainne (LXV §§61–4; CXV §44; Lec.15ra11–12); *Fiachrach Laibrinne* (gen.) in Poppleton.

Oengus Olmucaid (LXV §67, the last king of Ireland named in the poem; CXV §46; Lec.15ra15–16); *Oengussa Olmochada* (gen.) in Poppleton.

Rothechtaid (CXV §48; Lec.15ra19–20); *Rodchada* (gen.) in Poppleton.

Sírna (CXV §61; Lec.15ra25–6); *Sirna* (gen.) in Poppleton.

Giallchad (CXV §64; Lec.15ra31–2); *Elchada* (gen.) in Poppleton.

Nuadu Fáil (CXV §65; Lec.15ra35–6); *Nuadat Fail* (gen.) in Poppleton.

Simón Brecc (CXV §71); *Semoin Bricc* (gen.) in Poppleton.

Muiredach Bolgrach (CXV §73); *Muredaich Bollgreich* (gen.) in Poppleton.

Dui Ladgrad (CXV §87) (appears elsewhere as Duach Ladrach); *Duach Lograich* (gen.) in Poppleton.

Úgaine (CXV §94; Lec.15rb40–1); *Ugaine Moir* (gen.) in Poppleton.

Cobthach Coel Breg (CXV §97; Lec.15rb42–3); *Cobthaig Coelbreg* (gen.) in Poppleton.

Meilge (CXV §99; Lec.15rb46–7); *Moalgi* (gen.) in Poppleton.

Irereo (CXV §102; Lec.15va3–4) (elsewhere Irero or Eirora); *Erero* (gen.) in Poppleton.

Conlaeth (CXV §104); *Conlaith* (gen.) in Poppleton.

may be noted that the king-list poems by Fland Mainistrech and Gilla Coemáin were concerned not only to list kings of Ireland but to record how each king died. This kind of king-list poem, which has been characterised as a series of summarised death-tales, was subsequently composed for 'provincial' kingships; there are two by Gilla na Naem Ua Duinn (d.1160) for Connacht and Leinster respectively, and a similar anonymous poem on kings of Ulaid (probably composed in 1165/6).[233] The Scottish king-list denoted as τ in the stemma, datable probably to the twelfth century (and maybe 1124 in particular), would also have been a list of this type, in so far as its author was concerned to record the circumstances of each king's death. Whether or not it existed as a Gaelic poem, it would appear to be another example of a major Gaelic kingship furnished with a king-list in line with a fashion set, it would seem, by Irish historians in the mid-eleventh century. That the work of Eochaid ua Flannacáin/Flainn, Flann Mainistrech and Gilla Coemáin was influential should be no surprise. Their poems in which the vision of an ancient Irish kingship was elaborated (or, rather, consolidated) may seem dull and monotonous to modern ears, but were presumably written like that to fulfill a function – as a way of packaging an array of detailed information which could thus be more easily learned and retained by Gaelic men of learning as part of their training.[234]

Scottish men of letters, therefore, looked to Ireland for the legitimating ancient history of their kingship, and would have enjoyed the reflected glory which kings

Ailill Casfiaclach (CXV §105; Lec.15va7–8); *Elela Casiaclaig* (gen.) in Poppleton.
Eochu Altlethan (CXV §107; Lec.15va11–12); *Echach Altlethin* (gen.) in Poppleton.
Oengus Tuirmech (CXV §109; Lec.15va15–16); *Oengusa Turmig* (gen.) in Poppleton.

233 Byrne, '*Clann Ollaman*', is an edition, translation and discussion of the Ulaid poem; for the dating, see 59. At 60–1 there is a discussion of this type of king-list poem, which he described as 'a series of summarised *aideda*'. Another poem of this type is *Ériu óg, inis na naem* on Christian kings of Ireland up to Toirrdelbach Ua Conchobair (datable therefore to 1122x56), by Gilla Mo Dutu Ua Casaide (*LG*, V. poem CXXXVI); see Scowcroft, '*Leabhar Gabhála*. Part I', 130. For discussion of other 'veritable catalogues of *aideda*', see Mac Cana, *The Learned Tales*, 71.

234 See especially the perceptive remarks by John Carey that 'these are evidently school poems, meant to be memorised as a means of retaining large quantities of data: the very form of the verse would have aided rote-learning and indeed catechesis, thanks especially to such ornamental features as internal rhyme and linking alliteration' (Carey, *The Irish National Origin-Legend*, 20). It may also be recalled that there may have been a particularly close link between Scotland and Armagh, in which case Gaelic men of letters in Scotland would presumably have come into contact with the work of Eochaid ua Flannacáin/ ua Flainn (d.1004), brother and ancestor of abbots of Armagh, if this Eochaid was, indeed, one-and-the-same as the author of the earliest extant text which gives a detailed account of the earliest pseudo-historical kings of Ireland, and who was apparently a key figure in developing the impressive historiographical edifice of Irish history which, in the mid-eleventh century, became *Lebor Gabála*. (See esp. Scowcroft, '*Leabhar Gabhála*. Part I', 120 and n.114. On Eochaid ua Flainn's family ties with Armagh, see T. Ó Fiaich, 'The church of Armagh under lay control'.) I am grateful to Professor Francis John Byrne, however, for alerting me to his serious reservations about the identification of Eochaid ua Flainn with the pseudo-historical scholar Eochaid ua Flannacáin.

of Scots would have acquired from the fashioning of a comprehensive and coherent history for the kingdom of Ireland in the eleventh century (if not earlier). Before the Scottish king-list was reinterpreted as a succession of more than a hundred kings by the author of the β archetype of the origin-legend-plus-king-list text, the lustre of antiquity which the kingship required as an expression of its legitimacy evidently rested chiefly on the king's Irish ancestry proclaimed in the royal genealogy.

IX

FROM IRISH IDENTITY TO A SCOTTISH NATION

The Scottish kingship in the twelfth and thirteenth centuries acquired deep roots by its identification with Ireland articulated in the royal genealogy. The genealogy was the most obvious expression of the kingship's authenticating antiquity, and its importance was powerfully reflected in the ceremony of royal inauguration when, according to the account of Alexander III's inauguration in 1249, it was read out as soon as the king was enthroned. It should not be surprising, therefore, that when a historian during William I's reign sought to attach the Dál Riata king-list to the established account of the royal succession which began with Cinaed mac Alpín, he went to some trouble to ensure that this extended king-list was compatible with the royal genealogy, and that the king's descent could be traced within it.

Irish identity would also have been crucial for the Gaelic learned orders, especially as their status presumably depended on their ability to participate in a culture based on a standardised literary vernacular shared by men of letters throughout the Gaelic world. As has been noted already, Scottish men of letters went to Ireland (and perhaps Armagh in particular) to achieve the highest standards of learning. It is apparent, however, from accounts of Scottish origins underlying the works of Fordun, Grey and Wyntoun, that Irish identity retained a significant degree of its vitality in the thirteenth century among men of letters who were illiterate in Gaelic and had no apparent links with Irish historians. For them, Irish identity continued to furnish the kingship with a legitimating antiquity sufficient for its status. It is significant that so many of the origin-legend accounts that can be traced to the thirteenth century were accompanied by the king-list. The role of Irish identity in the kingdom's claim to be a kingdom at all would explain why these authors were keen to portray Ireland as the homeland of Scottish kings and of their people.

The thirteenth century saw some important developments in the way the kingdom's past was portrayed. A new dimension was created by focussing on Mael Coluim Cenn Mór and his second wife, St Margaret, as dynastic founders, rather than Cinaed mac Alpín. The earliest extant king-list which took Mael Coluim as its first king was written at the tail-end of a roll inserted into the Chronicle of Melrose.[1] This was subsequently updated at Melrose;[2] the original

1 Anderson and Anderson, *The Chronicle of Melrose*, 25–6; xxii and xl for discussion. The roll became fo. 13 of the Chronicle. See above, 138–9.

2 Certainly from the notice of Alexander II's marriage in 1221. The same scribe made a series of calculations at the bottom of fo. 13v; it appears he made these calculations initially in or about 1243 (perhaps in connection with the birth of Alexander III in September, 1241); these were then altered by him in 1264 (probably in connection with

scribe's activity extended to the notice of the birth of the future Alexander II (in 1198), and therefore may be dated to 1198x1214. The text is more than just a plain list of kings and reign-lengths. It is emphasised that the legitimate heirs to the throne are the descendants of Mael Coluim and Margaret; Domnall Bán, Mael Coluim's brother, is thus branded a usurper, and Donnchad mac Maíl Choluim, whose mother was Mael Coluim's first wife, is dismissed as illegitimate.[3] A more elaborate account of the royal succession focussing on the descendants of Mael Coluim and Margaret is found in a Dunfermline manuscript dating to the reign of James III (1460–88).[4] This royal history continues up to James III himself, but the final section from Alexander III to James III is so peremptory compared to the rest of the text that there can be little doubt that its exemplar was written during Alexander III's reign (perhaps not long after his accession). The intimate knowledge of the location of royal burials in Dunfermline Abbey which is revealed in the text suggests that it was written at Dunfermline.[5] A striking aspect of this history is that its account of Mael Coluim and Margaret's children is heavily dependent on the *Genealogia Regum Anglorum* by Ailred of Rievaulx.[6] Ailred's *Genealogia* was largely concerned not only to describe David I's qualities as a king, but to give an account of David's glorious royal ancestors through his mother, Margaret. This raises the likelihood that a focus on Mael Coluim and Margaret as dynastic founders allowed kings of Scots to be portrayed as successors to a prestigious line of English kings – a view expressed for instance by Adam of Dryburgh writing in 1180.[7]

The new prominence accorded to Mael Coluim and Margaret can readily be understood as reflecting a tighter dynastic structure, whereby succession to the kingship was confined to the representative of the eldest male line descended from their union. This was firmly secured when William I's younger brother, David earl of Huntingdon, did homage to William's young son Alexander in 1205, four years after the other magnates had done so.[8] The family's success as members of the

---

the birth of Alexander III's eldest son, also Alexander, in January 1264). (On all this, see Anderson and Anderson, *The Chronicle of Melrose*, xl–xli.) Another hand, not otherwise found in the Melrose Chronicle, updated the original to the accession of Alexander II in 1214 (ibid., xl).

3 This claim had been made earlier: William of Malmesbury (in book V of his *Gesta Regum Anglorum*) described Donnchad as *nothus*: Stubbs, *Willelmi*, II. 476.

4 Madrid, Royal Palace Library MS II. 2097, fos 21v–26r. For discussion of this manuscript and an account of its contents see MacQueen, MacQueen and Watt, *Scotichronicon*, III. xvii–xviii.

5 The royal burials so described in the abbey church in Dunfermline are those of St Margaret herself, Mael Coluim Cenn Mór, his eldest son Edward, Edgar, Alexander I, David I and Mael Coluim IV. No such detail is offered concerning royal graves elsewhere: Henry (son of David I) at Kelso, William I at Arbroath, and Alexander II at Melrose.

6 For Ailred's *Genealogia*, see Migne, *Patrologiæ*, CXCV. cols 711–38; the section on Mael Coluim and Margaret's children is at 735–6.

7 In his *De tripartito tabernaculo*: Migne, *Patrologiæ*, CXCVIII. cols 609–792, at 722–3. For the date of *De tripartito tabernaculo*, see Bulloch, *Adam of Dryburgh*, 11.

8 Anderson and Anderson, *The Chronicle of Melrose*, 51–2; Anderson, *Early Sources*, II. 354, 365; Stringer, *Earl David*, 43, and David Sellar's suggestion (*apud* Stringer, *Earl*

expanding Anglo-French world would also explain the desirability of advertising their descent from pre-Conquest kings of England. This aspect would no doubt have been especially attractive for Anglo-French men of letters who were established in the kingdom as a result of the initiative of kings of Scots in promoting Anglo-French bishops and in founding Benedictine Dunfermline and a significant number of monasteries of the new orders.

There is little indication in extant or traceable historiography, however, that these developments had a negative impact on the kingship's Irish identity expressed in genealogy and origin-legend. The only surviving rumble against Irish identity generally is found in a cut-and-paste collection of extracts from Isidore's *Etymologiæ* on Pictish and Scottish origins written sometime between 1202 and 1214 somewhere in the east midlands.[9] In one place its author added the comment that '*Scoti* are now wrongly called *Hibernienses*', but unfortunately the exact meaning of this is not straightforward to interpret.[10] King-lists which began with Cinaed mac Alpín continued to be copied – one was inserted piecemeal into the margins of the Chronicle of Melrose sometime in the mid-thirteenth century;[11] and, as we have seen, expressions of Irish identity in the royal genealogy and origin-legend are an important feature of royal historiography in the thirteenth century. It would appear, therefore, that the focus on Mael Coluim and Margaret and the access Margaret provided to English royal ancestors added a new dimension to the kingship's identity without changing the fundamental significance of the appeal to Irish roots.

Another change which proved to have a more direct effect on the kingdom's Irish identity was the inclusion of a Pictish king-list by the author of ξ writing sometime during the reign of Alexander II (1214–49). The immediate significance of this was that Alexander II was portrayed as successor of whoever had ruled in Scotland (or at least 'Scotland proper', i.e. Scotland north of the Forth), rather than simply as the latest in a line of kings of *Scoti* who had originated in Argyll (and ultimately Ireland), which is how they had been portrayed in the source-list of ξ. The Pictish past now played a valid part in providing the kingship with a legitimating antiquity. This suggests an increasing desire to focus on the kingdom as a territory or country rather than simply emphasise the kingship's genealogical roots in Ireland; the Pictish king-list, sporting sixty kings, thus provided the kingdom of Scotland with an impressive history which would not have been so obviously appropriate if the kingship was identified exclusively as a kingship of *Scoti*. It is noteworthy that list ξ was written at much the same time as *Scocia* began to be used

David, 284) that a memory of a formal resignation by Earl David of his right to succeed may have lain behind the claim to the throne made by Floris V, count of Holland, during the Great Cause, 1291–2: see Simpson, 'The claim of Florence'.

9 Edited in Anderson, *Kings and Kingship*, 243–5; discussed in Miller, 'Matriliny by treaty', 138–42. She suggests Scone as a possible provenance. See also Broun, 'Recreating ancient *Alba*'.

10 It is difficult, for instance, to determine whether *Scoti* as *Gaídil* or *Scoti* as inhabitants of *Scocia* was at issue. The situation is made worse by the scholar's own lack of consistency: *Scocia*, for instance, is found referring to Scotland north of the Forth, Scotland north of the Forth but east of Argyll, and as an alternative name for Ireland.

11 See above, 136–7.

consistently for all the territory within the kingdom by Melrose chroniclers, who first described Galloway and the south-east borders as within *Scocia* in 1216; hitherto *Scocia* (or *Albania*) had in a variety of sources denoted chiefly the core region of the kingdom, which in its most restricted sense meant the region bounded by the Forth, the central highlands and Moray.[12] The idea that the kingdom was also a country was a new one.

The more enduring significance of the incorporation of the Pictish king-list was that it paved the way for a more spectacular statement of the kingdom's antiquity. This occurred when the author of the β archetype of the origin-legend-plus-king-list text assumed that the later stages of the Pictish list did not run parallel with the Dál Riata list (as stated in ξ), but followed the Dál Riata list as part of a single succession of kings of Scotland, which as a result totalled more than one-hundred-and-ten kings. It is unfortunate that β itself cannot be dated more precisely than 1214 x *c*.1300. Some indication of the currency of this new long list may be gained by considering when texts of this type first become visible, and when texts written in Scotland which conformed with the older arrangement (akin to ξ) ceased to be maintained. The earliest extant text[13] which saw Dál Riata and Picts as a single series is γ datable to 1292x1304. The extant texts which presented Dál Riata and Picts as parallel successions are preserved as **F**, **G** and **I**, and can be dated respectively to 1251 or soon thereafter, in or soon after 1286, and *c*.1290. On the face of it, therefore, the most likely period when β was written, or at least gained currency, would have been the 1290s. The search for an ancient past that was exclusively Scottish may, therefore, only have intensified after Edward I began his assault on Scottish independence in May 1291.[14]

During the course of the war which ensued from 1296 a number of attempts were made to refashion the origin-legend so as to promote Scotland rather than Ireland as the homeland of *Scoti*. The versions produced by Bisset in 1301 and in the Declaration of Arbroath in 1320 were brief, however, and were produced by royal officials with immediate political objectives in mind. Their authors would appear to have been prepared to alter their source-material quite radically for the sake of making their defence of Scottish independence unassailable. In more general histories of the kingdom and its people (spanning from origins to the present day) Scotland was portrayed as the homeland of *Scoti* in a far less intrusive fashion. The author of *Liber Extrauagans* achieved this simply by reserving the term *Scoti* for the first colonists from Ireland to reach Scotland, rather than by making this idea a central theme in a rewriting of existing material.[15] The author of γ may have had a similar idea in mind when he described how the first *Scoti* in Scotland readopted the name *Scoti* for themselves. A different consciousness of Scots as distinct from Irish may have been elaborated by the author of δ, if he was responsible for the passage preserved in Wyntoun's chronicle in which we are informed that the Scots come from Scota and the Irish come from Scota's son,

12 This is attested for the last time in a record of William I's itinerary in 1214. See Broun, 'Defining Scotland'.

13 Although the text is only extant translated into French.

14 On the events of May 1291 see now Duncan, 'The process of Norham'.

15 In contrast, the authors of the 'Éber' and 'Partholón' accounts rewrote their sources in such a way that Ireland as homeland of *Scoti* was a key element in their narrative.

Éber. The origin-legend material in β itself was not, as far as we can tell, rearranged at all by its author for such a purpose. The most influential history, at least in the long term, was the synthesis of origin-legend, genealogy and king-list which underlies Fordun's chronicle. Its author's determination to combine different accounts within a unifying chronological structure, however, meant that he, too, did not produce a radical reinterpretation of existing materials. As a result he retained origin-legend material focussing on Ireland as well as elaborating his own vision of the Scottish kingship as an ancient institution in its own right. What is striking, therefore, is that in this case, as in *Liber Extrauagans* and also β, γ, and δ, there was no attempt at a radical refashioning of the origin-legend itself along the lines sketched out by Baldred Bisset and in the Declaration of Arbroath. The link with the Irish continued to be relevant politically throughout the war, after all; there may have been no perceived need, therefore, to recast the origin-legend as unambiguously Scottish in works whose purpose was more general and which were not conceived with an immediate political objective in mind. Their chief concern was to proclaim an impressively ancient history for the Scottish kingship in Scotland.

Not everyone followed the author of β, however, in the radical step of regarding Dál Riata kings as predecessors of the Picts. The author of *Liber Extrauagans* seems to have gleaned from a king-list like β the notion of Scots' inhabiting Scotland about one thousand years earlier than the Picts, but apparently felt some disquiet about accepting such an early date for Fergus Mór and his successors, and thus had his cake and ate it by sticking to the older view that the Dál Riata kings were actually contemporaries of the Picts. The author of the impressively coherent statement of Scottish history which underlies Fordun's chronicle found his own way of endowing the Scottish kingship with an ancient past BC without going so far as supposing that kings of Dál Riata preceded the Picts. It would appear, however, that he shared with the author of *Liber Extrauagans* some serious reservations about employing the Dál Riata king-list in the manner of β, but was not averse (it seems) to adopting the idea of an early date for the arrival of *Scoti* in Scotland nonetheless (although in his case he was notably agnostic about whether *Scoti* arrived in Scotland earlier than the Picts). In different ways, therefore, Scottish authors found ways of projecting an ancient Scottish past – back to 443 BC in *Liber Extrauagans*; back to 330 BC in the case of the synthesis behind Fordun's chronicle; a continuous series of kings dating back 443 BC in the case of δ; or in the case of γ a stated history of 1,976 years, 9 months and 8 days as a kingdom on the day John Balliol was inaugurated as king on 30 November, 1292. This effectively overtook the original function of the kingship's Irish identity which had underpinned the view of the kingship's past expressed in king-list, genealogy and origin-legend. The emphasis was now on the kingdom's antiquity; in the process the royal genealogy had in some cases (notably β and its derivitives) become obsolete, and the origin-legend now functioned as a prelude to the king-list, serving principally to locate the ancient Scottish kingdom and people in relation to the biblical past.

If this vision of an ancient people and kingdom may be recognised as the idea of a nation,[16] then it must be acknowledged that Scottish historians did not begin to

16 As argued above, 7–9.

think of their kingdom in these terms until the thirteenth century. King-list ξ may be seen implicitly as marking an initial shift of focus in the portrayal of the kingdom's past away from Ireland and on to Scotland itself; but it was not, it seems, until Edward I began his assault on Scottish independence in the 1290s that serious efforts were made to articulate a sense of a Scottish nation when writing the kingdom's history. Unfortunately the most impressive work in this respect – the synthesis underlying Fordun's chronicle – can not be dated precisely to that decade.[17] What makes this work different from others at that time is its intimate understanding of the royal genealogy. This might suggest that its author was from an older generation of scholars who acquired their knowledge when the genealogy was still regarded as a key element in the kingship's past; it might, however, simply mean that its author was a much more accomplished scholar than was the author of β, and made effective use of the wide range of materials at his disposal. Some uncertainty must remain about the dating and contents of this lost history which was to prove so influential; and, because of this, our understanding of when and how Scottish historians constructed a national past must also remain significantly incomplete.

Scottish historians had constructed a national history without the benefit of an origin-legend which focussed chiefly on the people of Scotland. There had, indeed, been no established sense of the Scots as an ancient people in their own right whose homeland was Scotland. It is perhaps significant that over succeeding centuries Fordun and the scholars who expanded, edited or copied his work were content to repeat origin-legend material which had been designed originally to emphasise the kingdom's Irish identity. Possibly this had become a largely academic exercise. The idea of a Scottish nation as expressed by Scottish historians by the end of the thirteenth century was, indeed, focussed predominantly on the kingdom and its claim to antiquity. It would be unwise, nevertheless, to draw too clean-cut a picture of Irish identity giving way completely to the idea of a Scottish nation in the 1290s.[18] The question which remains is whether this idea of a Scottish nation can be explained chiefly as a response to the immediate crisis of the 1290s, or was rooted in a more general change in the nature of Scottish society in the thirteenth century. It is also unclear to what extent it reflected more than just a change in how men of letters in general thought about kingdoms and peoples.

[17] If its author knew of a text like β (see above, 107), then this may suggest that he was also working in the 1290s.

[18] This would appear to show that perceptions of what constituted a primordial people, and how this related to kingdoms, had developed to the extent that a sense of being a primordial people could be expressed simply in terms of being kingdom, without necessarily invoking a unique origin-legend amplified by the notion of a distinct culture and custom.

BIBLIOGRAPHY

AMORY, Patrick, *People and Identity in Ostrogothic Italy, 489–554* (Cambridge 1997).

AMOURS, F. J. (ed.) *The Original Chronicle of Andrew of Wyntoun*, Scottish Text Society, 6 vols (1903–14).

ANDERSON, Alan Orr, and ANDERSON, Marjorie Ogilvie (edd.), with index by DICKINSON, William Croft, *The Chronicle of Melrose from the Cottoniam Manuscript, Faustina B ix in the British Museum: a complete and full-size facsimile in collotype* (London 1936).

ANDERSON, Alan Orr, (collected and trans.) *Early Sources of Scottish History A.D. 500–1286*, 2 vols (Edinburgh 1922).

ANDERSON, Benedict, *Imagined Communities: Reflections on the Origin and Spread of Nationalism*, 2nd edn (London 1991).

ANDERSON, M. O. 'Dalriada and the creation of the kingdom of the Scots', Whitelock, McKitterick and Dumville, *Ireland*, 106–32.

ANDERSON, Marjorie Ogilvie, *Kings and Kingship in Early Scotland*, 2nd edn (Edinburgh 1980).

ANDERSON, M. O. 'The lists of the kings', *SHR* 28 (1949) 108–18.

ANDERSON, M. O. 'The lists of the kings – II: the kings of the Picts', *SHR* 29 (1950) 13–22.

ANDERSON, M. O. 'St Andrews before Alexander I', Barrow, *The Scottish Tradition*, 1–13.

ANDERSON, M. O. 'The Scottish materials in a Paris manuscript, Bib. Nat. Latin 4126', *SHR* 28 (1949) 31–42.

ATKINSON, Robert (ed.) *The Book of Ballymote*, photolithographic facsimile (Dublin 1887)

BABBINGTON, Churchill (ed.) *Polychronicon Ranulphi Higden Monachi Cestrensis*, II, Rolls Series (London 1869).

BANNERMAN, John, '*Comarba Coluim Chille* and the relics of Columba', *IR* 44 (1993) 14–47.

BANNERMAN, John, 'The king's poet and the inauguration of Alexander III', *SHR* 68 (1989) 120–49.

BANNERMAN, John, 'Notes on the Scottish entries in the early Irish annals', *Scottish Gaelic Studies* 11 (1968) 149–70.

BANNERMAN, John, *Studies in the History of Dalriada* (Edinburgh 1974).

BARRELL, A. D. M. 'The background to *Cum universi*: Scoto-papal relations, 1159–1192', *IR* 46 (1995) 116–38.

BARRELL, A. D. M., CRAWFORD, B. E., and ORAM, Richard (edd.) *Church and Chronicle in Late Medieval Scotland* (Edinburgh, forthcoming).

BARROW, G. W. S. 'The idea of freedom in late medieval Scotland', *IR* 30 (1979) 16–34.

BARROW, G. W. S. *The Kingdom of the Scots. Government, Church and Society from the Eleventh to the Fourteenth Century* (London 1973).

BARROW, G. W. S. *Robert Bruce and the Community of the Realm of Scotland*, 3rd edn (Edinburgh 1988).

BARROW, G. W. S. *Scotland and its Neighbours in the Middle Ages* (London 1992).

BARROW, G. W. S. (ed.) *The Scottish Tradition. Essays in Honour of Ronald Gordon Cant* (Edinburgh 1974).

BARTLETT, Robert, *Gerald of Wales 1146–1223* (Oxford 1982).

BELL, Alexander (ed.) *An Anglo-Norman Brut (Royal 13.A.xxi)* (Oxford 1969).

BEST, R. I., and O'BRIEN, M. A. (edd.) *The Book of Leinster, formerly Lebar na Núachongbála*, III (Dublin 1957).

BHREATNACH, Edel, *Tara: a Select Bibliography*. Discovery Programme Monographs 1 (Dublin 1995).

BOARDMAN, Stephen, *The Early Stewart Kings: Robert II and Robert III 1371–1406* (East Linton 1996).

BOECE, Hector, *Scotorum Historiae* (Paris 1527).

BOYLE, A. 'The Edinburgh synchronisms of Irish kings', *Celtica* 9 (1971) 169–79.

BOYLE, A. 'St Cadroe in Scotland', *IR* 31 (1980) 3–6.

BREWER, J. S., and DIMOCK, James F., and WARNER, G. F. (edd.) *Giraldi Cambrensis Opera*, 8 vols (London 1861–91).

BROUN, Dauvit, 'The birth of Scottish History', *SHR* 76 (1997) 2–22.

BROUN, Dauvit, 'Defining Scotland and the Scots before the wars of independence', in Broun, Finlay and Lynch, *Image and Identity*, 4–17.

BROUN, Dauvit, 'Dunkeld and the origin of Scottish identity', *IR* 48 (1997) 112–24.

BROUN, Dauvit, 'Gaelic literacy in eastern Scotland, 1124–1249', Pryce, *Literacy*, 183–201.

BROUN, Dauvit, 'A new look at *Gesta Annalia* attributed to John of Fordun', Barrell, Crawford and Oram, *Church and Chronicle*, forthcoming.

BROUN, Dauvit, 'The origin of Scottish identity', Bjørn, Grant and Stringer, *Nations, Nationalism and Patriotism*, 35–55.

BROUN, Dauvit, 'Pictish kings 761–839: integration with Dál Riata or separate development?', Foster, *The St Andrews Sarcophagus*, 71–83.

BROUN, Dauvit, 'Recreating ancient *Alba*: the seven Pictish kingdoms in *De situ Albanie*', Cowan and McDonald, *Alba* (forthcoming).

BROUN, Dauvit review of Taylor and Watt, *Scotichronicon*, V, and Shead, Stevenson and Watt, *Scotichronicon*, VI, *SHR* 73 (1994) 132.

BROUN, Dauvit, 'A third manuscript of *Vita Sancti Servani*' (forthcoming).

BROUN, Dauvit, FINLAY, Richard, and LYNCH, Michael (edd.), *Image and Identity: the Making and Remaking of Scotland through the Ages* (Edinburgh 1998).

BROUN, Dauvit, and SCOTT, A. B. (ed. and trans.) '*Liber Extravagans*', Watt, *Scotichronicon*, IX (Edinburgh 1998), 54–127.

BROWN, D. E. 'The Scottish Origin-legend before Fordun', Ph.D. dissertation, University of Edinburgh, 1988.

BULLOCH, James, *Adam of Dryburgh* (London 1958).

BYRNE, Francis John, '*Clann Ollaman Uaisle Emna*', *Studia Hibernica* 4 (1964) 54–94.

BYRNE, Francis John, *Irish Kings and High Kings* (London 1973).

CAREY, John, *The Irish National Origin-Legend: Synthetic Pseudohistory*, Quiggin pamphlet no. 1 (Cambridge 1994).

CAREY, John, 'The Irish vision of the Chinese', *Ériu* 38 (1987) 72–8.

CAREY, John, *A New Introduction to Lebor Gabála Érenn, The Book of the Taking of Ireland*, ed. and trans. R. A. Stewart Macalister, Irish Texts Society (London 1993).

CAREY, John, 'On the interrelationships of some *Cín Dromma Snechtai* texts', *Ériu* 46 (1995) 71–92.

CARNEY, J. and GREENE, D. (edd.) *Celtic Studies: Essays in Memory of Angus Matheson, 1912–1962* (London 1968).

A Catalogue of Additions to the Manuscripts of the British Museum in the Years MDCCCC–MDCCCCV (London 1907; repr. 1967).

COLGAN, John, *Acta Sanctorum Veteris et Maioris Scotiae, seu Hiberniae Sanctorum Insulae*, ed. John Colgan (Leuven 1645; facsimile reprint with intro. by Brendan Jennings, Dublin 1948).

COLKER, Marvin L., with intro. by O'SULLIVAN, William, *Trinity College Library Dublin: Descriptive Catalogue of the Mediaeval and Renaissance Latin Manuscripts*, 2 vols (Dublin 1991).

CORNER, David J., SCOTT, A. B., SCOTT, William W., and WATT, D. E. R. (edd. and trans.) *Scotichronicon by Walter Bower in Latin and English* vol. IV, books vii and viii (Edinburgh 1994).

COSGROVE, Art (ed.) *A New History of Ireland*, II, *Medieval Ireland, 1169–1534* (Oxford 1987).

COSS, P. R. and LLOYD, S. D. (edd.) *Thirteenth Century England V* (Woodbridge 1995).

COWAN, E. J. 'Myth and identity in early medieval Scotland', *SHR* 63 (1984) 111–35.

COWAN, E. J. 'The Scottish chronicle in the Poppleton manuscript', *IR* 32 (1981) 3–21.

COWAN, E. J., and MCDONALD, R. Andrew (edd.) *Alba: Medieval Celtic Scotland* (East Linton, forthcoming).

CRAIGIE, W. A. *The Asloan Manuscript*, Scottish Texts Society, 2 vols (Edinburgh 1923–25).

CRAIGIE, W. A. 'The St. Andrews MS of Wyntoun's Chronicle', *Anglia* 20 (1898) 363–80.

CRICK, Julia C. *The Historia Regum Britannie of Geoffrey of Monmouth*, III: *Summary Catalogue of the Manuscripts* (Cambridge 1989).

CRICK, Julia C. *The Historia Regum Britannie of Geoffrey of Monmouth*, IV: *Dissemination and Reception in the Later Middle Ages* (Cambridge 1991).

DAVIES, R. R. (ed.) *The British Isles, 1100–1500* (Edinburgh 1988).

DAVIES, R. R. 'The Peoples of Britain and Ireland 1100–1400. I: Identities', *TRHS*, 6th series, 4 (1994) 1–20.

DAVIES, R. R. 'The Peoples of Britain and Ireland, 1100–1400. III: Laws and Customs', *TRHS*, 6th series, 6 (1996) 1–23.

DAVIES, R. R. 'The Peoples of Britain and Ireland, 1100–1400. IV: Language and Historical Mythology', *TRHS*, 6th series, 7 (1997) 1–24.

DAVIES, Wendy, *Wales in the Early Middle Ages* (Leicester 1982).

DENHOLM-YOUNG, N. (ed. and trans.) *Vita Edwardi Secundi Monachi cuiusdam Malmesberiensis* (London 1957).

DREXLER, Marjorie, 'The extant abridgements of Walter Bower's Scotichronicon', *SHR* 61 (1982) 62–7.

DREXLER, Marjorie, 'Fluid prejudice: Scottish origin myths in the later middle ages', in Rosenthal and Richmond, *People, Politics and Community*, 60–76.

DUFFY, Seán, 'The Bruce brothers and the Irish Sea world, 1306–29', *CMCS* 21 (1991) 55–86.

DUFFY, Seán, 'Ireland and the Irish Sea Region 1014–1318', Ph.D. dissertation, Trinity College, Dublin, 1993.

DUFFY, Seán, *Ireland in the Middle Ages* (Basingstoke and London 1997)

DUMVILLE, D. N. (ed.) *The Historia Brittonum*, 10 vols, III, *The 'Vatican' Recension* (Cambridge 1985).

DUMVILLE, D. N. 'Kingship, genealogies and regnal lists', in Sawyer and Wood, *Early Medieval Kingship*, 72–104.

DUMVILLE, D. N. 'The peculiarity of the Annals of Tigernach, A.D. 489–766: the Clonmacnoise redaction of the "Chronicle of Ireland", Grabowski and Dumville, *Chronicles and Annals*, 109–152.

DUMVILLE, D. N. 'Some aspects of the chronology of the *Historia Britonum*', *BBCS* 25 (1972–4) 439–45.

DUMVILLE, D. N. 'The textual history of 'Lebor Bretnach': a preliminary study', *Éigse* 16 (1975–6) 255–73.

DUMVILLE, D. N. 'The West Saxon genealogical regnal list and the chronology of early Wessex', *Peritia* 4 (1985) 21–66.

DUMVILLE, D. N. 'When was the 'Clonmacnoise Chronicle' created? The evidence of the Welsh annals', Grabowski and Dumville, *Chronicles and Annals*, 207–26.

DUMVILLE, D. N. 'Where did the 'Clonmacnoise Chronicle' originate? The evidence of the Annals of Tigernach and *Chronicum Scotorum*, A.D. 974–1150', Grabowski and Dumville, *Chronicles and Annals*, 153–205.

DUNCAN, A. A. M. *Scotland: the Making of the Kingdom* (Edinburgh 1975)

DUNCAN, A. A. M. 'The process of Norham, 1291', Coss and Lloyd, *Thirteenth Century England V*, 207–30.

DUNCAN, A. A. M. *Regesta Regum Scottorum*, V, *The* Acta *of Robert I 1306–1329* (Edinburgh 1989).

DUNCAN, A. A. M. 'The Scots' invasion of Ireland, 1315', Davies, *The British Isles*, 100–17.

ENGELS, L. J. 'Bower's Latin', Watt, *Scotichronicon*, IX. 281–314.

FERGUSSON, Sir James, *The Declaration of Arbroath* (Edinburgh 1970).

FOOT, Sarah, 'The making of *Angelcynn*: English identity before the Norman conquest', *TRHS*, 6th series, 6 (1996) 25–49.

FOSTER, Sally M. (ed.) *The St Andrews Sarcophagus: a Pictish Masterpiece and its International Connections* (Dublin 1998).

GALE, Thomas (ed.) *Historiae Britannicae, Saxoniae, Anglo-Danicae, Scriptores XV*, 2 vols (Oxford 1687–91)

GEARY, Patrick, 'Ethnicity as a situational construct in the early Middle Ages', *Mitteilungen der anthropologischen Gesellschaft in Wien* 113 (1983) 15–26.

GELLNER, Ernest, *Nations and Nationalism* (Oxford 1983).

GOLDSTEIN, R. James, *The Matter of Scotland. Historical Narrative in Medieval Scotland* (Lincoln, Nebraska, 1993).

GOLDSTEIN, R. James, 'The Scottish mission to Boniface VIII in 1301: a reconsideration of the context of the *Instructiones* and *Processus*', *SHR* 70 (1991) 1–15.

GOODALL, Walter (ed.) *Joannis de Fordun Scotichronicon cum Supplementis et Continuatione Walteri Boweri*, 2 vols (Edinburgh 1759).

GRABOWSKI, K., and DUMVILLE, D. *Chronicles and Annals of Mediaeval Ireland and Wales: the Clonmacnoise-group Texts* (Woodbridge 1984).

GRANSDEN, A. 'A fourteenth-century chronicle from the Grey Friars at Lynn', *EHR* 72 (1957) 270–8.

GRANSDEN, Antonia, *Historical Writing in England*, I, *c.500–c.1307* (London 1974).

GRANSDEN, Antonia, *Historical Writing in England*, II, *c.1307 to the Early Sixteenth Century* (London 1982).

GREENWAY, Diana (ed. and trans.) *Henry, Archdeacon of Huntingdon. Historia Anglorum. The History of the English People* (Oxford 1996).

GRIFFITHS, Jeremy, and PEARSALL, Derek (edd.) *Book Production and Publishing in Britain 1375–1475* (Cambridge 1989).

GWYNN, A. 'Brian in Armagh (1005)', *Seanchas Ardmhacha* 9 (1978/9) 35–50.

GWYNN, Edward (ed.) *Book of Armagh. The Patrician Documents*, facsimile edn (Dublin 1937).

GWYNN, John (ed.) *Liber Ardmachanus. The Book of Armagh* (Dublin 1913).

GWYNN, Lucius, '*De Maccaib Conaire*', *Ériu* 6 (1912) 144–52.

GWYNN, Lucius, '*De Síl Chonairi Móir*', *Ériu* 6 (1912) 130–43.

GWYNN, Lucius, 'The recensions of the Saga "Togail Bruidne Da Derga"', *ZCP* 10 (1915) 209–22.

HEARNE, Thomas (ed.) *Johannis de Fordun Scotichronicon Genuinum, una cum ejusdem Supplemento et Continuatione* (Oxford 1722).

HENNESSY, William M. (ed. and trans.) *The Annals of Loch Cé. A Chronicle of Irish Affairs from A.D. 1014 to A.D. 1590*, 2 vols (Dublin 1871).

HENNESSY, William M. (ed. and trans.) *Chronicum Scotorum. A Chronicle of Irish Affairs from the Earliest Times to AD 1135, with a supplement, containing the events from 1141 to 1150* (London 1866).

HENNESSY, William M., and MACCARTHY, B. (edd. and trans.) *Annála Uladh: Annals of Ulster; otherwise Annála Senait, Annals of Senat; a Chronicle of Irish Affairs from AD 431, to AD 1540*, 4 vols (Dublin 1887–1901).

HERBERT, Máire, '*Fled Dúin na nGéd*: a reappraisal', *CMCS* 18 (1989) 75–87.

HERBERT, Máire, *Iona, Kells and Derry: the History and Hagiography of the Monastic* Familia *of Columba* (Oxford 1988; paperback edn, Dublin 1996).

HUDSON, Benjamin T. 'Historical literature of early Scotland', *Studies in Scottish Literature* 26 (1991) 141–55.

HUGHES, Kathleen, *Celtic Britain in the Early Middle Ages. Studies in Scottish and Welsh Sources*, ed. D. N. Dumville (Woodbridge 1980).

INNES, Thomas, *A Critical Essay on the Ancient Inhabitants of the Northern Parts of Britain, or Scotland*, 2 vols (London 1729).

JACK, R. D. S. (ed.) *The History of Scottish Literature*, I, *Origins to 1660* (Aberdeen 1988).

JACKSON, K. H. 'The Duan Albanach', *SHR* 36 (1957) 125–37.

JACKSON, Kenneth Hurlestone, *The Gaelic Notes in the Book of Deer* (Cambridge 1972).

JACKSON, K. H. 'The poem *A eolcha Alban uile*', *Celtica* 3 (1955) 149–67.

JACKSON, K. H. Review of Anderson, *Kings and Kingship* (1st edition, 1973), in *Medium Aevum* 44 (1975) 98–101.

JAMES, Montague Rhodes, *Descriptive Catalogue of the Manuscripts in the Library of Corpus Christi College, Cambridge*, I (Cambridge 1912)

JAMES, Montague Rhodes, *The Western Manuscripts in the Library of Trinity College, Cambridge: a Descriptive Catalogue*, 4 vols (Cambridge 1900–4).

KELLEHER, John V. 'The pre-Norman Irish genealogies', *IHS* 16 (1968–9) 138–53.

KERR, N. R. *Medieval Manuscripts in British Libraries*, 3 vols (Oxford 1969–)

KNOTT, Eleanor (ed.) *Togail Bruidne Da Derga* (Dublin 1936)

LAING, David (ed.) *The Orygynale Cronykil of Scotland by Androw of Wyntoun*, Historians of Scotland, 3 vols (Edinburgh 1872–9).

LAWLOR, H. J. 'The absolution of Robert Bruce', *SHR* 19 (1921–2), 325–6.

LAWLOR, H. J. 'Notes on the library of the Sinclairs of Rosslyn', *PSAS* 32 (1897–8) 90–120.

LEGGE, Dominica, 'La Piere d'Escoce', *SHR* 38 (1959) 109–13.

LEHMANN, Ruth (ed.) *Fled Dúin na nGéd* (Dublin 1964).

LINDSAY, W. M. (ed.) *Isidori Hispalensis Episcopi Etymologiarvm sive Originvm*, 2 vols (Oxford 1911).

LINEHAN, P. A. 'A fourteenth-century history of Anglo-Scottish relations in a Spanish manuscript', *Bulletin of the Institute of Historical Research* 48 (1975) 106–22.

LYALL, R. J. 'Books and book owners in fifteenth-century Scotland', in Griffiths and Pearsall, *Book Production*, 239–56.

LYALL, R. J. 'Fifteenth century Scottish manuscripts: a revised checklist', unpublished report prepared in 1980 for the Conference of Medieval Scottish Historical Research.

LYALL, R. J., and RIDDY, F. (edd.) *Proceedings of the Third International Conference on Scottish Language and Literature (Medieval and Renaissance), University of Stirling 2–7 July 1981* (Stirling/Glasgow 1981).

LYDON, James, 'The impact of the Bruce invasion, 1315–27', Cosgrove, *A New History*, II. 275–302.

MAC AIRT, Seán (ed. and trans.) *The Annals of Inisfallen (MS Rawlinson B.503)* (Dublin 1951)

MAC AIRT, Seán, and MAC NIOCAILL, Gearóid (edd. and trans.) *Annals of Ulster to A.D. 1131, Part I: text and translation* (Dublin 1983).

MACALISTER, R. A. S. (ed. and trans.) *Lebor Gabála Érenn, The Book of the Taking of*

Ireland, 5 vols (Irish Texts Society vols 34, 35, 39, 41 and 44) (London 1938–56; rev. impr., 1993).

MAC CANA, Proinsias, *The Learned Tales of Medieval Ireland* (Dublin 1980).

MAC EOIN, G. 'On the Irish legend of the origin of the Picts', *Studia Hibernica* 4 (1964) 138–54.

MAC MATHÚNA, Séamus (ed.) *Immram Brain: Bran's Journey to the Land of Women* (Tübingen 1985).

MACQUARRIE, Alan, 'Lives of Scottish saints in the Aberdeen Breviary: some problems of sources for Strathclyde saints', *RSCHS* 26 (1996) 31–54.

MACQUARRIE, Alan, *The Saints of Scotland: Essays in Scottish Church History AD 450–1093* (Edinburgh 1997).

MACQUEEN, John, and MACQUEEN, Winifred, 'Latin prose literature', in Jack, *The History of Scottish Literature*, I. 227–44.

MACQUEEN, John, and MACQUEEN, Winifred (edd. and trans.) *Scotichronicon by Walter Bower in Latin and English*, I, books i and ii (Edinburgh 1993).

MACQUEEN, John, and MACQUEEN, Winifred (edd. and trans.) *Scotichronicon by Walter Bower in Latin and English*, II, books iii and iv (Aberdeen 1989).

MACQUEEN, John, MACQUEEN, Winifred, and WATT, D. E. R. (edd. and trans.) *Scotichronicon by Walter Bower in Latin and English*, III, books v and vi (Edinburgh 1995).

MASON, Roger A. 'Scotching the Brut: politics, history and national myth in sixteenth-century Britain', Mason, *Scotland and England 1286–1815*, 60–84.

MASON, Roger A. (ed.) *Scotland and England 1286–1815* (Edinburgh 1987).

MAXWELL, Sir Herbert, Bart (trans.) *Scalacronica: the reigns of Edward I and Edward II and Edward III by Sir Thomas Gray of Heton* (Glasgow 1907).

MEYER, Kuno, 'Partholón mac Sera', *ZCP* 13 (1919–21) 141–2.

MIGNE, J.-P. (ed.) *Patrologiæ cursus completus . . . series Latina*, 221 vols (Paris).

MILLER, Molly, 'The disputed historical horizon of the Pictish king-lists', *SHR* 58 (1979), 1–34.

MILLER, Molly, 'The last century of Pictish succession', *Scottish Studies* 23 (1979) 39–67.

MILLER, Molly, 'Matriliny by treaty: the Pictish foundation-legend', in Whitelock, McKitterick and Dumville, *Ireland*, 133–61.

MULCHRONE, Kathleen (ed.) *The Book of Lecan. Leabhar Mór Mhic Fhir Bhisigh Leacain, with descriptive introduction and indexes*, facsimile edn (Dublin 1937).

MURPHY, Denis (ed.) *The Annals of Clonmacnoise, being Annals of Ireland from the Earliest Period to A.D.1408, translated into English by Conell Mageoghagan* (Dublin 1896)

NICHOLSON, Ranald, 'A sequel to Edward Bruce's invasion of Ireland', *SHR* 42 (1963) 30–40.

NYBERG, Tore, PIØ, Iørn, SØRENSEN, Preben Meulengracht, and TROMMER, Ange (edd.) *History and Heroic Tale: a Symposium* (Odense 1985).

O' BRIEN, M. A. (ed.) *Corpus Genealogiarum Hiberniae*, I (Dublin 1962; 2nd edn. 1976).

Ó CATHASAIGH, Tomás, 'On the *Cín Dromma Snechta* version of *Togail Brudne Uí Dergae*', *Ériu* 41 (1990) 103–14.

Ó CONCHEANAINN, T. 'A Connacht medieval literary heritage: texts derived from Cín Dromma Snechtai through Leabhar na hUidhre', *CMCS* 16 (1988) 1–40.

Ó CORRÁIN, Donnchadh, 'Irish origin-legends and genealogy: recurrent aetiologies', Nyberg, Piø, Sørensen and Trommer, *History and Heroic Tale*, 51–96.

O' DONOVAN, John, *Annála Ríoghachta Éireann. Annals of the Kingdom of Ireland by the Four Masters, to the year 1616*, 2nd edn, 7 vols (Dublin 1856).

Ó FIAICH, T. 'The church of Armagh under lay control', *Seanchas Ardmhacha* 5 (1969) 75–127.

Ó RIAIN, Padraig (ed.) *Corpus Genealogiarum Sanctorum Hiberniae* (Dublin 1985)

O'SULLIVAN, Anne (ed.) *The Book of Leinster, formerly Lebar na Núachongbála*, VIII (Dublin 1983).

PRYCE, Huw (ed.) *Literacy in Medieval Celtic Societies* (Cambridge 1998).

QUIN, E. G. (ed.) *Dictionary of the Irish Language, Compact Edition* (Dublin 1983).

REID, N. H. 'Alexander III: the historiography of a myth', in Reid, *Scotland in the Reign of Alexander III*, 181–213.

REID, N. H. (ed.) *Scotland in the Reign of Alexander III 1249–1286* (Edinburgh 1990).

REYNOLDS, Susan, *Kingdoms and Communities in Western Europe* (Oxford 1984).

REYNOLDS, Susan, 'Medieval *origines gentium* and the community of the realm', *History* 68 (1983) 375–90.

ROSENTHAL, J. and RICHMOND, C. (edd.) *People, Politics and Community in the later Middle Ages* (Gloucester 1987).

ROYAN, N. R. 'The *Scotorum Historiae* of Hector Boece: a Study', D. Phil. dissertation, Oxford University, 1996.

SAWYER, P. H., and WOOD, I. N. (edd.) *Early Medieval Kingship* (Leeds 1977).

SCOTT, A. B., and WATT, D. E. R., with MORÉT Ulrike and SHEAD, Norman F. (edd. and trans.) *Scotichronicon by Walter Bower in Latin and English*, VII, books xiii and xiv (Edinburgh 1996).

SCOTT, W. W. 'Fordun's description of the inauguration of Alexander II', *SHR* 50 (1971) 198–200.

SCOTT, W. W. 'John of Fordun's description of the Western Isles', *Scottish Studies* 23 (1979) 1–13.

SCOWCROFT, R. Mark, '*Leabhar Gabhála*. Part I: the growth of the text', *Ériu* 38 (1987) 79–140.

SCOWCROFT, R. Mark, '*Leabhar Gabhála*. Part II: the growth of the tradition', *Ériu* 39 (1988) 1–66.

SHEAD, Norman F., STEVENSON, Wendy B., and WATT, D. E. R., with BORTHWICK, Alan, LATHAM, R. E., PHILLIPS, J. R. S., and SMITH, Martin S. (edd. and trans.) *Scotichronicon by Walter Bower in Latin and English*, VI, books xi and xii (Aberdeen 1991).

SIMPSON, G. G. 'The claim of Florence, count of Holland, to the Scottish throne, 1291–2', *SHR* 36 (1957) 111–24.

SKENE, Felix J. H. (trans.), SKENE, W. F. (ed.) *John of Fordun's Chronicle of the Scottish Nation*, Historians of Scotland (Edinburgh 1872).

SKENE, W. F. *Chronicles of the Picts, Chronicles of the Scots* (Edinburgh 1867).

SKENE, W. F. 'The coronation stone', *PSAS* 8 (1868–70) 66–99.

SKENE, W. F. (ed.) *Johannis de Fordun Chronica Gentis Scotorum*, Historians of Scotland (Edinburgh 1871).

SKENE, W. F. 'Notice of an early MS of Fordun's chronicle', *PSAS* 10 (1872–4) 27–30.

SKENE, W. F. 'Notice of the existing MSS. of Fordun's Scotichronicon', *PSAS* 8 (1868–70) 239–56.

SMITH, Anthony D. *National Identity* (Harmondsworth 1991).

SMITH, Anthony D. 'The problem of national identity: ancient, medieval and modern?', *Ethnic and Racial Studies* 17 (1994) 375–99.

SMYTH, Alfred P. (ed.) *Medieval Europeans. Studies in Ethnic Identity and National Perspectives in Medieval Europe* (London 1998)

SIMS-WILLIAMS, P. P. 'Some functions of origin stories in early medieval Wales', Nyberg, Piø, Sørensen and Trommer, *History and Heroic Tale*, 97–131.

STEVENSON, Joseph (ed.) *Scalacronica: a chronicle of England and Scotland from A.D. MLXVI to A.D. MCCCLXII* (Maitland Club 1836)

STOKES, Whitley, 'The Annals of Tigernach: the third fragment', *Revue Celtique* 17 (1896) 119–263.

STOKES, Whitley, 'The Annals of Tigernach. The fourth fragment, AD 973 – AD 1088', *Revue Celtique* 17 (1896) 337–420.

STOKES, Whitley, 'The Destruction of Dind Ríg', *ZCP* 3 (1901) 1–14.

STOKES, Whitley (ed. and trans.) *The Tripartite Life of Patrick with Other Documents Relating to that Saint*, 2 vols (London 1887).

STONES, E. L. G. (ed. and trans.) *Anglo-Scottish Relations 1174–1328. Some Selected Documents* (London 1965).

STONES, E. L. G. 'The appeal to history in Anglo-Scottish relations between 1291 and 1401. Part I', *Archives* 9 (1969) 11–21.

STRINGER, K. J. *Earl David of Huntingdon 1152–1219* (Edinburgh 1985).

STUBBS, William (ed.) *Radulfi de Diceto Opera Omnia*, Rolls Series, 2 vols (London 1876).

STUBBS, William (ed.) *Willelmi Malmesburiensis Monachi De Gentis Regum Anglorum Libri Quinque, Historiæ Novellæ Libri Tres*, Rolls Series, 2 vols (London 1887–9).

SWANTON, M. J. 'A fragmentary Life of St Mildred and other Kentish royal saints', *Archaeologia Cantiana* 91 (1975) 15–27.

TAYLOR, A. B. 'Cape Wrath and its various names', *Scottish Studies* 17 (1973) 61–9.

TAYLOR, John, *The Universal Chronicle of Ranulf Higden* (Oxford 1966).

TAYLOR, Simon and WATT, D. E. R., with SCOTT, Brian (edd. and trans.) *Scotichronicon by Walter Bower in Latin and English*, V, books ix and x (Aberdeen 1990).

THOMSON, D. S. 'The Harlaw Brosnachadh: an early fifteenth-century literary curio', Carney and Greene, *Celtic Studies*, 147–69.

THORNTON, David E. 'Power, Politics and Status: Aspects of Genealogy in Mediaeval Ireland and Wales', Ph.D. dissertation, University of Cambridge, 1991.

THURNEYSEN, Rudolf, *Die irische Helden- und Königsage bis zum siebzehnten Jahrhundert* (Halle 1921).

THURNEYSEN, R. 'Synchronismen der irischen Konige', *ZCP* 19 (1933) 81–99.

TYSON, Diana B. 'Handlist of manuscripts containing the French prose *Brut* chronicle', *Scriptorium* 48 (1994) 333–44.

TYSON, Diana B. 'Les manuscrits du Brut en prose française', Wilkins, *Les manuscrits français*, 101–20.

VAN HAMEL, A. G. (ed.) *Lebor Bretnach. The Irish Version of the Historia Britonum ascribed to Nennius* (Dublin [1932]).

WATSON, Fiona, 'The enigmatic lion: Scotland, kingship, and national identity in the wars of independence', in Broun, Finlay and Lynch, *Image and Identity*, 18–37.

WATT, D. E. R. 'Editing Walter Bower's *Scotichronicon*', Lyall and Riddy, *Proceedings*, 161–76.

[WATT, D. E. R.] 'Fordun: appendices I and III and *Gesta Annalia*', unpublished paper dated 30 November 1993 circulated to members of the *Scotichronicon* editorial team.

WATT, D. E. R. (gen. ed.) *Scotichronicon by Walter Bower in Latin and English*, 9 vols (Aberdeen/Edinburgh 1987–98).

WATT, D. E. R. (ed. and trans.) *Scotichronicon by Walter Bower in Latin and English*, VIII, books xv and xvi (Aberdeen 1987).

WATT, D. E. R. (ed) *Scotichronicon by Walter Bower in Latin and English*, IX [critical studies and general indexes] (Edinburgh 1998)

WEBSTER, Bruce, 'John of Fordun and the independent identity of the Scots', Smyth, *Medieval Europeans.*

WEBSTER, Bruce, *Scotland from the Eleventh Century to 1603* (London 1975).

WEST, Máire, 'Leabhar na hUIdhre's position in the manuscript history of *Togail Bruidne Da Derga* and *Orgain Brudne Uí Dergae*', *CMCS* 20 (1990) 61–98.

WHITELOCK, Dorothy, MCKITTERICK, Rosamund, and DUMVILLE, David N. (edd.) *Ireland in Early Mediaeval Europe: Studies in Memory of Kathleen Hughes* (Cambridge 1982).

WILKINS, Nigel (ed.) *Les manuscrits français de la bibliothèque Parker, Actes du Colloque 24–27 mars 1993* (Cambridge 1993).

WOLFRAM, Herwig, 'Gothic history and historical ethnography', *Journal of Medieval History* 7 (1981) 309–20.

WOLFRAM, Herwig, '*Origo et religio*. Ethnic traditions and literature in early medieval texts', *Early Medieval Europe* 3 (1994) 19–38.

WRIGHT, Neil (ed.) *The Historia Regum Britannie of Geoffrey of Monmouth*, I: *Bern, Burgerbibliothek, MS. 568* (Cambridge 1985).

WRIGHT, Neil (ed.) *The Historia Regum Britannie of Geoffrey of Monmouth*, II: *The First Variant Version: a Critical Edition* (Cambridge 1988).

INDEX

Abbreviations:

(*c.*)	*circa*
(d.)	died
(dep.)	deposed
(f)	reference to figure in text
(*fl.*)	floruit
(g)	reference to edited text of the Scottish royal genealogy
(k)	reference to edited text of Scottish king-list
(o)	reference to edited text of Scottish origin-legend
(res.)	resigned
(s)	reference to stemma

STUDIES IN CELTIC HISTORY

Already published

I · THE SAINTS OF GWYNEDD
Molly Miller

II · CELTIC BRITAIN IN THE EARLY MIDDLE AGES
Kathleen Hughes

III · THE INSULAR LATIN GRAMMARIANS
Vivien Law

IV · CHRONICLES AND ANNALS OF MEDIAEVAL IRELAND AND WALES
Kathryn Grabowski and David Dumville

V · GILDAS: NEW APPROACHES
M. Lapidge and D. Dumville (edd.)

VI · SAINT GERMANUS OF AUXERRE AND THE END OF ROMAN BRITAIN
E. A. Thompson

VII · FROM KINGS TO WARLORDS
Katherine Simms

VIII · THE CHURCH AND THE WELSH BORDER IN THE CENTRAL MIDDLE AGES
C. N. L. Brooke

IX · THE LITURGY AND RITUAL OF THE CELTIC CHURCH
F. E. Warren (2nd edn by Jane Stevenson)

X · THE MONKS OF REDON
Caroline Brett (ed. and trans.)

XI · EARLY MONASTERIES IN CORNWALL
Lynette Olson

XII · IRELAND, WALES AND ENGLAND IN THE ELEVENTH CENTURY
K. L. Maund

XIII · SAINT PATRICK, AD 493–1993
D. N. Dumville and others

XIV · MILITARY INSTITUTIONS ON THE WELSH MARCHES: SHROPSHIRE, AD 1066–1300
Frederick C. Suppe

XV · UNDERSTANDING THE UNIVERSE IN SEVENTH-CENTURY IRELAND
Marina Smythe

XVI · GRUFFUDD AP CYNAN: A COLLABORATIVE BIOGRAPHY
K. L. Maund (ed.)

XVII · COLUMBANUS: STUDIES ON THE LATIN WRITINGS
Michael Lapidge (ed.)